Bring back the
BIRCH

The **Alan Birchenall** Story
with Paul Mace

Published by **Polar Publishing**

First published in Great Britain 2000 by Polar Group Ltd
9-17 Tuxford Road, Hamilton, Leicester LE4 9TZ

Text copyright © 2000 Alan Birchenall & Paul Mace
Design copyright Polar Group Ltd © 2000

ISBN 1 899538 17 8

British Library Cataloguing in Publication Data. A catalogue record for this book is
available from the British Library.

General editing by Julian Baskcomb and Julia Byrne
Layout & design by Neill Staniforth
Designed & Printed by Polar Group Ltd
9-17 Tuxford Road, Hamilton, Leicester LE4 9TZ. Tel: 0116 274 4700

Stats: Dave Smith
Cover Photograph: Stu Williamson
Photographs courtesy of: Neville Chadwick Photography, Denis Clarebrough,
Colorsport, Empics Ltd, The Leicester Mercury, Raymonds.

Most remaining photographs are from Alan Birchenall's private collection or from
scrapbooks/albums kept by his family. The publishers have, perhaps inevitably,
been unable to trace the sources of all these pictures, but any photographer
involved who has been inadvertently omitted is cordially invited to contact them in
writing providing proof of copyright.

Forewords

If The Birch gives me one more rendition of 'Wilkie Eye', I swear I'll swing for him!

Alan's singing talents are almost as legendary as his footballing abilities. Down the years he's fancied his chances as a cabaret singer as much as a player. Well, sorry Birch, but I have to say you made the right career choice all those years ago when you donned your football boots.

I've had the privilege - if that's the word - of singing a few duets with Alan. Let's just be polite and say his tones weren't exactly velvet. As he recounts in this book we had some memorable nights together at the Costa Brava restaurant, along with various other 'dens of iniquity'.

From the moment I first met Alan in the Bull's Head pub in Leicestershire, we got along famously. All joking aside, he's been a fantastic friend to me down the years and is the sort of bloke who's always there when you really need him.

As someone who watched him playing football, not just at Leicester but Hereford and Trowbridge too, we've stuck together through thick and thin. Alan truly is one of the game's great entertainers.

Dave Bartram (*Lead Singer, Showaddywaddy*)

Mention The Birch and I'll instantly think of the crazy language we always used to greet each other. It's unintelligible to anyone else. Come to think of it, we don't understand it either!

Alan will shout at me: "her der fer!" and I'll reply: "say der four". Madness, I know, but I think its origins date back to mimicking the stereotyped Scottish pub singer who slurs his words into a dodgy microphone on the Glasgow cabaret circuit.

It was Birch's way of making me feel welcome when I left home in Scotland for the first time as a young 19-year-old to join up with Leicester. From the very first day Birch went out of his way to introduce me to everyone and make me feel part of the Leicester family. He did it brilliantly. We've kept in touch ever since and I even had the privilege of playing alongside him in testimonial matches (Birch told me to put that in!).

I'm afraid I never saw Alan play 'live' but, don't worry, Birch has filled me in on every goal and every pass he ever made in his career (that lasted all of two minutes!). Without doubt, Birch is one of the most colourful characters I've ever met and his book is certain to be a belter.

Gary McAllister (*Ex Leicester City and Scotland*)

Macey and Birch don their Wembley togs for the Worthington Cup final victory over Tranmere Rovers.

Co-author Paul Mace (37) will never forget the time, when as a 12-year-old schoolboy on the terraces of Meadow Lane, he first set eyes on Alan Birchenall.

Alan had just missed a crucial penalty for Notts County in a top of the table Division Two clash against Sunderland and a junior Mace was among those hurling abuse in Birch's direction from the Meadow Lane stand. Seventeen years later their paths were to cross again when Paul joined Leicester City as Press Officer.

In between, Paul (unable to rise above the dizzy heights of the Greenwood Dale Comprehensive and the Forest Fields College football teams and Sunday morning parks sides) cut his teeth as a sports journalist and sports editor with the *Retford Times, Peterborough Evening Telegraph* and *Birmingham Daily News*. He also worked as a sports broadcaster with *Radio Trent* before arriving at Filbert Street.

Macey and Birch have developed a keen sense of banter in their 10 years together with Paul kindly allowing Alan to share his office at Filbert Street and the training ground *(you mean my office! - Birch)*. Paul is now Director of Media and Communications at Leicester City and is responsible for the club's award-winning match-day magazine, publications, internet and other communication mediums and overall strategies. He is also chairman of the Football Press Officers' Association, a governing body representing officials working in media departments at English football clubs. *(What a load of cobblers! - Birch)*.

Contents

My book is dedicated to
My Mum, Dad and sister Christine.

In his fledgling years the Birch and 'sis' seldom went short of anything we asked for. My family were my biggest supporters and whether I wanted a pair of new football boots, a racing bike or an army cadet uniform, my parents somehow provided for me. It was only when I grew older that I truly appreciated the sacrifices they made. My thoughts too are always with Christine. Her tragic early death helped shape Birch's attitude to life. Live for the moment, that's what I say, because you may not be around too much longer.

PS Mum, you still make the best egg butty in the world.

My Childhood Years

Chapter 1

IF you're expecting this to be a footballing epic of League Championship triumphs, European glory nights and international clashes with the likes of Brazil, Argentina and Germany, then I'm afraid my humble offering may disappoint. There are precious few League Championship medals, European trophies and navy blue England international caps in the Birchenall trophy cabinet. Well, to be honest, there's not even one!

I was no George Best, Bobby Charlton nor Kevin Keegan. I never made that top drawer but, with a mix of determination and honest endeavour, I was able to carve out a soccer career spanning almost twenty seasons and over 500 League appearances, principally in the First Division.

The trophy cabinet may be bare but I was proud and privileged to play in an era when football was blessed with an abundance of genuine characters. Most of all, I have a tremendous treasure-trove of memories and stories and it is those I would like to share with you.

I played against and with the Shiltons, the Bests, the Charltons and the Keegans... and they usually gave me a good tonking. I can never begin to compare with those greats when they talk about the fantastic games in which they were involved, but I can tell you what football was like off the park in the truly remarkable era of the late sixties, seventies and early eighties.

I'm no embittered old footballer. I've had a fantastic life, travelled the world, brought up a family and like to think I've had my fair share of laughs on the way.

Where I truly hope to be different is in producing a publication that gets to grips with the real life of a footballer, not a sports book which details every last kick of my footballing career: about how I nutmegged two defenders at Old Trafford and *larruped* one into the top corner from 30 yards, or the moment I scored my first-ever hat-trick in front of a baying crowd of 55,000.

Oh, before I get too carried away, you're probably wondering what *larruping* means. Well, over the years the Birch has devised his own language enabling him to engage in conversation with other like-minded persons. I may inadvertently drop into *Birch-ese* but all the words are in italics. A glossary of these phrases is to be found at the end of this book.

In my autobiography I want to talk about the real me - my experiences away from the football pitch, my life, my loves (but not too many of those, please) and the kind of things that really make me tick. Football, as a 90-minute game, is not particularly important to me but the whole football environment has unquestionably shaped my character. It has allowed me to develop from a shy, lanky, buck-toothed teenager into, as many people will tell you, an amiable, modest guy not exactly lacking in the self-confidence department.

Enough of the high-sounding, noble sentiments, it's time to get on with my story. It's not my intention to bore you rigid with a day by day account of the Birch's existence. Crikey, such a chronology, spanning as it would the past five decades from the East End of London to Nottingham, Sheffield, Chelsea, Crystal Palace, Leicester, America, Notts County, Blackburn, Hereford and all stations to Trowbridge Town, would send **me** to sleep. No, I'll hopefully be choosing topics and themes which you find just a shade more interesting and a little less difficult to read.

■ **YOU GOT THE CUTEST LITTLE BABY FACE**
...I needed a considerable amount of persuading from my co-author before I decided to let this little gem go in. A true piece of history because this is the first photographic evidence of junior Birch at the tender age of six months. Please note the flowing blond locks which were already sprouting.

Unfortunately, I couldn't think of a way to deal with my childhood years other than by rambling on about my early life. To me, my days as a young boy in London and Nottingham were of tremendous importance in influencing just about every aspect of my future. So, before we get down to all those Birchy tales of adulthood, let's get the boring stuff out of the way.

Little Birchy came into existence on August 22nd 1945, just after World War Two had been won and shortly before victory over Japan. Indeed, some wags have subsequently said I was the cause of the ceasefire. My mum was Gladys and my dad Leslie, they met and married during the War. Dad hailed from Nottingham and came from a small family. During the war he served as a gunner in the Burma Star in Burma and India.

Dad remained a loyal serviceman throughout his life and I remember him attending the Remembrance Day parades on Nottingham's Victoria Embankment every single year without exception. It was from him I inherited a keen sense of discipline which has always stood me in decent stead.

Mum was one of seven children and

DEDICATED FOLLOWER OF FASHION
...two years old and look at the immaculately groomed hair as I pose at the entrance to our house on Ruskin Avenue in Manor Park. Not a hairdryer in sight *(see later chapters for details)*. The clothes may look a little tatty but I can assure you these were the height of designer fashion for all two-year-olds.

among many abiding memories of my days in the East End of London are the innumerable aunties, uncles and cousins who shared our house.

Home for the Birchenall family was a typically Victorian terraced property - 151 Ruskin Avenue in East Ham E12. Well, I always thought of it as East Ham although my mum assures me the district was actually Manor Park. Anyway, it was about a mile and a half from Upton Park, home of West Ham United, which was to be the first professional soccer ground I ever visited.

BRING ME SUNSHINE.
The back garden of 151 Ruskin Avenue where junior Birch spent many a happy hour. You'll notice I'm protecting my eyes from the sun. This was a problem I had later in life in front of the camera because, whenever my club was holding a team photo-call, the sun appeared to shine straight into my eyes and I used to squint terribly.

Indeed, the area was something of a post-war soccer hot-bed with former England manager Terry Venables growing up in the same London district. Little did I know our paths were to cross in the coming years.

At the age of four, my life was nearly over before I'd had an opportunity to kick a football in anger. Although I have no recollection of the illness, I was struck down by peritonitis and given no better than a 50-50 chance of survival.

My appendix burst and poisoned my system. Even today this is still considered a serious illness but in the immediate post-War years it could be life-threatening. Mum told me how a Sri Lankan doctor came around to Ruskin Avenue to diagnose the condition and warned her to fear the worst. The appendix was removed - I still have a two inch scar to prove it - and there were anxious moments until I managed to pull through.

A year later the Birchenall family left the East End and established a new life in Nottingham on a pristine council estate

Here we all are at 45 Montfort Crescent, Sherwood, Nottingham. It looks like we are off to audition for Enid Blyton's Famous Five minus one character. Look at the mac I'm wearing. There's my sister Christine with my best pal Micky Somers and his younger brother Tony. Mick and I were inseparable on the football pitch but while I went on to play for Sheffield United, he moved to Hartlepool, Chelsea and Torquay.

BROTHER AND SISTER.

There are, in truth, precious few photographs of myself and sister Christine. I was so preoccupied with football we rarely saw each other. Here, we are casting a quick glance through the family album although I am a trifle nervous that one of the very early copies of Playboy may fall from its pages. Christine and I always used to have a race to get back home from school. Mum and Dad were out working so the first home was able to grab the crust off the loaf, dunk it in the condensed milk and sprinkle on some sugar for a truly scrumptious tea-time snack.

in Sherwood. Dad held down a variety of jobs in those days and it was enhanced employment prospects which took us to the Midlands.

Not that our roots with the East End were ever severed. I would make trips back down to Ruskin Avenue for the summer holidays every year until the age of 14. I was - and still am - very proud of my connections with the area. I came from a working class background, typical of the era as Britain rebuilt itself after the War. Mum and Dad both worked hard and, though there was never an abundance of money, my parents ensured myself and my sister were always well provided for.

When I tell stories about our home in Ruskin Avenue listeners afford themselves a smile. There was certainly never any shortage of people living in our house. With no side entrance to our property, you went in through the front door off the street, walked through the living-room and out into a long terraced back garden. It was a three storey house, populated at various times by different members of our family.

Off the stairs on one floor was my Auntie Doll who lived with her family, while my Uncle Len had his own room. Uncle Bob and Auntie Myra were also often in attendance and, during my childhood years, I could never be quite sure which members of our extended family were in residence at any one moment. I suppose it was like something out of Charlie's family in the book *'Charlie and the Chocolate Factory'*. Our grandparents didn't quite share the same bed but I'm sure you get the broad idea. In those days, and I know I might sound like an old fogey, families were much closer knit and everyone really did pull together.

MUM AND DAD. Unquestionably my two greatest fans and, without their unstinting efforts, my footballing career would never have got off the ground. Dad Leslie worked on the buses with Bartons Transport and introduced me to professional football at Meadow Lane. Sadly Dad passed away a few years ago but Mum still lives in Top Valley in Nottingham. Once a week I pay a visit there to have the best egg butty in the world. I tell Mum I'm passing through on business but really I make a special trip just so I can sample her superb home-cooking.

Out in the back garden you could look to the right and see a row of twenty houses. Glance to the left and there was another identical row of twenty - all with exactly the same long, thin, twenty-yard strip of garden. At the bottom of ours was an air-raid shelter where I spent many happy hours. As these were the immediate post-war years, there was a variety of memorabilia which I was able to lay my hands on.

Uncle Len used to give me lessons in target practice with an air rifle. We would lean out of his bedroom window and aim at various items I had placed on top of the shelter. This might sound a bit on the adventurous side for a four-year-old. However, it was child's play compared to the games we played with a wickedly-sharp bayonet which my father had brought home.

Uncle Len used to take the bayonet down from his wardrobe and we would have fights together on his bed. I shudder to think how just one false 'Corporal Jones of Dad's Army-style' lunge with the bayonet could have caused either myself or my uncle to arrive at a prematurely pointed end.

I suppose all boys look back on their childhood and recount tales with fond affection. In my case, I invariably seemed to be at the centre of attention for my elders' money-making enterprises. It is a bone of contention to the Birch that people have consistently made money at my expense, a trend apparently instigated at the tender age of three.

In those days Guy Fawkes' Day was seen as a fairly lucrative money-spinner around the East End and no self-respecting youngster would be seen dead with a stuffed immobile Guy. The problem was, which gullible toddler could be dressed up as Guy and paraded in a pram?

For my cousins and young neighbours, I was the answer to their prayers. So, every year in the week before Bonfire Night you could glimpse junior Birch, dummy in mouth, being wheeled up and down the streets of East Ham in a coach-spring perambulator to the shouts of 'Penny for the Guy.'

Not that my elders were any less fazed by the prospect of exploiting junior Birch as a source of child labour. Remember *Steptoe & Son,* the old rag and bone men in the BBC telly series of the sixties and seventies? Guess what job I was lumbered with...

Uncle Len - when not giving me lessons in marksmanship or brandishing bayonets - was to be seen riding around on his customised bicycle which had a little trolley attached to the back. He would time his cycling activities to co-incide with the twice-weekly visits in our locality of the rag and bone men.

'Rag and bone' went the cry as the horse trundled the cart on its winding way around the East End. In tow was Uncle Len, and yours truly armed with a shovel. Sure enough, when the horse crapped on the street, there was I with my trusty spade ready to load the offending mess into the little trolley. Strikes me I've been shovelling shite for the past 50 years, but that's another story!

Ever the entrepreneur, Uncle Len had a little round lined up whereby we would immediately deliver the steaming horse manure to keen East End gardeners looking to improve the quality of their roses. The only slight problem with this arrangement was that every house was a Victorian terraced affair with a single access to the rear garden. So junior Birch would knock on the front door and then walk through the living-room, out through the back door and deposit the manure on the garden.

Uncle Len used to get a penny a shovel-load, although I must admit it wasn't easy to walk through the house without spilling some of the smelly stuff on the carpet. Those East Ham residents had some fantastic roses and tomatoes, but the price to pay was a living room that didn't half *pen and ink.*

Gradually I grew out of making a living from horses' bowel motions but my uncles were quick to conjure up more money-making activities using my labours.

On my visits for summer holidays, from the age of nine onwards, Uncles George and Bob seconded me to help out with meat and vegetable deliveries. The pair had a thriving business supplying fresh produce to local schools and shops. We used to get up at 4am to go to Smithfield and Convent Garden markets in order to load up. After a short apprenticeship spent watching from the sidelines, I helped with order-packing and delivering. Occasionally, I would be paid pocket money but, in truth, I really enjoyed myself. It was great to ride on a lorry and I considered myself a real man doing a grown-up's job.

Inbetween these money-making enterprises, junior Birch liked his own free time playing around the place. I did all the usuals, like Saturday morning cinema clubs, but my firm favourite was the twice-weekly trip to East Ham baths. My pals and I would catch a bus for the short ride to the pool. Of course, swimming was great fun but the highlight for me was munching my way through the tastiest toast in the world afterwards. Up we would go to the snack-bar counter and I would order two slices of hot toast at a penny each. I don't know what kind of butter or bread they used but the taste was simply magical. Since then I have eaten toast in just about every country in every continent around the world but nothing has ever come remotely close. It's ironic that most professional footballers have tea and toast as part of their pre-match routine, and I have probably consumed many slices more than any other 53-year-old, yet I have no hesitation in pronouncing the scrumptious toast from Manor Park East Ham baths is truly in a league of its own!

On the way home I'd spend the rest of my swimming money allowance from Mum on a bottle of Tizer. In those days you couldn't get Tizer, or any other fizzy stuff, in a can - it came in a bottle with a flip-top and was truly delicious. I still drink Tizer today - now there's an admission to shatter the Birch's street cred - but the taste doesn't even begin to compare. So, there you have it, as a youngster Birch's idea of heaven was two slices of hot buttered toast and a bottle of tingling Tizer. Easily pleased, wasn't I?

To this day, I retain a great affinity with the people of East London. Yes, I suppose I have got the Cockney 'rabbit' and I received a wonderfully warm response from West Ham supporters when I recently returned to Upton Park for a sporting function with Hammers boss Harry Redknapp. Many of the Birchenall clan have long since left the area; Uncle Len became a printer in Bradford and most of the family relocated to Canada (probably to get as far away from me as they could!).

There are, however, a couple of cousins who continue to live a stone's throw away from Upton Park. When my beloved Leicester City play there, I'm invited to use the space outside their house because parking in that area can be a total nightmare. Unfortunately the police close off the roads and it's immensely difficult persuading an officer of the law that you really do have a cousin living at the bottom of the road. Or at least it is on the particular afternoon you've got a big 'Foxes Never Quit' sticker in the back of your car.

My East End experiences were confined to about three weeks on annual summer school holidays. For the other 49 weeks of the year home was 45 Montfort Crescent in Sherwood. In the early years Mum worked at the 'Nibbits' factory making savoury snacks before moving on to the looms at Meridian clothing on Haydn Road in Sherwood.

Dad worked on the buses as a driver and conductor for Bartons Coaches. He had a fantastic head for figures and, when his bosses discovered this talent, he was moved into the offices at the bus depot in Chilwell. Around about the age of six I was introduced to the world of professional football. Although I had been to my first game at Upton Park a year earlier, Notts County were to become my team.

In those days Nottingham Forest were still the bigger club but it was Notts to whom my dad swore his allegiance and I was to follow in his footsteps... quite literally. Although Dad worked on the buses, he would always prefer to walk rather than take advantage of a free ride.

His walking ability was legendary - Sherwood to Meadow Lane was a distance of approximately six miles and we used to cover half of those on foot. Every Saturday afternoon we'd hop on a bus to Slab Square, as we used to call the centre of Nottingham in front of the main Council House. Bartons ran football specials to the ground from there. I would cast an envious eye at them but dad would shout: "Come on, we're not getting the bus," and off we went... on foot. En route to the ground, we would stop off at Auntie Anne's in The Meadows area for some tea. I was usually in desperate need of refreshment by that stage.

Now, don't get the impression my dad was a fitness freak. He smoked his Woodbines as well as the next man but he loved to walk. Not ordinary walking but a real fast pace and young Birch had a hard job keeping up. By the time I arrived at Meadow Lane I was absolutely knackered. At the ground I'd be despatched to the kids pen, to the right of the goal on the Kop End, and Dad would take up his position in the heart of the Kop. The places in a football ground where supporters sit or stand are very territorial. Some thirty years later one of Dad's dreams came true when the Birch got to play in a Notts County shirt at Meadow Lane. I offered him

Directors' Box tickets. "No thanks son, I'll go where I've always stood," he replied and duly watched the game from the Kop.

Our walking was not solely confined to pre-match activity. After the game we'd yomp past those football specials and go into Slab Square. On rare occasions we would walk past the buses in the square and go for the 'Full Monty' all the way back to Sherwood. To this day, I maintain that one of the reasons I had more stamina than skill throughout my professional football career was because of those walks to and from Meadow Lane.

LEON LEUTY
My original hero, Leon was one of the great centre halves. His sudden and premature death at the age of 35 upset me immensely.

Dad and I were football fanatics. We attended every home game, me with a little rattle and completely in awe of anyone who sported a black and white Magpies shirt. My first hero was Leon Leuty, one of the game's great centre halves. We were walking across Slab Square one night to catch a bus back to Sherwood and bought a *Nottingham Evening Post*. In huge headlines was the news that Leon had died suddenly. I cried my eyes out.

It's funny how I can still picture those players I watched 45 years ago. Peter Broadbent was a powerful winger and there was a big strong centre half called Pete Russell. He was the hardest of all the hard men and made the likes of Norman 'Bites yer legs' Hunter, Billy Bremner and Ron 'Chopper' Harris look like Lionel Blairs. Playing with his shorts rolled right up to the tops of his thighs, he was an absolute animal who could trap the ball further than he could kick it. By contrast there was little Ron Wylie, a deft and pacy inside forward.

Unfortunately, I just missed seeing the Notts and England centre forward Tommy Lawton. Dad told me all about him on many an occasion, how he was the best header of a ball in the history of the game and how he scored goals with his head from the half-way line.

One stroke of luck we had was that Dad knew one of the Notts players - a guy called Aubrey Cresswell. He never really made the first team but every year he would get me all the players' autographs on a team photo. I was in heaven, and the photo took pride of place on my bedroom wall. In return for these services, Aubrey didn't have to worry about paying for rides on Bartons buses.

When I wasn't watching football at Meadow Lane, I would be playing it. Right from my first few months on this planet Mum tells of my fascination with any kind of ball. Before I even reached my first birthday, one of my favourite pastimes, apparently, was for dad to lift me up and swing me between his legs to kick a miniature football along the path.

My heading skills were first honed indoors where Dad would blow up balloons for me then ping one across the room. I had to jump up and head it back to him. If you've ever tried heading a balloon, you'll realise how hard it is to get any real power behind one.

Naturally, though, most of my footballing practice took place outside when, come wind, rain or shine, you'd find me in our back garden in Sherwood. I spent literally hours and hours there. Dad devised a game for me involving a ball and a dustbin. He'd take the lid off the bin and I'd have to chip the ball in from a few yards. Then the bin would be moved a yard further back and so the game went on. Mostly, I was left to my own devices and I'd wellie the ball around all four corners of the diamond-shaped garden... and beyond.

Everyone on the estate took a great deal of pride in looking after their houses and gardens and our neighbours spent hours trimming their hedges into perfect shape. A council estate it may have been, but everywhere was spotless and well-cared for. Well, almost. Unfortunately, *the claw* would occasionally wellie a ball a shade too hard and through onto somebody else's patch. Sometimes it would end up in the allotments at the bottom of our garden and I'd merrily trample across the carrots and cauliflowers to retrieve it. Other times it would end up in a neighbouring garden. On the first occasion I'd go and ask: "Can I have my ball back please, mister," in time-honoured tradition. On the second, third, fourth, fifth and sixth times, I'd begin to feel a little embarrassed so I'd wade through these perfectly-kept hedges to get my ball back. Down the years, many gaps developed where I'd dived through.

In truth, football was all that mattered to me. Every night I would be out with my pals, our main meeting point a circular patch of land in the middle of the estate. This green was roughly eighty yards in diameter and perfect for seven-a-side games. Down went the clothes for goalposts and we would play, day after day, night after night. This really was where I learned my football, my soccer education which was to set me up for the rest of my career.

Every evening it was the same group of guys, and no fewer than three of us went on to become professional footballers. There were the Turton brothers: Barry was deaf and dumb but what a fantastic goalkeeper he was and his brother, Ian, was a nippy little sod. Terry Bell later went on to become a pro at Portsmouth and then there was Mick Somers who became my best friend.

Mick played for Chelsea and moved on to Torquay and Hartlepool where he was with Brian Clough and Peter Taylor. Now he's a plasterer living only a few miles

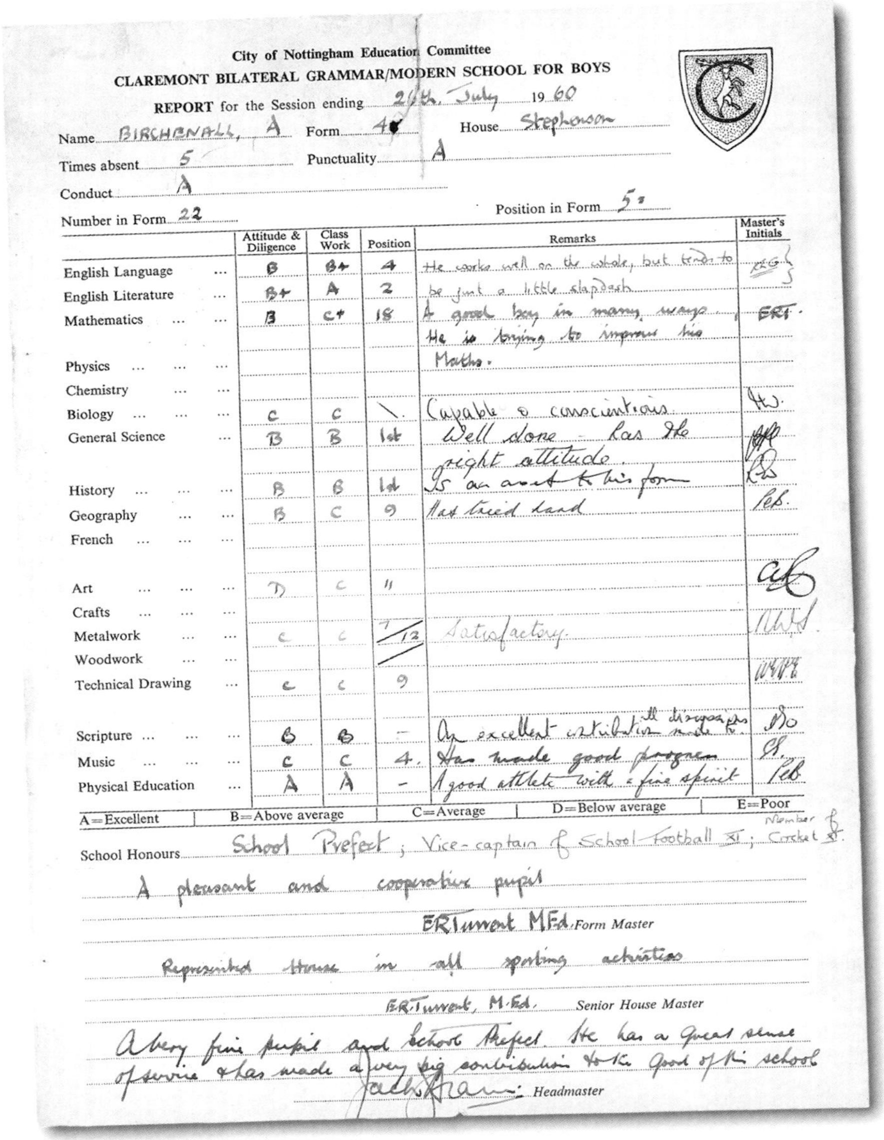

City of Nottingham Education Committee
CLAREMONT BILATERAL GRAMMAR/MODERN SCHOOL FOR BOYS

REPORT for the Session ending _26th, July_ 19 60

Name _BIRCHENALL, A_ Form _4¢_ House _Stephenson_

Times absent _5_ Punctuality _A_

Conduct _A_

Number in Form _22_ Position in Form _5?_

	Attitude & Diligence	Class Work	Position	Remarks	Master's Initials
English Language ...	B	B+	4	He works well on the whole, but tends to	
English Literature ...	B+	A	2	be just a little slapdash	
Mathematics	B	C+	18	A good boy in many ways. He is trying to improve his Maths.	ERT.
Physics					
Chemistry ...					
Biology	C	C	\	Capable & conscientious	4J.
General Science ...	B	B	1st	Well done has the right attitude	
History	B	B	1st	Is an asset to his form	Feb.
Geography	B	C	9	Has tried hard	
French					
Art	D	C	11		
Crafts					
Metalwork	C	C	7/12	Satisfactory.	
Woodwork					
Technical Drawing ...	C	C	9		
Scripture	B	B		An excellent contribution made all discussions.	Bo
Music	C	C	4.	Has made good progress	
Physical Education ...	A	A	-	A good athlete with a fine spirit	Feb.

A=Excellent | B=Above average | C=Average | D=Below average | E=Poor

School Honours _School Prefect ; Vice-captain of School Football 3[; Cricket 8[. Number 6_

A pleasant and cooperative pupil

ERTurner MEd Form Master

Represented House in all sporting activities

E.R.Turner, M.Ed. Senior House Master

A very fine pupil and school prefect. He has a great sense of service & has made a very big contribution to the good of this school : Headmaster

Schoolwork was not really my forte but I was always a trier though and you'll see I got A's for punctuality and conduct as well as physical education which was perhaps not surprisingly my best subject. This I have to say was one of my better school reports!

18

away in the Mapperley district of Nottingham. Mick's family were slightly better off than the rest of us which meant he was the one to supply the football.

He also had a bit of a temper and, about once a week, if things weren't going his way, the games would come to a premature end and he'd take his ball home. Fortunately, he used to come around to my house for lunch and I wouldn't let him eat any food until he agreed to bring the ball back!

Another happy hunting ground for us boys was Woodthorpe Park in Sherwood on a Sunday morning, the real mecca of football kickabouts. Between thirty and forty people would gather to play, including the ex-Nottingham Forest professional Ken Simco. Ken was an icon at the time and the morning used to attract the best amateurs in the city. Play was of a really high standard and Mick and I had to serve our apprenticeship by watching from the sidelines before we were allowed to take part.

We were only about 13 or 14 and everyone else was fully-grown, so not surprisingly we were the last picks. It was a tremendously high standard and games would go on for two hours or more, none of this 45-minutes-a-half lark. Tangling with grown men taught me a lot, they took no prisoners. Then, on Sunday afternoons I'd head off to Valley Road playing fields and start all over again with boys my own age.

While I took to football and other sports like a duck to water, the same could not be said of junior Birch and academia. I make no apologies for saying that I found school extremely hard work. Studying certainly did not come naturally to me.

My first seat of learning was Seeley Infants and Juniors. It's still there today and is next to Nottingham Prison - it recently attracted nationwide media attention as the school next door to a planned paedophile unit. After Seeley, I went to Haydn Road and it was there I was asked if I wanted to take eleven-plus examinations in order to move on to grammar school. My parents left the final decision to me but I said I'd rather not sit the test, my principal objection being if I went to a grammar school I would have to play rugby as the main sport rather than football.

Other than physical education, school was one big mystery to me. To this day, I still have a mental block when it comes to Maths. All the other academic subjects such as Geography, History and English passed over my head. Don't get me wrong, I wasn't bottom of the class and a complete 'thicko', it was just very slow going. I didn't rebel, though, by playing truant, I was always conscientious and never bunked off.

Lack of academic ability was surpassed only by my complete ineptitude when it came to crafts such as woodwork and metalwork. Ham-fisted attempts at producing useless tools and ornaments from these two disciplines gained legendary status among my family. One of my most celebrated pieces of handywork was a wicker

■ Here's the first-ever football team photo involving junior Birch. I'm the chubby-faced eight-year-old on the front row, second from the left. In the centre holding the ball is my best pal Micky Somers This was Haydn Road Junior School where I collected the first of my schoolboy trophies.

basket. It took weeks to make in woodwork lessons although all I'd had to do was weave willow strips in and out to form a basket. It looked like a piece of surreal art manfactured by Salvador Dali and was somewhat warped. Why on earth my teacher allowed me to take it home, I'll never know. "Mmmm, very nice, Lal," said Mum when I proudly presented it to her. Only much later in life did she tell me the whole family fell about giggling as soon as I was out of earshot.

Undeterred, the school suggested I try metalworking and I was charged with making a poker. All I had to do was get a steel rod, make a handle and flatten out one end but, again, I made a complete pig's ear of it. Perhaps this was why I constantly leaned towards sport instead. Academically, I wasn't very bright and, by my own admission, utterly useless with my hands, all of which meant my self-confidence took a bit of a battering.

In the gymnasium and on the sports field, however, it was a different matter. I can't say, though, that school gymwear did much for anyone's sartorial presence - white army surplus vest and shorts, and a pair of black plimsolls with a rubber toe at the end. It was in the gym though that I first discovered sexual urges. I was shinning up a rope one day and suddenly felt a stiffening in my loins. "Mmmm... that's rather pleasant," I thought, and proceeded to clamber up and down at every available opportunity. Tarzan had nothing on me when it came to swinging on ropes!

I used to perfect all possible ruses to ensure I spent less time studying and more time involved in sport. One of the most successful came at Claremont Secondary Modern when I was playing for the school teams.

We had double maths on Friday afternoon, about the worst possible ending to the school week as far as I was concerned. Saturday mornings were school football matches and, in those days, balls needed to be dubbin-ed. I volunteered to perform these duties... which had to be done on Friday afternoons. Many a time my maths teach would shout out: "Where's Birchenall?". Back would come the reply in unison: "Dubbin-ing his balls, sir!".

Claremont, a concrete jungle of Nissan huts, was a most intimidating school. It looked more like the Bastille than a place of learning and I still afford myself a wry smile today when I drive past. The headmaster, Jack Aram, and I were on fairly close terms. I was regularly called to his room to receive a friendly greeting from a strap he affectionately dubbed 'Joey'.

My 'crime' was organising games on the courtyard. Balls were banned so I used a large stone, which was fine until it went flying through the windows of the technical drawing room. "Birchenall! Get in here immediately!" he bellowed and in I went for a few lashes. Other times in lessons I'd spend most of the period concentrating on

■ CAN YOU SPOT ME? I'm on the back row, second from right. A real little shortarse at the time, wasn't I? Actually, I look smaller because of the gentle giant with the *wingnuts* on the left. This was the Claremont School team which lifted the Bentinck League Division Two championship.

swapping football cards. If it wasn't cards, then it would be my sweet tooth getting me into trouble. I loved sherbet dips. You know the ones I mean - bright yellow and you sucked the powder through a liquorice stick. The only problem was I used to get the powder on my hands, which was a dead giveaway. A whack across the knuckles with a ruler was deemed sufficient punishment for those misdemeanours.

Sport, in contrast to academic studies, did bestow a certain amount of street cred in school. At Claremont I was invariably in the top five for football, cricket and general physical education activities. I was looked upon as a leader and this status was reflected by the fact I had my own special space in the bike shed. Usually, it was a case of first come, first served but woe betide anyone who parked their wheels in my slot.

Cycling and junior Birch went hand in hand. I asked my parents for a bicycle and, sure enough, Mum obliged. Money was far from plentiful in our household but my parents were absolutely brilliant. I asked for a bike with derailleur gears because I wanted to join a cycle club with Mick Somers.

My mum, bless her, went along to the cycle shop. "Excuse me," she said to the assistant, "I'd like a sporty bicycle with Disraeli gears." The assistant fell about laughing and it's a story she still tells today. Anyway, the Birch soon became the proud owner of a ten-speed racing cycle so I joined Nottingham Cycling Club in Daybrook for eighteen months, during which time I clocked up hundreds of miles.

One of our most famous long-distance jaunts was to Uttoxeter, a round trip of the best part of a hundred miles. To this day, whenever I drive along the country's motorways and see Uttoxeter signposted, I have a laugh to myself and immediately recall the summer day we cycled there. At the time I was so pleased with my achievement, it was as if I had cycled to the ends of the earth.

To establish your street cred as a cyclist you also had to turn your hand to a bit of theft. The ultimate status symbol was to carry a Wall's ice-cream bag on the back of your seat but these could only be obtained from your local shop where the bag formed part of a Wall's advertising display. Needless to say, junior Birch managed to purloin one.

The more I think about it, the more I believe youthful interests helped shape my football career. I considered myself a reasonably talented player, but I was renowned for stamina and a never-say-die attitude. I'm absolutely certain that cycling, and walking to Meadow Lane, contributed enormously to my 'engine' which was to stand me in such good stead for the rest of my life.

Look at my *hampsteads* on this team photo of Claremont Soccer School in 1958. Yours truly had now been elevated to the status of school captain hence a ball at my feet and a central position in the front row. I was just beginning to perfect the poses which were to stand me in good stead on team photographs at the likes of Chelsea and Leicester in later life. Look at our footwear and the fact that we're all wearing odd socks. On the left of the photo is school headmaster Jack Aram. We were actually quite close. Only a strap called 'Joey' separated us on the several occasions I was hauled into his office.

Here's the Birch looking a right little short-arse in the Nottingham Boys team which won the Cobbin Cup in 1960. I'm the one with the baggy shorts (extreme right, back row). My best pal Mick Somers is an even shorter-arse. Check out the ugly sprog on the extreme left of the front row - none other than my old pal David Pleat. Pictured above: *Back (l to r): Lannon, Weatherall, Williams, Vickley, Potts, Birchenall; Front: Pleat, Gregg, Noon, Watson, Somers.*

Although my directional sense never let me down when on a bicycle, the same could not be said when I joined the Notts Battalion of the Army Cadet Force Association.

Following in my father's military footsteps, I thoroughly enjoyed dressing up in army gear and I did genuinely approve of the discipline, so much so that I considered becoming a full-time soldier.

One of my first trips was up to Catterick where I used a real gun on the rifle range and a few months later I returned to North Yorkshire for further exercises. We had to yomp across the moors using our map-reading and orientation skills, but the next thing Mum and Dad heard of me was when a policeman knocked on their door, to deliver the news their precious son had gone missing while on manoeuvres. I was eventually found the following morning, having yomped half-way across Yorkshire! Ironic, isn't it, that in twenty years as a professional footballer I pride myself I never 'went missing' on the pitch, but on my very first attempt at army cadet manoeuvres I disappeared without trace.

Meanwhile, my footballing ability at schools level began to shine through when I was at Haydn Road. We had an excellent team, winning all the various divisions before going on to lift the Nottingham Cup. Representative honours with the Nottingham Boys and Nottinghamshire Boys sides followed and I was fortunate enough to be named captain from the Under-12 side upwards.

There were plenty of other excellent schoolboy footballers too. One young fellow from Mundella School, in particular, caught the eye. Such was his skilful trickery, even at that tender age he was being hailed as the next Tom Finney. You may have heard of him - his name was David Pleat. Playing for Claremont we often used to cross swords although I'm pleased to report our school normally won.

Unfortunately, a serious injury curtailed his playing career with Nottingham Forest but he became a great manager, particularly with Luton Town and Tottenham Hotspur.

We were team-mates in the Nottinghamshire Boys side along with Mick Jones from Worksop, who was my strike partner at Sheffield United before he made a name for himself with Leeds in the great Don Revie era. There was also a nifty little wing half called Maurice Bembridge who subsequently went on to become a very successful European golf professional.

```
                NOTTINGHAM BOYS v. LEICESTER BOYS
At St. Alban's Road, Bulwell. Tuesday, September 22nd 1959. Kick-off 5.45 p.m.
        NOTTINGHAM BOYS                          LEICESTER BOYS
          Green & Gold                             Blue Shirts

                            11.Somers      7.Smith B.
                             (Claremont)
              6.Birchenall                               4.Day.
               (Claremont)
        3.Chaplin          10.Webster    8.Boyce           2.Hough
        (Fairham)           (Highbury)
  lliams      5.Gregg        9.Pleat      9.Payton    5.Smith R.  Caithness
  untingdon)  (Berridge)    (Mundella)
      2.Potts               8.Bolsher    10.Tewley        3.Ford
      (Mundella)            (Wm.Crane)
              4.Bickley      7.Hales     11.Bilsden    6.Beazeley
               (Claremont)  (Deering)

   Referee:  Mr.E.Pickering (Bulwell).  Linesmen Mr.H.White. Red Flag.(Bulwell)
                                                  Mr.E.Botham.Orange Flag.(Bulwell)
```

Here's the team sheet as it was typed for a Nottingham Boys v Leicester Boys fixture in 1959. It includes yours truly and a certain other notable name at number 9 - David Pleat

Playing for Nottingham Boys had its advantages. Training sessions were held twice-weekly in West Bridgford in the evening and we were given tokens from school to make the journey via bus and trolleybus. I would inform our school secretary we needed to be there a couple of hours earlier than actually required and that way we managed an afternoon off school!

This is perhaps an appropriate time to pay tribute to Mum and Dad for their unstinting support in getting my football career off the ground. They followed me all around the county, cheering from the sidelines. I remember one representative game at Newark when David Pleat fell over and broke his arm. My mum was a mite too close to the accident for comfort and duly fainted.

Football boots were expensive then but my parents insisted on buying the best. I wore a brown model made by Arthur Rowe which cost two and a tanner a week from a catalogue. When I was selected for the County Boys side, my mum said they would really have to push the boat out for me and she invested in a pair of Adidas boots, at a time when it was exceedingly rare for any youngster to own a pair because they were so darned expensive. It cost them a small fortune but they managed it and I'll always be eternally grateful for their support.

If you haven't already guessed, football was my life. So far, I have made only the briefest of mentions of my sister Christine. Like all brothers and sisters growing up we had our fights but, to this day, I really don't know how she spent her time. I was hardly ever in the house and lived only for my sport.

■ Here's another of Birch's football clubs as a youngster. I turned out for Bestwood Youth Club and I have to admit we didn't enjoy the greatest of facilities. On our pitch we spent more time avoiding dog muck than trying to get the ball. Next to me on the front row, wearing black shorts and national health glasses, was our star striker. Many a time *junior claw* whipped in a cross only for 'four eyes' (as he was affectionately known) to completely miss the ball. Needless to say, this was before the advent of contact lenses which could have done much to improve our striker's game.

Football gave me an identity at school. The headmaster would read out the results from weekend matches at Monday morning assembly and my name would frequently be mentioned. It gave me a sense of status and I was immensely grateful for that. Believe it or not, I was quite a shy youngster and football gave me the self-confidence I lacked.

Sadly, my prowess did not stand me in much stead with the girls! As school captain you'd think that would be a good starting point with which to impress the opposite sex. Remember, in those days, it was still all-boy and all-girl schools. Claremont Secondary Modern didn't have so much as one girl in its ranks and I had to wait until I was 13 before I even got my first kiss!

> Claremont Secondary Boys' School
> HUCKNALL ROAD
> NOTTINGHAM
>
> 24ᵗʰ March 1959.
>
> Congratulations on the award of your School 'A' Team Football Colours for the 1958-59 season.
>
> S. H. Heathcote M.A.

Football gave me a sense of status and added to my self confidence.

I'll spare the girl's blushes and refer to her simply as Christine D. At the time I looked on her as an absolute goddess, although in reality she was probably a *clagthorpe*. To be fair, she did have a bit of a reputation around Daybrook but at the time I was bowled over by her. I invited her around to my house one Sunday afternoon when both my parents were out. Not a great deal happened because I was petrified Mum and Dad would walk in, but nevertheless, it was quite an education for me and, as they say, a real eye-opener.

I would hesitate to call her my first girlfriend; without sounding too brutal she was more of an adolescent experiment. I know that sounds terrible but I was so obsessed with football nothing else mattered - I was 15 before I began to pay serious attention to the opposite sex.

At this stage I would also point out that modern 14 and 15-year-old girls look vastly different to their counterparts of the 1950s. As far as I was concerned the nearest to them had ben Christine D. and she was my sole experiment for a game of doctors and nurses.

If truth be told, the Birch was far from an oil painting and lacked self confidence and assertiveness. I started to show an interest in girls at 15 and wandered down to the local chip shop after football on a Friday night. There was one girl there called Christine Worthington who I had a mad crush on. She was a real knockout and was captain of all the sports teams at Manning Girls School, where my first real girlfriend, and future wife, Heather also went. My fantasy girl Christine dated my friend Terry Bell. He was a good-looking guy, whereas I was a lanky lad with buck teeth and a terrible complexion. As a result of my childhood peritonitis scare, I'd been pumped full of penicillin for years and I swear that drug was to blame for the unsightly boils and painful carbuncles which formed on my neck as a teenager.

If I was a late starter with girls, then I was positively backward in the drinking stakes. I always swore I would never drink alcohol. My favourite tipple was mixed fruit but there are only so many pints of mixed fruit you can drink. Eventually I graduated to shandies, tops and, finally, bitter and lager in later life.

As for drugs, we'd never heard of them. In many ways, being a schoolkid was far easier then than now. There were considerably fewer distractions for a young lad, and for me the fewer the better meant I could concentrate more on football.

Like all growing boys I loved my food. When it came to eating greens I wasn't too pernickety but I did have a few food vices. One of these was a fondness for two different types of sandwiches, but not conventional ham or cheese. No, I loved condensed milk sandwiches and, best of all, sugar butties. I'd pile on loads of butter and then pour a mound of sugar into the middle. Absolutely scrummy! Remember, in those days there were no McDonald's or Burger Kings so these sandwiches were our 'burgers of the '50s.

Kids won't be surprised to learn that school dinners tasted worse than they do now. The only edible fayre was the caramel sweet. The rest, I'm afraid, was absolute garbage - mashed potato, served with an ice-cream scoop, was lumpy beyond belief and, no matter what other items were on the menu, they would always be accompanied by lashings of over-cooked cabbage.

When I look back on my childhood one of the single biggest events was the arrival of the television set. I can perhaps best put it into perspective by saying it was the equivalent of a Martian landing in your back garden. I was about 11 when the Birchenall family took delivery of a John Logie Baird masterpiece. A pokey little black and white set it may have been, but what an attention-grabber - an electrical device in the corner of the room which showed moving pictures and was alive!

Its fascination was such it succeeded in interrupting my football and I'd spend an hour or two watching children's programmes - Muffin the Mule and the Flowerpot Men were my favourites. There was no sport in those days but I sometimes watched our neighbours' television because theirs boasted a special magnifying glass over the screen which made the picture look bigger.

The neighbours retaliated by popping round on Sunday nights. One chap in particular had a portable puppet theatre with a lantern from which he would make animal shadows. Sad, I know, but I found it enthralling.

By now the Birch had finally managed to graduate from helping other people

JUNIOR MAGPIE: My official call-up papers from Notts County to play for their 'A' youth team in the Midland Intermediate Youth League.

make money and had belatedly grasped the concept of making his own. I decided to take a morning paper round, but made one fundamental mistake. Most kids take on a round close to their home, but not me, I had to walk two miles to get to the newsagents before I even started deliveries.

I had noticed a paper-boy vacancy advertised but conveniently ignored the fact the shop was nowhere near where I lived. Still, I must have made a reasonable success of the job because one of the ladies on my round was moved to write a letter to the *Nottingham Evening Post*. Hilda Nation-Draper was her name and she waxed lyrical about my delivery talents, so much so that the letter was spotted by our headmaster who read out its contents at morning assembly.

In my closing years at school, football began to assume increasing importance. Much of my time was now spent training and playing with the City Boys and County Boys squads in Nottingham. This meant training up to three times a week and playing up to four games a week.

Academically, at 15, main examinations were looming. I sat the first batch and passed. The second set, however, co-incided with a rather important trial for Nottinghamshire Boys. When Claremont headmaster Mr Aram learned I was planning to miss them, he called me into the office. "The likelihood of you becoming a professional footballer is a million to one, I suggest you re-think," he told me. I doggedly explained it was highly unlikely the county selectors would make an exception for me not turning up.

My parents were again excellent and allowed me to choose. This was probably the first really major decision of my life and, to this day, I believe I made the right choice. I was never going to reach college or graduate to university. I wanted to taste 'real life' and even if I wasn't going to make it as a footballer then I was going to get a job immediately. Oh, and by the way, I did get called up to the County team.

Scouts from Nottingham Forest and Notts County regularly kept a close eye on all who played for the representative City and County sides. To be honest, although becoming a professional was my dream, I was never completely convinced I would be good enough to make the grade. Forest were the bigger of the two clubs and in Division One, while the Magpies languished in the old Third Division. In those days, clubs did not have apprentices or youth trainees, instead you joined what was called the groundstaff, normally for a two-year period.

My dilemma arose in that I had grown up a Notts County supporter but it was Forest who showed the greater interest in me. I had been playing for Notts in the Midland Intermediate League side for twelve months and, naturally, my father was both tremendously delighted and proud. Being the poorer of the two clubs, Notts' entire groundstaff only amounted to two youngsters and I was not one of them. Forest, by contrast, had a much bigger groundstaff of about a dozen and it was they who offered me an opportunity to join them.

Just before I was about to leave Claremont I received the following letter from the then Forest manager Billy Walker. It's a letter I have always kept and it's reproduced here in full.

July 27 1960

Dear Alan

Mr Hamilton and Mr Gordon, two schoolmasters whom you know, have combined to drop us a line about your ability as a footballer and your deep interest in maybe one day becoming a professional if considered good enough. We are pleased to hear about this and also the fact that if you could make the grade, Nottingham Forest would be your main ambition.

You already know that several of your ex-school colleagues in soccer, Pleat, Niblett and Somers (to mention but three) are with us and we would be delighted to have you join us too as soon as you leave school and are free to come down training either during the days of your holidays (starting at 9.30am) as Pleat is doing at the moment or on Tuesday and Thursday evenings each week (from 5.15pm) as Somers is doing. In either case we shall be pleased to see you.

We are enclosing an amateur form for your possible signature (where marked X) and return to us, together with your personal details on the card provided. When replying, perhaps you'd like to let us know if you have made any plans for your future, off the field, when you leave school.

Meanwhile, we shall be holding the first of our pre-season trial games on Saturday August 6. If you would like to report to City Ground at 1pm you can be included if you would like a run out with us. We hope that you'll be able to take advantage of our training sessions, during the day or the evening, and will look out for you then.

May we just say that if we think you have the required ability to make the grade in professional football we shall not hesitate to say so and suggest plans which will help you along the hard road to success just as, on the other hand, if we feel we cannot offer you anything here we would also tell you straight away. However, in closing let us say that if you maintain the kind of form you showed in the school teams then you ought to make the necessary progress.

Looking forward to hearing from you and to the return of the enclosed cards. Kindest regards and all future good wishes for your success on the field and off.

yours sincerely

Billy Walker
Manager Nottingham Forest

Telephone No. 88236

Established 1865

NOTTINGHAM FOREST
FOOTBALL CLUB

English Cup Winners 1897/98

F.A. Cup Winners 1958/59

CITY GROUND, NOTTINGHAM

Secretary :
G. NOEL WATSON, J.P.
Home Phone 85101

Manager: W. H. WALKER
Ground Phone: (Private) 89914
Home Phone : Ruddington 488

WHW/DM

Alan Birchenall, Esq.,
45 Markham Crescent,
Sherwood,
NOTTINGHAM.

16th August, 1960.

Dear Alan,

Looking through our files we find that we have had no reply to our letter to you of the 27th July in which we asked you if you were interested in the prospects of becoming a footballer eventually.

We wonder if there is any further information you need from us or if you would care for one of our representatives to call on you.

Looking forward to hearing from you in due course.

Yours sincerely,

Acting Manager.

p.s.

We have sent a copy of this letter to Mr. Hamilton a former master of yours, as we did the first one we wrote to you.

Forest had no reply from me to their letter. It is one of my few regrets that I couldn't pick up the courage to tell them my decision.

This was truly a tremendous honour, and a letter my friends and schoolmates would have died for. But, having been brought up a Notts County fan, something didn't feel right. I talked it over with my dad and, again, my parents were brilliant, as they allowed the final decision to rest with me. It was unheard of for any youngster to turn down a professional club, but I did. My allegiance to County meant I clearly couldn't sign for their arch-rivals. I told my dad and said I wanted to go out into the real world and find a job. At that stage I genuinely thought my chance of a professional football career had gone, you didn't get two bites of the cherry... or so I thought. But don't get the impression Forest expended any effort in trying to persuade me to change my mind. Far from it, there were many youngsters queueing up to replace me. So, that was the end of that. Perhaps my only regret in later life was my next move - I went on holiday to London with my relatives and, basically, 'did a runner' being unable to pluck up the courage to tell the club of my decision.

So, within days of finishing school and without a single academic qualification to my name, I had turned down the possibility of a professional career with Nottingham Forest and desperately needed a job.

I had hoped to be taken on at my father's company, Bartons Transport, but there were no vacancies. I thought about an apprenticeship as an electrician but, and don't ask me why, I didn't pursue it. Then, out of the blue, I noticed a vacancy in the local paper for work at a conveyor belt factory in the Carlton area of Nottingham. I went for an interview and got the job. My extensive duties including punching holes on a production line and the pay was good. I earned a basic £3 per week which rose, with overtime and bonuses, to nearly £5. At the time, my dad was only earning £12. Half my wages I gave to Mum for board and lodgings, the rest I spent on myself having discovered the delights of going out on the town in Nottingham, to places like the Palais, Locarno and Colemans.

One of the major attractions of working in Carlton were the lunch-hour football matches in the yard, on a pitch the like of which I had never come across - it was L-shaped with a fence running along one side. There I was in my overalls getting a real 'dab' on in my industrial boots. We couldn't use a leather ball because of the concrete surface but a Fido ball or tennis ball sufficed and this became the highlight of my working day.

After about six months a vacancy came up in the unit repair shop at Bartons Transport in Chilwell and Dad was able to give me the nod. As the youngest guy in the store, various unsavoury jobs befell me. Firstly, let me point out that Sherwood to Chilwell is a distance of around ten miles. Occasionally, I would take the bus, but mostly I cycled. I got up at 5am and, armed with sandwiches and thermos flask, pedalled for an hour, along the boulevards and past Nottingham University, to get to work. On arrival my first job was to get some coke, shovel it into the boiler, douse it with petrol and get the fires going. I was as black as the ace of spades by the time I'd finished. When they were glowing, I would stand in front of the fires and belatedly warm myself.

A ginger-haired chap named Ted would invariably arrive and push me out of the way. "Are you going to move your arse Birchenall, and stop day-dreaming about becoming a footballer?" he would sneer. This ritual took place nearly every morning.

My main job was to scour out the brake drums with a guy called Fred Kitching. Bear in mind that Bartons used mainly double decker buses, so you can imagine the state these brake drums were in. We had to crank the drum onto a special machine and scour all the muck out. Then I had to take off the old brake pads and rivet on

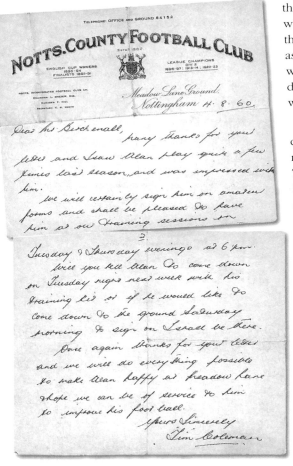

A letter to my Dad from Tim Coleman spelling out what would be required at Meadow Lane.

the new ones - a practice not without its health hazards. Inside the brake linings was a layer of asbestos but in those days we weren't fully aware of the dangers, and I never bothered to wear a breathing mask.

Apart from his own tasks, my dad was also responsible for running the works football team. These days every city has literally hundreds of Sunday morning sides but Bartons Transport were one of the first dozen in Nottingham. Dad's side and a team call 'The Hungarians' were the two big clubs vying for honours. I got all my mates to turn out for us, but we preferred to play for Bartons Reserves which played in an expanded Division Two of the Notts Sunday League. Within a short space of time we were better than the first team.

During this time I was still playing for Notts County in the Midland Intermediate League. Matches took place on Saturday afternoons and we would play against other League clubs like Rotherham, Port Vale, Aston Villa and Barnsley. I was tremendously proud to be playing for County but it was hard work... and getting harder all the time. I was working a 55-hour week but was still expected to train on Tuesday and Thursday evenings. On those days I would get up at 5am, cycle to work, dash off to Meadow Lane for two hours of training and get back home at 9.30pm and then start all over again the following day. Naturally, my dad loved it and I would tell him stories of senior players I bumped into at the ground.

Saturdays, too, became increasingly difficult. I had to work until 12 noon which invariably made me late for the Notts matches. I could just about make the home games but often failed to catch the bus for away venues. I got a rollocking or two for not turning up and Notts told me I really could not continue missing every other match. By this stage I had no chance of joining the Meadow Lane groundstaff so I decided to call a halt to that ambition. It was a difficult decision because of my allegiance but I felt I was going nowhere.

At the same time I was being courted by two of the leading Saturday afternoon youth teams in Nottingham - the quaintly-named Parliament Street Methodists and Thorneywood Athletic. I talked it through with my dad and explained that work and playing for the Magpies was becoming too much to handle. He was great and told me to do whatever I felt was best. I began playing for Parliament Street on Saturday afternoons before I was approached by Thorneywood manager Colin Baines.

They were the top youth team in the county and won every honour going. I was enjoying my football and all thoughts of becoming a professional had subsided.

Arguably the most quaintly named team I ever played for was Parliament Street Methodists. They were second in Nottingham only to Thorneywood Athletic for whom I was to subsequently sign. I'm occupying my accustomed position second from the right on the front row. The Meths (short for methodists and nothing to do with methylated spirit) had religious affiliations, although I'm not aware that any of us actually went to the church.

■ All-conquering Thorneywood Athletic line up for the camera. We were the undisputed kings of youth football in the county winning a whole host of leagues and cups. We were obviously quite successful because we could afford a set of matching socks. In the background you can just see a trolleybus at the Colwick terminus. Our home pitch was a stone's throw from Nottingham racecourse. It was whilst playing for Thorneywood I was spotted by Sheffield United.

I played with Thorneywood until I was 17... and one eventful afternoon Sheffield United's assistant manager Archie Clark came along to watch. He'd been eyeing me up for half a dozen games before the approach came.

I'll never forget it. The final whistle had blown and I was walking off the pitch when I noticed an old guy wearing a trilby hat, sports jacket and gold waistcoat. He came up to me and asked: "Would you be interested in having a trial with Sheffield United?" I was dumbfounded. United wanted me to go to Bramall Lane for a three-month trial. I was on a works apprenticeship at Bartons and needed their permission to leave temporarily. I had to go and see the managing director who, whilst most accommodating, obviously didn't fancy my chances of making the professional grade.

"Don't worry lad, you go with our best wishes. We'll keep your job open for you for when you return," was his response to my request for three months' leave.

I went back to the unit repair shop for the rest of the week and was determined to exact some revenge on my ginger-haired colleague Ted. Right on cue, he had a poke at me for dreaming about becoming a pro as I warmed myself in front of the furnace at 7am.

Hardly able to contain myself, I blurted out: "That's right, I am. I've got a three month trial with Sheffield United, so there!" Stunned into temporary silence, he then retorted: "You'll be back, you'll be back." I clearly remember vowing to myself that I would never return, I just had to make it work. I would not give this old whinger the satisfaction of seeing me crawling back on my hands and knees. It was the motivation I needed. I knew I was incredibly lucky to be given a second chance to make the professional ranks and it really was a case of now or never.

But, you know, I did go back a couple of years later, only instead of turning up on a bicycle wearing dirty overalls, I arrived in a shiny flash car sporting a smart new suit. Everyone else was delighted to see me but there was Ted, hiding away behind the gearboxes. He didn't say a word. Cruel, I know, but he made my life a misery for a year or more.

The mucky and unattractive environment of the factory floor drove me steadfastly on when I went to Sheffield United. I didn't relish the thought of returning to scour out dirty brake drums or feel greasy sump oil dripping onto me. When I had turned down Forest, I was still at school and had not experienced paid employment, I just wanted to go out and sample the real world. But I'd done that now for the past eighteen months and realised exactly how hard it was to get out of bed at 5am every morning. My second chance, with Sheffield United, was not one I was going to discard lightly.

■ **ON THE BOTTOM OF THE WORLD.** Invercargill in New Zealand marked the most southerly inhabited spot of the planet. London is a mere 11,820 miles away as we enter week three of Sheffield United's six week tour of New Zealand, Australia and Hong Kong. The South Pole is just two miles short of 3,000 away, while Sydney is a stone's throw 1,250 miles distant. Under the famous directional sign are: Gil Reece (Sheffield United and Wales), a pipe-smoking Jimmy Armfield (Blackpool and England), Tony Waiters (Blackpool and England goalkeeper), and Alan Hodgkinson (Sheffield United).

All over the World

Chapter 2

Adventurers like Michael Palin, in his excellent television series, have shown us how much easier it is to navigate the world nowadays. While I haven't quite circumnavigated the globe in eighty days, I have been fortunate enough to play football across all five continents during a twenty-year career. From arduous month-long tours of South America to New Zealand, from North America across Europe and Asia to Hong Kong, I've merrily whacked footballs around to my heart's content. The game truly has given me a valuable opportunity to see the world.

These days you will probably have to travel a long way to find a teenager who has not been on at least one 18-30's week of debauchery in some Balearic hot-spot, and good luck to them too, but back in the sixties our holiday horizons were slightly less ambitious. If you lived in Nottingham, the staple holiday diet was a week at the bracing East Coast resort of Skegness. If you were a little more adventurous you might travel further up the coast to Mablethorpe and Sutton on Sea - the Birch once managed to reach the Butlin's holiday camp in Filey. However, this excursion was blighted by a dust-up involving my friend Micky Somers. A group of twelve lads went there and Micky, a little the worse for a pint or two of alcohol, decided to take on a group of bouncers. Needless to say he lost, and it took our combined diplomatic endeavours to ensure the entire group wasn't kicked out of the camp.

From such humble travelling expeditions, I was thrust into the world of football tours with Sheffield United and how quickly times changed. Within a matter of weeks, I was selected for the Blades' youth team which was to travel to Holland for an international youth tournament in Gröningen, an excellent competition which, I understand, is still running today.

■ **FILEY, HERE WE COME.** Our first teenage holiday away on our own and one I'm unlikely to forget. I'm the silly plonker wearing the sailor's cap and in the middle is my short-arse pal Mick Somers who almost got us all thrown out for starting a fight. On the right is our pal Eddie McGlory. A total of eight of us (main pic) shared two chalets and it's fair to say we all did a bit of growing up in North Yorkshire during that week.

Train and ferry were our mode of transport and I remember the team proudly lining up in club blazers on Sheffield railway station ready to embark on a journey I considered to be to the ends of the earth. In truth, we probably looked more like a bunch of evacuees but we did have quite a talented squad which included Mick Jones, who I'd played alongside for Nottinghamshire boys, and also Alan Woodward, Charlie Bell and Len Badger who all graduated to senior level.

Upon arrival in Amsterdam we were herded into a big community hall. At this point you can dismiss all thoughts of luxurious five-star accommodation. We were to be lodged with local families and waited apprehensively for our names to be called. Assistant manager Archie Clark shouted them out and when 'Alan Birchenall' was heard a friendly couple stepped forward and escorted me to their car. When I arrived at their pleasant house, I immediately spotted one particularly welcoming feature - their teenage daughter who was exquisitely pretty and about my age. My room for the next few days was a loft conversion with a neat little single bed and I have to say that everyone - especially the daughter - went out of their way to make me feel at home.

The following morning it was my misfortune that my hosts were unable to drive me to the training ground and instead pointed me in the direction of the local bus stop and gave me a handful of guilders. There I stood, a spotty 17-year-old innocent in Sheffield United training kit, waiting patiently by the tulip fields in Dutch countryside, for a mysterious bus which would hopefully pull up and convey me to a training ground I had never before visited. I was growing up fast, I can tell you.

Thankfully, as all us Brits pray for in such desperate times, most of the natives spoke English and I was able to arrive safely at my destination. Unfortunately though, on the return journey all the Dutch houses looked exactly the same to me and, after getting off the bus, I wandered up and down the flower fields for a while trying to find my lodgings before I eventually bumped into my hosts' daughter. She, you might say, showed me the lie of the land.

This was the photo of the Sheffield United line-up that appeared in the Youth Tournament programme in Gröningen in May 1964. I'm next to my mate Mick Jones in the middle of the front row.

The Gröningen Youth Tournament programme was a lavish 12 page issue with photos of all the teams taking part.

My problems with Dutch geography, though, were nothing to the ones I encountered on the obligatory tour to the red-light district of nearby Amsterdam. Although most aspects of society have changed in the past thirty years, the Canalstrasse was just as brazen and up-front as it is today (or so I'm told, having never gone back there since this particular experience). On the eve of the final in which we were playing Leicester City, a group of us United lads decided to pay a visit to the area.

You can imagine the looks of surprise on our fresh little faces as we clocked the glamorous ladies of the night for the very first time. Everywhere we turned we could see women in windows with their *borussias* hanging out and others *semi clothed-off* beckoning for trade. Eight of us sat down with a coke apiece and hit upon the bright idea that we should pool our guilders and choose one hapless individual who would visit a prostitute. How did we choose? We decided to draw straws, and guess who copped the short one? Needless to say, I tried hard to back out but the other lads wouldn't have it.

Eventually, I plucked up the (Dutch?!) courage to walk over the bridge and approach one of the ladies. Picture the scene. I was a spotty little oik in my Sheffield United tie, club blazer and flannels and, at the tender age of 17, I was about to attempt the most nerve-wracking task of my teenage life. My *'arris* was going like a *fiddlers elbow*. I went up to the lady and held out my hand which was overflowing with crumpled guilders. "How much?" I muttered, almost unintelligibly.

In surprisingly good English, she replied: "Go away little boy, and come back when you're a man." It was the ultimate put-down and I stood there completely mortified. Obviously, upon clocking the blazer, lapel badge and tie, she had mistaken my United gear for a school uniform. The lads, watching from the other side of the bridge, creased up in fits of laughter.

At least there was a happy ending to the trip because in the final against Leicester the following day we managed to win on a penalty shoot-out. So you see I didn't return to England completely empty-handed. Despite my rejection by a Dutch lady of the night, I still maintain that Holland is one of the friendliest of all the countries I have visited.

If my eyes were opened by the trip to Gröningen, then I was in for a real shock twelve months later after breaking into the The Blades' first team at the tender age of 18. Let me preface this story by saying that any tour lasting over a week is considered a marathon by today's professional soccer clubs. Even trips to Australia

■ **DUTCH DELIGHT.** It's all smiles as the Sheffield United youth team return home triumphant from an international tournament in Holland. Yours truly is holding what appears to be a white handbag but is actually my 'duty-frees'. This was my first-ever trip abroad and I'm pleased to say we were rather more successful on the pitch than off it. However, I'm ashamed to say I returned 'empty-handed' from a visit to the red light district of Amsterdam. On the far left is Archie Clark, the man responsible for launching my professional career. Archie, assistant manager at United, spotted me as a teenager playing for Thorneywood Athletic in local league football in Nottingham.

■ **HAWAII FIVE 0:** Well, six of us managed a few hours on Waikiki beach in Honolulu during a stopover on our around-the-world tour between Canada and New Zealand. Just look at that lithe, supple Birchy torso (I'm the one on the extreme left, can't you tell). Oh for a body like that now. Left to right are my United team-mates Reg Matthewson, Ken Mallender, Bob Widdowson, Gil Reece and (sitting) Barry Wagstaff.

and the Far East don't take more than seven days. Sheffield United and Blackpool had lined up a twelve-game around-the-world series of exhibition matches lasting six weeks and encompassing Canada, New Zealand and Hong Kong. Michael Palin would not have looked out of place on this trip. Anyone organising such a tour these days risks being classed as certifiable but United boss John Harris loved his long end-of-season journeys.

As an inexperienced teenager I did not fully understand the enormity of what lay ahead, I was just pleased to be in such illustrious company as the Blackpool captain and former England international, Jimmy Armfield, and my United team mates. The flight from London to Vancouver, on a BOAC Comet aircraft, was my first ever trip on an aeroplane. I was slightly nervous but my trepidation was outweighed by a sense of excitement and keen anticipation. I felt like royalty as meal after sumptuous meal was smilingly served up by glamorous air hostesses. Today's stewardesses are no *clagthorpes* but the attractive hostesses of that era were held in the same high esteem as today's sought-after supermodels.

Match-fixing allegations have, regrettably, been all too commonplace in recent times, with unsubstantiated allegations against leading players. For the very first time, I can reveal that match-fixing is nothing new. Our entire tour series with Blackpool was supposed to have been fixed. United skipper Graham Shaw and Blackpool captain Jimmy Armfield got together before the first game to thrash out a deal. After a long, hard season the last thing both sides wanted was to be running around like wombats on a exhibition series around the world. So, it was agreed that each side should win specific games and results would be mapped out in advance.

Graham gave us the instructions for the first match in Vancouver's Olympic Stadium - it was to end in a 3-3 draw. I was to net a goal and, after an uncharacteristic mistake by the Blackpool defender, I duly scored. Lovely jubbly. The game went ahead as planned and, with a couple of minutes remaining, the score was 3-3. We were contentedly playing out time when, all of a sudden, a Blackpool lad let fly with a 20-yarder that scorched into the top corner of the netting. We couldn't believe it. Blackpool were 4-3 up and seconds later the final whistle blew. Back in the dressing room we all laid into Graham. "'Ere, we thought it was supposed to be 3-3. What's going on?" we asked. "I know. I know. I've spoken with Jimmy and he says his player shouldn't have done it." Bear in mind at this stage that our agreement had been struck without the knowledge of the two managers.

Off we flew from Vancouver, half-way across the world to New Zealand, to play the next round of matches. We were due to appear at eight locations - Wellington, Auckland, Dunedin, Invercargill, Napier, Palmerston, Nelson and Christchurch. In the first game, in Auckland, John Harris gave us our pre-match pep talk. He laced into us about our diabolical defending in the game in Vancouver, not knowing we had allowed them to score as part of the deal. After the team talk, the lads made a beeline for Graham because according to our schedule we were due to lose this game. "Don't

■ Playing Blackpool all over the world!

45

NOT ANOTHER FOKKER. New Zealand airlines Fokker Friendships weren't the most comfortable of planes and many's the time we touched down on grass landing strips... but John Docherty can still afford us a cheery wave as we board another Fokker.

INSPECTING THE LOCALS. On our tour of New Zealand we visited a real-life Maori settlement. They were very friendly but I found one of their habits particularly unsettling. Instead of giving you a great big *'gregory's'* they insisted on rubbing *bugles.* Not that I've got a complex about the size of my bugle, you understand.

Invercargill, New Zealand, June 2 1965. Gil Reece and I survey the scene on the seventh match of the New Zealand leg of our tour. The crowd in the stadium was about 1,500, while in the hills behind are about 4.7million sheep!

Wellington, Auckland, Nelson, Christchurch or Palmerston? To be honest, I haven't a clue. More fans than usual so it must have been a decent-sized town. By now, the fatigue factor was beginning to set it. After you've played Blackpool eight times in four weeks, you're beginning to get fed up of the sight of them. *N.B. If you know where this is, please drop me a line at Leicester City football club. The first correct answer wins a signed copy of this book.*

worry,'" he said, "the gloves are off, let's sort those bastards out!" For the remaining eleven games of the tour it was as if third world war had broken out. Across the length and breadth of New Zealand, us and Blackpool kicked lumps out of each other desperately trying for victory in every game. I'm not totally sure but I think we edged the series in the end with six wins, two draws and four defeats.

Whilst travelling Down Under we certainly didn't enjoy the luxury of a BOAC Comet. Instead, New Zealand Airlines ferried us around in an old war-time Dakota to airports that barely lived up to the name and, indeed, outside of Wellington and Auckland, we frequently touched down on grassy landing-strips. One airport resembled a scene from the Wild West and actually had a hitching pole for the horses outside the arrival lounge!

One abiding memory I have was of a lengthy plane-hop in Australia from Sydney to Darwin. On touching down, I looked across the barren landscape to be greeted by the sight of mile upon endless mile of red clay. It was a roasting 130 degrees Fahrenheit in the shade and I asked myself: "Birch, what are you doing here?"

So long away, and so far from home, by this time everyone in both camps was beginning to feel more than a little homesick. Telephoning across the world was an impossibility and pigeon post was the fastest way to communicate with the UK. Although the junior member of United's squad, I was quickly entrusted with the job

■ **A BAR SOMEWHERE IN NEW ZEALAND.** Who cares where. I've always said if you plonk a few footballers down anywhere in the world and give them a few beers, they'll be in heaven. The young quartet in question are (left to right) Ken Mallender who went to to play in Hereford's famous giant-killing FA Cup team, Welsh international winger Gil Reece, John Docherty who enjoyed managerial stints at Brentford, Cambridge and Millwall, and yours truly.

of social secretary to liven up the nights. From this tour brief glimpses emerged of my innate organisational skills which were to stand me in good stead among fellow professionals - and get me into so much trouble - in my future playing career. We'd discovered New Zealand possessed an abundance of sheep... but the country's nightlife was decidedly threadbare. In each new city we visited, the extent of social activity was a welcoming night in the town hall with a bunch of local dignitaries only one step away from mummification.

Very quickly we realised the best way to attract some female company was to contact the local hospital and so, on arrival, Birch was charged with the task of ringing up to explain we were professional footballers on tour and could we arrange a party. Our modus operandi was that we would supply the drink and food if the girls could supply themselves and a venue. It seemed to work quite well. Obviously, we didn't mention this to the Blackpool players because we didn't want them spoiling our fun.

These parties soon became the highlights of the tour but inevitably led to friction with the Seasiders camp. They cottoned on to our idea and tried to steal it for themselves so there was quite a race to be first to contact the hospitals upon arrival.

Unfortunately, at one venue the Blackpool lads gatecrashed the Sheffield party and there was a bout of fisticuffs. Not only were we kicking lumps out of each other on the park, but tempers were boiling over off it as well.

Looking back, it's not surprising really. Two clubs living in each other's pockets for such a long time were always going to cause a few problems. The idea of a similar tour would not be entertained at all today. And rightly so.

On the way back, we stopped off in Hong Kong. Of all the countries I had visited so far, this was the one which made the biggest impression on me. Later, in my business life, I was to return there several times but the first occasion I saw the island was the most impressive - the combination of the sight of thousands of people bustling around at midnight, the sounds, the smells and the overwhelming feeling of busy-ness. We took a ride on the famous Star Ferry, sailed out to Kowloon and chose fresh live lobsters from enormous tanks on the picturesque floating restaurants.

When it came to football, the Hong Kong team were not quite so impressive. They were skilful and tricky but their principal problem was lack of inches - their tallest man was only five feet four inches! We played them in a game and, for the opening quarter of an hour, it was quite tight. Then came orders from the bench to 'lump it in the air'. Alan Woodward proceeded to launch a barrage of far-post balls for the Birch to meet, and we won at a canter with me scoring a couple of headers in a 4-2 victory.

When we finally returned home and I regaled my friends in Sherwood with the trip around the world they could scarcely believe their ears. I was having difficulty myself, since only twelve months earlier I'd been stuck under a Bartons bus with oil dripping all over me. This, however, was only just the beginning. Blades manager John Harris specialised in these long tours. Come to think of it, he should have been a travel agent for Michael Palin.

We toured South and Central America in back-to-back seasons. First John put together a natty little schedule which took in Mexico, Chile and Paraguay, then, a year later, he produced another fascinating trip - five weeks of country-hopping between Chile, Peru, Argentina, Ecuador, Bolivia and back again to Mexico.

John, you see, was the typical English gentleman. Unmarried, he didn't smoke or drink, went to church regularly and never swore. I defy you to find a manager in the modern game who doesn't fall foul of at least one of those vices. And, as you can probably gather, he loved to travel.

John was obviously unsure whether our 1965-66 end-of-season jaunt to three Latin American countries was sufficiently long enough, so he arranged a two-game trip to

Norway to face club sides in Oslo and Bergen as a warm-up. Three days after the fjords of Bergen we touched down in Mexico City for an international tournament.

We had been sent over as the English guinea pigs in advance of the 1970 World Cup being hosted by the Mexicans. There was much talk about the effects of the high altitude and rarified atmosphere on a footballer's body and we had to report back exactly how difficult it made things. Damn difficult, I can tell you.

We played two matches in Mexico City and a third in Guadalajara against the Mexican national team and two club sides. Forget about playing football, breathing was a difficult enough feat in itself. Oxygen masks and cylinders were placed at various points along the pitch and we spent more time putting those on than we did chasing the ball. As a special dispensation we were allowed continuous use of substitutes and we kept having to come off after every ten minutes. Needless to say,

in the three games we didn't score but we did manage a goalless draw with the Mexican national side in our final fixture. This proved an excellent result because it helped us slot in a never-to-be-forgotten holiday in Acapulco.

Manager John Harris was highly delighted with our showing and suggested we all took a short break in the Mexican holiday paradise.

■ **SELF SERVICE LOBSTER, HONG KONG STYLE.**
My Sheffield United manager John Harris looks a trifle sheepish, or should that be lobster-ish, during a stroll down the famous floating Aberdeen restaurant in Hong Kong. I've taken a particular liking to this lobster and, from what I can remember, jolly nice it tasted too.

Even in those days Acapulco was considered something extra special. We were due to fly out the following morning but disaster struck when we were informed all flights to Acapulco were fully booked. John gave us the option of driving but pointed out it was an arduous six-hour journey by road. Undaunted, we unanimously decided to travel by car and a fleet of taxis was chartered. The skips carrying our kit were wedged in and off we went. Acapulco here we come!

Now, in truth, the whole ride was probably only two hundred miles but the roads were diabolical, winding their way though the desert and mountains. It did, though, offer us a fantastic opportunity to see the unspoilt natural countryside of Mexico. There were five of us in our car and I sat in the front, arm dangling out of the window, catching the rays from the fierce midday sun. We passed stereotypical Mexican hombres perched on donkeys, wearing sombreros and ponchos, and sporting enormous zapata moustaches. Invariably walking behind them, were their wives carrying huge bales of hay on their heads (these Mexicans have the right idea!).

"Hombre," shouted my taxi driver, "put your arm inside." I was too busy getting a suntan to listen. After six hours of driving through terrain from which I expected Clint Eastwood to emerge at any moment, we finally reached Acapulco. We pulled into the main drag and our hearts rose as we passed The Hilton and Sheraton. Which top hotel would we be staying in? We drove straight through the town and up into the mountains before finally pulling into a shaded building set back from the road. I hesitate to use the word 'hotel' because it was a complete dump. The man on reception offered a clue as to just how bad things were likely to be. A Mexican version of Manuel, the Spanish waiter in Fawlty Towers, he was busily spitting whilst calling everyone 'Gringo'.

The hotel itself was grimy, insects were crawling everywhere and the place stank. I was rooming with Tom Fenoughty, a neat little inside forward on amateur forms with the club. By this time, six hours of constant exposure of my arm to the midday sun was beginning to have a dramatic effect. I watched horrified as the limb literally exploded into a sea of red while a massive water blister formed along the length of my arm from shoulder to hand. It was pure, unadulterated agony. Tom wafted the area with a piece of paper in a vain attempt to keep it cool before the club doctor arrived to administer gallons of soothing calamine lotion.

The pain was excruciating so I decided to put my arm under a cool shower and turned on the water. None was forthcoming, but a couple of lizards popped their heads out of the pipe. Then I decided to go down to the pool but the water there was covered in slimy green algae and frogs had already chosen to go for a midnight dip ahead of me. Wearily I trudged back to my room and lay on the bed, unable to sleep because of the pain. As I looked upward, more lizards were scurrying across the ceiling. Yes, this was Sheffield United on tour in Acapulco.

Next day the squad made a bee-line for John Harris to voice their complaints but he thought the place a palace! By then, my arm was feeling less painful so I rounded up some of the lads for a night out in Acapulco town. Off we went to our first port of call - The Hilton. As we walked in we instinctively knew we had arrived. This was obviously the place to be. A piano player tinkled away in a far corner and there was a terrific ambience.

We had a few drinks and struck up a conversation with the pianist. "Australian?" he asked. "No, we're English," I replied and then staged the first of my impromptu cabaret acts for which I was to command legendary status in later life. I belted out a few tunes such as "Roll out the Barrel" and soon the whole place was humming. I was in the mood now and the last place I wanted to be was back in our fleapit of a hotel. "Let's book into here," I said. "Four each in a room, we should be able to afford that." Using the spenders we'd been given by the club we pooled our money and paid for two rooms up front. Spacious bathroom, comfortable double bed, air conditioning... this was the life. Now we were ready to hit the town.

First, we sampled the 'Whisky A Go Go'. Fortified by a few tequilas, we sat back to enjoy the sight of nubile, scantily-clad girls gyrating in cages suspended above the bar. We beckoned them over and Bernard Shaw and me replaced them, performing our own versions of dirty dancing. The Mexican police didn't see the funny side of this unscheduled cabaret and asked us to come down. "No chance, get lost!" we cried, at which point two revolvers were produced and grimly pointed in our direction. In less than half a second we'd obeyed, hastily jumping out in fear of our lives. We got booted out of the bar but, at 2am, the night was still young. One of the lads ripped off his shirt, rolled it into a ball and we started playing football with it down Acapulco high street.

Eventually, we staggered into another bar . There were only four of us by then and we ordered drinks. Around us, we noticed a group of six rather suspicious-looking Mexicans. Time passed, and one of them beckoned to me: "Gringo, over here. You Americano?" "No, English," I said. "Eeengleez!" he spat menacingly, flicking cigarette ash on the top of my head. Then he grabbed hold of my arm and tried to walk me around the back of the bar. I ripped my arm away, turned to my friends and said "Let's get out of here!" In a split second, we were surrounded by a group of twelve Mexicans. It was reminiscent of a scene from a Western movie.

I knew, at this point, we were in deep trouble, but a split second later the cavalry arrived when a number of American Marines stepped out of the shadows. There were a fair few Marines in Acapulco because several US Warships were carrying out manoeuvres in the Gulf of Mexico. "You guys having trouble?" they drawled. "Go call yourselves a taxi and we'll sort this lot out." The Marines formed a human shield and escorted us from the bar. At best they saved us from a beating, at worst they saved our lives. I will always be eternally grateful to those Americans.

However, our Acapulco adventure was not yet over. There was the small matter of reporting back to John Harris the following morning. As we expected, he gave us an almighty rollicking when we finally arrived back. We argued that we had paid for the overnight stay at The Hilton ourselves but that didn't stop him fining us. "You, Birchenall, you're always the ringleader!" he accused.

Next stop on the South American skylark was the Chilean capital of Santiago where we took

■ **GIANNI RIVERA** was the 1960's midfield superstar in the legendary red and black of AC Milan.

on the Chile and Mexico national squads, Seville from Spain and Italian giants AC Milan. I can remember being totally in awe of the Italians when we met together for a pre-match luncheon. Gianni Rivera and Co. sat down to their meal and what surprised me most was their choice of drink. We were all on Coca-Colas while the Italians sipped a glass or two of red wine. I thought they'd all be drunk, and maybe they were, because we went on to beat them 4-0 to clinch second place in the tournament.

Arguably the most chilling of all the adventures came at our final port of call on a five week 'Magical Mystery Tour' of Latin America. Paraguay, and the city of Asunción, was our last stopping-off point for our eighth fixture. How John Harris ever managed to arrange a game of football in that god-forsaken place I will never fathom out to my dying day. Asunción in the sixties made the Third World look distinctly modern.

We had been lined-up to play a Paraguayan local team called Guarani (I know this, not because of my incredible photographic memory but because the Sheffield United club historian gave me a full list of fixtures and results to help me write this book!) and arranged to go for a training session on the morning of the match. We arrived at the ground which was, to say the least, primitive.

There were tin huts doubling as stands on two sides of the ground, one completely open and, at the other end, a concrete wall. Our local English guide explained that we were very honoured to be playing here. Apparently, our game marked the official re-opening of the ground after it had been closed for several months. We asked why, but immediately wished we hadn't!

"There was a revolution here and fifty of the ringleaders were rounded up, taken to the far end of the ground, lined up against the wall and shot dead." Gulp! We walked over and, sure enough, there were the bullet holes and traces of blood still spattered on the wall. I've heard of some deadly finishing in football but this really took some beating. It was certainly much better than our finishing though as, still shell-shocked from the grisly news, we were beaten 3-1 by the local side. Somehow, though, it all seemed strangely academic.

Undeterred, John had us all back again the following year, and this time we visited the countries we'd missed twelve months earlier. Chile, Peru, Argentina and Ecuador were our first four ports of calls. We country-hopped so much that most of the time the lads genuinely didn't know where we were. In Lima I had the misfortune to leave my club blazer behind in the hotel. I got a right rollocking from John Harris about not looking after club property as we touched down in Buenos Aires, a most 'English' city if I remember correctly. I needn't have worried too much, however. Two weeks later we made an unscheduled return stopover in Lima and I was able to collect my missing jacket from a bemused hotel receptionist.

Bolivia, though, sticks out in my mind from the rest of the South American countries for two particular reasons. Firstly, its capital La Paz, where we were based, is one of the highest altitude capitals in the world and, as a result, there's a distinct lack of oxygen. Secondly, I've never seen such a large concentration of *clagthorpes* in my life. The women were absolutely horrendous. They wore unbecoming pieces of headgear similar to miniature bowler hats, their clothes consisted of multi-coloured shawls and drapes and, to cap it all, they were mostly sitting astride mules or llamas.

Our flight to Bolivia was an event in itself as we weaved our way through the mountains and bounced onto the runway. And, within hours of settling down in the hotel, we were warned we could be in the middle of a revolution. At this time the British Government did not deem Bolivia worthy of an Embassy, so instead they had a missionary. He came to see us and delivered the sort of 'welcome meeting' you never want to hear again.

He explained that each year the Bolivian tin miners gathered together in the hills and marched on La Paz demanding an improvement in their working conditions and rights. This had been going on for the past fourteen years but some gatherings had

■ **WHERE ARE WE NOW?** Here's yours truly (left) outside a cathedral in Lima, capital of Peru, with Ken Mallender, Harry Latham, Bob Widdowson and Bill Punton.

been more violent than others - approximately four had involved major clashes with soldiers and police. "At this stage we're not sure yet whether it's going to be a bloody coup or a peaceful meeting," he said, with typically understated English diplomacy, "but don't go out because they're marching into town tomorrow."

This, of course, was disturbing enough news, but then we were advised that, due to the high altitude and consequent lack of oxygen, newcomers should acclimatise very gently over several days. Under no circumstances must we even consider walking up the stairs because we could collapse due to the physical exertion necessary. "Great," we thought, "we're playing against the top two Bolivian club sides in the national stadium in the next twenty-four hours."

As top English sportsmen we did initially take his advice with a pinch of salt and, ignoring the hotel's lift, jogged up the stairs. Two flights later we were prostrate, and convinced we were all about to expire. Needless to say, an economy of effort was employed in our two matches, losing the first 3-1 to Bolivar before mustering a second wind to beat Santa Cruz 3-1.

THE GREAT PETER OSGOOD!
Ossie's novel methods of paying club fines were an education!

Chelsea's pre-season tours weren't quite so ambitious, the London club contenting themselves predominantly with trips to Europe. One of the first I went on, after my £100,000 move from Sheffield United, was to Kaiserslautern in the 'old' West Germany. We stayed in a Gothic 'Stalag 17' type building forty-five minutes from the city and in the middle of nowhere.

After drawing the game 1-1, manager Dave Sexton informed us we had until midnight before we embarked on the coach home. Off we went in pursuit of action, as many other professional players have, and always will, in such circumstances.

The town appeared as dead as a Dodo until I heard the faint strains of Oompah... *oompah... oompah* drifting along on the night air. Where there's music, there's life and my nose soon sniffed out the bierkeller a few streets away. In our merry gang was me, Peter Osgood, Joe Fascioni and Marvin Hinton. The place was *minging* and in a matter of moments we were sinking thirst-quenching steins of Bavarian nectar. In came Dave Webb, and Peter Bonetti for his obligatory half of lager.

The midnight hour fast approached and the goody two-shoes amongst us prepared to leave for the coach. "You're staying here," instructed Ossie as I prepared to join them. I'd only just got married and was still the new kid on the block at Stamford Bridge. By then we had become friendly with a German couple and they offered to run us back to our hotel in their car. No problem. So, at about 3am we all clambered into the Mercedes and it cruised along the autobahn.

After half an hour, however, a cry went up from the back seat where Marvin Hinton was feeling decidedly the worse for wear. "Stop the car! Stop the car! I've got to get out for a *Belle Vue,*" he gurgled. We screeched to a halt and were treated to the sight of Mavs spewing up at 3.30am in the middle of the autobahn. He got back into the car but, after ten minutes, another cry came from him. "Do you want to be sick again?" said our German driver. "No, turn around and go back. I've lost my tooth!"

Mavs, you see, had a single false tooth on a dental plate and this had fallen out as he was throwing up. We told him not to bother but Mavs was insistent so we turned around. Eventually, after much moaning from his team-mates, we whizzed back up the opposite carriageway and, by trial and error, found the spot where Mavs had been ill. Out he jumped and, aided by the headlamps of the car, squelched his way through the puke before finally plucking out his prized tooth. A quick spit and polish later he popped it back in his mouth, as pleased as punch, while we continued our journey!

We eventually arrived at our hotel, but by this time it was 4am and pitch black and we daren't ring the front door bell for fear of waking Dave Sexton. We did a quick

MARVIN 'MAVS' HINTON who lost his false teeth laying down a 'pavement pizza' on an autobahn in the middle of the night.

reconnoitre and found a back entrance with a skylight above the door. The smallest among our group was Joe Fascioni so we volunteered him to clamber through the skylight. Up he shinned but, although not very tall, we had reckoned without his above-average sized arse. His head, shoulders and upper body slithered through the space with no problem, but his arse was wedged tight. Joe, by now, had half his body in the hotel and the other half dangling outside, but try as we might we couldn't heave his arse through the window. Eventually, we grabbed him by his legs and gave one enormous great shove. I tell you, he shot through that window like an Exocet missile and we heard a wailing sound, swiftly followed by an enormous crash as Joe landed on the pots and pans in the scullery. Seconds later, there was a massive commotion upstairs, the lights went on and down came Dave Sexton in his dressing gown. All hell broke loose while Joe lay concussed on the floor. "Get to bed, I'll see you lot in the morning!" barked Dave as we were all dispatched upstairs.

The following day he gave us a terrible rollocking and fined us all two weeks' wages. I was distraught. Recently married, a Chelsea new boy, a terrible reputation as a result of our escapade and now I had been fined. Was it all worth it? Ossie, by contrast, seemed remarkably calm about the entire episode, as if it were a regular occurrence. I kept chuntering away while Ossie told me everything would soon be sorted.

My wife and I had just moved into a brand new house in Ascot, Ossie lived a few miles away in Windsor. Having flown back, we shared a car for the drive home and after a few miles we pulled into a lay-by where there was a telephone kiosk. "Now listen, this is all part of your education," Ossie told me. He dialled a number and asked to be connected with the Sports Department of the *Daily Express* newspaper. "Want an exclusive?" he asked the reporter. "Four Chelsea players fined two week's wages after bust-up on pre-season tournament in Germany Back page exclusive, maybe even front page." I couldn't believe my ears and immediately broke out in a cold sweat.

It was bad enough being fined, but now it would be plastered all over the papers. I was a gibbering wreck by the time Ossie got back into the car and declared: "Sorted!" "Sorted?" I said, "What do you think you are doing?" Ossie told me to shut up and went on to explain how he had sold the story for a sizeable fee - not only adequate, but more than enough to cover the total fines we had all been docked. Sure enough, the following day we were back page headline news in the *Daily Express* and, a week later, Ossie handed out the monies from the paper which perfectly covered our fines. As Ossie said, it was a real education.

Undoubtedly, one of the most disappointing moments of my career was missing Chelsea's FA Cup final victory over Leeds in 1970. A bad knee injury meant I was sidelined for the final at Wembley and the Old Trafford replay... but the after-match celebrations and tour to Barbados did go some way towards atoning for my misery. One of the top fashion photographers of the day was a guy called Eric Swain who snapped many of the 'Page Three' topless models. A friend of the players, he generously threw a celebratory party for us on the night before we jetted off to Barbados.

Eric had booked a top private restaurant in Notting Hill Gate and in trooped eighteen footballers to be greeted by a bevy of Page Three beauties - fully clothed I hasten to add! The food was delicious and the dessert excellent. Only joking. Afterwards we went to a club before finally staggering back home, waking bleary-eyed the following morning. Most of us looked much the worse for wear as we raggedly assembled at Heathrow Airport.

For one of our number, in particular, life was a little uncomfortable... especially when he was sitting down. A Chelsea player, one of the single lads I hasten to add, had what appeared to be four bullet holes in his 'arris. They were, in fact, a set of ladies false fingernails which had embedded themselves into his buttocks! Incredibly, they were so well buried inside the flesh the player didn't know they were there. In the showers the others clocked his problem immediately but for the next three days in Barbados the poor soul wandered around in his briefs unaware of his predicament. I'm sure you can work out exactly how the fingernails came to be there!

Whilst out in the Caribbean I was accredited with saving the life of Chelsea chairman Brian Mears' wife. Myself and reserve goalkeeper Tommy Hughes went out water-ski-ing in the tropical waters. I attempted it first, only to find I was utterly useless. Tommy was a shade better at the sport than me and then June Mears, who had accompanied us on the speedboat, tried her luck. She was doing quite well until she lost her footing and, as she fell, one of the skis caught her a thumping smack on the head. She was left lying face down on the water so we raced to her rescue. I dived in and pulled her into the boat and we zipped speedily back to the shore.

■ 'Whoh... I'm going to Barbados', went the famous song from KC and the Sunshine Band. And here's the Chelsea squad - fresh from winning the FA Cup against Leeds in 1970 - after touching down in Barbados following a 10-hour flight from Heathrow. Despite a bit of jet-lag, you can see the Birch was still game for a laugh. I'm the joker on the back row sticking my fingers out of the back of the head of Ian Hutchison. This was a tour made especially notable for my antics in a wheelchair.

She was semi-conscious by this time, but after medical treatment on the beach was allowed to retreat to her hotel room. In the evening Brian Mears called me over to thank me for saving his wife's life. Actually, he tried to make a joke of it and said he would be putting me on the transfer list because I might have been doing him a favour by leaving June out there. Brian did, in fact, have the last laugh because a few months later I was sold to Crystal Palace. So, the moral of this story is don't save a chairman's wife unless you want a transfer!

Instead of being in the right place at the right time, a few days later the Birch found himself in the wrong place at the wrong time as I dozed beside the hotel swimming pool, glass of lager in one hand and a book in the other. At the bar was an admirably attractive but frosty-natured young lady who had been attracting much attention from some of our newly-crowned FA Cup winners. None had received much encouragement so far in their attempted conversations with her so Eddie McCreadie and a few others - Ron Harris was one, I recall - decided to hatch a little plot.

While I lazed semi-conscious in sunny blissful ignorance, Eddie told the woman I had suffered a terrible accident and was paralysed from the waist downwards. Subdued and lonely as I was, perhaps she wouldn't mind talking to me for a little while. Eddie tipped me the wink as the girl approached, intent on having a chat and hopefully cheering my spirits. Practically unprepared, I was forced into playing along with this scam, which quickly spiralled out of control and was reminiscent of the main scene in the film *Dirty Rotten Scoundrels* featuring Michael Caine and Steve Martin, who played the two confidence tricksters.

"Can I get you a drink?" the young woman asked. "Please don't be too down, I know you are seriously injured," she went on. "I'm frightened my career may be over," I said, playing the sympathy line perhaps a little too strongly.

The lads, meanwhile, were clocking everything from behind a bunch of palm trees twenty yards away. Out stepped Eddie to announce that they were all off to a club. "Coming with us, Birch?" Eddie shouted. "No, I'll stay here. I don't want to interrupt your enjoyment," I said plaintively. "No problem, Birch. We'll fetch your wheel-chair!"

As luck would have it (for them!), in the lobby of the hotel stood a wheelchair, supplied for the use of disabled guests. By this time, my new female companion was determined I should not be left out of the partying. "You **must** come. If I come with you, will you go? I insist. You shan't be left on your own." Reluctantly I agreed to come along, despite maintaining I would not be good company. She asked the lads to bring me the wheelchair and proudly declared: "Alan is coming."

The lads were struggling to keep a straight face. "This is not a laughing matter. Be grateful this has not happened to you," she instructed. I was bundled into the wheelchair and trundled through the foyer to wait for a taxi. The lads got into the cabs and the lady pushed me into the last one, stashing the wheelchair in the boot. "It's such a pity you have been struck down, you are such an interesting person," she said, as she held my hand on the back seat.

A few minutes later we pulled up outside Alexandria's Nightclub in Bridgetown. Twenty-four hours earlier I had been in the same nightclub, dancing around like a demented wombat to sounds of the Rolling Stones. The manager recognised us so the lads raced up the steps, ahead of my companion and I, to let him in on the ruse.

"Ah, Alan. We are delighted you have come. I have reserved you a special place," he said, as my newly-found friend wheeled me through the doors and into the VIP area where drinks were laid on for us. The lads dashed off at this point to check out the action.

"Don't stay with me all night, go and enjoy yourself," I said benevolently. "No," she replied, "I have come with you and I am going to stay with you. You must not be on your own."

Laying on the sympathy card rather heavily, I said she should go and have a dance and not worry about me. And then came the real choker "I like to dance, but not tonight. Maybe one day we will be able to dance together," she proclaimed.

What had started out as a five-minute jape had now lasted three hours and showed no signs of abating. I was, in truth, beginning to feel rather guilty about the whole episode. Not quite guilty enough, though.

At this point, my favourite Stones record - 'I Can't Get No Satisfaction' - came on. As the music became louder, I said: "I think I'm beginning to sense some feeling in my left leg. And it's in my right leg, too!" She virtually screamed with delight. "This is absolutely fantastic. Can you stand up?" she asked, ordering two complete strangers to help me to my feet. I tottered about and said: "I am going to try my hardest to dance. Please help me." She supported me as far as the dance floor where I took a few stumbling steps before breaking into my best Mick Jagger strut as I bopped across the floor.

At this point, she finally tumbled everything. All the lads were creased up. "You bastard!" she screamed loudly at the top of her voice. She was hysterical for five minutes and the club manager had to calm her down but after ten minutes she came back up to me and, to her immense credit, admitted it had been a great con-trick. "I know I've been a little snooty and perhaps I did deserve it," she said.

Some people might find this anecdote offensive. That prank is all part of a footballer's sense of humour and there was genuinely no malice intended by any of the lads. It was one of those japes that carried on longer than any of us imagined but ultimately no harm was done.

After my exploits with Sheffield United and Chelsea I thought I had experienced everything, but I reckoned without my days with Leicester City. I am often asked which club was the most riotous when it came to off-the-field activities. My answer is, they all were. At Leicester, perhaps, I was looked upon as more of a ring-leader. From my early days as social secretary at Sheffield United through to my education at the hands of Ossie and the London boys at Stamford Bridge, I was able to put all of these to good effect at Filbert Street.

Leicester manager Jimmy Bloomfield was another boss who loved his tours. These tended to take place in pre- rather than close-season. The only difference between the two was that there was actually some training involved in pre-season.

Unlike John Harris at Sheffield United who so loved South America, Jimmy had a soft spot for Scandinavia in general, and Sweden in particular. There was one training camp we visited on more than one occasion - Hindus Garden, a purpose-built training retreat less than an hour from Gothenburg. Set in picturesque surroundings, there was an obligatory ski jump, cool clear lakes, towering mountains and clean, pure Scandinavian air. Our wooden accommodation was pretty basic - a dining area, a football pitch surrounded by an athletics track, and lots and lots of Swedish conifer trees.

Of course, training camps are invariably based in the middle of nowhere for obvious reasons. The last thing managers and coaches want is to work the players relentlessly all day on fitness, only for them to undo their hard-won efforts by hitting the highspots in the evening. Hindus Garden certainly came into this category.

Unwilling to be beaten, the Leicester lads managed to devise an evening's entertainment of sorts. We clubbed our spending allowance together to buy a crate of beer and smuggled it down to the lakeside in a plastic bag. There, we idled away the evening, our feet dangling in the icy cold Swedish waters. Also submerged were our bottles, suspended on lengths of string. Hey presto, we'd invented our own fridge for chilling beers and when we fancied a drink, we simply pulled up another bottle.

On this occasion, Wolves were also staying at the same establishment. Jim McCalliog, Willie Carr, Derek Parkin and Co. lacked our ingenuity and vision, though. Full marks to them for making it down to the fjord with us... but they bought bottles of Coca-Cola.

After whiling away a few hours one evening, we wandered back to the main building and, as we passed reception, a call came through for Frank Worthington. It was Frank's first wife Birgitta, a partner well-known for her ability not to beat about the bush. As soon as Frank picked up the phone we could hear the barrage of abuse. Birgitta was shrieking to such an extent Frank was obliged to hold the earpiece five yards from his face. He had forgotten to ring her earlier in the evening and his wife thought he had been out on the town.

Eventually, Frank put her on to me. "Don't worry, we've been sitting down by a fjord near the boat house having a nice quiet drink," I explained, but this only served to inflame the situation as Birgitta accused me of being a downright liar and laced heavily into me as well! By this time quite a crowd had gathered and Frank spent the next half an hour vainly trying to calm his beloved.

Now, had Birgitta chosen another night to ring she might have had more genuine grounds for complaint. On this tour we were playing Wolves, German side Stuttgart and hosts Gothenburg in a four-team tournament. Please don't ask me the results because I haven't a clue, as I've already explained, I can only remember the interesting bits. I think we won one, drew one and lost one, which left Jimmy Bloomfield reasonably satisfied.

After the final game, he declared the coach home would set off at 11pm. He was not unduly concerned about whether we were all on it, but expected everyone to be ready for training at 10am the following morning. Jimmy, bless him, was very good in this respect, he treated the players like adults and gave us a fair amount of licence which hopefully we did not abuse excessively... at least not all of the time.

We found a lively nightclub, where even the exorbitant alcohol prices in Sweden did not deter us from getting steamboated, and a hard-core of us Leicester players were still to be found there come the early hours. One by one we slowly weaved our way to Gothenburg station to camp out for the night before catching the early morning train out to Hindus Garden. Some of us slept in the waiting-room, others on the platform.

One of our party, who shall remain nameless, arrived shortly before the train was due to leave at 7am. He looked considerably less dishevelled than the rest of us except in one respect - he had lost his tie. On quizzing him about this, he revealed all. Apparently, he had been quite successful with a local Swedish girl who had invited him back to spend the night at her apartment but whilst in her bedroom she had produced a pair of scissors and cut off his neckwear. Initially, thoughts of a bondage session crossed his mind but the young lady merely pinned up the tie on her living-room wall, where he noticed a long string of them adorning the wallpaper.

The cheeky young nymph collected football club ties as 'trophies'! Apparently, she had neck-pieces from soccer clubs all around the world but this was the first she had obtained from Leicester City.

Our collective adventures were not quite over, yet. Although Jimmy was very fair, we didn't want to advertise the fact that we were arriving in from our night out while everyone else was about to sit down for breakfast. I spied Derek Parkin in the hotel and motioned him to let us in through a rear fire escape. He opened the door and in we scampered. Unfortunately, we bumped straight into the Wolves management team of Bill McGarry and Sammy Chung. Bill's face was a real picture. He was just preparing to tuck into his kippers, while we were coming in from the night before!

On pre-season and post-season tours, especially, it has been remarked that no-one was safe from the Birch. This was an adage which unfortunately proved all too true for one of the Leicester directors, a lovely man called Sid Needham. I really looked up to Sid and called him 'Dad'. On another trip to the Hindus Garden, myself and Frank Worthington were playing tennis. I loved the sport although I wasn't particularly good at it. Like my football, I gave it my all while Frank was one of these fancy-dan merchants, full of drop shots and the like.

Chasing down one of Frank's racy flicks, I steamed up determined to return the ball. I whacked it off the racket but my return was lacking in accuracy and the ball veered away at a right angle, cracking a watching Sid Needham right in the eye. Poor Sid, who was in his seventies, was completely pole-axed. Our trainer George Preston raced over to give him some urgent medical treatment. Suffice to say, Sid spent the next month in a Swedish hospital with a detached retina and his wife was flown over to sit by his bedside while he made a recovery. So, while the rest of us flew back home fighting-fit a few days later, poor old Sid had to wait another three weeks before the Swedish medical authorities would allow him to return. When he did eventually come back, he very kindly accepted my profuse apologies but I did warn him not to watch quite so closely when the Birch was playing tennis in future.

Physio George also suffered a major health scare on the same trip, again thanks to the Birch. George fancied himself as a runner and the lads never wasted an opportunity to wind him up. Frank and Lenny Glover baited him one day about how they felt he could beat the Birch over a three-mile course just outside the training camp. George approached me and I bragged I could easily out-run him but, if he had the bottle, we would have a race, the stipulation being I found it difficult to run alongside anyone and therefore we should have staggered starts. George, being extremely gullible, readily agreed so I went first with a 30-second start. All the lads turned up to watch and off I raced into the woods but as soon as I was out of view, I dived behind the nearest tree. Thirty seconds later, George came racing by

ANYONE FOR TENNIS? Although I was no Tim Henman, I always liked a game of tennis. Unfortunately, I was a little too over-zealous during a Leicester City pre-season tour of Sweden. Attempting a sizzling back-hander, I crashed the ball over the baseline and hit our director Sid Needham straight between the eyes, causing him to spend an additional three weeks in a Swedish hospital suffering with a detached retina. I doubt even Greg Rusedski could have hit the ball harder for that shot.

like a bat out of hell. I casually strolled back to the finishing line and waited idly with the rest of the lads.

Just before George was due back, I retreated a few hundred yards down the course to a blind corner. George steamed steadily up the hill, pouring with sweat and, at that moment, caught his first glimpse of me. In the meantime I had splashed my clothes with water and, as the lads egged George on, I raced to the finish. George collapsed over the line, his body contorted in pain. I had done my sums wrong, however, and forgotten about my thirty-second start. As George finished only ten seconds behind me, he had effectively won. Realising this, he jumped for joy and it was well worth handing over the prize money just to see the expression on his face. Poor old George, it was three years before we finally told him the truth.

Another of the more memorable Leicester pre-season tours took us to the Italian island of Sardinia and a prestigious game against Serie 'A' side Cagliari. Again, I can't remember much of the action on the pitch, except the sight of members of the groundstaff picking out weeds from the turf an hour or two before kick off. We stayed at the Forte Village complex, still a favourite to this day with top footballers and music and film celebrities. While we were there a fashion photographer was doing a glamour shoot with a quartet of quite famous 'Page Three' models. We got talking to them over breakfast and arranged to see them in the nightclub the following evening. Sure enough, we met up and had an entertaining time.

Jimmy Bloomfield was signing Frank Worthington back in England so he had put his assistant, Dave Coates, in charge of us. Dave was a great guy but not the strongest of characters. He told us all there was an 11pm curfew. Sure enough, down he came at 11pm but we managed to negotiate a half-hour extension and, thirty minutes later, the lads started to file reluctantly upstairs. The girls begged us not to go and asked me to join them for a swim. I whispered to Lennie Glover that I was going for a dip and would be up in the room shortly.

Off we went and there then followed one of the most incredible sights I have ever witnessed: greater than an eclipse; more incredible than Peter Bonetti opening his wallet to buy a round, or Leicester's Alan Woollett forsaking Milletts and buying a suit from Armani. At the poolside these four beautiful babes just stripped off and dived into the waters which were illuminated by underwater lighting.

"In you come," they giggled so, rather bashfully, I *clothed off* and jumped in. Surrounding the pool was a large privet hedge and, seconds later, a head forced its way through while a voice shouted: "Birch, you're in BIG trouble this time. You're already on a fine. Get back in your room NOW!" It was Dave Coates. I was in a bit of a dilemma. There I was enjoying a moonlight skinny-dip with four gorgeous girls but the boss was telling me to come straight out and leave the fun behind. "Dave, what would you do?" I shouted back. Dave cast his beady eyes around the pool, clocking the bevy of beauties. "See you in the morning, Birch." he retorted. And with that he was gone.

One part of the world I have not yet touched upon is the Middle East. Don't worry, I went there as well on more than one occasion and, not unsurprisingly, there are a few tales to tell. During my Sheffield days, we visited Israel and Kuwait. Given the political differences between these two countries at the time it was a most unlikely double and a couple of the lads made the mistake of getting an Israeli stamp on their passport. Thankfully, I didn't bother and the Kuwaiti customs officers allowed me to proceed through the green door unhindered. Unfortunately, the same could not be said for Len Badger and Bernard Shaw who were whisked away by the authorities and spent an anxious few hours locked up by armed guards.

This, however, was small fry compared to the diplomatic incident provoked when I returned a few years later with Leicester. We were all well aware that most of the Middle East was 'dry' and this filled some of us with more impending doom than it did others. I'm talking here about directors rather than players. Sid Needham, in particular, was fond of a tipple or two.

"How are you going to get through the week without a drink?," I asked. "Don't worry, son, it's sorted." was all he would say. After a fairly uneventful flight we touched down in Kuwait and hung around by the baggage carousel. In those days, our kit used to be ferried around in large wicker baskets and training gear and boots were piled high in these skips. Normally when we travelled there were about two skips, but on this occasion, although our tour consisted of only sixteen players, I counted four heavy baskets. Ever willing to lend a hand I dragged the last of these skips off the carousel and pushed it towards the customs channel.

The first three had sailed through without a problem but, just my luck, a customs officer picked on me. He pointed at the basket and motioned me to open it. There was a massive Chubb lock on the catch and, as I did not have the key on me, I had to go and find the kit manager. The lock was duly opened and the official began rummaging through. Underneath a thin covering of bibs and balls, the officers produced bottle after bottle of scotch, vodka and whisky. Further inspection produced crates of lagers, beers and mixers. My 'arris was twitching a little by this time. A number of armed guards now surrounded the skip and there was much shouting in Arabic accompanied by excited gesticulating.

Those players already esconced on the team coach were hauled off and we were lined up inside the airport. Also present was a delegation from the Kuwaiti Football

Association. As many of these were oil sheikhs and not without influence there was much heated debate for more than an hour. Eventually, we were allowed to leave with three skips, but not the one containing our alcoholic contraband. Three days later we got a surprise call from Sid enquiring if we would like to attend a pre-drinks reception before one of our nights out, courtesy of the Kuwaiti FA. We arrived at his hotel and there, slap bang in the middle of his room, was the missing wicker basket. "Get stuck in, lads," he said.

We were all mesmerised and helped ourselves to lagers and bitters, while the directors poured a few shots from the spirits. Sid never did tell us how he managed to get the basket back, all he would say was: "Ways and means." But he did admit it was a few bottles of brandy lighter when it finally reached his hotel room!

Later in the tour we were invited to an evening function at the Kuwaiti Hilton. On the coach to the hotel we noticed our directors were all toting identical carrier bags under their arms and, when we'd seated ourselves for dinner, realised the reason. Whilst the players were served non-alcoholic Coca-Colas and Fantas, the directors proceeded to pour illicit drinks from the bottles contained in the carrier bags stashed under the table, the spirits topped up with non-alcoholic mixers. It was a similar story with the Kuwaiti hierarchy who trooped in, each with a carrier bag tucked under their arms. Apparently, the authorities knew this went on but were prepared to turn a blind eye as long as it wasn't too blatant.

Five days into the tour, one bottle of lager courtesy of Sid apiece, the lads were gagging for a *sherbet*. We played a series of matches against regional sides in various oil cities. Coach for one of these days was ex-player Bobby Kellard, who moved in the opposite direction in the £100,000 deal which took me from Crystal Palace to Leicester.

After the game (don't ask me the score. Who cares?), Bobby invited us back to his apartment for a little *libation* and about half a dozen lads took up his offer. Settled at his place he shouted to us to help ourselves, and we all began looking around for the booze until he indicated the dustbin. Great, I thought, loads of bottles bobbing up and down in a bin filled with iced water. Lovely jubbly. Pulling off the dustbin lid, I was not greeted with the sight of a single bottle. Instead, the bin was swimming with a thick, treacle-like, brown goo. There was also a big ladle which stood up straight in the liquid.

"Get stuck in!" offered Bobby. "You must be joking," we all cried. This, you see, was Bobby's home-made special brew. He explained how risky it was to smuggle in bottles and cans - a much safer bet was to slip in a sachet or two of DIY home-brewing beer in his luggage. I'd like to point out it was still very much the early days

BOBBY KELLARD moved to Palace when I joined Leicester but his home brewed rocket-fuel over in Kuwait was out of this world!

of home-brewing so the drink was something of an acquired taste. However, it only took us about two glasses to adjust to the flavour by which time we were extremely merry. Beer? - this was more like rocket fuel and seldom had a glassful tasted so good.

Only one thing was harder to come by in Kuwait than beer... and that was female company. To Frank Worthington, however, this was not an insurmountable problem. In Frank's autobiography, the quaintly-named *One Hump or Two*, he talks about a pleasant interlude with a British guest in one of our hotels. There has been considerable speculation about the identity of the two mystery players hiding in the wardrobe while Frank entertained a 'friend'. As we have now reached the second chapter of my book, I judged it about time to produce a further world 'exclusive' after the New Zealand match-rigging scam.

Allow me to set the scene for you...

Staying in our hotel was a honeymoon couple, although the husband was combining his nuptials with work as a telephone installer. He was often sent to the middle of the desert to lay cables, leaving his wife on her lonesome - not the most sensible plan of action when Frank was around. The ever-gallant Mr Worthington befriended her over a couple of days to help combat her loneliness as she began married life.

In the meantime, myself and partner-in-crime Lenny Glover had decided to spruce up Frank's room by varnishing the inside of his wardrobe. We were busy painting away when Frank made a surprise return with his female companion. Not wishing to embarrass them, Lenny and I barricaded ourselves in the wardrobe. Fortunately, for air-conditioning purposes I hasten to add, we were relieved to discover some slats in the door through which we could breathe more easily.

Thanks to the antics of Frank and his paramour, our breathing became heavier as the afternoon wore on. Eventually, we decided enough was enough and burst into the room. Frank and friend were astonished. "We've finished varnishing the wardrobe, but don't forget to keep the doors open to let it dry properly," we explained as we turned on our heels, making a sharp exit. Frank didn't even notice we'd left our paint-brushes behind!

There is one part of the world, extremely popular with Brits, that I have not yet mentioned and now seems an appropriate time to rectify that omission.

Many a pleasant moment has been enjoyed by my fellow countrymen, supping sangria and San Miguels on Spain's sunshine coast and, on a short visit to Torremolinos, we were no different. Manager Jimmy Bloomfield had been called back to England, leaving his coach Bill Dodgin in charge. Jimmy had left orders for us to do a really hard session one afternoon. Unfazed, Bill did exactly that... but with a difference.

Now, if Jimmy was laid-back, Bill was completely horizontal. He ordered us to change and then lined us up on the tarmac in the fierce midday sun. "See that building right up there at the top of the hill?" he said. Our hearts sank to our boots as we contemplated a series of shuttle-runs up and down the road. "The last one in buys the first round!"

We were off like a flash. None of us had ever run as fast in our lives as we swiftly sprinted that mile-and-a-half uphill and flung ourselves into the bar. The locals certainly gave us a few funny looks as, clad in Leicester City tops and shorts, we waited patiently for our drinks. Bill jogged up gently and dutifully ordered the first round. For the next seven hours we were ensconced in the bar, until Bill finally said enough was enough. With that we wended our way slowly back to the hotel. "Phew! That was one heavy session," he told us.

In between games on the tour, Bill would give us an afternoon or two off to allow time to explore the town. On one occasion I went shopping with Frank Worthington. It was the first and only time - shopping with Frank is worse than with any woman. He wanted to buy a Stetson and an Elvis Presley belt but I suggested the place to buy an Elvis belt was in Memphis, not the back-streets of Torremolinos. Frank was having none of this and we trawled around every shop imaginable.

He was even worse with the Stetson and must have tried on over a hundred hats in an attempt to find one he really fancied - white ones, brown ones, camel ones, ones with studs, ones with corks. On and on he went before eventually picking up one he liked.

On our second afternoon off, six of us went to a local bar. The usual suspects were all there - myself, Frank, Dennis Rofe, Lenny Glover, Steve Earle and Steve Whitworth. We couldn't help but notice one hapless Spanish local sitting a few yards from us. He was wearing arguably the worst *syrup* I have ever seen in my life - his sideburns were spindly and grey but on his bonce was this big, thick, black, shag-pile of a carpet. I noticed that when he moved his head, his *ferret* didn't budge.

Hatching a dastardly plot, I told the lads I would go outside and stroll past the window where he was sitting. As I walked by I shouted "Oi" at the top of my voice.

Like a startled rabbit, the Spaniard turned around, but I swear his *syrup* stayed in exactly the same place with his centre parting now running down the middle of his right ear. It was just like the Spitting Image puppet of Paul Daniels where his hair-piece whirls around on top of a pole coming out of his head. The lads were in hysterics. Schoolboy humour, I know, but when you get a group of lads together this is what they are like. Or at least they were in my day.

■ **FRANK WORTHINGTON:** Only 'Elvis' could try on a hundred stetsons in, of all places, Torremolinos to make sure of that perfect 'Dallas' look.

From Torremolinos we made a return visit to Barbados and as luck would have it, I ran into one of my pals from the world of showbiz. Brian was quite a famous actor and was making a film on the island at the same time as were playing a tournament with Ipswich. The film was *The Tamarind Seed* and the two principal stars were Omar Sharif and Julie Andrews. Now Julie was a big name from *The Sound of Music* and Omar was one of the most famous of movie greats - *Dr Zhivago* and the like. Brian suggested I get a group of the lads together and he would arrange a meet.

Myself, Frank, Dennis Rofe, Lenny Glover and Steve Whitworth were like schoolboys off to see our hero as we were ferried to the far side of the island to meet the legendary Egyptian. We got there at 2pm - four hours before a planned evening training session. Brian bought us a round of beers and we waited to be introduced. One beer became two, became three, became four but still no sign of Omar.

I had clocked a procession of attractive women going into a particular chalet for the two hours we had been there, but gave the matter no more thought. As we got closer and closer to training time, Brian admitted that Omar was in there too. I had counted between six and ten women going in or coming out. "I don't know what he's doing but it's not humanly possible," I murmured.

Eventually Omar, clad only in a silken dressing-gown, emerged. Referring to him as an Egyptian peasant, Brian explained we were professional footballers with Leicester City and had come to meet him. Brian introduced us all one by one. With impeccable timing, associated only with the acting profession, Omar studied us all intently, uttered "So moved," bowed politely and then simply walked away. We were completely gobsmacked, not to mention slightly inebriated after six bottles of lager. None of us said a word. To this day, I don't know whether he was being sarcastic or genuine. "Sorry about that but Omar has got to rush off to learn his lines. There's a big scene tonight," Brian proffered, by way of an apology.

The day was far from finished, though, as we had to dash back to our hotel for the 6pm training session. I was distinctly the worse for wear and quite a few people noticed this. Jimmy had decided we would train on a tennis court. Throughout the trip we had watched Ipswich train, and they in turn had watched us go through our paces, and a few of their lads were now sitting on a grassy knoll overlooking the court, laughingly looking forward to seeing how I would cope. Jimmy, keen to impress our rivals, had a quiet word about us giving our all.

I intended to keep a low profile and the lads covered for me as we did a few warm-up laps, but when the bibs were handed out for the five-a-side I decided to stay out of the way. If I got the ball, I would pass it first time and contribute as little as possible. Nothing new there then, I can hear you saying. After a couple of minutes of successfully avoiding the ball, the first pass was aimed towards me. I went to play it down the line, but as I drew my left foot back it got caught in the wire netting surrounding the court. There was an almighty crash and I let out a yelp as my foot got completely stuck in the mesh. Everyone was in hysterics - except for Jimmy - and the game had to be stopped for ten minutes while the lads extricated my foot. If you remember my antics when last in Barbados, this was a time when I really did need that wheelchair as I was helped off the court.

My footballing career can probably be split into two distinct halves - my times with Sheffield United, Chelsea and Leicester in the top flight, and my spell in the nether regions with Notts County, Blackburn Rovers, Luton Town and Hereford when I was, by my own admission, rather less effective. This gulf is no better illustrated than with the Magpies at Meadow Lane, the club I had grown up supporting as a boy.

I had been fortunate enough to travel the world, sampling some of the most attractive holiday hot-spots and sun-drenched islands, before I touched down in Nottingham once more. Mid-way through the season there was talk of a tour. If we were able to get a couple of results, then it would be on.

"Great," I thought after we managed two draws which were enough to swing it. Manager Jimmy Sirrel called all the lads together one morning and, in his pronounced Scottish accent, confirmed a four-day event had been booked. At great expense to the club, he went on, we were off to Skegness. Now, I had been bracing myself for the fact that Notts County might not make Acapulco or Hawaii, but I had been thinking in terms of temperate resorts such as Malaga or Benidorm rather than the wind-swept English East Coast in February.

I was gutted and my first reaction was to say: "No way!" but, before I'd had the chance to make up an excuse, Brian Stubbs came along with his clipboard. It was now that I was to find out why all the lads called him 'hon sec' (short for honorary secretary).

Stubbsy was a fearsome centre half who could walk through brick walls and not bat an eyelid. He was a real working-men's club sort of guy, completely at home with a pint and a set of dominoes, so it came as something of a surprise when I saw him, armed with a clipboard and pen, coming down the coach as it rattled along the A46 to Skegness. "What can I put you down for?" he asked. I looked at him gone out, only to be offered a selection of dominoes, darts, bar-billiards, pool or table-tennis. "You must be joking!" I said. But, as David Needham told me, he was being deadly serious.

Stubbsy was the social organiser for the trip and loved every minute of it as he plotted the first rounds of each pub sports competition. I rather foolishly asked if there would be a water ski-ing competition. Water ski-ing in the North Sea off the coast of Skegness in February? Enough said. They say the Lincolnshire town is so bracin'. Bracin'? The gale-force winds almost blew us away the whole time we were there.

■ **BRIAN STUBBS** was a pint and dominoes sort of a guy - and Social Organiser of Notts County's trip to... wait for it... *Skegness!*

On the first evening we decided to suss out the local nightlife. Myself, Stubbsy, David Needham, Steve Carter, Eric McManus, Les Bradd and Ray O'Brien all popped into the nearest pub. We were the only customers. I asked the barman if there was anywhere we could go after closing time. "You're struggling, mate. Wrong time of year, my duck," he said. We managed to find a bar/club but, again, we were the only ones there. In truth, this was one of the longest weeks of my life. The lads at County were absolutely brilliant but this was not what I had been used to. I was also particularly crap at all of Stubbsy's games. Mind you, after the amount of dominoes practice he had at his local club throughout the year, it was virtually impossible to beat Brian.

If my previous trips with Sheffield United, Chelsea and Leicester had been first class, this outing was very much a Wheeltappers & Shunters special. But it was still another experience... and my life has certainly been filled with those. No doubt you are now asking yourselves: "What about his touring experiences with Blackburn, Luton and Hereford?" Do me a favour! I was either not there long enough or the clubs could not even afford a jaunt to the East Coast. As you might have guessed, tours were among the highlights of my footballing career. I had a few tales to tell, but I always maintain they were invaluable when it came to fostering team spirit. One of my favourite sayings is that you can plonk a group of footballers and a crate of beer down on just about any place on this planet and they'll have a good time. I know I certainly did.

75

A Manager's Life

Chapter 3

In the current era of the professional game, I can think of few more precarious careers than being a football manager. Whilst writing this chapter, Ruud Gullit became the first Premiership managerial casualty of the 1999-2000 season - and the campaign was only five games old.

When I opened a local hostelry in the Leicestershire village of Swithland four years ago, I asked my friends in soccer management to drop me a line and a signed photo to be hung up in my back passage (of the pub). Do you know, of the twenty managers to reply no fewer than sixteen are no longer employed by the same club?! So, when I look back on my own playing career it surprises even me that I played under so few managers.

In my first twelve years in the game, with Sheffield United, Chelsea and Leicester, I served under three. Indeed, it was not until the fifteenth year of my professional career - by which time it was very much in the twilight stages - that I was playing for clubs when they sacked their managers. Mind you, Blackburn Rovers did more than make up for the previous years of stability. Jim Iley signed me on a Friday at Ewood Park but was dismissed by the Monday!

Though there may not have been an abundance of quantity, there was definitely plenty of quality in the managers I had the good fortune to serve. I always maintain that I played the game when there was a shift in the balance of power in the way a manager went about his work. On the one hand there was the boss you never saw, except on a Saturday afternoon doing the team-talk. He was always dressed in a suit and was usually aloof. On the other was the track-suited manager, who was always on the training ground, practising drill after drill. I certainly do not have the authority to say who was right and who was wrong but that perhaps is one of the great strengths of this game of football. There is no single right way, and no single wrong way.

Let's deal first with John Harris, my first and only manager at Sheffield United. When they made John, they threw away the mould. A fiercely proud man, he never once smoked a cigarette, didn't touch a drop of alcohol, never swore, remained a bachelor throughout his life and attended church on Sundays. Sounds a real boring old dummy, doesn't he? But nothing could be further from the truth.

Of all the managers I played under, I had more respect for John than any other. I looked up to him almost as much as I did my dad. John lived in Dore, a posh southern suburb of Sheffield and drove either a Hillman or a Rover (dependent on the year). I know this well because when I joined the Sheffield groundstaff one of my jobs was to wash the gaffer's car after training on Friday afternoons. This was a

particularly prestigious task given that my previous 'job' had been to unload coke from a lorry, a distinctly grimy experience.

John was, in many respects, years ahead of his time. It is one of my earnest views that there are very few things in life which are completely new, most are simply old ideas recycled and repackaged.

John inherited an ageing United team and his vision for a successful future at Bramall Lane was to bring in younger, home-grown players who graduated through the club's youth system. Does any of this sound familiar with the recently established Football Association Academy blueprint whereby Premiership clubs are asked to invest millions in producing their own players, rather than import large numbers of foreigners?

■ **JOHN HARRIS** - a Teetotal, non-swearing, God-fearing Scot. "You's bloomin' useless you bloomin' bean poles" was the full extent of his vitriol.

While researching this chapter, I dug out one article which summed up John's philosophies perfectly. He told shareholders in 1964 that high fees and wages did not necessarily bring success and *"I would sooner persevere and try to bring on our own boys so that we can have players who eventually will win one of the top honours for our club"*. Introducing young players not only promoted loyalty but also fostered a wonderful team spirit, he said.

As a result of John's philosophies I was given my chance at the age of 17 along with Len Badger, Barry and Tony Wagstaff, Mick Jones, Bernard Shaw, Ken Mallender, Alan Woodward, Frank Barlow and David Munks who all made the transition through the youth and reserve ranks. The end result was that we had one of the youngest teams United had ever fielded in Division One, and all this was down to John Harris.

Now don't get the impression that John was a soft touch. As a player, he made a name for himself as an uncompromising centre half at Chelsea. He relished regaling us with the story about how he met up with Cardiff hard-man Trevor Ford. On the morning of the game, John was going for a pre-match walk in town when he was spotted by Trevor. "I was marking him that afternoon and Trevor shouted across the road: 'Morning Johnny'". John went on: "I looked him in the eye and told him not to bloomin' morning me cos I was going to bloomin' well break both his bloomin' legs in the afternoon!"

Although he never swore, John's one little weakness was to use the word 'bloomin' at every available opportunity. Myself and Mick Jones - two players he signed for no fee and was to eventually sell for £100,000 apiece - often copped a volley from the boss. Our Monday morning debriefings used to take place in the billiard room at the ground. We'd all be huddled around the baize tables while John tore us off a strip. "You's blooming beanpoles. You's bloomin' useless, you bloomin' namby-pambies," was how he would dismiss the efforts of yours truly and Mick. That was the sum total of his vitriol. Some of our current Premiership managers find themselves incapable of not 'effing' every other word.

Not only did John cut a unique figure in his selective use of the English language but he also stood out from the crowd, you might say, with his dress sense. Many a morning we used to see him emerge onto the Ball Road training-ground clad in duffle coat and beret with grey strides tucked into his wellies. John would berate us all from the sidelines.

There was one player not blessed with the brightest footballing brain - his name was Garth Lee. He would run down the line in a practice match as a number of shouts were directed towards him. Above all the others, we could hear John Harris saying: "Hold the ball! Hold the ball!" Just about every person who has ever kicked a football knows this is soccer-speak to retain possession. Garth, unfortunately, took John's instructions literally and picked up the ball with his hands! John very nearly swore but was instead content to let rip with a stream of 'bloomin's'.

Really, myself and the rest of the teenagers were looked upon as John's babes-in-arms. If truth be told, he took us under his wing and nurtured us well. In those days to have half a team of teenagers was a rarity and, at the risk of sounding like an old fuddy-duddy, the game was much more physical. Late tackles were not illegal, they were obligatory. It didn't matter who you were, when you were about to touch the ball for the first time, you were whacked. The Bolton back four, in particular, was a breeding ground for the SAS. But John would stick up for us and get us through. Hence, when I booked four of the lads into the Acapulco Hilton on our trip to Mexico, he was more concerned with how he would break the news to our families should the hotel have burned down.

There are perhaps more than a few parallels with John's approach and that of Alex Ferguson's at Manchester United. At the time, I was lodging with Len Badger and his widowed mum in the Badger family home, a large three-storeyed Victorian house on Woodseats Road in Sheffield. Being young lads with the world at our feet, we liked the occasional night out. One evening we sallied forth together wearing our PFA blazers, ties and badges and ended up in The Locarno nightclub on The Moor in Sheffield. Yes, I suppose we thought we were big time. We had a few *sherbets* before finally walking home. This was in midweek, I hasten to add, and not before a weekend match.

Len's mum had a bedroom at the top of the stairs while Len and I had rooms on the other side of the landing. It was quite late when we got back and we crept silently up the stairs like a pair of timid dormice. As we arrived at the landing, however, on came the light and down came a well-aimed blow from a hair-brush which caught the Birch firmly on the head. Whack! Another stinging blow rained down on Len. At first we thought it was Mrs B, but nope, it was John Harris waiting for the pair of us to come in! "You's bloomin' good-time charlies. You's bloomin get in that room and I'm seeing you tomorrow!" he raged.

He left shortly after and Mrs B came to our room to explain that John had arrived at 8pm wanting to see us and had stayed for the next five hours. She had given him dinner and tea while he waited. We were absolutely petrified and got the rollocking of our lives the following day. Obviously, he wanted to keep on top of us and make sure we didn't stray from the straight and narrow.

It was probably a similar story with Alex at Old Trafford when he kept a tight rein on the likes of Giggs, Sharpe and Beckham when they were teenagers at United

Here we are with Blades' boss John Harris at the start of the 1965-66 season. Back: Brian Richardson, Len Badger, David Munks, Reg Matthewson, Barry Hartle. Centre: John Short (Coach), Len Allchurch, Ken Mallender, Mick Jones, Alan Hodgkinson, Cec Coldwell, Graham Shaw, Joe Shaw, Archie Clark (Asst. Manager). Front: Me, John Docherty, Gil Reece, John Harris (Manager), Tony Wagstaff, Alan Woodward, Keith Kettleborough.

making their way in the game. He, I understand, was not averse to paying a few house calls when the players least expected it. Again, John Harris was ahead of his time.

There was also a second theory subscribed to by several players at Sheffield. John certainly did seem to spend more time at Mrs Badger's home than others. There was talk that he had a soft spot for that good lady and would use us as an excuse to have a cup of tea with her. He helped get her a job serving teas down at Bramall Lane on matchdays and always dropped his gruff exterior when in her company. Here, of course, John and Alex were poles apart. I'm sure Alex never wanted to get off with Ryan Giggs' landlady. (Only joking, Alex. Please don't sue, cos my testimonial only made one thousandth of yours and I can't afford it).

As I mentioned earlier in the chapter, this was around the time when a real revolution was going on between old and new-school types of manager. John Harris was one of the last of the old breed, while my new boss at Chelsea, Dave Sexton, was one of the first of the new school. In the space of just a few weeks I was able to sample both ends of this cultural revolution and what a shock it proved.

Not quite as big a shock as the actual day of my transfer out of Sheffield to the bright lights of London. If truth be told, Sheffield United had a bit of a reputation for being a selling club. Invariably, a player would be sold every season to enable the Blades to fund some new ground improvements at Bramall Lane. My close friend and strike partner Mick Jones had already been sold to Leeds United that season for £100,000. Leeds were a magnificent side and it was a great move. Although I only found this out in later life, Leeds manager Don Revie had come in for both of us and offered a £200,000 double package. John Harris needed the £100,000 but he daren't let us both go so he gave Leeds the option to choose one. They chose Mick and they were absolutely right - he was a proven goalscorer and had already broken into the England team.

MICK JONES: Leeds United wanted both of us but when told they could only pick one quite rightly chose my mate Mick.

I put in a transfer request shortly after Mick's departure and, a few weeks later, I received a call from trainer Harry Latham to go and see John Harris out on the terraces. I'd been out late the night before and thought I was in for another rollocking.

In those days, Bramall Lane was three-sided and we set off on a walk together. Putting his hand on the inside of my palm (this was one of John's little foibles), he told me there was only one club he was prepared to let me go to. He had agreed terms with them but did not want me to leave. I was gobsmacked and wondered what on earth was going on.

By now, we had reached the open-ended cricket side with him still holding my hand. We walked into the pavilion and he told me to wait in the secretary's office. As I sat down, I heard the key turn in the door. John had only gone and locked me in! Strange, I thought. I waited a few minutes and then tried to use the telephone but the line was dead. The mystery deepened. Eventually the door opened and John announced a surprise guest. As he came in I was staggered to see it was none other than Dave Sexton, who had taken on the Chelsea job a few weeks earlier and now wanted me to be his first signing. "You's bloomin' talk with this man and you let me know what you's doing," said John.

Dave explained that he had booked us a table at a new hotel in Sheffield, Hallam Towers, and after some preliminary small-talk told me he had agreed terms for my signature with Sheffield United. "Would you like to join Chelsea?" he asked. Wow! The big names at Chelsea, the King's Road, Carnaby Street, the metropolis ... "Of course, I would," I replied.

A comparable transfer these days would involve agents and lengthy meetings, yet here was yours truly sitting down to an informal lunch, with the manager, all by myself. "Don't you want to know your terms?" he said. "Yes please," I replied. When Dave outlined the wages, my jaw dropped open six inches - the basic was £60 a week plus £30 per point, and Chelsea frequently played two games a week! Quickly doing some mental arithmetic I calculated that, if Chelsea won both games, I could be earning £180!

I was on £35 a week plus £5 per appearance with the Blades so the Chelsea offer was serious money. Although the figures might sound paltry in today's market-place, back in the late sixties the average wage was £12 per week - my dad was only earning that much as a clerk at Bartons.

Having agreed terms, we got back in the car and Dave asked if I was happy with everything. I was a little concerned about how to address him. "Now you've agreed to sign for me, you'd better call me boss," he replied.

By this time, a lot of things were happening to me. I'd banged in a few goals for United and my name was bandied around as a possible for the new generation of England players preparing for the 1970 World Cup. The Chelsea offer, though, surpassed all expectations. Then, out of curiosity, Dave asked what fee I thought he had agreed with Sheffield United for my services. This was a difficult question. Mick Jones had gone to Leeds for £100,000, so based on his valuation I replied: "Maybe as much as £50,000, boss." That was the valuation bandied about in the newspapers. "Nope. I'll put you out of your misery. I've paid £100,000 for you."

I couldn't believe it. There had been a few six-figure transfers before this but for talented players I considered top drawer - Mick Jones and Denis Law to name but two. However, there was one minor drawback to my dream move. I went straight home and phoned my future *tank commander* Heather to impart the good news. She was delighted but quick to remind me of a rather rash pledge I had made to her. Engaged at the time, I had promised we would be married as soon as I moved on from Sheffield United. Heather pointed this out during the 'phone call and, less than a year later, we tied the knot.

In the meantime, my first day's training at Chelsea is one I shan't forget for the rest of my life. Understandably, as the new £100,000 kid on the block, I was a little nervous. Training at United had been fairly primitive. Basically, it involved hard running, followed by training sessions with lots of crosses being put in. It was the job of myself and Mick Jones to make a variety of runs and clatter into 'keeper Alan Hodgkinson as we endeavoured to get our heads onto the ball. Essentially, that was it. At Chelsea, it was as if I had moved to the continent.

But if I thought the morning session was different, I was in for even more of a rude awakening later. Dave asked me, but no-one else, to stay behind for an afternoon session. I wondered what was going on. Why did I need extra training? I'd just become one of the first players ever to be transferred for a six-figure sum. By this time, most of the lads had finished their shower and were outside watching as Dave asked me to collect a bag of balls and a corner flag. Off we walked to a pitch and I set up camp on one of the corner spots. A flag was positioned on the goal-line one yard behind the near post. "Right," said Dave, "by the time you finish this training session I want you to be able to curl three crosses out of ten into the one-yard gap between the post and the corner flag."

My first bag of balls was a complete failure. I was struggling to curl one cross into the whole of the goal, let alone into such a narrow area. After about twenty minutes I'd wellied over fifty balls but all with the same lack of success. I could feel the rest of the lads laughing at me as they watched from the verandah. All sorts of things were going through my mind. Was this exercise designed to belittle me? Did they want to bring the new £100,000 signing down to earth with a bump? What was the point of spending all that money just to destroy a lad's confidence? Surely, there was some purpose to all this.

Eventually, taking pity on me, Dave called a halt to the practice and suggested I had not done a lot of skill-work in my years at Sheffield. Reluctantly, I had to agree. He then showed me how to align my body and create the right shape as I kicked the ball. As far as I was concerned this was rocket science, and a completely different approach to coaching. After a few more punted crosses, it began to feel a little easier and I received some encouragement from Dave. Then, he showed me how to kick the ball and exactly where, on the inside of my foot, it should make contact. Bear in mind, by this time I had already played four years in the First Division, was an England Under-23 international and had become one of the handful of £100,000 players.

But his advice began to bear fruit. My knee hurt from kicking the ball so often, but eventually I caught one cross perfectly and the ball flew neatly into the net between post and corner flag. My sense of elation was unsurpassed and, after a couple of hours, I managed the required three in ten.

■ **DAVE SEXTON** Welcome to Stamford Bridge. Chelsea boss Dave Sexton shares a laugh and joke as he shows me around Stamford Bridge for the first time after my £100,000 arrival from Sheffield United. To say I was impressed would have been an understatement. I've always maintained that I learned more from Dave than any other manager. He was a fantastic coach, years ahead of his time. The only criticism that could be levelled against him was his choice of players, after all, I was his first signing for Chelsea!

By this time, all the lads had gone home with the exception of a disgruntled Peter Osgood. Ossie was the king of Stamford Bridge, but he had offered me a lift that afternoon so had no option but to wait. It was the first and last time I ever did that particular practice. On the way home in the car, I told Ossie: "I've never done anything like that before." "There's plenty more to come." he replied, and never spoke a truer word.

Another of those early lessons, during which Dave took me 'back to school', was on how to time my forward runs. As a striker of some repute, I thought I was doing okay. I got caught off-side a fair amount but banged in the goals without any problems at Sheffield United. Dave completely re-educated me. In training, he would come onto the pitch and hold my hand whilst Eddie McCreadie would be charged with supplying the through-ball for me to run onto. I'd want to run straight away but Dave wouldn't let go of my hand. "Wait, wait," he'd command, then he'd walk with me across the back line and, just when I thought it was far too late, he'd let my hand go and off I would run.

From a coaching and technical point of view, Dave was truly fantastic, he expected us to do the obligatory hard work in the first part of training, but then he'd work on special drills and tricks. He was the manager who taught me how to chest-trap a ball correctly, and about how to hit a ball down the middle with the outside of your foot. You only had to look at the Chelsea side of that era to see the individual skills which bore Dave's hallmark.

Dave was also years ahead of his time when it came to using an extended squad and rotating players to contest a large number of competitions. Manchester United and Arsenal are two current Premiership sides who bid for honours using a pool of players, rather than relying on twelve or thirteen men. Dave had a first team squad of eighteen which helped him lift the FA Cup and Inter-City Fairs Cup, as well as producing regular top six finishes in the First Division. Any one of those eighteen players would have held down regular places at every other First Division club but Dave would swap them around and only a very few were ever-presents.

If Dave did have a failing, it was his man-management skills. Managing Chelsea at that time - and maybe to this day - was far from easy. There were many strong characters in the dressing room who all wanted their input and later on, after my departure, I think Dave did find it a little hard to cope. I hasten to add he never had any problems with me. In many respects, there was a special relationship, given that I was Dave's first signing after he'd taken over from Tommy Docherty. To this day, we still have a bit of Birchy banter about it. Dave often comes to Filbert Street and I always apologise to him. "What for?" he asks. I reply: "I was your first-ever signing and everything was downhill after that. Did you ever recover from signing me?"

Dave and my next manager, Crystal Palace boss Bert Head, were like chalk and cheese. Bert was very much 'old school'. A certain amount of frustration had set in with me at Chelsea. I wasn't always getting a regular game because of the squad system and, one day, myself and Bobby Tambling got a surprise call to say Palace were interested in us. We knew the Eagles were a well-supported club in South London who had just been promoted to the top flight, but neither of us really thought we would leave Stamford Bridge.

We arrived at Selhurst Park together and I went in first. Talks didn't last long but in the time I was with Bert I was offered over £100 a week basic for the first time in my career. The bonus there was even more fantastic - £60 per point. I went out, saw Bobby, told him he would be signing and we'd chat about it in the café up the road. A few minutes later he duly arrived and confirmed his signing. Even by Chelsea standards the points bonus was out of this world. Obviously, as newcomers to the First Division, Palace felt they wouldn't get too many victories. How wrong they were. We got off to a flier and were top of the table for two months before reality set in. In the meantime, though, we enjoyed excellent wage packets.

In truth, we saw very little of Bert. Most of the training was undertaken by George Petchey. Twice a week, George would take us down to the Crystal Palace athletics track where fully-trained athletics coaches would take us for special sessions. They would attach us to special harnesses and we would attempt to run with a harness flapping behind us. One coach, in particular, took a special interest in me. He used to do the BBC commentary and told me I could have made a serious runner - he liked my technique and natural running style. Mind you, he said little about my footballing abilities.

Bert only showed his face on a Saturday morning, when we met for our pre-match meal at the Selsdon Park hotel. I often felt sympathy for George; it must have been very difficult for him during the week because he was not given any advance knowledge about the team until Bert announced it on Saturday. I would frequently ask George if we could prepare special routines, like free-kicks, in training. "Not worth it, Birch, I don't know who will be in the team," George would reply.

BERT HEAD: All he needed was a parrot on his shoulder to complete his Long John Silver team talks!

My initial direct contact with Bert came when he delivered the team-talk before my first match. It was a capacity crowd at Selhurst Park and I was a little nervous as I changed for the first time with my new team-mates. I remember being next to Steve Kember. Elsewhere in the dressing room was Mel Blyth, goalkeeper John Jackson, John McCormick, my striker partner Gerry Queen and David Payne. We weren't a top class side but Bert had done a great job getting the club into the top flight. After my days at Chelsea, I was used to quite specific team talks about who to pick up, timing my runs and the opposition low-down. Steve Kember warned me I was in for an eye-opener and he was quite correct.

I was sitting by the door when Bert came in, wearing his customary three-piece suit. "Right, listen up you bastards," he delivered in his Wiltshire accent, which always made me think of Long John Silver. " Hit 'em hard and hit 'em often. They'll come at you like a bunch of Arabs for the first 89 minutes. If you get 'em, get 'em in the last minute. Have a good game, my hearties." With that, he turned around and left the dressing room. All he needed was a parrot on his shoulder and my mental picture would have been complete. I was stunned into silence but Steve confirmed this was the basis of Bert's team-talk for just about every game.

I was at Palace for about eighteen months and in that time enjoyed very few, if any, conversations with Bert. We saw precious little of him. If we won a game, he'd come into the dressing room and congratulate us, but that was about it. Bert always kept a good distance between himself and the players and, to be fair, it certainly seemed to work for him.

Probably the longest conversation I ever managed with Bert was when I left to join Leicester City. He called me into his office to explain that the Foxes had made a move for me, and he would be keen to do the deal with Bobby Kellard coming in the opposite direction. At all of my clubs, I was proud the managers had said they didn't want me to go but would be prepared to release me. Bert said he needed to strengthen his midfield and that's why he would let me go. I'd heard of Leicester's interest and had subsequently learned the club had wanted to sign me when I was at Sheffield United. With mine and my wife's families in Nottingham, we already had good connections with the East Midlands.

I drove up to Leicester and met Jimmy Bloomfield who did a great job of selling the club to me. I signed for £125 basic but with a reduced bonus structure of £30 per point. Potentially, I was taking a pay cut to come to Filbert Street but Jimmy was a great talker. Leicester had just signed Jon Sammels from Arsenal and Jimmy told me the way he wanted to play the game. Of all the managers I played under, I admired him more than anyone else - he was a purist. He wanted to play the beautiful game. He wanted to go out and put on a great display as well as win.

A lot of managers these days live and die by results and that, ultimately, is all that matters. Jimmy was different - he wanted results but he also wanted to entertain. He was a real gentleman, but throughout my time at Leicester I very rarely saw him display any emotion. One of Jim's successors at Filbert Street, Martin O'Neill, is famed for his touchline activity. That, I think, helps Martin release his pent-up anger and frustrations. Jimmy, by contrast, had no release valve. He always seemed to bottle things up and never really displayed his true emotions. When we won, he would permit himself a smile. When we lost, he would try to put a brave face on it all but, deep down, you knew he was hurting. Sadly, Jimmy died, having developed cancer a few years after I left the club. It is my theory that his approach may, in some small way, have had a detrimental effect on his health.

Jimmy really was a lovely fella - some might say too pleasant to have been a football manager - but, like Dave Sexton at Chelsea, he encountered a few problems with the players. In truth, some would take liberties with Jimmy but he didn't seem to let it worry him unduly. Unquestionably one of the all-time classics concerned a coach-ride back from a First Division trip to Newcastle. We were trounced 3-0 and Malcolm Macdonald ran us ragged. Despite the long return journey, at least we could look forward to a good Saturday night out. As social secretary, the responsibility fell on me to organise the activities.

The plan was to go to our favourite Spanish restaurant, the Costa Brava, where owner Ramon used to look after us really well. Discreetly, as the coach trundled along the A1 through Wetherby, I walked up the aisle to establish who was coming out on the town. Weller, Whitworth, Earle and Co. were all up for a night out but when I asked Frank he explained he couldn't make it because he had been unable find a babysitter. Birgitta, his very attractive Swedish wife, was staying in and Frank would not be allowed out. Now remember, in the seventies mobile phones had not been invented. The only item of modern technology we had on the coach was a cassette machine which belted out Elvis Presley hits. None of us really liked Elvis but because Frank wanted to listen to his hero that was the end of the story.

Half an hour later Frank came over and asked where we were meeting. "The Old Horse pub, over the road from Victoria Park," I replied, "but I thought you couldn't make it." "Oh well, it's changed, I'm out now," said Frank.

I was more than a little surprised. Having had no contact with the outside world, Frank had managed to magic up a babysitter. "Hold on a minute, how have you got a baby-sitter sorted," I asked. "Jim's doing it," he replied in a very matter-of-fact tone. All of us were sat there scratching our heads. The only Jim we could

■ **JIMMY BLOOMFIELD** was a purist who loved to see football played to entertain.
By the looks on our faces here we're all wondering if Humpty Dumpty is Jimmy's latest signing!
Left to right are physio George Preston, Jon Sammels, Keith Weller, Jimmy, Frank Worthington and Birch.

think of was the manager. "That's right," said Frank. We were gobsmacked. Frank had spoken to Jimmy and he had agreed to it. I don't know whether we were more surprised that Frank had the bottle to ask the manager, or that Jimmy had acceded to the request.

So, there we were; we'd lost an important First Division game 4-0 but our manager was going home after an overnight trip to Newcastle, to say hello to his wife, drive straight over to Frank's house and then very kindly baby-sit for the evening. It spoke volumes for Jimmy... and for Frank. I mean, can you imagine it happening today? Dennis Wise goes up to Gianluca Vialli and asks if he will baby-sit so he can have a night out on the town. Unbelievable! Only Frank could have got away with it.

Jimmy felt football could only be played one way, and he always urged us to go out and express ourselves. He was not quite up to the coaching level of Dave Sexton at Chelsea, as Dave had obviously picked up a lot of his ideas from the continent, whereas Jimmy was more your English-style skill. Jim wanted his teams to win with style, and even in training was very innovative. For warm-up sessions, he would often play a tape of the Haarlem Globetrotters theme music and there we would be, jogging around the gym believing we were the footballing equivalent of Meadowlark Lemon.

One of Jimmy's finest hours was unquestionably a 4-0 victory over Luton Town at Kenilworth Road in the fifth round of the F.A. Cup. It was one of those days when we could have beaten Manchester United, Barcelona and Inter Milan combined, such was the quality of our performance. Keith Weller capped the scoring with a stupendous goal and there was a real party mood in the dressing room afterwards when we heard a knock at the door. In came a familiar figure - none other than Malcolm Allison who had helped take Manchester City to the First Division championship and other major trophies.

"Do you mind if I say a few words to the boys?" Malcolm enquired of Jimmy. "Lads, that was one of the greatest displays of attacking football I have ever seen in my life. You were absolutely superb." This was unheard of, rival managers did not come into dressing rooms to praise you. As Big Mal made his exit, Jimmy sported a massive grin from ear to ear. That day we had won, and in fine style. Jimmy could ask for no more.

Throughout my career with Sheffield United, Chelsea and Crystal Palace, I prided myself on having good working relations with my bosses. Sure, I overstepped the mark with an occasional late night but I considered that to be all part of the game. Although I admired Jimmy more than any other manager, there was a rocky period between the two of us which culminated in an FA inquiry. I had missed a few games with a knee injury. Unfortunately, although a number of doctors investigated it, they could find nothing visibly wrong. I subsequently believe it to have been 'housemaid's knee'. Sounds wimpish, I know, but the joint kept filling with fluid and I wasn't able to play for several weeks.

Eventually, I managed to get over it and expected to return to the first team. I played a few obligatory reserve games and thought I would be put on the bench. On the contrary, Jimmy signed Brian Alderson and I didn't a get a look-in. I asked to see Jimmy but, by this time, reports had got back to him that there had been nothing wrong with me. They suggested I was malingering. Now, down the years, the Birch could be accused of a lot of things but cheating was never one of them. I was furious with Jimmy and had a blazing argument. When I get a bee in my bonnet, I'm not one to stand down and I felt very disappointed about the whole affair.

Jimmy took the matter one stage further by fining me, because I had declared myself injured when he thought me fit. This was like the proverbial red rag to a bull. I appealed against the fine and called for a full FA inquiry - big news at the time. The inquiry was to take place at Filbert Street with several FA bigwigs travelling up from London. I prepared my own case and secured medical evidence of my injury from several leading experts. I was confident of winning. How naive.

My confidence, however, started to wane a little on the day of the inquiry. As I waited to be summonsed, I noticed Leicester secretary John Smith taking in a tray of drinks to the inquiry team - not coffees or teas but stronger, alcoholic, drinks. I was eventually called in and prepared to submit my evidence, but I was stunned when the chairman of the inquiry ruled that written evidence was inadmissible. I suppose I should have then simply read it out but, unable to think quickly enough on my feet, I ummed and ahh-ed and spoke for a few minutes. In truth, it would not have made the slightest difference. I got the impression it was a fait accomplit and not only did I lose the appeal but I had to pay the full costs of the whole inquiry.

Needless to say, things were never quite the same with me and Jimmy again. Our relationship was soured and it was not long before I was bundled off to America, and a stint with Notts County. I am eternally grateful, though, that I made my peace with Jimmy before his death.

Of all the managers I have served, Jimmy Sirrel was arguably one of the more colourful characters. There are, quite literally, hundreds of Sirrel stories to come out of Meadow Lane. Returning to the club I supported as a boy was obviously an emotional experience but I could never have braced myself for my encounters with Jimmy. Originally, I went there on three-months' loan before spending a full season with the club. Jimmy was a little guy with a heavily-pronounced Glaswegian accent. When it came to movie-star looks, I'm afraid he was some way down the pecking order. On coach journeys to away games, we used to while away the time by drawing up 'Ugly XI' football teams. From week to week, the players might change but there was always a unanimous vote for the manager.

But, before I get ahead of myself... When I returned for my full season with the Magpies it was Jimmy's former assistant, Ron Fenton, who was in charge. I got on well with Ronnie and it was a real shame when he became the first manager to be axed whilst I was playing for a club. We didn't get off to the most successful of starts in the old Second Division and Ronnie quickly found himself under pressure. Ironically, I did my utmost to prevent him facing an FA charge for attacking a referee, only for him to get the bullet a couple of weeks later.

The incident occurred in a game against my former club, Luton, at Kenilworth Road when one of the most blatant handballs I had ever seen in my career took place. It wasn't just handball, it was an intended punch off the line. The referee missed it and at the end of the game - we lost 2-0 - Ronnie was determined to get to grips with the official. I managed to manhandle Ronnie away before he got himself into real trouble. Sadly, we lost at Sheffield United 4-1 the following week and Ronnie got the push. He was quickly given another job by Brian Clough, over the river at Nottingham Forest, and I wished him all the very best.

JIMMY SIRREL: The Notts County manager had a penchant for practising penalties … and licking the top of the tomato sauce bottle.

Jimmy Sirrel was installed for his second managerial spell at the club and you could never question his commitment. He was a winner in everything he did and could not abide losers. So much so, that after one defeat he unleashed his fury on long-serving physiotherapist Jack Wheeler. Jimmy was lacing into us about how we weren't being competitive enough. "You gotta get your foot in," he told us. "Ere, Jack son," as he would always refer to the genial giant, "this is what I mean." And with that Jimmy decided to offer us a graphic lesson on his preaching. In shorts and boots, he walked over to Jack who was innocently leaning against the dressing room wall minding his own business. Jimmy then proceeded to go over the top, raking his studs all the way down Jack's legs. Jack crumpled up and, afterwards, showed us the painful red weals. The manager had just topped his own physio in the dressing room. Unbelievable!

For some weird, unknown reason, Jimmy was quite a fan of yours truly. He was pleased to have brought in a First Division player and waxed lyrical. This became a little embarrassing, particularly when we had lost. After another defeat (I can't remember too many wins in a Magpies shirt, unfortunately), Jimmy was lashing into the whole side with one exception. "Ere, Birchy, he's played at a higher level but he still wants to play. He wants to put his foot in. He's not come here for an easy ride. This is what you lot should be striving for." Needless to say, the lads gave me a right ribbing.

Jimmy's competitive edge was never better illustrated than with his rather novel penalty routines in training. Up until this point in my career, I had experienced high-quality facilities for training, but County's locations alternated between a field behind a sewage farm and Nottingham's equivalent to Hackney Marshes, a massive expanse by the banks of the River Trent called Victoria Embankment. This particular day we were on the Embankment, but it might just as well have been Antarctica. Colin Murphy, the former Lincoln and Notts manager, was warming us up in twos.

As we jogged around the pitches, I spied a little figure in the distance carrying a bag of balls. It was Jimmy. He strode up to an empty pitch, unloaded the balls and placed one on the spot. "Just watch what happens next," whispered Les Bradd to me. Jimmy had a whistle tied to the top of his arm. He bent to blow the whistle and then rushed forward to blast a penalty into an empty goal. As the ball hit the back of the net he clenched his fist and jumped up into the air as if he had just scored the winner in a European Cup final.

He had repeated these actions another ten times when physio Jack Wheeler appeared on the scene and was motioned into goal by Jimmy. Jack had been a 'keeper at Huddersfield Town prior to becoming County's physio. Jimmy gathered up the balls and took a further set of penalties, blasting another one into the net as Jack went the wrong way. Jimmy banged in all ten as Jack was left clutching thin air. I looked at Les Bradd incredulously. This was our gaffer. After the penalty shoot-out, I also collared Jack. "You used to be a goalkeeper, but you got nowhere near any of them." He replied: "That's right, Birch. That's why I've been here for the last 20 years."

Fair play to Jimmy, though. He was one of the fittest managers I have ever come across. Before training he would do ten laps of Meadow Lane, but a problem arose in that Jimmy seemed to have an aversion to washing machines when it came to his sweat-soaked training kit. At Meadow Lane, there was a huge plunge bath located under the main wooden stand. After training, we would all dive in and I thoroughly enjoyed soaking up to my neck in warm soapy water. However, the bath would be vacated in double-quick time when Jimmy appeared, removed his sodden, whiffy, training gear and threw it straight into the water. The kit floated around on the surface while we all made a sharp exit!

Our gaffer's eating habits also attracted their fair share of attention, especially on away trips. Forget all this boiled chicken and pasta for pre-match meals lark, in our day we munched our way through succulent juicy steaks. On my first trip, Dave Needham marked my card and warned me to watch out for the ketchup bottle. The lads always tried to ensure the sauce was placed out of reach at the furthest corner of the table from Jimmy. As soon as Jimmy was served his steak he would demand the ketchup. "Eh lads, pass me the ketchup," went up the shout. Mesmerised, I watched Jimmy transfer half the contents of the bottle onto his food. "Have some steak on your ketchup," I whispered to Dave. "Wait for the best bit," said Dave. Jimmy then proceeded to lick all the way around the top of the sauce bottle before putting the top back on!

Now I'm sure that Jim Iley, then boss of Blackburn Rovers, was a great guy. And I'll bet there are a million and one stories to tell about him. But I'm afraid my recollections of Jim at Ewood Park will have to be considerably shorter than the rest of the managers I have played under - principally because he lasted only two days after signing me before getting the sack. I will forever be indebted to Jim, however, for rescuing me from one of the worst nightmares of my life.

After Notts County I went off to America to play in the North American Soccer League (NASL) for a year before returning to Leicester. With no offers forthcoming from English clubs, I was faced with the humbling prospect of signing on the dole for the first time in my working life. Down I went to the local Labour Exchange - a drab, grey, faceless building - and took my place in a long line of unemployed folk waiting to register. I could see one or two people in the row staring at me and thinking: "Is that really you, Birch?" But before I reached the end of the queue, I could take no more, so I turned around and walked out. I vowed never to go to a place like that again, and thankfully, I've been fortunate enough to have avoided them ever since.

A day later I got a 'phone call from Jim at Blackburn asking if I would like to come up to the club. I travelled up on a Thursday and was signed at the same time as Joe Craig from Celtic. We had a training session on Friday, lost 2-1 at home to Charlton Athletic on Saturday and by Monday Jim had been given the bullet by the

JOBS FOR THE BIRCH: This was me opening a Job Centre in 1976 but I faced a thankfully brief taste of life on the dole towards the end of my footballing career.

chairman. I've subsequently joked to Jim that my signature must have been the straw that broke the camel's back.

His assistant John Pickering took over but my time there was not the happiest. I stayed up in Lancashire for three nights a week but in my six months with Rovers we only won two games. One abiding memory of Blackburn was the hot pies we consumed after training. Forget all this healthy food stuff. After a session, one of the apprentices would be despatched to the local takeaway and he'd return with a trayful of piping hot meat & potato pies and pasties. They were absolutely delicious but quite possibly contributed to the undermining of our fitness levels.

It was my old Nottingham Schoolboys team-mate David Pleat who rescued me from Blackburn. David, who had seen his own promising playing career cut short by injury at Nottingham Forest, had tentatively taken his first steps on the managerial rungs. He was in charge at Luton and I got a call from him to ask whether I fancied moving down south to Kenilworth Road. We had kept in touch over the years and agreed to meet at Trowell Services on the MI. Our negotiations didn't take long.

Travelling down to Luton from my Leicester home took an hour and was considerably preferable to the journey across the M62 up to Blackburn where it always seemed to be raining. Foolishly, I thought David had signed me because he felt I still had something to offer the game. Not a bit of it, I was signed because I possessed the right character and temperament to give everyone a lift in the dressing room - but this I only discovered on the day I left for Hereford, just ten games after signing for The Hatters.

David's coach Dave Coates told me the story and to say I was stunned would have been a severe understatement. Apparently, Pleaty had been concerned about a lack of spirit in the dressing room. On the pitch he was putting together a very talented team - subsequently to gain promotion to Division One - including the likes of David Moss and Brian Stein. At this time, though, they were still struggling in the Second Division and I was chosen as the perfect person to inject some carefree humour and gee up everyone's spirits. Birch the player had become Birchy the court jester.

At this stage, of course, I was in blissful ignorance, so much so that I really gave it everything in pre-season training. Pleaty, I imagine, felt I was just at Luton for the ride and, in any case, he hadn't acquired me for my footballing abilities, but he was suitably surprised by my undoubted commitment. David was still very much a young, unproven manager but I was impressed with his coaching techniques. Our relationship could have been fairly difficult given that we had begun as schoolmates but he was now my boss. He was one of the few people in the game who didn't refer to me as 'Birch'. Instead, he always addressed me as 'Lal', the pet name given me by my family. But we got along fine.

I had a healthy respect for Pleaty as a manager and I would put him up there alongside Dave Sexton and Jimmy Bloomfield when it came to coaching. He would mix up the sessions and constantly change around things we did in training. He was innovative and kept everything fresh. Tactically he was clever, and could spot many aspects of the game others would miss. Another strength was his knowledge of players, not just in England but probably throughout Europe as well. Even in those days you could see an inquisitive side showing through. Pleaty has an encyclopaedic knowledge of footballers - he knows everything about everyone, and there is hardly anything that happens in the game he misses.

Despite my promising pre-season, I failed to last beyond October at Kenilworth Road. Hereford made an approach for me and it was agreed I would travel to Edgar Street to speak with manager Mike Bailey and his coach Bobby Gould. I wasn't too keen and insisted I still had plenty to offer at Luton. "No, your job in the dressing-room is done," said Pleaty. I wondered what on earth he meant. What about my job on the pitch? Dave Coates filled me in on the tawdry details and I was left with little option but to head westwards across the country and discover what Hereford had to offer.

I agreed terms with them and, at this stage, insist on dispelling any theories readers may be harbouring about 'brown-paper bags and motorway service stations'. I know from other salacious stories and biographies that all sorts of under-the-counter payments were supposed to have taken place. Hand on heart, I can safely say these all passed me by when I moved from club to club. There were no envelopes stuffed with bank notes, I simply turned up and signed on the dotted line. It was exactly the same with my last League port of call, Hereford.

Mike and I agreed I would travel over to the club from the Midlands for one training session a week, and stop overnight before a game. The rest of the time I was left to maintain my own fitness in the Leicester, an arrangement which suited us both. Where, however, this scenario broke down was when Mike took up a coaching post at Brighton and his assistant Bobby Gould also left, approximately two months after I had joined.

Mike's successor at Hereford was a guy called Frank Lord, who had previously been playing in South Africa. Frank and I did not, it's fair to say, hit it off. He saw me as the ageing senior pro just along for a ride, turning up for one training session a week and a match on Saturday. He thought I was a disruptive influence on the younger players. I admit I had again been appointed social secretary of the club, even though I was only there for one day a week.

My relationship with Frank was not improved by a night out I organised in Hereford - when we all got completely wrecked - on the eve of my solitary weekly training session. Unfortunately, the gaffer spotted us out on the town. The following day was supposed to be a light, gentle session but, intent on making us pay, Frank hauled us through one of the most physical sessions of my entire career. I ended up physically sick and in a distinctly bad way and never played for the club again. Frozen out of the team, I was only ever called up for one more match. It was away at Lincoln but the game was postponed at the last minute because of an unfit pitch. Eventually, my contract was cancelled in January 1980 - three months after I had joined the club. I maintain I was not there for the ride but, in hindsight, I can understand Frank's situation and, in his position, I would have done exactly the same.

So, there you have it, a complete who's who of all the managers I have played under during my twenty years in the English game. Strangely, the entire total only comes to ten and seven of those were when I was playing outside the top flight. My respect for John Harris rivalled that which I afforded my own father, Dave Sexton was a coach many years ahead of his time from whom I learned the most, and dear old Jimmy Bloomfield was the manager I particularly admired. Some were track-suit bosses, some from the old school but, in my Public Relations Officer position over the past two decades at Leicester City, I have noticed one underlying trend which differentiates current managers from those I played under.

In my day there was always a bigger divide between player and boss. Nowadays, most managers seem to want to be one of the pack and mix far more. Take meal-times for example. Once upon a time, after training, the gaffer would eat a solitary lunch alone in his office but now managers sit in the canteen along with the rest of the playing personnel. Those impenetrable barriers which used to exist have been broken down. I'm not saying it's right, but equally I'm not saying it's wrong. It's just a way the game has developed.

■ **DAVID PLEAT** - Signed me for Luton because I was the right character to give the dressing room a lift - and I thought he'd bought me for my outstanding array of skills!

I can honestly say there was not a manager under whom I played that I did not learn something from. Later in this book, I will tell you about my own managerial experiences at non-league level, establishing little Trowbridge Town in the old Alliance Premier League. And, maybe then, you'll be able to gauge whether I did actually absorb any of the lessons!

■ **INTERNATIONAL BIRCH.** My England U-23 caps are among my most treasured possessions.

Confessions of a Cabaret Artiste

Chapter 4

Arguably one of the more famous chapters in football biographies was 'penned' by the great Sunderland and England striker Len Shackleton. In his memoirs, Len left a blank page when it came to the section about directors and their knowledge of football! Though not quite as succinct as Len's offering, I'm afraid this fourth chapter, describing my international career, is not as lengthy as my other ramblings.

There are, of course, many reasons for this, but mainly, in order of importance:
1. Bobby Charlton;
2. My mother and father getting their act together two days late;
3. My karaoke version of Mick Jagger and the Rolling Stones' "Satisfaction".

Not the usual set of excuses, are they? Indeed, I'm sure you must be admiring my creativity although you're probably a little puzzled, but please read on and all will be revealed. Oh, and by the way, *a general lack of international ability probably has something to do with the chapter's brevity too.*

I consider myself a shade unfortunate that, at a time when my career was at its peak in the late sixties and early seventies, breaking though into the full England squad with Sir Alf Ramsey was probably harder than at any other time in the modern era. England had won the World Cup on home soil in 1966 and were to defend their trophy in Mexico four years later.

Around this time I was winning caps in the England Under-23 squad but I was destined never to make that final jump into the seniors. Sir Alf was a fiercely loyal manager and stuck with a small but select band of players. Even when they did not necessarily play their best football at club level, it invariably seemed they retained their places in the national squad. It was a difficult closed shop to break into and, given the results we obtained, rightly so. Yes, Sir Alf would experiment by bringing in one or two new players from time to time, like Rodney Marsh and Mick Jones, but the nucleus of the side remained unchanged.

For those over 40, I hope you will understand the scenario I am trying to paint, although my younger readers may get the impression I'm a guy with a chip on his shoulder. Honestly, I'm not. I'm simply trying to explain how I read the situation at the time. In truth, it is one of my biggest regrets in football that I never represented my country at full international level. I've already mentioned that my trophy cabinet is hardly brimming with medals, but some of my most treasured possessions are the England caps and shirts I collected at Under-23 level.

Indeed, for many years I felt I was destined never to win international recognition at any level. My problems started when I was still at school. I was nominated by Nottinghamshire Boys to contest regional trials for England Schoolboys. In those days there were trials in the North, the Midlands and the South. I went along to the Midlands trials at Worksop and was selected for the final national trials. This was quite an honour and again I was successful.

Unfortunately my arrival, on August 22nd 1945, could not have been more badly-timed by my parents - apparently, I was two days too old. So, when the selectors checked my date of birth, and realised I was over the date limit, I was not allowed to represent my country at schoolboy level. This was a considerable disappointment but worse was to follow when I signed on at Sheffield United.

After a difficult start in the youth team, I went on to crack in over fifty goals for United in the Northern Intermediate League. I received a surprise call from manager John Harris, inviting me to see him and, with some trepidation, went to his office, only to be told I had been selected to play in the England team for the European Youth Championships. This was a fantastic honour... and I was even more made up when I discovered the venue for these championships... the Canary Isles. I had to forward sizing details for my made-to-measure England suit and England bag. Sir Alf Ramsey was going to send us off from Lancaster Gate and I was tremendously excited.

About a week before I was due to fly out, I was summoned by John Harris again. In a quiet, matter-of-fact voice he explained: "Bad news, Sherman (his nickname for me) we had to send off your passport and it would appear that, when they checked it, you were two days over the age limit for the tournament." I was absolutely gutted. I walked home to my lodgings on Woodseats Road and bawled my eyes out for the rest of the evening. First, the Schoolboys and now England Youth as well.

Thankfully, I was able to put those disappointments behind me and, a couple of years later, I was knocking on the England selectors' door again. The next age group was the Under-23s and, thankfully, with a couple of years to spare I didn't have to worry too much about an extra two days.

My first call-up into the squad came in April 1965 when I was named as a reserve for a game against Czechoslovakia at Leeds' Elland Road ground. Although I wasn't brought on, I do however recall one rather humorous incident in the England dressing-room before the game.

Flame-haired Alan Ball, soon to be a World Cup winner, was having a run-out with the Under-23's. He stood in a corner of the dressing-room, flicking up a ball and trapping it neatly on the back of his neck. I was mightily impressed and decided to follow suit. I wellied up the ball but, instead of catching it as planned, it shot across the room and sent all the tea cups crashing to the floor! I yearned wholeheartedly for the room to swallow me up. Sadly, it's a trick which has eluded the Birch to the current day. Still, of what practical use is it, anyway?

I got my second Under-23 call-up when I was 20 years old, in the season leading up to the 1966 World Cup. It was a game against France at Carrow Road, Norwich in November '65. I was on the bench and distinctly remember being in some pretty illustrious company, and feeling more than a trifle nervous. Also in the dug-out was the England manager Sir Alf Ramsey and an Everton goalkeeper by the name of Gordon West. Gordon was a jovial prankster and, midway though the first half, one of our players sustained an injury. West dug me in the ribs and told me the manager wanted me to warm up. I shot from the dug-out like a startled rabbit and proceeded to sprint up and down the touchline in my England track-suit.

I did all those exaggerated stretches, like touching your toes, side strains, hamstring stretches and so on and really worked up quite a sweat, if I remember rightly. From the corner flag, I flew smartly past the bench in an attempt to persuade the England manager that I was fit and ready to be introduced for my very first taste of international football.

Unfortunately, these actions didn't elicit the required response. Instead, Sir Alf leant out of the dug-out and, in perfectly modulated English, exclaimed: "What on earth are you doing, Birchenall?" "I'm warming up, boss," came my bemused reply. "Well, young man, nobody has requested you to warm up so kindly get back in the dug-out and take your seat," commanded Sir Alf. I sat down feeling slightly sheepish. It was all Gordon West could do not to collapse in fits of convulsive laughter. He'd done me up like a well-smoked kipper. "Thanks a lot, Gordon," I said. I couldn't help but ponder that I hadn't made the best of initial impressions on the famous England manager.

■ **TERRACE TALK.** I was never short of club colleagues when I was called up for international duty with the England under 23s. My Sheffield United team-mate Len Badger was the most capped under 23 international of his era. He should have won full honours but his loyalty to his home-town club may well have held him back. To this day Len has kept his roots in the area and now runs a hostelry in Sheffield. This photo was taken on the terraces of Bramall Lane and shows me getting some advice from Len after my first call-up to the England under 23s. Also pictured is 'Bongo' Smith.

Although I didn't get introduced as a substitute in that game, I was given my chance a few months later when I was named in the starting line-up for the Under-23 game with Turkey at Ewood Park - just two months before the World Cup was due to begin. It was appropriate that I should be handed my first cap alongside two of my Sheffield team-mates, Len Badger and Mick Jones.

Also in the side for the game was soon-to-be World Cup winner Martin Peters and a young Alex Stepney, then of Millwall but shortly to move on to Manchester United. The England team for the game was: Stepney (Millwall), Badger (Sheffield United), Thomson (Wolves), O'Neill (Burnley), Cross (Leicester), Peters (West Ham), Summerbee (Manchester City), Hunt (Wolves), Jones (Sheffield United), Birchenall, Armstrong (Arsenal). We all received a match fee of £20, no small sum in those days.

I cannot begin to describe my feelings of pride as I pulled on the England shirt and stood smartly to attention while the national anthem was belted out before kick-off. I had a good game too and we won 2-0, although my abiding memory of the match is not particularly savoury.

Now, even at that early stage of my career, I was quite used to being on the end of some pretty harsh treatment from opposing defenders. I had been kicked from pillar to post, punched, had my hair pulled, my nuts grabbed, my ribs poked, the full works in fact, and I had managed to take it all calmly without seeking retaliation. But there is one thing I find totally abhorrent and that is spitting.

I was defending a corner where I was marking a Turkish player but, just as the flag-kick was about to be delivered, he spat straight into my face at point-blank range. There was phlegm all over my face. I saw scarlet and completely lost my temper. As the ball was cleared out to the right, the offending Turk ran away to the left. I raced after him and it must have looked quite comical to spectators as twenty players went rushing to the right while a single mad Englishman set off in the opposite direction in hot pursuit of a fleeing Turk. Unfortunately, he was a little swifter than me and I wasn't able to catch him.

At half-time Sir Alf went absolutely potty and slaughtered me for pursuing an individual vendetta. I tried to explain that he had spat in my face. "But you spent a minute chasing after him. You went completely berserk. You are no good to the team like that. You should have been concentrating on the game," ranted Sir Alf.

I was able to exact retribution in the second half, however, when I scraped my studs down the back of his Achilles tendon and he left the pitch squealing like a stuck pig. After the game, I asked all the players to sign my programme and, to this day, it's taken pride of place in my soccer scrapbooks.

My second full appearance in the Under-23's came after the World Cup. I was picked for the England side to face Wales in Swansea on November 1st and the players were requested to meet at 1.30pm under the 'Big Clock' on Platform One at Paddington Station. It was like some massive blind date!

One of my abiding memories of this game was the clothes sense of one of my team-mates, Peter Knowles from Wolverhampton Wanderers. Peter, later to become a Jehovahs Witness, arrived punctually at the station wearing a sombre three-piece suit and carrying a furled umbrella. Actually, the brolly came in useful because it was pouring with rain and I borrowed it to ensure we didn't get soaked during the walk from the hotel to the nightclub after the match! The game, if truth be told, was far from a classic. I think we won 2-1 but the Welsh Under-23's were hardly a world force with which to be reckoned. Come to think of it, nothing's changed now, has it?

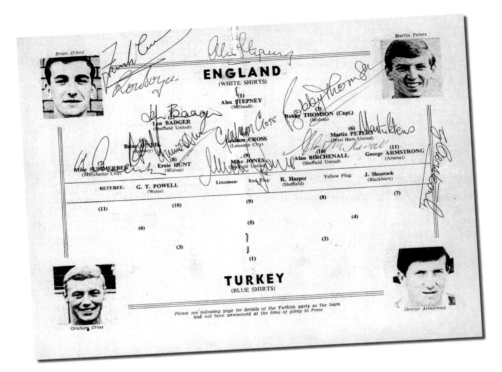

■ Here's one of my most treasured programmes, the one from my full debut for England in the Under-23 international against Turkey at Ewood Park. It cost the princely sum of one shilling and, as you can see from the centre spread, I got all the lads to sign their autographs on the team sheet.

Our England team for that game was: Clemence (Liverpool), Wright (Everton), Hughes (Liverpool), Kendall (Everton), Sadler (Manchester United), Hurst (Everton), Rogers (Swindon), Knowles (Wolves), Osgood (Chelsea), Birchenall, Kidd (Manchester United).

My first two England Under-23 caps had taken me to the footballing hot-spots of Blackburn and Swansea. Things definitely improved, though, when I was called-up for an end-of-season trip to Italy, Hungary and West Germany in the spring of 1968. The full squad was: Springett (Sheffield Wednesday), Jones (Bournemouth), Badger (Sheffield United), Wright (Everton), Hughes (Liverpool), Hollins (Chelsea), Smith (Liverpool), Kendall (Everton), Stephenson (West Ham), Doyle (Manchester City), Sammels (Arsenal), Royle (Everton), Osgood (Chelsea), Chivers (Tottenham), Baldwin (Chelsea), Sissons (West Ham), Harris (Chelsea), Shaw (Sheffield United).

I received a letter from FA secretary Denis Follows and events brightened considerably when I heard we would all be supplied with special tour suits. Even in those days the Birch was something of a fashion icon (in my own mind, at any rate). Suit arrangements, though, were done rather differently then than today. There was no chance of going down to the local designer store for an Armani or a Hugo Boss. No, the FA supplied you with the fabric which you then passed on to your tailor.

The following instructions were contained in the letter:

"The FA, in addition to supplying the fabric, will allow up to £17.10s.0d towards tailoring expenses. It is important that the suits are ready for the tour and to ensure a uniform style among all members of the tour party, the following specification must be adhered to: Two piece, single breasted, three buttoned (uncovered) suit, with a single vent at the back, no more than six inches in length and no lapels on pockets."

Now, bear in mind this was the swinging sixties. *Floral dickies* and *kipper peckhams* were all the rage, accompanied by 20-inch *Tony Blairs*. By this time I had just completed my £100,000 move from Sheffield United to Chelsea so my fashion sense had been even more uplifted - us Chelsea boys did our shopping down Carnaby Street. However, this fashion-conscious free-spirit had to be balanced against the discipline of Sir Alf Ramsey and the FA. It was no contest.

Myself, 'Chopper' Harris and Tommy Baldwin all took delivery of our roll of grey fabric and carried it down to our

favourite tailor in Carnaby Street. It was arguably the most 'boring' suit he had ever been commissioned to cut, but none of us dare upset Sir Alf so we followed the instructions to the letter. Completing the look was a sober white shirt and a narrow navy blue tie complete with three light blue lions. Believe it or not, I've still got not one but two of those ties in my wardrobe. Don't ask me why, but I nicked one while on the tour. At the time we wouldn't be seen dead in them, unless it was on the strict instructions of the FA.

We were to report to White's Hotel at Lancaster Gate on Wednesday May 22nd 1968 at 3pm. On arrival I was delighted to see a friendly face amongst all the FA officials, none other than Chelsea club doctor Dr Boyne who was to be our medical officer for the trip. The doc was a colourful character; he drove a gleaming Rolls Royce, dressed in the finest clothes from Saville Row and possessed a calm, relaxed disposition. We all, including the senior England squad, assembled at Lancaster Gate for a pre-tour briefing.

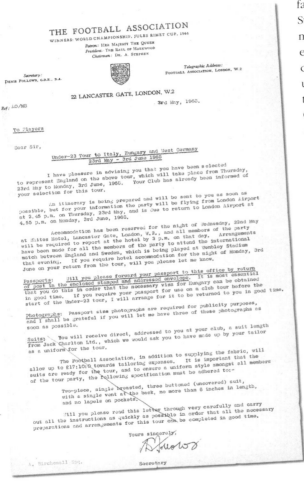

■ YOUR COUNTRY NEEDS YOU: This is the official letter I received from the F.A. informing me of my call-up for the Under-23 tour of Italy, Hungary and West Germany. Of particular interest, towards the end of the letter, are the instructions for the tailoring of our club suits.

The Under-23 manager was Spurs boss Bill Nicholson and his assistant was Wilf McGuinness. Sir Alf was present, of course, together with eminent FA luminaries. It was traditional for the touring party to be addressed by the doctor, who would warn players of the dangers of drinking unsterilised tap water and advise in general how to look after their bodies abroad, what with different foods and the like.

Sir Alf introduced Dr Boyne. "Right lads," said Dr Boyne taking centre stage in the middle of the room. "We're on a trip. We all hope we have a good time and a jolly up and, if anyone gets a dose of the clap, come and see me and I'll sort you out." The lads were stunned into silence. Sir Alf gave him a withering look and, it's worth pointing out, that was the doc's one and only trip with England.

On the evening of our get-together, we all went to Wembley to watch the senior international between England and Sweden. My eyes were well and truly opened on the coach the following morning. It only travelled from Lancaster Gate to Heathrow but, during that time, I saw more monies being gambled on cards than in the whole of my previous lifetime. I'm not a card player but I could not believe the sums wagered. Joe Royle, Peter Osgood, Ron Harris and Tommy Wright were betting megabucks. In one round, a week's wages were put on the table. I was absolutely gobsmacked and ensured I stayed out of the way.

As the young kid on the block, I was keen to impress. On these trips I invariably liked to look around and drink in the atmosphere. Once at Heathrow airport, the players disappeared to the four corners of the building. I spied Johnny Sissons and Johnny Hollins in the paper shop but couldn't locate the others. However, when I glanced across to the bar there sat quite a few of them - Peter Osgood, Tommy Baldwin, Bernard Shaw and company. The Birch has always made it one of his unwritten rules not to drink before getting on a plane, but this obviously did not apply to the rest of the players and by the time we made our way to the boarding gate more than a few pints had been sunk.

We flew out to Venice, then travelled by coach the remaining 100 miles to Trieste in Northern Italy for our first game against a talented Italian team, which was to subsequently supply a large percentage of their senior squad. We earned a 1-1 draw and I started the game. Aside from one rather uneventful night out, Trieste went very much according to plan. Little could anyone have guessed what was to happen in the next few nights as we prepared to march on to Hungary.

Don't ask me why but the Football Association decided to forsake air travel and instead booked the whole party onto an overnight train. The players were herded together into a sleeper coach, on the midnight express out of Trieste, for the 15-hour journey to Budapest. At 00.25am we set off, playing cards to while away the hours in our first-class sleeper car. Halfway through the journey the Hungarian authorities decided to detach our carriage from the train and parcel it away in a remote siding, miles from anywhere. Apparently, there were some problems with the passports.

We were indebted to John Sissons, the West Ham player who we nicknamed Reuters, for this information. Reuters was an international news agency and we'd given John this nickname because he always seemed to know what was going on. Suddenly there was a commotion down at the far end of the carriage as a group of Hungarian guards marched onto the train. Three of them, who were carrying sub-machine guns, came into the compartment and asked for our passports. I showed them my grubby one and they gave it the once over, then pointed to the top bunk where Bernard Shaw, my former Sheffield United team-mate, was sleeping.

Now, to be truthful, Bernard was a miserable bastard at the best of times. He was clearly unfazed by the whole scenario. "They want your passport," I told him. Bernard remained unimpressed and said it was somewhere in his bag and he couldn't be bothered to look for it. By this time the guards were becoming irate. Patience definitely wasn't one of their virtues. "Ahhh... show them this, Birch." And, with that, Bernard peeled back the bed clothes, lowered his big fat arse over the side of the bunk bed and did a moonie at the guards. What a sight!

Bernard had suspended his buttocks six inches away from this Hungarian guard's sub machine gun. The guard was unsure whether to fire the gun or use it as a bayonet. Of course, Bernard had still not realised they were carrying guns, in his semi-comatose state he had thought they were just ordinary customs officers. I warned him of his predicament and, like a shot, he bounced from the bunk and found his passport. I'd never seen him move so fast in his life.

By now it was the middle of the night and we discovered we were to be kept in the siding until morning. The lads were mortified but then we hit on the bright idea of pooling our Hungarian spenders in the hope of bribing the guards to get us a few beers. Aided by our interpreter, we handed over fistfuls of cash that to us was nothing more than Monopoly money, but to poorly-paid communist guards it was the equivalent of winning the pools. From threatening to shoot us, they cheerfully leapt out into the countryside and ferreted around like wombats to find beer for us. An hour later they returned, staggering under the weight of three crates of Hungarian booze. We had a great night, playing cards and supping beers before a locomotive came to pick us up in the morning.

Feeling somewhat the worse for wear we finally arrived in the Hungarian capital. Budapest is a beautiful city and I enjoyed walking around the streets soaking up the culture, right down to numerous bullet holes in the concrete walls, embedded when the Russians had invaded several years earlier.

We were ensconced in the Hotel Sport, an old-fashioned establishment where, on the eve of our game against the Hungarians, Bill Nicholson read out the team. As it was current policy to rotate the squad, I was only on the subs bench, with Martin Chivers coming into the side. We sat down for dinner and afterwards Bill informed us there would be an 11pm curfew.

Taking advantage of the free time available, a group of us decided to go for a walk. As Hungary was a communist state, it's fair to say there was not a great deal to do. Budapest, in fact, made Skegness look like Las Vegas.

After an hour of fruitless walking, we decided to head back to the hotel. However, just as we were about to make our way through the rear entrance, I heard music wafting along the street. This was just the incentive I needed. Where there's music, there's a bar. Where there's a bar, there's a bit of life. Sure enough, a couple of blocks later we found a dingy little Hungarian dive where there was a live band. They weren't the greatest but they weren't too bad either and the place boasted a bit of an atmosphere, so we decided to pool our spending money - £2 per day per player while we were abroad - and buy a round or two.

In our party was me, Ron Harris, Martin Chivers, Tommy Baldwin, Len Badger and Bernard Shaw. We downed a few Hungarian beers and gradually got into the swing of the night. I had earned a certain notoriety for my ability to sing a few songs. Back in Sheffield (and there's more about this in the rest of the book) I had sung with Joe Cocker when he was taking the first steps in his colourful musical career. The lads were giving me a bit of stick, demanding I get up on stage with the band.

Over the public address system, an Hungarian - in his best broken English - announced that members of the England football team were among the crowd. The locals all broke into typically regimented Communist applause. And, went on the announcer, we hear that one of their players would like to sing a song for us, Satisfaction, by the Rolling Stones. I was manhandled on stage by the lads and the band broke into a pidgin version of the Stones' classic. I start doing my best Mick Jagger impression, gyrating my hips, pursing my lips and flailing my arms around like a madman. Very quickly, I got into the swing of it. No-one really understood the words I was singing, and the band struggled to keep up with me, but I was thoroughly enjoying myself.

Then I happened to glance across the bar and noticed none of the lads were around. "Strange," I thought to myself. It's very rare that footballers will tear themselves away from the tommy without good reason. I carried on for a few more

■ **I DID IT MY WAY.** Okay, okay, I know the jacket looks a bit loud even in a black and white photograph, but when I took to the stage I always liked to look the part. In this crooning session in my Leicester City days I was able to recognise most people in the audience. Unfortunately, the same could not be said when I made my singing debut on an England Under-23 tour of Italy, Germany and Hungary. In the crowd of Hungarians, unbeknown to me, were a group of England VIPs. Sadly, my impromptu concert in official England tie and blazer the night before a game in Budapest spelled the end of my international career.

minutes, throwing my jacket and tie into the audience, before I was completely knackered. I was given a standing ovation as I walked off stage and the lights in the room gradually brightened.

To my horror, as I looked across to my left, I saw a group of six men who definitely weren't Hungarian-looking in appearance. No, they were in fact six Football Association council members who were travelling on the trip and who went under such intimidating titles as Squadron Leader Hadley and Lieutenant Colonel Mitchell OBE. I was mortified. This was the night before an Under-23 international against Hungary and although I was only a sub, that didn't matter a jot. None of the six showed a flicker of emotion as I beat a hasty retreat back to my hotel room. I didn't sleep a wink that night and wondered what would happen the following day. Strangely, absolutely nothing was said and I began to think I just might get away with it.

We played the game and then flew out for the third and final leg of the trip, a match against West Germany in Kassel. Still, nothing had been said about the escapade. We had a couple of free days in Kassel and Bill Nicholson suggested we take an afternoon off and go ten-pin bowling. Bill called over Under-23 captain Ron Harris, handed over a fistful of Deutsche Marks and told us all to have a good time. Bill had obviously thought we would enjoy a pleasant relaxing afternoon knocking over some skittles, but when we arrived at the Kassel bowling-alley the first thing that attracted our attention was not the skittles but the German bar. We immediately waded over and started ordering round after round of drinks proffering the money Bill had given us.

Leading the way was my Chelsea team-mate, Tommy Baldwin. Tommy had earned the nickname 'Sponge' from Dave Sexton for his ability to soak up punishment from defenders. The lads also called him 'Sponge', but this owed more to his ability to soak up copious amounts of alcohol. With only infrequent games of skittles interrupting our drinking, a very merry afternoon was had by all, the only slight hitch being we ran out of cash midway through the session.

This was easily overcome when the bar manager, recognising us as English footballers, announced that drinks could go on the tab. We had arrived at 2pm and by now it was 6pm. As we had a team meeting at 7pm we reluctantly called some taxis to take us back to the hotel. With a classic sense of mistiming, the Birch was the last person to get into the final cab. As a result, just as I was about to clamber aboard, the lads inside told the taxi driver to drive off. This went on for about half a mile down the road and I became increasingly frustrated at their schoolboy prank. Suddenly, I noticed the bar manager, in his Mercedes, pulling up behind. "Where are you staying?" he asked. "Give me a lift and I'll show you," I replied.

We drove swiftly back to the hotel without the guy saying another word. At our hotel - the Parkhotel Hessenland - we all stumbled out of our respective vehicles to be greeted by the sight of Bill Nicholson and Wilf McGuinness in Reception. "Had a nice time all of you?" he politely enquired. "Yes, we had a great time," said Chopper, desperately trying to sound coherent, which he found difficult at the best of times. Then, shouting at the top of his voice, the bar manager made a dramatic entrance. "I want more money! You owe me money!" he continued. Bill turned to Chopper and said: "Ron, you must have played a lot of games of ten pin bowling." But the game was well and truly up when the bar manager continued: "Your drinks bill is over 100 marks. Pay me now!" We all decided, to a man, to make a sharp exit and left a startled Bill to settle the tab!

Nicholson called us all together for a team meeting on the night before the game was due to take place. "I've never been in charge of a party quite like this before. It seems to me to be a cross between Billy Butlins and Billy Smarts Circus. Some talented players, but discipline lacking a bit," he barked.

I was next to Martin Chivers as we waited for Bill to read out the team. Eventually, he came to Number 9 and announced it would be Chivs. But he did add a pointed rider: "I just hope he plays a darn sight better than he has done for me so far." Martin, you see, had just been signed by Bill from Southampton for £125,000.

"And at Number 10, Alan Birchenall." I thought to myself that I must have done okay in the first game against Italy, but my joy was short-lived. In his next breath, Bill delivered the immortal line: "How Dave Sexton ever paid £100,000 for a cabaret artiste I will never know."

Bill had known all along about my partying but had not said a word for forty-eight hours. Still, I was in the team and determined to do well. Things couldn't have gone better - I scored the winner, steering in a low cross from fifteen yards. This was my only ever international goal and I was understandably delighted. Sadly, it was also to be my final appearance in an England shirt. How many players can say they scored for England yet never played for their country again?

Several years later, I found out that a report had been sent back to Sir Alf Ramsey at FA headquarters stating I was deemed unsuitable for the squad. In those days, discipline was extremely strict and you were expected to be very regimented in your approach. The report, filed to Sir Alf, suggested I was too interested in enjoying myself to be an England footballer and was a bit of a jack-the-lad. I felt I could combine the two; I could enjoy myself and still be good enough to play for my country, but the powers-that-be decided otherwise.

Over the years I've been asked many times if I regretted the way I acted on the tour. Sure, I was bitterly disappointed that I never figured in an England squad again. There were one or two brief mentions of a recall later in my career but nothing concrete materialised. But I genuinely have very few regrets. That tour was a tangible sign of the development of my character. My ability to be out-going and put people at ease was beginning to blossom and my teenage shyness was developing into a more confident personality and that is not something I would have swapped for the world. Who knows? Had I been a quiet goody two-shoes I may well have earned a few more Under-23 caps but even then I might never have been good enough to make the step up to the full England squad.

At least I displayed the real me while I was with England, and if the price I had to pay was not to be involved again then so be it. I certainly didn't think I was a bad lad, my only crime was that I liked a good time and I don't think I caused harm to anyone. On the contrary, most people seemed to enjoy what I got up to. Even to this day, I pride myself on an ability to put a smile on people's faces.

You're probably asking yourself where does 'number one in my order of importance', Bobby Charlton, fit into this overall picture? Well, now we have to fast forward a few years. I had moved to Leicester via Crystal Palace and was preparing to travel down from the Midlands to London for one of the footballing social events of the year - the Annual Football Writers' bash in the capital.

As this is a story my Leicester team-mate Lenny Glover tells far better than ever I could, I thought it appropriate to hand over this section to Lenny. Over to you, Lenny.

Thanks, Birch. Well, this was a night when all the top stars converged on one venue and had a great night out. As social secretary for the players at Filbert Street - and the fact he was the only mug who would drive - five of us decided to go down to London in Birch's car. There was Frank Worthington, Dennis Rofe, me, Birch and Steve Earle. Off we trogged down the MI, excitedly looking forward to the night out. On the way, a big flashy car whizzed by us and we noticed it was carrying Bobby Charlton and his entourage. We all waved to Bobby and he waved back. The only person in our car not to acknowledge Bobby was Birch. He muttered something under his breath as he gripped hold of the steering wheel.

We all booked into our hotel and got ready for the night ahead. As usual, all the lads had a few drinks and everyone was in good spirits. On the way out of the hotel, we saw Bobby holding court with some reporters on the steps. Birch suddenly got the arse, rushed up to him and clipped him smartly over the head! Unfortunately, Birch was a little the worse for wear and stumbled down the steps after his assault on the soccer legend. Bobby looked around and couldn't believe it. We all apologised to Bobby and rushed Birch into the nearest taxi. On the following morning, Birch was quite subdued as he drove us all home. We asked him why he had clipped Bobby but he wouldn't answer. After much persuasion, he finally blurted out the truth. "He cost me my England place. If it hadn't been for him I could have been a World Cup winner with Sir Alf!" We all cracked up in hysterics.

Thank you, Lenny. As always, your memory gets the better of you but let's just say I felt I did have some cause for concern over my actions. For the next twenty years, I never really said much to Bobby. I suppose I was deeply embarrassed that I had cuffed him on the steps outside an official bash. It's not really the done thing, is it?

However, I did meet up with Sir Bobby a couple of years ago for the official opening of the Carling Stand at Filbert Street. He was the perfect gentleman and never said a word although I still wonder whether he recalls that incident all those years ago. Perhaps now, a quarter of a century later, might be the appropriate time to issue a full and sincere apology to Sir Bobby. So, if by chance you have been bought a copy of this book and are reading this chapter right now: "Sorry Bobby, you know I was only kidding."

And that, really, brings down the curtain on my international career. All that remains are my memories, and the shirts and caps my mum has dutifully hung on to all these years. I've also kept all the instruction cards we received for our call-ups. Elsewhere, in this chapter you'll see them reproduced. Of course, my games for England are ones I shall always cherish but, in truth, they were largely like the rest of my career in that I don't remember too much about them. As always, the Birch can recall far more about the social scene that accompanied the England get-togethers.

Being in the England squad meant I rubbed shoulders with many talented players who went on to enjoy far more illustrious careers. I'm not sure, though, how many can say they performed a Rolling Stones number in front of 350 screaming Hungarians. Many moved into management, and myself and Joe Royle still share a joke or two about our time in Italy, Hungary and Germany. Joe always reminds me of one story in particular. Unfortunately, it's not printable but I maintain it never happened anyway!

In summing up, appearing for my country probably gave me some of the biggest thrills of my career. I've not really got any regrets about not making more appearances. My four international caps are ones I will always treasure and cherish and I am grateful I was given the opportunity to wear the three lions with tremendous pride, a small amount of ability and a broad smile. And, as I'm sure even Bill Nicholson might concede, I wasn't a bad cabaret artiste, either.

Christmas Greetings 1965

WORLD CUP WILLIE

■ **WORLD CUP WILLIE.** Here's the only correspondence I received from England boss Sir Alf Ramsey in the run up to the 1966 World Cup finals. Sir Alf kindly signed and sent me this Christmas card from the Football Association. Suppose the invite to join Sir Alf's 22 for the finals must have got lost in the post. Mind you, I knew I had blotted my copybook after my singing sessions in Budapest.

American Dream

Chapter 5

America, it is often said, is the land of opportunity, and seldom has a truer word been spoken. Ostensibly I went there as a professional footballer but ended up holding down a number of jobs, the more unlikely of these included acting as a pizza delivery boy in San Jose, and performing the duties of an Elvis Presley tour guide for English ex-pats around Presley's Gracelands home in Memphis.

Unfortunately, at the age of 32 my soccer career was already well and truly on the wane so I was hardly likely to set the world alight with my talents. However, during two consecutive summers with San Jose Earthquakes and Memphis Rogues, my eyes were opened to the marketing and commercial approaches Americans give to their professional sports. These practices were to stand me in excellent stead throughout my business career and my role as Public Relations Officer with my beloved Leicester City. Even to this day it is worth pointing out that many of America's marketing ideas are only now being transferred across the pond into our own British sports such as football, rugby and cricket.

My entire American NASL career spanned less than fifty games with the Earthquakes and the Rogues but, as usual, there's a treasure-trove of stories to tell. Although the football was far from top-class, I lined up against world greats such as Pele, Beckenbauer and Eusebio (well, I was on the same astro-turf). Off the pitch, I had such diverse experiences as almost being 'topped' by a gang of Hells Angels, employing a gun-toting nanny for my children and having to escort a spaced-out *tank commander* home after she ate a cannabis biscuit mistakenly thinking it was a chocolate chip cookie!

My American dream started back home, in the office of Leicester manager Jimmy Bloomfield in the spring of 1977. Relations between the pair of us were rather strained as a result of my knee injury and both knew it was only a matter of time before I was shipped out to pastures new. I had missed much of the season because of the knee but was slowly coming back to some form of fitness.

Jimmy called me into his office one day. "I've had a number of approaches from American soccer franchises enquiring about the availability of my players and I thought of you because you have not played many games," he told me. It took me aback because, although I was only 31, I hadn't thought of America at all. Gradually I started to warm to the idea because popularity and hype surrounding the NASL was at its height. Virtually all the great veterans were plying their trade in the States led, of course, by Franz Beckenbauer and Brazilian legend Pele.

Four clubs had shown an interest in me - Vancouver Whitecaps, Chicago Sting, Detroit Express and San Jose. Unfortunately, no enquiries came from the Cosmos in New York so my dreams of playing with Beckenbauer and Pele remained unfulfilled. However, one club stood out from all the others. It was nothing to do with their respective footballing abilities but more a case of geographical location.

PELE: The legendary Brazilian star was with New York Cosmos. I couldn't get near him.

I got out my North American A - Z map book and soon spotted San Jose in sunny California, less than an hour's drive from San Francisco - a wonderful city I had visited earlier in my career. By this stage of the book, I think you've got the idea that the Birch loves the sunshine lifestyle. California, sun, Baywatch babes - forget football, this had to be the life for Birch.

I communicated my preference to Jim and, within twenty-four hours, received an offer from San Jose for my services - a six-month contract at £250 a week, plus company car, plus apartment. After brief discussions with the *tank commander* and the *dwarfs*, we made up our minds and I was on the next plane out to San Francisco.

Following a twelve-hour flight, I was met at the airport by San Jose's general manager Tom Mertons. "Welcome to America, Alan," he said in typical Yankee drawl. Marching through the arrivals lounge, he pointed to the parking lot and threw me a bunch of keys. "They're for your new car," he said. "No time like the present, you might as well get used to your wheels." He jabbed a finger in the direction of a huge red Cadillac. My eyes popped out of my head. It appeared only slightly smaller than 'Titanic'.

Up until this point in my life, I had driven a range of English sports and family cars - a Triumph Spitfire, a sponsored Fiat and, biggest of them all, a Jaguar. Even the Jag seemed a bubble car compared to this monster. I was still a little jet-lagged from the flight and the last thing I wanted to do was drive a car the size of an articulated lorry along American roads I was unaccustomed to.

However, as the new English import for the club, I countered my tiredness against the need to look ultra-cool and show no fear. "You have been used to driving an automatic, Alan?" queried

FRANZ BECKENBAUER: The Kaiser was the proud possessor of the largest mobile telephone I have ever seen.

Tom. "There's nothing to it, just put one foot on the brake and the other on the accelerator." But there was also power steering to contend with. Although the Cadillac was the size of a tank, you could spin it around with one finger. Sitting behind the steering wheel, the bonnet appeared to jut out for two miles in front of me. Not to put too fine a point on it, I was scared shitless.

"Let's go, Alan," said Tom. Remember the old dear from the BBC television series Driving School? I made her look like Stirling Moss. Turning out of San Francisco airport, I committed the first major driving error - I was still on the left-hand side of the road and only narrowly avoided a head-on collision. I often wonder to myself why there are not more multiple auto accidents in Florida when thousands of us Brits get into hired cars at Orlando airport and head off to Disney World.

"Perhaps we ought to try the right-hand lane," said Tom, trying not to sound overly concerned. We lurched our way onto a six-lane freeway. The Birch didn't have a clue what was going on let alone find the right lane for San Jose. Tom was busy talking football while I was busy trying not to write-off the Cadillac. "Slow down a bit, Alan, the speed limit over here is only 55mph," he told me, after I'd nudged 90mph through sheer nervousness.

I was weaving in and out of the lanes when I glanced to my right and saw a Hells Angel motorcyclist right alongside me. I looked to the left, only to find myself flanked by another. I wasn't too concerned until I heard Tom declare: "Goddam it! Whatever you do, just keep going at 55mph and stare straight ahead. You appear to have upset our brothers."

I looked in the rear view mirror and saw a gang of twenty leather-clad Angels in the slipstream. Here I was, in San Francisco a mere half an hour, and already being chased by a gang of mean-looking bikers. Apparently, I had been weaving in and out of the lanes and had inadvertently cut up one of their clan. They followed me for about five miles and I became increasingly concerned.

Tom barked at me. "Don't do anything! These kinda guys do NOT mess around. We're in big trouble here." I wanted to wind the window down and offer my apologies to the chap cruising alongside, but Tom almost had a heart-attack. "Leave the goddam window alone!" he bawled, but by this time, I had had enough. "Bollocks to this," I thought. "If I am going to get turned over on my first day in America I might as well do it my way." So, despite Tom's protestations, I wound the window down and shouted to this evil-looking biker. "Whatever I've done, I'm sorry. I'm English."

It's similar to the maxim followed by Basil Fawlty when he excuses his Spanish waiter Manuel's many failings by pointing out that he hails from Barcelona. A little puzzled, the guy dropped back into the pack trailing behind me. "Jesus Christ, we're in for it now," moaned Tom. All of a sudden, I heard a massive roar as twenty powerful Harley Davisons revved up in unison and roared off into the distance. Tom was sweating cobs. He heaved a huge sigh of relief and explained: "Alan, you don't realise how close we both came just there. It could have got very nasty indeed." Only later did I come to understand the power of Hells Angels in America and fully appreciate the enormity of the situation.

Having spent twelve hours on a transatlantic flight only to barely survive a brush with death by a gang of Hells Angels in a 90-minute nightmare drive, the last thing I wanted was to play a game of football. Desperately yearning to retire to a soft, comfortable bed I had little choice but to pull on my boots and play a special practice game which had been organised for me.

At the time I believed I was in America for a guaranteed six months. Not exactly true. In the small print were disclaimers which meant the Americans could get rid of you in a matter of days if they didn't like your looks. Effectively, I had been signed on the strength of a few videos they had seen but now they wanted to take a look at me in the flesh, and if I didn't come up to scratch I would be on the next plane back to London. Fortunately, without realising the importance of the game, I did reasonably well.

My performance was capped by a spectacular 40-yard chip over the head of the opposition's goalkeeper. It was enough to convince them I was here to stay. San Jose's owner, Milan Mandaric, was a particularly tough task-master and, over the next few months, I was to see dozens of imports jet in from all around the world only to be flown home a few days later. Mr Mandaric is now in England where he has bought a controlling interest in Portsmouth, and already a couple of managerial heads have rolled at Fratton Park.

After the game I was shown to my temporary home, where I would live until the family flew out to join me. I was sharing a condominium with three Yugoslav team-mates. Now, I've got nothing against the Slavs but they don't party like us Brits. They were playing cards but I wanted to sample an American bar or two and, if truth be told, pose in my new Cadillac. I was like a kid in a sweet shop.

The guys told me about a nearby bar and I hopped into the car. Roaring out of the underground garage, in a scene reminiscent of 'Starsky and Hutch', I blazed down the freeway. What should have been a five-minute journey lasted an hour and a half but I didn't care, I loved the new wheels and felt I was a star - even if half the American population also had red Cadillacs.

I eventually found the bar which was called the 'Frog and Toad', a Pizza Hut-type of place and dimly lit. Over came the barman and I ordered my drink. "Australian?" he queried. "No, English." Striking up a conversation with him, I casually imparted the information that I had just signed for the Earthquakes. With that he rushed to the telephone behind the bar and started ringing his mates. "Guess who I've got in here right now? It's Alan Bircumballs the new signing for the Earthquakes."

Unwittingly the barman had started what was to become two amusing traits for the Birch while he was over in the States. Firstly, I had never realised it was possible to manage so many mispronunciations of my surname and, secondly, because of the blond barnet everyone thought I hailed from Down Under.

Even by American standards, San Jose were one of the poorer teams. We were a new professional franchise, one of the first pro clubs the city had ever been awarded. San Jose itself was a sprawling region of around half a million inhabitants, almost a suburb of San Francisco.

After a couple of weeks spent settling in, wife Heather, daughter Laura and son Dean flew out to join me. We moved into a lovely bungalow in a delightful area called Los Gatos. In the morning when you woke you could stick your arm out of the window and pluck an orange from the groves outside. What a life! So good in fact that the earth would shake under your feet! Well, actually, it did and that was the only drawback.

Located directly on the line of the San Andreas Fault, there was to be many a murmur while I was there. What the locals considered a gentle rumble, I interpreted as a full-blown earthquake. During the first week of my stay, and in the middle of the night, I suddenly felt the building quiver and shake. I was absolutely petrified. Everyone told me not to worry but that was easier said than done. In the six months of my stay, the biggest 'quake we experienced measured 3.5 on the Richter Scale - more than enough for me.

The Earthquakes' manager was a Yugoslav called Gaby Gabrowicz. Aside from the English, the most popular imports were Serbs and Croats, and our most famous player was Tony Simoes, a World Cup team mate of Portuguese superstar Eusebio. Tony had played for Benfica and was a member of the Portugal side beaten in the semi-finals of the 1966 World Cup. He was a charming guy and my abiding memory of him is the way he always smoked his cigarettes through a long, elegant holder.

My fellow ex-pats included former Wolves defender Laurie Calloway, centre half John Rowland who had played in the English lower leagues, and striker John Childs who was always banging in the goals for us. We also had several Americans in the squad. Their commitment and passion for the game could not be faulted. They would have run through brick walls. However, this overabundance of enthusiasm was not matched by equal amounts of natural footballing ability.

I always found it surprising the way their pre-game routines differed totally to those of the Europeans. While we Brits were cool, calm and collected, reading our matchday programmes, and the Yugoslavs indulged in their never-ending card games, the Americans would race about and head-butt the walls. They'd rush up, give you a bear-hug and shout in your ear at the top of their voices: "Let's kick ass!" I got tired out just watching them carry out these barmy routines in the dressing rooms.

Mind you, the Birch is not in an ideal position to talk about pre-game preparations after the fiasco of my debut in the San Jose stadium. Inside was a capacity crowd of 18,000 and a real carnival atmosphere, as there always was for any soccer game in the States. Half an hour before the game, I was ensconced in my usual position in the dressing room - on the khazi. I always liked to read the match programme in peace and, secondly, it kept me out of the way of those crazy Yanks running up and down head-butting the walls. I could hear their histrionics and, above the din, the announcer reading out the teams. I heard him declare: "Number 16, a veteran of fourteen years from England, Alan Birchenheimer." Damn, the silly sod had gone and got my name wrong again.

A few moments later, our trainer, Obie Oberower, rushed into the dressing room and called out to me. I reluctantly unhooked the toilet door catch, and peered around the door. "Alan, Alan, everyone is waiting for you," he shouted. "Kick-off's not for 20 minutes," I replied. "But you have to go out for the national anthems." "Oh shit," came my retort. In one swift motion, I'd wiped my arris, pulled up my shorts and dashed off into the arena.

As I ran onto the pitch, through a crowd of cheerleaders, there was a mixture of cheers for the new debutant but quite a few laughs as well. As I took my place in the side for the anthem, one of my team-mates pointed to my shorts and indicated a ten-yard trail of toilet paper sticking out of my arse. Who needs Andrex puppies when you've got the Birch? To turn it into a joke, I started waving the tissue and the crowd went wild.

That sort of spectacular entrance was nothing new. In fact, it was one of the more mundane. What about the time there was a circus in town and the eagle-eyed marketing boys - always quick to spot an opportunity - borrowed four elephants and had the team conveyed onto the pitch resplendently seated on these gigantic mammals? On other occasions we were paraded on Harley Davisons, in Lamborghinis and in jeeps. The match ball was often dropped in by sky divers or helicopter. Everything was razzamatazz, and so American.

However, even the San Jose marketeers had to take their hats off to probably the ultimate entrance dreamed up by their counterparts at Fort Lauderdale Strikers. The Florida franchise had not been enjoying the best of fortunes. They had lost their first four matches which put them about on a par with Lee Harvey Oswald in the popularity stakes.

We arrived in the afternoon to be greeted by a front page headline in the local evening paper "Is Newman Dead and Buried?" The Newman in question was John Newman, English manager of the Strikers. We thought little more about it but then, while we were warming up for the game, we noticed the Strikers were not making their usual noisy entrance.

Upbeat pop music was replaced with the sombre strains of a funeral march. Out came four players dressed as pall-bearers, carrying a brass-handled wooden coffin. Solemnly, they marched into the centre circle whereupon the lid was thrown open. Was Count Dracula about to make a rare daylight appearance? No, out of the coffin popped John Newman holding a microphone. "I'm not dead yet!" he roared, "Let's go out and WIN!" The crowd erupted, and I fell about laughing.

Unfortunately, it was the Strikers and John Newman who had the last laugh. They ended their four-game losing streak at our expense. I mean, could you see Bill Shankly or Don Revie going out in front of the Kop or Elland Road and carrying out that improbable stunt? This, though, was all part of the American psyche.

At the time it seemed incredibly outlandish. Even the unusual names of the clubs gave me a chuckle - Earthquakes, Lightning, Cosmos, Whitecaps, Quicksilvers. It was like something from a different planet. Yet take a look at the most conservative of our English sports, cricket. In the past couple of seasons they've caught the American habit. There are the Warwickshire Bears, the Sussex Sharks and the Notts Outlaws. WG Grace must be turning in his grave. Rugby League has taken a similar route - London Broncos, Hull Sharks, Wigan Warriors, the list is endless.

Squad numbers in the Premiership and Nationwide League have only recently been introduced by soccer's ruling bodies, but as soon as I arrived in the States in 1977 I was given a squad number of 16 and my name was plastered across the back of my shirt. Come to think of it, that was the only time they managed to spell it correctly! All these initiatives have been copied from the U.S. and aggressive promotion has also been imitated in recent years.

On only my third day in America the club's Public Relations Officer shook me rudely from my bed at 5am and whisked me off for a breakfast television interview in Los Angeles. It was a total embarrassment as the interviewer knew nothing about football. "Who's that with the flags?" was one of his first questions. "They're the linesmen," I replied. "What do they do?" he asked.

"Tell me, to score a goal do you have to get the ball over the crossbar?" was another choice offering. Came my caustic reply as I began to lose patience with the buffoon: "No, under the bar, that's why there is a net." What a shambles, but this was all part of the San Jose philosophy of generating interest in soccer.

To a certain extent, it was always a losing battle given the popularity of the mainstream sports of American Football, basketball, baseball and ice hockey. This, though, was a philosophy with which I was completely at ease. I was told that most English players who came over to America found it immensely difficult to co-operate with the numerous media and promotional requests from the club. I loved it. I would frequently be out and about in shopping malls, at barbecues and conducting innumerable radio and television interviews. I took to it all like a duck to water and was really in my element. My footballing skills may have been borderline but I was a dab hand with the microphone.

The lessons learned from this exposure helped me considerably when I returned to England and my role as Public Relations Officer at Leicester City. I'm not saying we should translate everything they do in America over to here, but there are many lessons to learn and, twenty years later, it would appear we are doing exactly that.

As well as a completely different marketing and public relations culture, the social side was also diverse. Tailgate parties were all the rage. After each game, the fans would return to their cars in the huge parking lots and start up a barbecue which would continue for several hours. Indeed, I attribute much of my popularity with the Earthquakes fans to my ability to lead the singing in the after-match parties. The fans loved it.

The players also had their own little bar in a corner of the stadium. We'd all have a little drink after the game, although the *tank commander* was never completely at ease. American women, you see, were rather more pushy than their English counterparts. We were standing at the bar after one game when two cheerleaders - still wearing their ra-ra skirts - came up to me, grabbed hold of my 'arris and planted a kiss on either cheek (of my face, unfortunately!). "Gee, what a great game, Alan. You were absolutely fantastic." It didn't matter if I had played my worst-ever game of football, they hadn't a clue. Needless to say, I was hastily escorted off the premises by the tank commander in double-quick time.

Not that every woman in San Jose and California was the glamorous Baywatch babe you might expect. As a family, on a day out we would drive to the nearby Santa Cruz California beach resort and there we would lounge on the boardwalk, watching the world go by. Don't get me wrong, there were some fantastic babes but there was also a large percentage of beached whales who had obviously been overdosing on McDonald's and Kentucky Fried Chicken. Irrespective of their looks the *tank commander* never quite got to grips with their forthright ways.

So far, I've done pretty well in this chapter, haven't I? Half-way through, and I've not mentioned a single football match! Well, it's time to redress the balance. Heard the one about the Birch and Eusebio? No? then please read on.

The Portuguese legend played for the quaintly-named Las Vegas Quicksilvers. The Quicksilvers versus the Earthquakes - sounds like a wrestling tag match out of the WWF rather than a game in the North American soccer league! Midway through the match I embarked on a run down the left wing only to be brought down in full flight by Eusebio. I fell quite heavily and, as the incident was quite close to the fans, tempers became a little frayed. While I was getting treatment, a hail of cans and bottles were thrown onto the pitch in Eusebio's general direction.

■ **LIKE FATHER, LIKE SON:** Son Dean is held up by my right arm, while my left grasps a bottle of beer and a ciggie. For what more in life can a man ask? This was a scene to be repeated after many a game in the parking lot of the San Jose Earthquakes stadium. After matches, everyone would retire to the car park where fans and players would put on a series of barbecues, a band would play and we would party until nightfall. The Birch was often a central figure in the entertainment department and would line up on stage with the band. Quite a change from after-match activities in England. I mean, could you imagine throwing a barbecue on the streets outside Old Trafford?!

I was quite a crowd favourite, due as much to my ability to sing melodiously with the band in the raucous tailgate parties as to my pacy footballing talents. Tony Simoes, a Portuguese team-mate of Eusebio's, came over and asked me to try and calm down the crowd. I picked up one of the cans, pretended to have a large swig and then swayed gingerly to my feet, acting as if I was tipsy and ready to fall. The crowd thought it was fantastic, hostilities subsided, and myself and Eusebio made it up with a hug and a kiss.

To me, this was one of those early occasions where I used a spot of casual humour to diffuse a potentially serious situation. It's something I like to think I have gone on to do throughout my career with a modicum of success. Not everyone in the 18,000 sell-out crowd, however, was pleased. Owner Milan Mandaric failed to see the funny side, so much so that he fined me two week's wages and banned me for the next two matches. "Godammit, Birchenall, we brought you here to play football, not to be an entertainer. We're not running a circus, you know," he ranted.

This was to prove the start of an irrevocable breakdown in our relationship which resulted in me becoming the team's pizza boy. Funny, but he always struggled to share my sense of humour. On another occasion, after being fouled, I stuffed the ball up my jersey and gaily raced to the other end of the pitch. The fans loved it, but not Mr Mandaric. That one cost me a week's wages although I did escape a club suspension.

On days before a long road trip - when we would play two or three consecutive away fixtures on the opposite coastline of America - all the players would meet at the chairman's luxury Californian mansion. We'd play a few games of head tennis and generally chill out. It was traditional to order pizzas, and muggins would always be entrusted with the job of collecting twenty-five of them. "Go and get the pizzas, Birchenall," the chairman would bark. There I was in my red Cadillac, reduced to the role of collecting box-loads of pizzas, garlic bread and coke.

I contented myself, however, with the knowledge I was one of the few imports to last the full duration of their contract. Mr Mandaric was not noted for his tolerance of foreign stars so I must have impressed him with my footballing skills or, more likely, I made him laugh now and again. I afforded myself a wry smile when I saw he had taken control of Portsmouth football club. I will genuinely look forward to meeting up with him again ... and asking him to fetch me a Pizza Margherita from Dominoes.

Unquestionably one of the highlights of my time in America was lining up on the same pitch as the great soccer legends Franz Beckenbauer and Pele. They both played for the New York Cosmos - the Manchester United of the NASL. The club had conscientiously assembled a collection of the biggest names ever to grace a football pitch.

My first visit with the Earthquakes to Meadowlands Stadium in New York was a breath-taking experience. A capacity crowd of 60,000 was in attendance and the teams were on the pitch warming-up. The announcer spoke over the PA system to unveil the Cosmos team. It was a Who's Who of world soccer - the very best names from Brazil, Germany, Italy, Holland and Argentina. Each player was such a big name in their own right it took the announcer twenty minutes to go through the team and catalogue their glittering array of trophies. They left Pele until last and when he came out the crowd went wild.

For the next 90 minutes I never got near Pele or Beckenbauer. Beckenbauer was a Rolls-Royce of a player and glided around the pitch as gracefully as a galleon. Pele was awesome; although he was in the twilight of his career this was equivalent to the start of any other mere mortal's career path. His ability to jump from a standing start was fantastic. I went up for a header with him and he finished two foot above me. I even tried to boot both of them to say I'd made my mark but I was left kicking thin air. Needless to say, we lost the match 3-0.

They say you are never too old to learn and, at the age of 31 and two weeks into my American career, I certainly learned a lesson from my first away game in Earthquakes colours. At San Jose we played on grass, but many of the NASL clubs performed on artificial surfaces. Seattle Sounders played at the impressive King Dome where the pitch was plastic.

In the locker room before the game, I noticed most of our players smearing themselves with tubs of vaseline. They slapped it on their knees, thighs, calves, arms, elbows, bollocks and just about everywhere. My pre-match routine was to put a couple of dabs of petroleum jelly over my eyebrows to stop sweat from running into my eyes, and after a fourteen-year career in the English game I saw no need to change now.

In the first couple of minutes I was up against the Sounders' former Spurs and Scotland winger Jimmy Robertson. He raced down the line and I charged after him. Determined not to let him outrun me, I performed the perfect sliding tackle for ten yards across the plastic. My professional satisfaction quickly subsided in favour of some of the most excruciating pain I have ever known.

I was in absolute agony and screamed like a banshee as the plastic stripped away layers of skin all the way from my hip down to the side of my knee. My outer skin gave way to a raw red patch dotted with thousands of little pieces of green plastic. In fact, during all my time in the States the scars never healed up properly. The lads had already told me not to tackle but I just carried on regardless. You stood up and shepherded opponents into channels. Suffice to say, I learned quickly. It was the one and only sliding tackle I made on astro-turf during my two summers in America.

Every away game in America was an event in itself. I loved visiing the big cities but there was one game on the NASL calendar which stood out above all others - the trip to play Team Hawaii. Suffice to say, there weren't too many injured players who ruled themselves out for this little jaunt. We flew out to the holiday isle four days before the game - purely for acclimatisation purposes and also to give the lads an opportunity to recover from the arduous four-hour flight! Nothing whatsoever, of course, related to the fantastic Hawaiian nightlife.

The late, great, England World Cup captain Bobby Moore was the mainstay of the Hawaiian team, with several other ex-West Ham players such as Tommy Taylor and Harry Redknapp in the squad. It was baking hot and, standing at one end of the pitch, the heat haze made the other set of goalposts wobble around in a blur. We partied for most of the time we were there and, speaking with Bobby, we were keen to get the game out of the way and get down to Waikiki Beach and enjoy a great night out. We flung in quite a lot of early crosses which the Hawaii 'keeper struggled to deal with. He missed the first by a mile, didn't move for the second and, in attempting to punch a third clear, only succeeded in knocking out his team-mate. I looked across to Bobby who explained: "Nothing unusual there. He's been on the waccy-baccy for the past three days. He doesn't know what day of the week it is." Neither did we, we couldn't even get one goal past him.

One of the few drawbacks to Californian life was the drug culture which permeated the social scene. Within a week of my arrival I was unwittingly exposed to drugs. One of my English team-mates, Laurie Calloway, organised a special party to celebrate my arrival and over two hundred people turned up. The party was really swinging and, after a few sherbets, the Birch was in need of a sprinkle. I made my way to the toilets but noticed a three-deep queue.

As I was unable to contain myself any longer, one of the guests offered me the use of her toilet in the house across the street. I made my way there but, while in the bathroom, I heard giggles and strange noises emanating from a nearby bedroom. Anxious to check the house wasn't being burgled I stuck my head around the door and was greeted by the sight of a dozen naked women on the bed, obviously spaced out of their minds. I went back to tell the house-owner that a group of people were high on cannabis but she treated the information as if they were enjoying a glass of orange juice.

On another occasion, I popped into one of my neighbour's garden where I noticed he had a king-sized padlock on the greenhouse. "Crikey," I thought, "he must have some prize-winning cucumbers and tomatoes stashed away in there". He offered to show me inside. It was about 100 degrees and all I could make out were some big green leafy plants, not a garden vegetable in sight. "Great weed, man," he told me. They were his prize-winning cannabis plants.

Even when we put our daughter on the school bus, we could see older students on the back seats lighting up their cannabis spliffs. Ultimately, this was to prove one of our reasons in deciding to return to England. I had received several offers to stay on in America - the way of life suited me and I fitted in better than most other English sportsmen. There were also opportunities to go into sports footwear and manufacturing but we decided to return to the old country.

After a season with Notts County in the First Division, I fancied another summer in the U.S. where plenty of people wanted me back in San Jose - the players, the fans, the band in the tailgate parties but not, I'm afraid, Mr Mandaric. San Jose wasn't big enough for both of us.

My former Chelsea team-mate Eddie McCreadie, though, had been appointed manager of a new NASL franchise club, the Memphis Rogues. Eddie had succeeded the charismatic Malcolm Allison. Malcolm, never noted for his frugality, had lasted only a few weeks. In that time, however, he had spent the entire annual budget on an assortment of players from all four corners of the world's nightclubs. Consequently, the Rogues had to cut their cloth accordingly and I was next choice on their slimmed-down list.

San Jose and Memphis were like chalk and cheese. Probably, like most other people in the world, I knew of Memphis for only one reason; it was home to the late, great Elvis Presley. I had been in San Jose when Elvis died. Like all famous historical moments you always seem to remember exactly where you are when you hear the earth-shattering news. I was in a supermarket in San Jose when the radio report of Elvis' death was broadcast and a cashier burst into tears. The death of Elvis in America was comparable to that of Princess Diana in Britain.

My only link with Elvis was Frank Worthington. I christened Frank 'Elvis' because of his love for the rock legend and to this day, Frank still answers to the nickname. However, it is my personal view that it is actually Frank who is buried in Gracelands, while Elvis is still alive and kicking, masquerading as Frank on the English sporting after-dinner circuit!

Our arrival in Memphis was a memorable one... for all the wrong reasons. A terrible cyclone had whipped up and torrential rain was lashing down. Streets were

■ **GOING FOR GOAL**. In truth my goalscoring record in the North American Soccer League was not exactly earth-shattering, for the Earthquakes or the Rogues. In a total of less than 50 games, I managed a measly four. I'm afraid this was not one of them. Still, admire the posture and the style as 'The Claw' cracks one inches wide in action for the Rogues.

turned into rivers and, as we pulled into our condominium, I noticed a dark shape on our driveway. I froze. There, curled into a tight ball, was a three-foot long snake. Thankfully it was dead but that didn't stop the reptile from frightening the shit out of me.

The Rogues were predominantly an English team. As well as myself, Eddie brought over Bobby Thompson from Wolves and Phil Holder from Spurs. Neil Smillie arrived from Brighton, my old Chelsea team-mate Charlie Cooke had a short spell with us and ex Everton man Jimmy Husband and Luton's Max Faulkner were a few others I can remember. Although the stadium capacity in Memphis was 40,000, we struggled to average crowds of more than 8,000. Football certainly wasn't as popular in Memphis as it was in San Jose.

If my part-time job in San Jose as a pizza deliverer was a shade unusual, then my out-of-hours duties in Memphis were truly sensational. I became a tour guide in Gracelands for all the English soccer players who flew in with opposing clubs to play the Rogues. Whenever a club arrived, they were bound to have an English player and they were equally bound to want to be shown around the home of Elvis. Dennis Tueart (New York Cosmos), Jon Sammels (Vancouver Whitecaps), Rod Marsh and Lenny Glover (Tampa Bay) and Trevor Francis were just a few who booked Gracelands tours with the Birch. The clubs would invariably stay at the Hyatt Hotel, less than a mile and a half from Presley's house.

You would imagine the home of music's greatest legend to be a luxurious and desirable residence in a salubrious neighbourhood. Not exactly. Gracelands was situated on its own on Elvis Presley Boulevard and, even though the great man had only died twelve months earlier, there was already a cluster of tacky little huts selling Elvis merchandise outside the gates. There was always a queue of 200 yards and, for

■ **A FLOWER FOR AN ENGLISH ROSE.** Well, not exactly, but the Birch is taking delivery of a rose from his own personal supporters' club in Memphis. A group of waiters and friends from the local restaurant I frequented banded together and formed 'Birch's Bowery'. They sat in the same section of the ground for every Rogues game and, in this picture, I'm being presented with a red rose from one of the 'Bowery' founder members. If you're wondering what bowery means, it's American for 'gang'.

the first few times, I had to wait to get in before circumstances changed, courtesy of a chance meeting in a Memphis restaurant with one of Elvis' bodyguards.

I got talking to the guard who said he recognised me as one of the Rogues players. The bodyguards enjoyed their football and came to our matches. I explained that if they ever wanted tickets they were to give me a call. "Thanks a lot," he replied, "and the next time you come to Gracelands just ring this phone number." I was made up.

The next time I had a group of players to escort I called the number and was told to come straight to the main entrance. Up we sailed in my car, past the long queue, and were beckoned in through the gates before being shown around the grave and given a tour of the estate. This continued for several weeks. I had become quite friendly with the bodyguards over the summer and was nearing the end of my contract. "Elvis' dad is going away soon. We'd like to give you a farewell present. Come round next Wednesday before you fly out, but come on your own." So, I drove in through the gates as usual to be greeted by the bodyguards.

Now, at this time, the house was off-limits but my 'present' was a behind-the-scenes tour of the house, quite an honour as I was one of the first-ever outsiders to be shown the interior of Gracelands. I was taken through all the rooms and it was quite a humbling experience. The only places I was not allowed were his bedroom, and the bathroom where he had spent his last few hours. There were padlocks on both doors and I was told the rooms had lain undisturbed in accordance with his father's wishes.

After my special tour I made straight for the tacky memorabilia huts. I was under orders from Frank Worthington to bring back loads of Elvis merchandise. I obliged by buying up a skipload of the tackiest photos, T-shirts, sweatshirts, belts, hats, glasses and jump-suits I could lay my hands on. The whole lot only came to ten dollars but Frank was in heaven.

Memphis itself was more backward than San Jose. There was a big north and south divide. Being in the heart of the south, these cultural divisions were more widely emphasised in Memphis. On our squad we had a few American players who hailed from Detroit. When we went into restaurants I noticed they always had to wait longer to be served their food. We could come in an hour later and still finish first. They would be served eventually but there was definitely an atmosphere between them. "Hell, they're from the North. They can wait. We have to do the same when we go up there," explained a waiter to me one time.

Everyone in Memphis was so quaint. They were god-fearing folk who spoke politely in typical American Deep South drawl. "My, we just love your English accent," I was told often. Our babysitter was a case in point. Mary-Lou was about 30 years old and lived just over the road from our condominium. One Sunday morning, I was by the pool watching the world go by when I saw a procession of five different men pull up in cars and pick up Mary Lou's younger sisters and brothers one by one. I was intrigued and asked for an explanation. "Oh, that's easy. They're all our pappas. My mum was married to five different men and they all come around and pick up the children every Sunday," she explained in a quiet matter-of-fact voice.

On another occasion, Mary Lou came around and asked if it would be alright if she took Laura and Dean to the cinema for the afternoon. We were only too pleased and settled ourselves down for an hour or so of peace and quiet. This was shattered less than thirty minutes later when a visibly distressed Mary Lou returned with our children. "I'm so sorry Mr Birchenall," she blubbed. "There was so much profanity in that film we had to come home early. I'm so, so sorry to have exposed your children to it. Please forgive me." We assured her no lasting damage had been done, sent her home to calm down and asked the kids what had happened. Came the reply from Laura and Dean. "It was a Walt Disney film and one of the characters said goddammit!"

Despite her demure appearance and love of God, however, Mary Lou could certainly pack a punch. One day I noticed she appeared to be carrying a gun in her handbag. Hardly believing my eyes, I asked if she possessed a firearm. "I most certainly do, Mr Birchenall," she said with more than a hint of pride. "And what's more I ain't afraid to use it. If some slimeball comes near me then I'll smoke him!" The statement seemed so incongruous to the rest of her gentle persona but in America, even twenty-five years ago, there were few who didn't carry weapons. So, there you have it. Our baby-sitter was a gun-toting female who was distraught at the Lord's name being taken in vain in a Walt Disney film!

As usual, I can't remember too much about the football but one of my special memories was the visit of New York Cosmos, and Franz Beckenbauer, to Memphis. Franz, however, could not have been too impressed by what he saw. He didn't bother to ask for a tour of Gracelands and the first I saw of him was in the players' tunnel an hour before the game. It was a steamy red-hot night, as usual, in Memphis. Franz came out, took a look at the pitch then walked off again. In his hand was one of the world's earliest mobile telephones. Not the compact nifty little number of nowadays, this was a machine the size of a suitcase with a three foot aerial sticking out of the top. I've seen more portable 26 inch television sets! As he made his way down the tunnel I overheard Franz say: "I can get a flight out of here in an hour. See you soon." He obviously didn't fancy the game and flew home early, but the Cosmos still beat us 2-0.

All in all, I had more than my fair share of problems with my NASL debuts. After the toilet-roll episode at San Jose, I suffered the ignominy of the only sending-off of my career in my first game for the Rogues. We were playing Fort Lauderdale Strikers in Florida and I was becoming increasingly frustrated by the antics of one of their players, Colin Fowles. Fowl by name and foul by nature. I decided to call him 'carpets' because he spent as much time on the floor. If I tackled him, he made a meal of it, so I dived to the ground to show to the referee he was being conned. The official, however, did not see the funny side of the incident and gave me a red card. In America they did not say you had been sent off, they said you were ejected.

■ **ON THE BALL.** In America, players were expected to take part in a great many community and marketing relations programmes. Here, I'm coaching at a local soccer school in Memphis. Although there was a wealth of talent at school and college level in the States, the standard and infrastructure of the professional game was not sufficiently high, or developed, for youngsters to fully realise their potential.

However, I must confess I still refuse to count this incident as a valid sending-off. Think of the worst referee in England (now there's a difficult one) and I guarantee you he is ten times better at his job than his counterpart in the States. Their officials truly were the lowest of the low.

I mentioned the drug scene in San Jose but only once did a member of the Birchenall family fall foul of this. Unbelievably, it was my wife Heather who unwittingly got spaced-out on stuff supplied by one of my Rogues team-mates in Memphis. We were in a bar one evening with Lewis, an American who wore a small leather pouch around his neck. Every so often, he would open the pouch and eat a little of what he called his 'special biscuit'. We had been having a few drinks and Lewis and I both decided to visit the gents. I have to admit I felt somewhat inadequate standing alongside him in the urinals, his manhood could be compared to a baby's arm holding an apple.

Out came the pouch, and he had a nibble of the contents. "Hey, Alan, your wife was asking me what I got in my pouch earlier," he said. "She said she wanted to try it so I gave her a cookie. She was only supposed to have a little nibble but she's gone and eaten the whole biscuit, man," he explained. Mortified, I rushed back into the room where the *tank commander* was completely spaced out. I bundled her into a hastily-summoned taxi, got her home and laid her out on the bed. She was floating on the ceiling, and suffered a king-sized headache the following day.

Before we left America we drove to Disneyland with the children, and went to California where we dined in Clint Eastwood's Hog's Head restaurant. My time in America, always exciting, exposed me to a different sporting culture and enabled me to learn a great deal.

There has been criticism concerning the lack of a credible top soccer tier in America for many years now but what should not be forgotten is the number of young Americans who play the sport. Even in my day there it was one of the more popular participation sports for under 18's. Lots of boys and girls played but once they reached 18 there was no further progression. If this were overcome, I am sure they would enjoy a successful future. America are the newly-crowned women's world champions so clearly some progress has been made.

At Leicester, we enjoyed the services of Kasey Keller, the American international number one goalkeeper, for three successful seasons and there are some top-class American soccer players now playing abroad in Europe. I have a feeling they will continue to develop and become quite a strong force in the world of football one day.

Aside from football, I also soaked up a good many ideas on the commercial side. On my return from Memphis I was shortly to take up a part-time position as Public Relations Officer at Leicester City. Although this has become the norm at most clubs, it was quite a revolutionary appointment at the time and my American commercial and marketing adventures stood me in great stead.

Blade-Runner

Chapter 6

Throughout our lives we are constantly reminded of the thin dividing line between success and failure. All of us, no doubt, can recall the defining moments which would have a profound effect on the rest of our careers. At the time, they invariably seem as if the outcome is decided on the toss of a coin. In football the difference between becoming a successful professional player and being dumped on the scrapheap as a teenager is perilously more marginal. Our national sport is littered with great names who were rejected as teenagers, while others destined for greatness as young boys never had the good fortune to make the grade.

I remember at Leicester City, back in the seventies, a great deal of debate about whether to hand a professional contract to a raw, young local kid from the city. Despite showing promise, the worry was whether he was strong enough. His name was Gary Lineker. Dave Buchanan, rated a better prospect, made his Leicester debut on the same afternoon. No disrespect to Dave, but look how their career paths subsequently differed.

Despite spending 18 years as a professional footballer in a career spanning over 500 appearances and almost 100 goals I remain convinced that the single biggest turning point in my career came when I was a fresh-faced 17-year-old apprentice at Sheffield United. At that early age I was to learn at first hand about the much talked about thin dividing line between delight and despair. Little could I have realised at the time, however, that my entire destiny was shaped by one five-minute meeting with Blades manager John Harris.

Plucked from Nottingham parks football with Thorneywood Athletic, I had found life really difficult during my first three months on trial with United. I had not settled

■ **LEAGUE AND CUP WINNERS:** Here's the lads who clinched the Northern Intermediate Cup and League double. Holding the League trophy is Mick Jones and, while the smaller cup is in the hands of the lads on the left. Spot the double take in the top right of the picture. Dead spits, aren't they. Those two are the pair I nicknamed the Bumblies and, who in a bid to avoid an initiation ceremony, spent an entire Friday afternoon clinging to the top of the Bramall Lane floodlight pylons.

in well at Sheffield and was feeling homesick. I was lodging with an elderly couple called Mr and Mrs Snooks in the Nether Edge area of the city. Although it was no fault of theirs, I felt lonely and despondent and did little most evenings but stare at my bedroom walls. I found the football quite hard going as well and, as my three months neared an end, I was beginning to fear the worst. Out of the blue I received a message to report to the manager from his assistant Archie Clark.

I was petrified and wondered what I had done wrong. I made the long walk down a dimly lit corridor which took me past the coke hole. Eventually, I reached a dingy little office and knocked timidly on the oak door. In I went to be greeted by the sight of John Harris sitting behind his desk, staring at a fixture chart immediately above him on the wall. He was wearing a blue sports jacket with brown leather padded elbows. He spun round in his chair and motioned me to sit down . "You's a blooming lucky man, Birchy," he began. "Why's that?" I enquired very politely. "Cos I's was all for sending you's back to Nottingham. You's not done particularly well. You's are borderline. However, Archie Clark wants to keep you's to the end of the season so that's what we are going to do. However, you's better make sure you's pull your finger out and don't let us down."

I didn't know whether to be happy or sad. To this day, I remain unsure whether or not he was playing mind games with me but at least I had another three months to win a contract and not have to return home, tail between my legs, to my old job at Bartons Transport working underneath double-decker buses. Just as importantly, the club also made a change in my living arrangements. They knew I was unhappy and moved me into a club house run by Mrs Badger in Woodseats Road. Mrs Badger's son Len was also a young player with the club and the two of us got along famously.

At the same time, Mick Jones was making the transition from youth to senior level. This freed up a place for a striker in the Northern Intermediate League side. The coaching staff decided I should be the one to fill that role. Up until that point, I had scored only a handful of goals from a series of largely uninspiring displays. For whatever reason, the transformation was incredible and I ended up setting a new scoring record in the League, finishing with 65 goals. Everything I touched found the back of the net and, quite literally, after my talk with John Harris and the change in accommodation, I never looked back. One game, in particular, sticks out in my mind. We beat Hull City 9-2 and I scored seven. After the game I shook hands with the Hull defender who had been charged with the task of marking me. "Thanks a lot, mate, you've just ended my career before it has even began," he said disconsolately. We went on to complete a League and Cup double against strong opposition from the likes of Newcastle, Sunderland and Leeds. Indeed, no fewer than seven of that team graduated to United colours in the First Division and a crowd of over 5,000 at Bramall Lane watched us lift the two-legged League Cup final at the expense of Leeds.

As things looked up on the pitch, I began to enjoy life much more in the Badger household. Friday evenings before Saturday games were always special occasions. Mrs B, a truly fantastic cook, would bring us our meals on a tray into the lounge while we watched television. Later in the evening, Len's girlfriend Diane - a real stunner - would come round and sit with us. I would be in the corner watching television while they canoodled on the sofa. This was the swinging sixties when mini-skirts were the height of fashion and Diane used to wear the full monty with stockings and suspenders. Len would always eat a bowl of grapes and had this annoying habit of spitting the pips at me across the room. I pretended to watch the tele but, in reality, I'd be clocking Diane's scotches and waiting for a glimpse of stocking tops. As the night wore on, her mini-skirt invariably used to ride up and,

■ **BLADE-RUNNER.** Just turned 18 and delighted to have broken into Sheffield United's First Division side... but how times change. No sign of commercialism on the kit in terms of a shirt sponsor or kit supplier. Look, too, at the way I wrapped my shiny white laces all around the boots three times. In the background the Kop is absolutely heaving with fans.

on rare occasions, I was even able to see her *alan whickers*. I know I sound like a pervert but it was all good harmless fun really. Len would walk Diana home at 10.30pm and later the two of us would lie in bed swapping stories as we prepared for the following day's matches.

I was enjoying life and my happiness was complete when I signed professional forms at the end of the season. I felt a tremendous sense of achievement when John Harris offered me my first contract - a contract I thought would never be forthcoming. I had turned my back on Nottingham Forest, never got a break at Notts County and, at the third time of asking, had finally made the grade. I signed for the standard young pro's contract of £15 a week and also received a £20 signing-on fee. I decided the best way to celebrate my new-found wealth was to invest in a made-to-measure suit. In those days only pop stars and film stars had special suits and, of course, impressionable young footballers. Although the money might not sound tremendous, the average wage was only £10 a week. Bear in mind that, at the age of 18, I was now earning more money than my dad at Bartons Transport. Off I went to a tailors in The Moor, the main shopping area of Sheffield. I felt like a million dollars as I picked out a roll of grey mohair cloth from which my suit would be made. It cost me £15 but was worth every penny.

Of course, as a 'new boy' I also had to endure certain initiation ceremonies. The customary one was for your private parts to be shaved but, unfortunately, I got a nasty cut due to a blunt razor. This was made considerably worse when liniment was rubbed liberally across my nether regions. Not that I can claim to be lily-white in this department. In my position as head of the groundstaff boys, I was responsible for a few initiations myself. One afternoon we decided to induct two local brothers who I had nicknamed the Bumblies. We searched high and low for them for three hours before 5pm came around and we decided to go home. Just as we were leaving, someone switched on the floodlights and there, clinging to the top of the pylons in the freezing wind, were the Bumblies.

At this stage I was bracing myself for a year or two in the reserves. Although I had enjoyed a meteoric rise in the second half of my apprenticeship, I expected to have to wait in the wings. I had certainly not braced myself for a remarkable turn of events in which I netted ten goals in my first twelve senior games for the club in the First Division and League Cup. It really was 'Roy of the Rovers' stuff.

The launch date for Birch's professional career was Wednesday September 2, 1964 when United were due to travel to Stoke City's Victoria Ground for a First Division fixture. As head of the groundstaff, I was merrily cleaning out the dressing rooms having been excused from training with the young pros. My calm was shattered when John Harris walked in, turned to me and said: "Birchenall, fancy travelling with

■ **THE HAPPY HOUSE OF HARRIS:** Here's the big family album shot of professionals and groundstaff alike at the start of my debut senior season in 1964-65. Manager John Harris (centre, wearing suit) graduated many players through the youth ranks into the First Division. I've got the pole position in the front row immediately in front of him.

us to the Stoke game tonight?". "Yes please, boss," came my reply as quick as a flash. I couldn't believe my ears. I was going to travel with the senior team for the very first time. Unbeknown to me, the normal striker, Derek 'Doc' Pace, had phoned in ill. Up went the squad on the dressing room wall although my name wasn't on it.

On his return from a light training session, I grabbed Len Badger to tell him the great news. We were all to meet at The Grand Hotel for a pre-match meal before setting off for Stoke in mid-afternoon. I was the new kid on the block and, determined to enjoy the lifestyle, when the waiter asked for my order I replied: "Fillet steak, well done please." I'd hardly seen a steak let alone eaten one. Mounds of toast and jam, orange juice, coffee and tea arrived. I devoured everything I could lay my hands upon. After polishing off my steak, I noticed Graham Shaw was only picking at his. "If you're that hungry you greedy little sod, go on and have it," he growled at me. "Thanks very much," I replied. Another unwanted fillet steak also made its way to my plate and, by the time I got up to leave, I had eaten two and a half fillet steaks, seven rounds of toast (although not as tasty as the toast from East Ham baths), two jugs of orange juice and half a gallon of tea.

The senior pros gathered downstairs to play cards while they waited for the bus. I was still a little peckish and went over to a nearby sweet shop to stock up on Mars bars, Bountys, Smarties, Maltesers and my favourite sherbet dabs. I returned with a huge bag of goodies and took my seat on the back of the bus with Mick Jones and Len. Throughout the two hour journey I munched my way through the entire assortment of sweets. Len warned me to go easy on the confectionery but I wasn't worried because I knew I wouldn't be playing... or so I thought.

We arrived at the ground and, as the junior travelling pro, it was my responsibility to help Harry Latham, our kit man, to unload. As strong as an ox with a big ruddy face, he was a great guy. Between us we wheeled the large wicker baskets off the coach, along the corridor and into the dressing room where I unpacked and hung up Doc Pace's boots and number nine shirt. I looked at the programme and saw a photograph of the legendary Sir Stanley Matthews. It was his final year at Stoke and, although he wasn't playing that night, it was still a humbling experience.

My next job was to collect the envelopes containing the players' complimentary tickets and deliver them to the ticket office. I was hanging around there when I felt a tap on the shoulder. It was coach John Short. "Son, you'd better nip off smartish and start getting changed," he instructed. I wondered what he meant and walked back to the visitors' dressing room. As I came through the door the players started clapping and laughing. My boots were hung up next to the number 10 shirt. Mick Jones, who normally wore 10, had taken Doc's number nine jersey and I was to be given my debut.

I was in a complete daze. In the dressing room were a number of small slatted windows, out of which you could see the pitch and the ground. I clambered onto one of the benches and stared out as the ground began to fill up. The biggest crowd I had played in front of was a few thousand, but tonight I was to perform before almost 28,000. In truth, the game passed me by. We won 1-0, courtesy of a goal from Mick Jones but I can't remember any incidents at all. I was on cloud nine and the game marked the fulfilment of all my footballing dreams.

My only disappointment was that my mum and dad - my two biggest supporters - were not there to witness the spectacle. They had followed me every step of the way from my Nottingham Boys days, to Notts County 'A' team matches, Thorneywood Athletic and the Sheffield United youth team. Everything had happened so quickly that I had not had time to tell them I was travelling to the game. There were no mobile phones those days from which I could have rang them whilst on the bus. To be fair, I had no inkling myself that I would be playing until an hour before kick-off which had obviously been John Harris's intention. The wily old fox had not wanted me to get too nervous before the game, although obviously he might have changed this tactic had he known I was going to eat half a cow's backside for my pre-match meal.

Although we didn't arrive back in Sheffield until well after midnight, I was up bright and early on the Thursday morning. Although the pros had been given the day off, I wanted to rush into the ground as quickly as possible and speak to all my pals on the groundstaff. I was as proud as punch and secretly hoped I might be recognised when I caught the bus into Bramall Lane. Sadly, I was to be disappointed.

At the ground, Archie Clark called me over for a quick chat. Archie, remember, was the man who spotted me in Nottingham and he told me the manager had been very pleased with my performance. Now all the speculation was whether I would retain my place for the big one against Sheffield Wednesday at Hillsborough on Saturday. As far as Sheffield fans were concerned, derby matches between the Owls and Blades were the most important games of the season. The local evening paper came around to take my photograph for a story in Friday's paper. I trained with the first team on Friday and rushed back into the dressing room. John Harris pinned up the team-sheet and there I was at number 10. I was going to play in the Sheffield derby. I had had only an hour to contemplate my debut at Stoke, now I had 26 hours to think about the second game.

Local derby matches exuded just as much passion in the sixties as they do now and the whole of Sheffield was talking about the forthcoming game. Happily, Lady Luck smiled down on me as I scored both goals in a 2-0 United victory. Midway through the first half Mick Jones unleashed a shot which rapped against the crossbar

■ **JUMPING FOR JOY.** The Sheffield Morning Telegraph took this photo on the eve of my first-ever derby match against Sheffield Wednesday. I'd made my debut on the Wednesday at Stoke and had retained my place for Saturday's game at Hillsborough. The photo was taken on Friday afternoon at the home I shared with the Badger family on Woodseats Road. Look at the outside toilet we had to use in the background. See, 'The Claw' could still control a ball even in winklepickers.

■ **GOALDEN DAYS:** One of the reasons I became so popular with United fans was my uncanny knack to score goals in the derby games with Sheffield Wednesday. In only my second game for the Blades, I scored both goals in a 2-0 win over the Owls at Hillsborough. I went on to score six goals in six derby matches. I had a particularly productive time in the 1965-66 season. I got the winner in round one at Bramall Lane in September and then scored both goals in a 2-2 draw at Hillsborough in March. Here, I'm pictured having just rammed the ball home for the first equaliser after the disconsolate Wednesday keeper Ron Springett (right) dropped the ball.

and, from the rebound, I managed to scramble the ball into the net. The second was a header from a corner. I climbed highest at the far post and powered in a cross which cracked into the net off the back of the stanchion. Suddenly I became a United hero overnight for sinking the arch enemy, and this time my mum and dad were in the crowd along with girlfriend Heather's parents.

Heather's dad had a Dormobile and, after the game, we all drove back to Nottingham together. He had

■ Young Sherman celebrates in the bath at Hillsborough after bagging another brace against arch rivals Sheffield Wednesday in 1966.

wanted to go directly to the MI but I insisted we made a detour through the centre of Sheffield so I could buy six early copies of the Green 'Un, the local sports paper, and read all about myself. We must have cut an unusual sight, myself, Heather, and both sets of parents crammed into a rickety old dormobile, avidly reading the newspaper.

Needless to say, we had a great weekend but it was back into the club as usual on Monday morning. Now, though, my life had changed forever. From being an anonymous face, I was recognised by United and Wednesday fans alike. Not only did I get praise from people I had never met before, I also had to take a fair amount of stick from the Owls' half of the city. There was an obligatory photo-call at the home of Mrs B. Local photographers came around to take snap shots of myself and Len sitting down to a home-cooked meal. In those days, there was still a reasonable amount of media coverage but nothing like today where the television stations, radio stations, sports magazines, internet sites, clubcall lines and newspapers seem to multiply daily. The next two months went like a dream for me as I not only maintained my place but managed to score regularly as well. Mick Jones and I became known as the two blond bombers, sharing 16 goals in just ten matches.

A highlight was the visit of Arsenal to Bramall Lane on a cold October night. The Gunners had just signed Frank McLintock for £80,000 from Leicester and I was wondering how on earth I was going to get by him. We played a blinder and Mick and I both scored two goals in a 4-0 rout of the Londoners.

Off the pitch we got a real result too. With myself and Len both doing well in the first team, the club offered Mrs B the chance to move to a bigger and better three-bedroomed club house in the Intake region of Sheffield. Now we had the luxury of a bedroom each. This really was utopia.

My first-ever trip to Anfield also brought me into contact with legendary Liverpool manager Bill Shankly. Despite my goals, I was still the junior pro and one of my responsibilities was to wheel in the wicker kit baskets from the coach to the dressing room. At Liverpool the dressing rooms were virtually

■ **BILL SHANKLY:**
"Eee, laddie it's a long way to come for nothing," the legendary Liverpool manager told me when I arrived at Anfield for the first time. He was right - we lost 3-1.

■ **MERSEYSIDE CRUNCH SEPTEMBER 1964:** Goalmouth action from a trip to Goodison Park to take on Everton - my first visit to Merseyside. My First Division career was less than a fortnight old at this stage, after a full debut against Sheffield Wednesday. I'm climbing on the back of defender Brian Labone who in turn is stood on my United team-mate John Docherty. With Everton keeper Gordon West also missing the ball, it's left to Mick Jones to get the touch. Mick scored our goal in a 1-1 draw in front of a massive 47,765 crowd. That, incidentally, was our biggest of the season - almost 5,000 more than watched us play Manchester United at Old Trafford three months later.

■ **SHEFFIELD UNITED 0 LEEDS UNITED 3:** This was the final game of my first senior season in 1965. Safety in the First Division was already assured but plenty of Yorkshire pride was at stake. Leeds were too good for us, however. I climbed above Paul Reaney to send in this looping header with (centre) Billy Bremner looking on but it was all to no avail.

■ **'THE CLAW':** The Birch's left foot was lovingly named 'The Claw'. Hours of practice went into perfecting this technique. Look at the arms in perfect symmetry as I do a few loosening exercise in front of the empty Bramall Lane terraces (right). My only problem was when my left foot came anywhere near the ball.

next door to each other and Bill, as I was to find out later, invariably stood in the corridor. I spotted him and tried to make a dash for the safety of the visitors dressing room but before I could get there, he delivered a fantastic one-liner in that harsh Glaswegian accent. "Eee, laddie, it's a long way to come for nothing."

Running up the famous Anfield steps will live with me for the rest of my life. You had to go down two steps before going back up a dozen more. The stairs were so narrow you almost had to go out in single file and, as you emerged onto the pitch, you were mesmerised by the crowd. The whole of the Kop used to sway. What a sight. I scored in my first appearance there but it all counted for nothing as we were crushed 3-1. Strangely, I have no recollection of the goal whatsoever.

A trip to Fulham in only my fifth senior game also provided an unforgettable experience with the strongest-smelling footballer it was ever my misfortune to come across. Players generally stink to high heaven of liniment and Ralgex. However, Fulham had a player by the name of Bobby Keech who smelt as if he had emptied the entire contents of a crate of aftershave over his body. You didn't need to see him coming, you could smell him a mile off. His hair was big and bouffant and he wore more jewellery than Mr T. He sported a big gold necklace and matching rings on his fingers and in those days the referee didn't even bother to tell him to take off the jewellery. He clanked while jogging up to me at a corner. "If you do anything, I'm going to break both your effing legs," he snarled. This was my first experience of what is now termed 'sledging'and although I had a strong enough character not to be intimidated by the threat it was still an eye-opener.

GOALMOUTH ACTION AT CRAVEN COTTAGE: Here I am looping a header goalwards for United against Fulham in September 1966. Although this effort missed, I did score the winner in a 1-0 win. Craven Cottage was certainly one of my happier hunting grounds. In my three visits there in a United shirt I scored in two games and we never lost. My opponent is John Dempsey who later joined me at Chelsea.

More frightening to me was when I had to line up in a wall during a First Division game against Birmingham City. Birmingham had a free-kick specialist called Stan Lynn. As hard as nails was Stan, with the physique of a brick outhouse and an air raid shelter rolled into one. There was no finesse with him. No Beckham or Zola top spin. Up he stepped and just wellied it like a rocket. I made the mistake of being on the end of the wall. Like an exocet, this free kick hit me in the chest and propelled me five yards backwards. For the rest of my career, I never stood on the end of a wall again.

I also learned at a very early stage to be careful where I applied the liniment and rubbing oils. As a young lad, I used to watch the senior pros smearing their legs liberally with liniment. Before one match I decided to take things a stage further and cover my face with it as well. In a matter of seconds I had turned a delicate shade of crimson and tears were streaming down my cheeks. All this was just a couple of minutes before the team was due to run out and the club doctor frantically tried to cover me in water and wash it off. When I ran out I must have looked like Coco the Clown and for the first ten minutes I could hardly see the ball.

Bolton Wanderers' back four had a certain notoriety at the time for being the hardest defensive unit in the sixties. They were the sort who had their pre-match steaks served red raw. Up at Burnden Park, I made the mistake of trying to go down the line when one of them bounced me 12 times along the gravel track around the side of the pitch. I don't know whether they had a tape machine stuck up their arris but after being whacked by any one of the four you always heard them snarl: "The ball might pass us kid but you aren't going nowhere." It was like coming up against four Blutos out of the Popeye cartoon, not that you ever dared tell them to their face.

With my new-found goalscoring prowess, my first nickname of Sherman was given a considerable airing by the press. Sherman was a type of tank to which the players likened me for my strong surging runs up front. This was how the Sheffield Morning Telegraph explained away my nickname in 1964. *"He is very tank-like in his approach to goalscoring and never gives up chasing anything which might represent half a chance. His progress in the scoring stakes will be followed closely and if Sherman is not very British it is a little easier for the tongue than Centurion or Conqueror."*

Bursting onto the scene in such a dramatic fashion, I inevitably found myself in a soccer spotlight. There was even talk of Mick Jones and I being a future England striking partnership. Strangely, I like to think that I never allowed all the talk to go to my head. Subsequently in life, I have noticed many young players bursting onto the scene in dramatic fashion but the acid test as far as I am concerned is whether you are still doing the same in two years time. When you first arrive, you are an unknown quantity. Opponents are not yet fully aware of your strengths and weaknesses. They

■ **NICE ONE, MICK.** My United strike partner Mick Jones (centre) celebrates his first full England call-up. Mick's United team-mates gather around on the Bramall Lane terraces to offer him our congratulations, I'm the goofy one on the end with his tongue out. *Left to right are, Mick Heaton, Birch, Ken Mallender, David Monks, Mick Jones, Joe Shaw, Tony Wagstaff, the unmistakeable quiff of Cec Coldwell and a young Alan Woodward before he went as grey as a badger.*

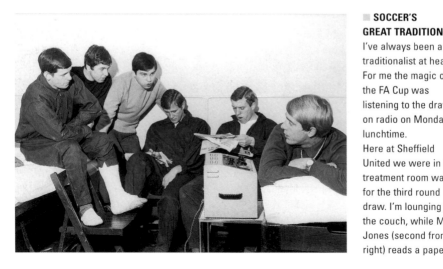

■ **SOCCER'S GREAT TRADITIONS:** I've always been a traditionalist at heart. For me the magic of the FA Cup was listening to the draw on radio on Monday lunchtime.

Here at Sheffield United we were in the treatment room waiting for the third round draw. I'm lounging on the couch, while Mick Jones (second from right) reads a paper.

don't know quite how you make your runs, what your first touch is like, whether you like to go to the left or right, can you head it, trap it, are you brave. All these questions remain unanswered. But in a very short space of time players wise up to your abilities and plot ways of stopping you. Your novelty value has been eradicated. There are only so many ways you can kick, cross a ball, tackle or shoot. What separates the top class from the average is the ability to perform their special little tricks supremely well so that opponents still cannot stop them doing it.

Despite my ten goals in twelve games, I knew I was not destined to be a natural goalscorer. I always saw myself as someone who could work hard alongside another striker, make channel runs for them and help create space. That's why I worked hard on other aspects of my game so that when defenders started to close me down more effectively and the goals dried up (as they did) I had something else to offer. I always afford myself a wry smile when I see a new young striker given banner headlines after grabbing a few goals. It's fantastic while it lasts but I think to myself that the hard work for them is only just beginning.

■ **KEYS TO THE DOOR:** United club captain Joe Shaw hands me the key to the door to celebrate my 21st birthday. Left to right are, Joe, Charlie Bell, Mick Jones, me and Jack Parks.

■ **MAN ABOUT THE HOUSE:** I've decided to swap the trusty blow-drier for the blow torch and engage in a little bit of DIY for my Sheffield United colleague Graham Shaw. Graham asked me around to strip some paint off his bannisters. Unfortunately, all I succeeded in doing was giving his children third-degree burns.

■ **ANGEL FACE.** I'm perfecting those film-star smiles for this portrait (below) of me leaning on the gate outside my digs in Woodseats Road.

■ **HOLDING THE BABY.** Now, despite what you may have been led to believe, the Birch definitely did not have any offspring while he was in Sheffield. Len Badger tells me this little bonny fella is definitely not his either so I can only assume this was one of those 'holding the baby' pics where the club was trying to court some free publicity.

■ **YOUNGEST SWINGERS IN TOWN**: A local golf professional at Dore and Totley GC gave us a crash course in the game, but as you can see our technique was a little on the shady side. From left to right, we are Len Badger, Mick Jones, Frank Barlow, Ken Mallender, Reg Matthewson, yours truly and Gil Reece.

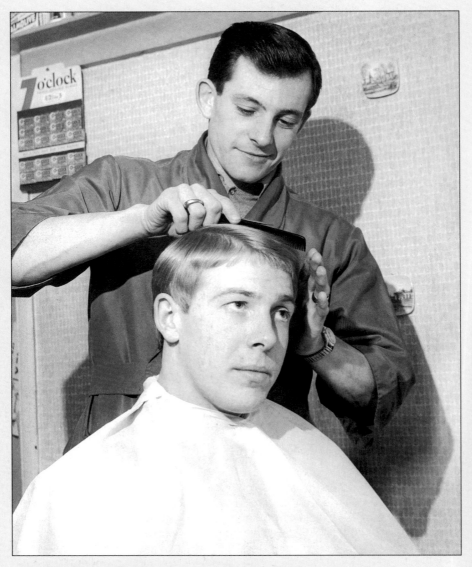

■ **SHORT BACK AND SIDES, PLEASE:** Going to the hairdressers was always a hair-raising experience, especially if you were a Sheffield United player and the person cutting your hair was a Sheffield Wednesday opponent. Here I am (above) getting the blond locks shorn by Owls inside forward Johnny Fantham. It was a special promotional photo taken by the local evening paper ahead of one of the Sheffield derbies.

■ Believe it or not, this little montage of photos (above) arose from the time we four young 'likely lads' from Bramall Lane were sent to a farm in Wiltshire. Arnold Laver, director of United, owned a big timber yard opposite the ground. Our manager John Harris decided that Birch, Mick Jones and brothers Tony and Barry Wagstaff all needed toughening up. As Arnold owned a farm down south it was decided to send this happy quartet to work on the land for a fortnight at the end of the season. We loved every minute of it. We worked in the fields during the day... and propped up the local hostelries at night, and you can tell we enjoyed a laugh or two. I'm doing my Laurel and Hardy impression with Barry Wagstaff, watched by Mick Jones. There were more high jinks as the Birch is pulled from under a car by Tony Wagstaff. In the driving seat is Mick. Thirdly, and perhaps most embarrassingly, the Birch found that the Wiltshire air brought out his cross-dressing tendencies. We've all heard about how young people experiment sexually as teenagers. In my case I can safely assure you this was as far as my transvestite yearnings ever went. Honest!

THE PIED PIPER OF BRAMALL LANE: Here I am leading the local youngsters a merry dance along the back of the main stand. Take a close look at the lads clothes and the price of admission to the terraces. Five shillings for adults. My, those were the good old days.

Not only did my arrival on the pro scene offer me instant recognition on the streets of Sheffield, it also afforded instant wealth. After my two goals against Wednesday, John Harris gave me a standard senior players contract. My weekly wage went up from £15 per week to £35. There were also bonuses of £5 for every appearance and £4 for every win. After beating Stoke and Sheffield Wednesday in my first week, I pulled a staggering £53 - five times the average wage. My only problem was that I didn't have a bank account.

I hastily went into town and opened one with Barclays (still my bankers today, incidentally) so that the money could be paid in. It was my original intention to withdraw the entire amount just so I could see what £53 looked like in hard cash. I also toyed with the idea of driving back to Nottingham and waving the wad under the nose of Ted - my miserable old workmate at Bartons who swore blind that I would never make a pro footballer. I did, however, think better of this.

I also decided now was the appropriate time to become the first ever Birchenall to learn to drive. My mum and dad didn't drive because we couldn't afford a car. I shelled out £50 to buy a second-hand Triumph Herald and had a series of ten driving lessons costing seven shillings and a tanner apiece. I'm not saying I was backward

KUNG FU FIGHTING: I'm doing my best to get to grips with Spurs centre half Mike England in the final game of the 1966-67 season at White Hart Lane. Mike was always a tough adversary... too tough in this one because we went down 2-0 but still finished in an excellent 10th position.

OFFICIAL TEAM PHOTO: Here's the official team group for the 1965-66 season featuring our 27 full professionals and, sat at the front, our eight young lads. I'm stood alongside Mick Jones on the back row, five in from the right.

PRIVATES ON PARADE: Me and Alan Woodward stand to attention at the Ball Inn training ground. We came through the youth ranks together and, for me, Alan had the hardest shot in the game. Only Leeds United's Peter Lorimer came close. They both could hit the ball like an exocet. Alan was also one of the finest crosses of the ball while on the run it was my good fortune to see or play alongside.

but it took me three weeks to open the boot. The principal source of conjecture about driving tests among the lads was the allegiance of your examiner. Get a Wednesday-ite and it didn't matter if you were Stirling Moss behind the wheel, you were bound to fail. Conversely, a United-ite was sure to turn a blind eye to your inability to perform a three point turn or how you jumped three sets of traffic lights. I took my test on the roads around Dore and Totley and spent most of the time worrying about the examiner's allegiance.

The test went okay and afterwards he asked me a few questions on the highway code. Very simple questions too. I braced myself. "Congratulations, Mr Birchenall you have passed the test," he said. I leapt up and punched the air in delight. "Tell me, Mr Birchenall," he went on, "did passing this test give you as much pleasure as you gave me when you whacked in two goals against Wednesday!"

A few months later Len Badger and I were walking past a Triumph dealership in the centre of Sheffield when we clapped eyes on two gleaming soft-top Spitfires. We looked at each other and walked inside. The salesman showed us around and we made up our minds there and then to buy one apiece. They cost £600 each, exactly the same amount of money I had saved in my bank account. Easy come, easy go. Our only problem was who should have which car. We decided to toss a coin; I got the red car, and Len the white one. We couldn't take delivery until next day and for 24 hours we were like expectant fathers.

After training the following day, we raced down to the showroom to pick up the cars. I recalled a year earlier seeing Tony Kay, a Sheffield Wednesday player, pose up and down The Moor in an enormous American car smoking a lah-de-dah. "Flash bastard, you won't ever catch me doing that," I thought to myself. Len and I then proceeded to screech up and down The Moor in our new cars hoping as many people as possible would see us. Mind you, at least we weren't smoking a la-de-dah.

Becoming a first team professional footballer also opened up social doors previously closed to me. Remember, though, that this was still the early sixties and nightclubs had not yet materialised. In fact, in my first season there was only one place in the whole of Sheffield where you could get an after-hours drink - a Chinese restaurant called the Rickshaw was the rather surprising venue. Graham Shaw introduced me to the delights of a 'chinkie' and a pint or three of John Smiths bitter.

After a midweek game, he invited his younger brother Bernard, myself and Len for a meal. In we went and started to partake of a few drinks into the small hours. I felt progressively worse, so much so that I had to go outside which was unfortunate because it was the coldest night of the year and I was only wearing a thin cotton shirt. For the next hour I was belle vue-ing all over the pavement and road before Graham and the lads bundled me into a taxi and home. The following morning I made the first of many vows that it was the last time I was ever going to do anything like that again.

Thankfully, Sheffield's social scene was soon to expand beyond a single licensed Chinese restaurant. The Pennyfarthing was the first nightclub to open in the city and, needless to say, Birch and his team-mates quickly starting making regular visits. This was the dawn of the 'Swinging Sixties', girls were into short skirts, white pvc knee-length boots and black stockings and sussies. The end of the week was out for us because we were preparing for matches but Monday evenings soon became established as the lads night out. The club also provided the backdrop for Birchy to improve his vocal talents alongside legendary singer Joe Cocker.

At the time Joe was a young kid who had recently formed a little-known group, The Grease Band, but they soon started to hit the big time with two chart successes 'A little help from your friends' and 'The long and winding road'. Joe had been performing at The Pennyfarthing for a few months and I got into the habit of joining him on stage to sing a few songs. In one corner would be the Wednesday lads - Eustace, Springett, Quinn, Smith and Fantham - supping their Coca-colas, while at the other end of the club the United lads - Mick Jones, the Wagstaff brothers and Len - quaffed pints of John Smiths. One of our favourite party pieces was the quaintly-named 'Walking the Dog' song from Joe. After a few lyrics, the choruses basically consisted of as many people as possible making barking noises. All the lads would bark away and then swallow a pint before spraying it over me on stage. Childish, I know, but at the time our antics brought the house down.

This was around about the time when I realised there was more to life than just football. I could be the centre of attention when I went out with the lads and, yes, I enjoyed the attention. Don't get the impression that I was out partying every night because I wasn't. I was very disciplined and knew I couldn't go out on the night before a match and get away with it. But when I went out - either on a Monday or after a game - I was determined to enjoy myself. I like to think that despite my rather outgoing personality I remained fundamentally the same underneath.

As a young soccer star there are a large number of problems waiting to trip you up. Drink is one of them, as we have seen in several high-profile cases in the current modern game. I was never much of a drinker. From my mixed fruit days I graduated to shandy and lager top. To be honest, I used to cheat a little because for many years I genuinely didn't like the taste of bitter or lager. I'd tell the lads I would have a lager but nobble the barmaid to give me a shandy. There was no drugs culture prevalent which there would appear to be today. I didn't find drugs readily available until I moved to America and by that time I was the wrong side of 30. Women, well, I was probably rather naive on that score. After whacking in a few goals I suddenly became the centre of attention with some of the female population of Sheffield. It wasn't like they were throwing their knickers at me but there was definitely more interest. Silly old me thought it was because of my good looks and athletic body. Nothing to do, of course, with me being a pro footballer who was being paid five times as much as most other blokes

There is, however, a completely different media culture in place today. Television, radio, newspapers, magazines - the list is endless, and they all want a different piece of the player. It's only in the past few seasons that Premiership clubs have started to employ press officers to help management and players deal with the media. It's a very busy role as my co-author in this book, Paul Mace, knows only too well having done the job for the past eight years at Leicester City, handling the likes of Steve Walsh, David Speedie, Neil Lennon and especially Robbie Savage.

In my day you would walk out of the dressing room and be met by a group of newspaper journalists. Although not as many, it still could still be daunting for a young teenage player making his way in the game. Where, of course, there is another fundamental difference is the way in which the newspapers report on the game, or more crucially, the off-the-field activities of professional sportsmen. Don't for a minute think it's only in the past couple of years that players have invented 'having a good time'. It's always been going on but now there is a media culture whereby you are far more likely to find your name plastered across the pages of the News of the World. I have a great deal of sympathy with today's young players who are just as likely to hit the front as well as the back pages. Thank goodness, the papers only turned up to report on sport when I was a lad in Sheffield.

I was also at the forefront in establishing a little social club of players which made regular outings to sample the Nottingham nightlife. Myself, Bernard Shaw, Len Badger, Ken Mallender and Jack Parks formed what my mum referred to as 'the Razzle Club'. We put in a pound each to pay our elder team-mate Harry Orr for the use of his Mini for a weekend. After a home game, we'd all cram into the car and head off to Nottingham, kipping down in various bedrooms or the sitting room in my parents' house in Sherwood. On Sunday, we'd get up bleary-eyed and head back north up the M1.

■ **MEET THE RAZZLE CLUB OF '63.** This was an unofficial United social club which made regular Saturday night trips to Nottingham. The five (l to r) are Jack Parks, Ken Mallender, Bernard Shaw, Birch and Len Badger. Our modus operandi would be to borrow a mini from one of the senior players for £5 and the five of us would pile into the car and hit the club scene in Nottingham. We'd all stay at my parents' house and then come back up on Sunday. Needless to say, it was quite a squeeze.

In my first full season I netted 13 goals although a disappointing end-of-term run saw us finish only two places above the relegation zone. Ten goals followed in year two and we ended in the top half of the table - a tremendous achievement. John Harris put the emphasis on youth with seven of us coming through the ranks. Wherever we went we were written off as no-hopers because we had very few big names in the team. That was always the case when we went to London where we were dismissed as country bumpkins. I always enjoyed trips to the capital because we went on a train and stayed overnight in a fancy hotel and had a nice meal. On the way back, if we had won, we had many an enjoyable wait in the St Pancras buffet bar with a drink or two. Of course, if we lost it was just a quick cup of tea and a sandwich before getting back on the train.

Bramall Lane was quite unique in one respect throughout the First Division - it was the only ground that didn't have four sides. We were surrounded by three stands and a cricket field, where the Yorkshire CCC ground backed onto the football pitch. This led to a certain amount of friction between the two groundsmen and a game plan adopted by clubs in the closing minutes of a match. If we were winning in the last few minutes, we were under orders to welly the ball at the cricket pavilion 200 yards away. No-one ever reached it but some went pretty close. In those days, you had to play with the same ball so we had some of the fittest ball-boys in the country. Mind you, the opposition employed the same tactics if they were winning so the last few minutes of Bramall Lane matches could be pretty tedious affairs. The cricket groundsman was furious when our ball boys kept trampling across his beloved cricket square leaving behind a trail of stud-marks but, equally, our groundsman was always put out at the start of the season when, despite manicuring the pitch as best he could, there was a set of brown footmarks left by Fred Trueman from his 50 yard run-up.

If you were forced to name three of England's all-time footballing greats, it's a fair bet that the names of Sir Stanley Matthews, Tom Finney and Jimmy Greaves would feature pretty high in many lists. Not too many fans will have had the privilege of being able to see all three play. And even fewer will have had the opportunity to play alongside all three.

In my first full season for Sheffield United I had the immense privilege of lining up against all three playing in the same team. The occasion was a testimonial game for long-serving central defender Joe Shaw. Joe was arguably the best uncapped defender of his generation. A genuinely nice man he amassed over 600 appearances for the Blades. I was included in the United side to face an All Star XI at Bramall Lane on Monday March 29 1965. To say I was awestruck would have been a monumental understatement. Sir Stanley, Greavsie and Tom Finney formed the All Star front line. It was no surprise they whacked six past us, including a hat-trick for Jimmy. I managed to score one in a 6-5 defeat but playing against those greats really was a once-in-a-lifetime experience. Or so I thought.

A few months later I got the chance to play in the same team as Sir Stanley. It was another testimonial game but the match was organised for a more sombre reason. A former United player John Niblo had been killed in a car crash. As he had also played for Stoke, it was decided to form a joint Sheffield/Stoke side to play his last

WEST HAM UNITED F.C.
Formed in 1900

Directors
R. H. PRATT, J.P. (Chairman) L. G. CEARNS (Vice-Chairman)
W. F. CEARNS R. G. BRANDON B. R. CEARNS, F.C.C.A.
Manager: R. GREENWOOD   Secretary: E. CHAPMAN
Honorary Consultant: W. ALEXANDER LAW, Esq., O.B.E., M.D., F.R.C.S.
Medical Officer: Dr. J. C. BELL, M.B., ch.B.

F.A. Cup: Winners 1963-4 Runners-up 1922-23 Semi-Finalists 1932-33
Football League (Div. II): Winners 1957-58 Runners-up 1922-23
F.A. Charity Shield: Joint Holders 1964
Football League War Cup: Winners 1939-40
Southern Floodlight Cup: Winners 1955-56 Runners-up 1959-60
London Challenge Cup: Winners 1924-25 1925-26 1929-30 1946-47 1948-49 1952-53 1956-57
American International Soccer League: Winners 1963
American Challenge Cup: Runners-up 1963
F.A. Youth Cup: Winners 1962-63 Runners-up 1956-57 1958-59 Semi-Finalists 1932-33

WEST HAM UNITED	SHEFFIELD UNITED
Colours:	Colours:
Claret Jerseys, Light Blue Sleeves	Red-and-White Striped Shirts
White Shorts	Black Shorts
1 Jim Standen	1 Alan Hodgkinson
2 John Bond	2 Len Badger
3 Martin Peters	3 Graham Shaw
4 Eddie Bovington	4 Brian Richardson
5 Ken Brown	5 Joe Shaw
6 Bobby Moore (Capt)	6 Reg Matthewson
7 Alan Sealey	7 John Docherty
8 Ron Boyce	8 Keith Kettleborough
9 Johnny Byrne	9 Mick Jones
10 Geoff Hurst	10 Alan Birchenall
11 John Sissons	11 Barry Hartle

Referee: Mr. L. CALLAGHAN (Merthyr Tydfil, Glam.)
Linesmen: Red Flag: : Mr. D. J. THOMAS (Solihull, Warwick.)
Yellow Flag: Mr. P. R. PARSONS (Cheltenham, Glos.)

WEST HAM V SHEFFIELD UNITED PROGRAMME:
Pictured above is the programme from only my eighth
appearance in the Football League with Sheffield
United. Take a look at the West Ham side which
included Bobby Moore, Geoff Hurst and Martin
Peters who were to all help England lift the World
Cup just 18 months later. We got beat 3-1 and ended
a run of seven
successive games
in which either Mick
Jones or I got on the
scoresheet.

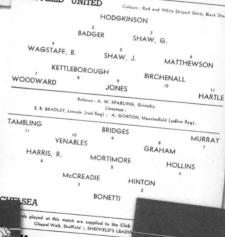

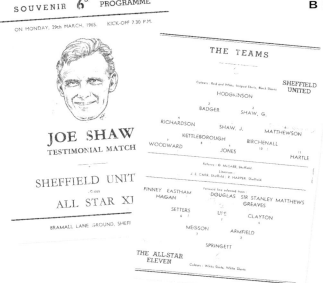

ON MONDAY, 29th MARCH, 1965.   KICK-OFF 7.30 P.M.

JOE SHAW
TESTIMONIAL MATCH

SHEFFIELD UNIT
ALL STAR XI

BRAMALL LANE GROUND, SHEFI

THE TEAMS

Colours : Red and White Striped Shirts, Black Shorts

SHEFFIELD UNITED

HODGKINSON

BADGER   SHAW, G.

RICHARDSON

SHAW, J.   MATTHEWSON

KETTLEBOROUGH   BIRCHENALL

WOODWARD   JONES   HARTLE

Referee : G. McCABE, Sheffield.
Linesmen
J. E. CARR, Sheffield : R. HARPER, Sheffield

FINNEY   EASTHAM   Forward line selected from:

HAGAN   DOUGLAS   SIR STANLEY MATTHEWS
GREAVES

SETTERS   LILE   CLAYTON

MEGSON   ARMFIELD

SPRINGETT

THE ALL-STAR
ELEVEN

Colours : White Shirts, White Shorts

FIELD OF DREAMS:
One of my dreams came true on Monday March 29 (left). I not only saw Jimmy Greaves, Sir Stanley Matthews and Tom Finney play, but I lined up against them in a testimonial game for long-serving United defender Joe Shaw who clocked up 20 years service at Bramall Lane. A crowd of 29,000 saw Greaves, Matthews and Finney join forces for the only time in an All-Star side which beat United 6-5.

Match programmes in the sixties weren't quite as colourful or informative as today's sophisticated publications. Scattered along the bottom of these two pages are just a selection from my Sheffield United days and those team line-ups are certainly informative and thought-provoking. Take a look at the Chelsea side which came to Bramall Lane in November 1964 and won 2-0. In midfield are former England boss Terry Venables and current Spurs manager George Graham. In the Liverpool side which arrived in Sheffield in April 1967 was one of their newest recruits, a £60,000 signing from Blackpool called Emlyn Hughes, plus such household names as Ian St John, Ron Yeats, Roger Hunt and Chris Lawler. Watch out for the Birmingham number two Stan Lynn. He had the hardest free-kick in the business and, on one occasion, almost knocked the Birch unconscious with a 20-yarder.

club Stockport County. Myself and Mick Jones were getting changed in the dressing room when Sir Stanley spoke to us. "You boys are doing quite well for yourselves," he said. "Don't forget, just pass it to my feet. I don't want to have to run for the ball because the legs ain't what they used to be." Meeting such a great soccer legend at such an early age was a very humbling experience.

But I'm also reminded of a piece of advice I received from Joe Shaw on the night of his testimonial. He was fortunate to attract a crowd of 29,000 but Joe reminded me: "If it was raining I'd have probably only got 5,000," he said. "Don't be like me, if you get the chance, move on to another club." Although I never moved from any club for the money it was good advice from Joe.

In total, I spent four tremendously happy years in Sheffield before my £100,000 move to Chelsea. Sheffield was a city I really did grow to love. The people were homely and the city itself I will always remember as one of terrific contrasts. Driving through north-eastern regions such as Tinsley proved a tremendous eye-opener. I always said to myself that in the highly unlikely event that I ever became manager at United I would take all the players on a guided tour of the many steelworks in the area. Life was tremendously hard for those people. I felt I could empathise a little because of my own background, working in a grimy coachyard in Nottingham.

Footballers do have a great lifestyle and it is all too easy to take for granted but the men working in those steelworks helped give us that lifestyle by coming to Bramall Lane and Hillsborough in their many thousands every Saturday afternoon. Conversely, on the other side of Sheffield, out towards Castleton and Baslow, was some of the most beautiful countryside I have ever come across in all my journeys throughout the world.

Sheffield was certainly a city of contrasts and I will always be eternally grateful to Archie Clark for initially spotting me in Nottingham parks football and, perhaps more significantly, for having a quiet word with manager John Harris to give me just a few more months to see whether I could make the grade. I have a great deal to be thankful to you for, Archie.

Treading the Kings Road

Chapter 7

IF any club typified the culture of the swinging sixties, then it had to be Chelsea. Make no mistake, the sixties was a time of vibrancy, glamour and a riotous film and pop culture. My experience of the sixties in Sheffield had been confined to the opening of a handful of nightclubs. Here in London we were at the very centre of the whole revolution. Chelsea, for me, was the club of the late sixties. The Beatles were at their height and the Kings Road was looked upon as the centre of the modern universe. Over in China, the local residents would never have heard of Bramall Lane, but from Moscow to Peking, they would have all known of the Kings Road. Chelsea was synonymous with the Kings Road, and Kings Road was synonymous with Chelsea.

Chelsea was where the world of football and show-business converged. Thanks largely to the club president Dickie 'Darling' Attenborough, most of Hollywood's great movie stars paid a visit to Stamford Bridge in my three seasons there. Chelsea was the club to be seen at, regardless of whether you had any interest in football. Steve McQueen, Paul Newman and Raquel Welch were just three who paid us a visit in the dressing room before a game.

As well as famous celebrities from the world of show-business appearing in abundance, footballers themselves were also beginning to adopt personality status. Eat your heart out Becks and Posh Spice, this was where the celebrity sport and showbiz era was born. And, at the heart of this conception, was Chelsea football club. I consider myself forever fortunate to have had the opportunity to be involved on the inside and tasted at first-hand a truly fantastic three years at the cutting edge of the footballing and changing fashion worlds.

■ **NEW KID ON THE BLOCK:** Getting to grips with the new training kit at Stamford Bridge for the first time after completing my £100,000 move from Sheffield United. It's Friday December 1, 1967 and I'm lacing up my boots in blissful ignorance of an initiation ceremony being planned for me by Ron 'Chopper' Harris.

Just a few years earlier I had been a mechanic in greasy overalls working under the oil sump of a corporation bus in Nottingham. Now I was stepping out in style as one of the very first £100,000 players in English football. The irony was never lost on me that I had spent many an enjoyable afternoon in Nottingham and Sheffield at the picture-house (that's the cinema, to all our younger readers). Now, those people who I considered to be demi-gods, were coming to watch me play football. I could never have envisaged that in my wildest dreams. And, in many ways, my time at Chelsea was a dream. Although I was still playing football in the First Division everything else had changed beyond recognition.

Chelsea were among the most fashionable clubs in Europe in more senses than one. Even the kit was different. At Sheffield United, if it rained your woollen shirts weighed twice as much at the end of the game. Chelsea used the best textiles and had special lightweight shirts for summer and heavier fabrics for the colder winter months. In this modern era such attention to detail is taken for granted but back then Chelsea were years ahead of their time. It was those sort of things that I felt proved Chelsea were one of the big league clubs.

Chelsea and Sheffield United were, to be honest, like chalk and cheese. And, in much the same way as I encountered problems settling in to my new lifestyle in South Yorkshire, I found London in the first instance to be a very intimidating environment. Upon my arrival as the new kid on the block from up north, I was told by Dave Sexton's assistant manager Ron Stuart that they had found some accommodation for me. In Sheffield all the players lived within a 20-minute radius of each other. At the drop of a hat, we'd be out on the town. At Chelsea, my digs were in a suburb called Barnes. I might as well have been in Bangkok. I was dropped off by Frank Blunstone at the front door of the house and told to report for training at 10am the following morning. My 'home' in the house of an elderly couple was an upstairs room - 12 feet by six feet with a single bed and bedside cabinet but no television or radio. I shared the family bathroom and dutifully came down to the dining room at mealtimes. My hosts were lovely people but I almost felt like a prisoner. Here I was - one of the country's most expensive footballers - living like a hermit in an upstairs bed-sit. The nearest Chelsea player to me was Joe Fascione and he lived 30 minutes away in Wandsworth. I was driven to distraction. I became so bored that, just to get out of the confines of the house, I would wander down to sit on a park bench by the pond in Barnes Common. But even the aquatic delights of the common became a little tedious after a while and, this is not meant to be an excuse, I was driven to going out on the town up to three nights a week. I'd wander down the King's Road and Old Kent Road and basically go into bars and sink a few *sherbets* just to enjoy some company. I remember listening to a young female singer at one particular club I used to frequent. I thought she was fantastic and a few years later she made a very famous single called 'Wheels on Fire'. Her name was Julie Driscoll. As a young professional footballer, this was not the ideal way to develop my career but I defy any young 20-year-old in London at the height of the sixties, unless they are a trappist monk, to sit in a room staring at four walls night after night.

Even to this day those early times in Sheffield and London live vividly in my mind. It amazes me that football clubs should invest such large sums of money on players and then dump them somewhere and take very little interest in their welfare. Take any young man and put him in new surroundings and he will need help to adjust to his new life. Just because a player has cost five million pounds does not mean he can cope any more easily with the change. I know from watching players arrive at Leicester City over the past 20 years that quite a few had their problems settling in. It

makes common sense to me for clubs to take those extra few strides to ensure their players are happy at home and are given every assistance they require away from the training ground, particularly when you are a single guy. My old Blades boss John Harris always used to like his players to get married at an early age. It's a philosophy that many Premiership managers still preach these days. "Get married early and you'll settle down and feel part of the community and not be going out every night," he used to say. Well, I did take his advice by getting married nine months after I first moved to Chelsea but those first few months were far from easy to endure away from the football pitch.

■ **HAVE WHEELS, WILL TRAVEL:** Here's the Birch proudly posing on his soft-top Triumph Spitfire after completing my £100,000 move to Chelsea. In those days a Spitfire held a fair amount of street cred although the car certainly hadn't helped my sense of direction. I got lost en route to Stamford Bridge from Sheffield and arrived late for my very first training session.

Indeed, I made a less than auspicious start on my first day with the London club. Travelling down to Stamford Bridge in my soft-top Triumph Spitfire, I quickly fell foul of the London traffic system. On all my previous visits to the Bridge, I had been on a team bus when you were either playing cards or concentrating on the game ahead. So, hopelessly lost, I wound down the window and asked the first person I could see for directions. He turned out to be a Chelsea fan and market stall holder plying his goods outside the World's End pub. Quick as a flash he recognised me and shouted out: "You're the new signing, aren't you?". "Yes I am," I replied rather proudly. "You're a centre forward and can't find Stamford Bridge. Not much chance of you finding the

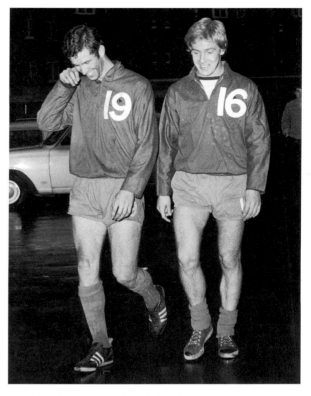

■ **I'M STILL STANDING** ...but only just. I enjoy a nervous laugh with strike partner Peter Osgood on my way back from my first training session on the concrete forecourt underneath the main stand at Stamford Bridge. Ossie congratulates me on the way I didn't react to an 'assault' by Chopper Harris. React? I should be so lucky, I was barely conscious.

back of the net, is there?" he quipped. "Any road, mate, go down this road for 100 yards and the ground is on your left." Welcome to Stamford Bridge, you might say.

Things, however, were destined only to worsen. As a result of getting lost en route, I arrived a few minutes late and had to hastily get changed for my first training session. Chelsea normally trained at their Mitcham training headquarters but on the day before a game the session was always held at Stamford Bridge. Today was a Friday and I was to meet up with Peter Osgood, Eddie McCreadie, Ron Harris, John Hollins and Peter Bonetti for the first time. I must confess to being in awe of them. I donned my training gear and as we walked out of the changing room I couldn't believe my eyes. That's when it dawned on me I had finally arrived. I found myself walking down with Ossie and he warned me to be careful. I didn't take much notice.

At this stage, you should forget all of today's high-tech training facilities. There were no indoor gymnasiums or astro-turf pitches. Our training session was to take place on the concrete forecourt underneath one of the stands. I remember seeing these massive steel girders jutting out from the ground at a 45 degree angle and thinking to myself "that could be dangerous". Dave Sexton threw me a bib and we proceeded to play an eight-a-side practice game. We'd done something similar at Sheffield United but in professional football these are looked upon as non-contact games for fear of injuring players for the following day's match. Thirty seconds into the game Peter Bonetti collected a cross, spotted me 30 yards away and threw the ball out to me. As the ball arrowed towards me I remember thinking that I had to make my first touch an impressive one.

The next thing that happened was that 'Chopper' Harris whacked me from behind, put me 12 feet into the air and sent me crashing to the concrete. I was unconscious for about 10 to 15 seconds before I groggily came around to be greeted by the sight of Chopper, or 'Buller' as most of the lads called him, bending over me. "Welcome to the Bridge, Birch, but

■ **SWEET 16:** I was awarded the number 16 for my training kit at Stamford Bridge. Why? I dunno, probably because the number 15 had already gone.

you still ain't on more money than me, you bastard," was Ron's immortal opening line. I dragged myself up and looked across to Dave Sexton and Ron Stuart expecting them to be highly concerned about the plight of their new big signing. Not a bit of it. They were laughing and joking like nothing had happened.

For the rest of the session I watched in amazement as everyone proceed to kick lumps out of each other. Charlie Cooke jumped 12 foot to avoid another Chopper tackle. I swear that Chopper even whacked the iron girders twice. As I walked back to the dressing room at the end of the session, I chatted with Ossie again. "You did really well there, Birch," he said. I looked at him quizzically. "If you'd jumped up and retaliated, Ron would have made your life a misery." "Retaliate?" I said, "I was out semi-bloody-conscious. I didn't even know where I was."

WARMING UP: My home debut against West Bromwich Albion, however, was to turn out to be a nightmare. We crashed 3-0 in front of just over 27,000 fans.

If you're wondering why Ron took such an immediate interest in my financial affairs, I'd better explain. Ron enjoyed more than a passing interest in other players' wages and, as I was to subsequently discover, he always knew what everyone else was earning. Allegedly, Ron was not averse to popping into the club offices and rifling through a few drawers to check out players' contracts. For the record - as Ron already knows - I was on £60 a week plus bonuses. Mind you, I never knew what Ron was earning... and I certainly wasn't going to complain if he was getting more. Ron's parents also used

■ **BEWARE THE IDES OF MARCH:** A chilly March morning in 1968 and I'm left to practise a few of my silky skills at an empty Stamford Bridge. I'd spent the previous two days in bed with a throat infection and Dave Sexton didn't want me to pass on the illness to the rest of the squad. He need not have worried... I would have mis-hit it anyway.

to pull the strings when it came to the running of the players' bar. They were responsible for the issuing of tickets so if you needed any extras it was always advisable to stay on the right side of him. Thankfully I did.

After such an eventful opening morning, we hopped on a train to travel up to Sunderland for my League debut for the Blues. At Sheffield United only the directors travelled first class but here the players sampled the high life as well. I was fortunate to make a winning start and get on the scoresheet as well. Peter Houseman broke down the flank, cut the ball back from the corner flag and I managed to steer the ball past Jim Montgomery for the opening goal in a 3-2 victory. Sunderland contained such greats as Jim Baxter and Charlie Hurley and it was a fantastic place to go and win at on your debut

Chelsea was not only a footballing hot-bed but the sporting showbiz capital of the country. I lost count of the number of Hollywood celebrities and English show-biz stars who were introduced to us. Chelsea, you understand, was the place to be seen. Like all clubs, we had a players' bar which ought to have been named the celebrity bar. On the domestic front the biggest disc jockeys of the era, Tony Blackburn and

■ **SWINGING IN THE SIXTIES**: I like to think that the Birch has always been something of a fashion icon (or should that be victim). Put together the swinging sixties and the Kings Road and you had a pretty fashionable combination. All the lads used to spend a few quid on a nice whistle. I'm feeling the quality of Peter Osgood's dark grey ensemble. I opted for a light grey number with matching silk tie and handkerchief. John Boyle cuts a pretty picture in a black two-piece.

■ **GOODISON DEFEAT:** I'm outnumbered here as Everton 'keeper Gordon West collects a cross during our 2-1 defeat on Merseyside in front of 47,000 fans in April 1968. On the right is Brian Labone but, left, take a look at the remarkable sight of Howard Kendall with a full head of hair (or is it a syrup?).

Ed Stewart, were regulars. Film and television stars Susan George and Joanna Lumley were always most welcome visitors, for obvious reasons.

But even our home-grown talent was eclipsed by the array of silver-screen stars which Dickie Attenborough brought to the club on an almost weekly basis. Stamford Bridge was akin to an English equivalent of the Oscars for star-spotting. Dickie 'Darling' was a typical 'luvvie' actor but he really enjoyed his football and I always found him to be a genuinely enthusiastic guy. Let's just be kind, however, and say that Dickie did not fully understand the normal etiquette of a match-day.

In the final half an hour before a game, the dressing room is sacrosanct. Players go into their own little world and prepare for the object of their entire working week. Our preparations would be routinely interrupted by a polite knock on the door. "Dave, is it all right if I bring in a guest to meet the lads," Dickie would enquire very

■ **LONDON DERBY:** It's Highbury, November 23, 1968. Peter Osgood (left) watches as Arsenal 'keeper and now television presenter Bob Wilson obligingly misses the cross for me to climb above Gunners defender Ian Ure and head goalwards. We won 1-0 in front of 45,588 fans courtesy of a goal from Peter Houseman.

politely of our manager Dave Sexton. Dave used to be livid but he didn't really have the heart to tell Dickie to go forth and multiply. In then would walk the latest big-name Hollywood star to be in London for a flying visit; Steve McQueen, John Wayne, Paul Newman, Robert Redford and Dustin Hoffman were all introduced to the lads. However, Dave Sexton was reduced to boiling point on one particular Saturday afternoon when we were playing Manchester United in front of a 55,000 capacity crowd and in walked Raquel Welch.

Even now she's still a stunner, but 30 years ago she was an absolute darling and probably the hottest female on the planet. She wore a mini-dress, high heels and a tight jumper which covered up her ample *borussias*. We must have looked a rag-tag bunch to her. Marvin 'Mavs' Hinton was in his customary position astride the 'bog' reading the programme with the door open. Chopper Harris was striding around in his jock-strap. Dickie patiently introduced Raquel to all of us. I was number 10 and

Ossie was nine so we were getting changed next to each other. I said a very polite hello but I noticed that Raquel was clocking Ossie. Now Ossie was a real athlete - six feet three inches tall with a physique to die for. Dickie explained that this was the man they called 'the King'. They had a brief conversation before Raquel turned out of the door and left us all to cool down a little.

The story is not over yet. With Chopper marking George Best out of the game, the match was hardly a classic. Midway through the second half a massive cheer went around the stadium. It was for Raquel who had decided to go for a stroll around the perimeter of the pitch.

In terms of male icons, Steve McQueen was on a similar plateau but he was a very unassuming guy. Unsure of the etiquette and not wishing to barge in, he stood by the dressing room entrance and casually reached for a packet of cigarettes. Closest to him was Eddie McCreadie who just happened to be one of the biggest smokers in the team. He dived into his suit pocket and produced a lighter for the Hollywood film legend. "Thanks," said Steve and proceeded to offer Eddie a ciggie just 15 minutes before kick off. Eddie was tempted but politely declined. As he said afterwards, he should have taken the cigarette and framed it.

■ **NICE ONE, LUVVIE:** Richard Attenborough shares a joke with David Webb in the dressing room. Dickie was a regular visitor and would bring with him a bevy of world-famous movie stars such as Raquel Welch, Steve McQueen and Paul Newman. Life was never dull before a game at Stamford Bridge. One of the biggest topics of conversation was who would Dickie bring in rather than which team you happened to be playing that afternoon.

Looking back now, it all seems so incredible. In truth, the Americans knew absolutely nothing about our football, and they didn't know us from Adam. They were into American Football and baseball. So, you had this nervous stand-off where they were famous in their world and we were famous in ours. We'd shake hands and exchange polite pleasantries, both parties no doubt feeling a little self-conscious. Because we were on our territory, I can't ever remember any of us asking for their autographs. They had come to see us and our own egos meant we felt we couldn't ask them, even though we considered them gods of the silver screen.

To this day, I've always felt you should judge everyone the same, regardless of their fame or wealth. I like to think I am as comfortable in the company of a managing director as I am a roadsweeper. People don't really faze me and perhaps the opportunity of meeting some of the world's most famous people at such an early age helped me formulate that viewpoint.

Throughout my three seasons at Chelsea, the club was destined to win an FA Cup final and never finish outside the top six. In my first season we ended sixth, went one better in 1968-69 to finish fifth, culminating in our cup-winning campaign when we also came third in Division One. One of the most popular criticisms levelled at Chelsea has been that the club lacks any real consistency. Flamboyant is the adjective which readily springs to mind when describing the club. Chelsea sides have invariably played with a fantastic amount of skill and this team was no exception.

One of the most outrageously talented was Charlie Cooke but he did have this annoying habit of calling everyone a 'diddy'. I'm not aware that it had anything to do with Ken Dodd and the mythical little dwarves from Liverpool. I believe it's a Scottish slang word and whenever Charlie was upset he'd dismiss you as a 'diddy'.

His best mate was journalist Hugh McIlvaney. They used to spend so much time together after training that I thought they were brothers. I also laboured for six months under the false impression that Charlie was the most obsessive trainer at the club. No matter how early I arrived at Mitcham training ground, Charlie's green Jaguar would always be in the car park. I asked Ossie about this and he laughingly told me to take a look in the back of the car. One day I took a peek inside and noticed a rail across the back seat with a whole range of changes of clothing. Apparently, Charlie would go out on the beer but rather than go home he would stagger back to the car at the training ground and kip down there for the night to ensure he wasn't late.

Peter Bonetti was a tremendous goalkeeping talent. Throughout my career I was fortunate enough to play in front of some truly great 'keepers and I quickly realised

■ **ROLL OUT THE BARROW:** Don't think that it's just the modern-day players who have to do the silly posed photographs for the tabloids. We were at it years ago. From left to right, Peter Bonetti, Bobby Tambling, Marvin Hinton and yours truly line up for an FA Cup photocall.

that a good goalie was the bedrock of any successful team. 'The Cat' was England number two behind Gordon Banks and although he was only three stone dripping wet his agility and grace was superb. Like many goalkeepers, he was rather quiet off the pitch and was not one of the great socialisers at the club.

The same, however, could not be said for Ron Harris. 'Chopper' was one of the legendary hard-men of the game but he had a tremendous footballing brain that was not always fully appreciated. Ossie once told me how Ron liked to play the percentages. Ron hardly missed any games through injury which, given his full-blooded approach, was little short of miraculous. But he would go in for real heavyweight challenges when the odds were stacked in his favour. He'd prefer a 60-40 or, even better, a 70-30. Ron knew that an awful lot of players were desperate to 'do' him because he had done them, so he always tried to stay one step ahead... and very successfully he did it too.

Johnny Hollins impressed me tremendously. He was one of the fittest players at the club and would regularly run past me on a forward run from midfield. He'd also very quickly go past me again on his way back into position. We used to call him Dave Sexton's love child because of his wholesome image. His nickname was Ena but what a fantastic player.

JOHNNY HOLLINS: He was one of the fittest players at the club. We used to call him Dave Sexton's love-child because of his wholesome image.

But, wherever you looked, the side was brimming with skill, and not just a fancy flick or two; the lads had great presence, great footballing minds. We could mix it or we could play it. We always had a few options on how to play the game. Eddie McCreadie, however, had one major flaw to his game - he was as blind as a bat. Eddie, rather unfairly, developed a reputation as a bit of a hard-man. There was nothing malicious in his tackles, they were just late... especially at night. During the day he wore glasses, and in the sixties was one of the first players to play with contact lenses. Floodlights then were not as powerful as they are now and in night matches Eddie had terrible problems seeing the ball. The end result was he spent more of the time kicking the opposition than he did the ball.

Arguably one of the very first names on Dave Sexton's team-sheet was Peter 'Nobby' Houseman. Nobby was a truly great crosser of a ball and a really nice guy. A quiet family man, you could spend a day in Peter's company and not hear him say more than two words.

CHELSEA FC 1968-69: Back row (left to right) Thomson, Boyle, Hollins, Bonetti, Webb, Hughes, Harris, Hinton, McCreadie; (front row) Cooke, Birchenall, Baldwin, Osgood, Houseman Tambling, Houston.

PETER OSGOOD had fantastic skill but hated training - especially when it came to going out on a run!

And, of course, there was the king himself, Peter Osgood. Ossie was supremely confident both on and off the pitch. Indeed, you would probably describe it as arrogance. For a big man, he had fantastic skill and a real presence. Like many great players, he did not suffer fools gladly and although not deliberate he might give the impression that he was looking down on you. There was a perceived arrogance about him, but I think that was part of his make-up and it helped make him the player he was. Ossie brought other players into the game so effectively as well as being a great finisher. Rodney Marsh was another of that era who had fantastic skill but was seen as a very strong-minded player.

Ossie did have one fundamental weakness. He hated training and absolutely despised running. There was one famous occasion when we were travelling back home together on a Friday after training. Ossie had been dropped for the following day's game and I was so embarrassed I didn't know what to say. Ossie had more skill in his little finger than I had in the whole of my body but I was in the team and he wasn't. "Birch," he said, "I wish I had your engine and could run like you." I was gobsmacked.

Ossie and running did not go hand in hand. As part of our pre-season fitness work, we went to Epsom Downs racecourse once a week for running practice and we'd have a timed run around the course. I don't know how far but it certainly seemed a long way. Off we galloped and invariably John Hollins and Peter Bonetti would hare off in front. I always made a point of staying in the middle of the pack for tactical reasons. Go up front and you would be expected to stay there every week, languish at the back and you'd be expected to improve, but stay in the middle and no-one would pay you much attention. Off the pace bringing up the rear would always be Ossie, Ian Hutchinson and Marvin Hinton. The early finishers would be cooling down on the bus when we arrived back and waiting for the stragglers to come home seemed like an eternity. It used to annoy The Cat and Ena immensely but they daren't complain when Ossie and Co limped home as if they had been out for a casual Sunday stroll.

One week Dave Sexton decided enough was enough. He told Ossie that if he finished last again the whole squad would come back for afternoon training. This was a serious threat. There were snooker games arranged, trips to the bookies or the prospect of watching the girls go by over pie and beans in the Markham Arms pub on the King's Road. We couldn't afford to lose that. I had a word with Ossie but he was playing his cards very close to his chest. "Gonna try properly now, are we?" I queried. "We'll see, Birch," he replied. I didn't hold out much hope and, sure enough, as we got ready for our Epsom Downs run the three main groups soon emerged.

The Cat and Ena raced out in front, I was in the middle of the main pack and Hutchinson, Mavs and Ossie brought up the field. Assistant manager Ron Stuart hid himself in the bushes half-way around and waylaid the trailing three. Mavs and Hutchinson managed to conjure a gallop and catch up with the pack.

Ossie, though, was nowhere to be seen. We turned into the home straight around Tattenham Corner fearing the worst. All of a sudden we heard this clumping of hooves and presumed some of the horses were still out on the gallops. We turned to look over our shoulders and there was Ossie, astride a thoroughbred racehorse, thundering past us two furlongs out. "Won't be last today, lads!" he shouted as the mighty beast flashed by us.

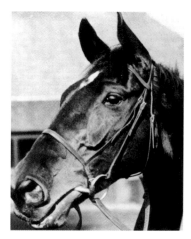

■ Ossie's thoroughbred has just spotted his jockey for the day!

Poor Dave Sexton didn't know whether to laugh or cry. Crafty Ossie had spoken with Peter Walwyn, one of his horse-racing friends. Peter had agreed to bring down a horse and hide him in bushes around the back of Tattenham Corner. While our backs were turned, Ossie darted off the track, mounted the horse and cantered by us. Thankfully, Dave saw the funny side and let us off that afternoon training threat.

■ **ACROBATICS:** One of the first examples of the bicycle kick in the modern English game (top).
Manchester City 'keeper Joe Corrigan is rooted to the spot as I send this effort over an empty net in a
goalless draw at Maine Road in September 1969.

■ **WHERE'S THE BALL?** I'm on a collision course with Stoke's England international Gordon Banks at the
Victoria Ground in October 1968 (above). In years to come the two of us were to play in the same Leicester
City geriatric XI but on this day Gordon had the last laugh as the Midlands boys ran out 2-0 winners.

■ **HOBBLING OFF:** I knew Nottingham Forest would always get their revenge. I turned down the chance to join the club as a youngster because of my allegiances to Notts County. So the Reds' back four exacted retribution with a crunching challenge which led to me being shouldered off in this First Division game at Stamford Bridge (left).

■ **ORDER, PLEASE:** What a shock, a Chelsea v Leeds game in which tempers flared (above). It could have been just about any encounter between the two clubs during my three years at Stamford Bridge. Tempers flared and the blood boiled as you can see from this 20-man melee. I'm trying to stay on the fringes in my number nine shirt. Not unsurprisingly, Ron Harris is at the centre of it all. The busiest people in these games were the two physios and the referee.

■ **MIND THE BOUFFANT:** With a swift glance I head the ball goalward against Southampton at the Dell in 1969, just ahead of Saints long-serving star John Sydenham.

■ **WALL OF SILENCE:** (Above) Recognise the face in the Arsenal shirt immediately to my right? Why, it's none other than George Graham. I always afford myself a wry smile when I hear George being described as a strict disciplinarian. I can't say that's the adjective which immediately springs to mind when we went out on the town together in London. How times change. This was a good day because I larruped in a couple of goals as we ran out convincing 3-0 winners in Division One action at Stamford Bridge in September 1969.

■ **CHELSEA PALACE:** Here we are in action against Crystal Palace at Stamford Bridge in August 1969 (right). I'm jumping for the ball with John Loughlan. Looking on is Dave Webb.

■ **BOBBY'S NUMBER ONE:** For me, not only was Bobby Moore one of the greatest footballers this country has ever produced, he was also one of the finest gentlemen ever to play the game. In this photo (below), he calmly dispossesses me in a Chelsea v West Ham First Division fixture (nothing new here, then). But what will always remain in my mind was in incident a couple of days after the birth of my daughter Laura. The first game after the happy arrival was against the Hammers. I dropped back for a corner and up came Bobby. As we jostled for position, Bobby very politely said to me: "I'd like to congratulate you on the birth of your daughter. "I was stunned. "Thank you very much," I said. A split second later he lost me completely and almost scored from the corner.

As a young player it is always easy to take everything in your career for granted. Your health certainly falls into that category. During my first six seasons in the professional game I had missed less than ten matches through injury. Sadly, however, it was to catch up with me at the worst possible time as Chelsea lifted the FA Cup in 1970 with their epic two-game defeat of arch-rivals Leeds. A series of knee problems meant I missed well over half the season and the opportunity to collect my only cup winners' medal. It taught me a salutary lesson and I will never forget the frustrations I had to endure that season.

Firstly, though, I must pay tribute to all the Chelsea players for the way they made me feel part of the team. I was involved in the cup final song (maybe that was not such a good idea!), the players' pool, and cup final events. I even took a place in the dug-out for matches.

My problems began back in October of the campaign when I suffered a persistent knee problem that would not subside. I kept getting a build-up of fluid inside the knee but in those days there was no such thing as MRI scans and basically it was your word

against the physio as to the extent of the problem. I missed out on a total of 15 First Division matches as Chelsea marched into the semi finals of the FA Cup with a date against Watford. I finally managed to get myself right and Dave Sexton told me I could still grab a starting place back in time for the final.

INJURY NIGHTMARE: One of the worst times of my whole career was having to sit out the 1970 FA Cup run. A gashed knee put me out for six weeks and I was never able to force my way back into the team for the finals with Leeds United.

We were playing Newcastle at Stamford Bridge and I went up for a cross with the opposition goalkeeper Ian McFaul. After the challenge, I got up and spun away only to feel a strange sensation in my knee. I looked down and saw this horrific gash across the top of my kneecap. There was no real pain but the blood was pumping out so I sat down and waited for trainer Harry Medhurst to come onto the pitch. I was carried off and taken to the medical room.

Apparently, as I subsequently found out, the goalkeeper's studs had ripped open the knee. In those days we all used to wear nylon studs which often chafed on concrete dressing room tunnel floors causing them to become very sharp. I was feeling rather sorry for myself because I knew my chances of being involved in the FA Cup were now almost non-existent. Blood was still spurting out but the doctor told me he could not give me an anaesthetic because I had drunk a pint of milk before the game. Instead, he gave me two rolled-up bandages and told me: "Grip onto these, son." There was still mud in the open wound as he proceeded to grab the two flaps of skin either side of the three inch gash and put in a couple of stitches to hold it all together until the ambulance arrived.

I was taken to St Stephens Hospital, still wearing my blood-spattered blue shirt and shorts, although my boots and socks had been taken off by this time. I waited outside the operating theatre for an hour and, as the game had been a night match, it was now nearly midnight. Two surgeons arrived and proceeded to ask me if I minded whether a group of student doctors came in and watched them perform the surgery. "No, I bloody well don't as long as you get on with it pronto," I replied. I was asked again about what I had to drink and they reluctantly agreed to give me a local anaesthetic, although normally the surgery would have been done under a general.

Here I was, prostrate on an operating table being studied by a group of student doctors who had somehow been assembled at an hour's notice at midnight. As the surgeons carried out the repair-work they commented on how unusual it was to find such clear muscle definition in the legs. "This is a typical athlete's quad. That's why it is so hard to pull the skin together because of the muscle development," the surgeon told the students. I couldn't believe what I was hearing. I needed a total of 40 stitches and the surgery lasted approximately an hour before I was transferred to an open ward.

On the following morning, I woke up with a pretty painful knee. A young lady physiotherapist introduced herself and explained she would be working on my rehab. I was more than a little surprised, especially when she said the stretching started immediately. I thought she was joking and had visions of all the stitches popping out. However, she was most insistent and I was made to shuffle down to

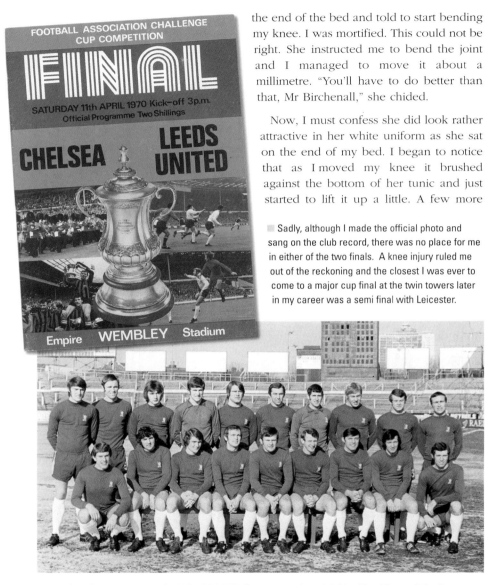

the end of the bed and told to start bending my knee. I was mortified. This could not be right. She instructed me to bend the joint and I managed to move it about a millimetre. "You'll have to do better than that, Mr Birchenall," she chided.

Now, I must confess she did look rather attractive in her white uniform as she sat on the end of my bed. I began to notice that as I moved my knee it brushed against the bottom of her tunic and just started to lift it up a little. A few more

▦ Sadly, although I made the official photo and sang on the club record, there was no place for me in either of the two finals. A knee injury ruled me out of the reckoning and the closest I was ever to come to a major cup final at the twin towers later in my career was a semi final with Leicester.

▦ **CHELSEA'S CUP FINAL TEAM GROUP PHOTO:** (back row, left to right) Ian Hutchinson, John Dempsey, Alan Hudson, Tommy Hughes, David Webb, Marvin Hinton, Peter Bonetti, Alan Birchenall, Eddie McCreadie, Ron Harris; (front row) Stewart Houston, Paddy Mulligan, Charlie Cooke, Tommy Baldwin, John Hollins, Peter Houseman, Bobby Tambling, John Boyle, Peter Osgood.

bends and I was now beginning to get a glimpse of her stocking tops. Whether this was very clever psychology on her part I'm not sure, but it certainly got me and my rehab going. My knee was soon going ten to the dozen. She came every morning for a couple of weeks and I never looked forward as much to getting up.

I was in hospital for almost three weeks and my stay was like something from a 'Carry On Doctor' film. In one of my first nights as a patient, the partitions were drawn around the next bed. I heard moaning and groaning and then the headboard started rattling against the wall. No, you dirty lot, it isn't what you are thinking. There was a drug abuse case in the bed and he had been handcuffed to the head-rest for his own safety. After nodding off to sleep, I was awakened by an almighty commotion. Police were everywhere, sirens were wailing and everyone was running around like headless chickens. "What happened?" I asked. "He's escaped," I was told. To this day I don't know how he managed it but at least his successor was a little quieter.

Mind you, I was responsible for keeping the ward awake on more than one occasion. After an away game, all the Chelsea lads came back to the hospital and, armed with a crate of beers, sat down on my bed and proceeded to watch Match of the Day, a programme that in those days was still very much in its infancy. The nurses were none too pleased at having to collect the empties but they turned a blind eye to our drinking.

I worked hard on my fitness but it was always an uphill battle. I did manage comeback games against Tottenham and Burnley either side of the two finals but was not included in either of the cup final teams. Ian Hutchinson had done tremendously well in my absence up front with Ossie and I was short of any real match practice.

In those days you were allowed only one sub so I did not even get on the bench. In the modern era with five subs I might have been one of those but it is not something I want to torture myself with. I felt as sorry for my mum and dad as I did for myself. They had watched me all those years from parks pitches playing for Nottingham Boys all the way through the professional ranks but they were to be denied a chance of seeing me in an FA Cup final at Wembley.

My own personal memories of the first game at Wembley were that the occasion was marred a little by the state of the famous Cumbrian turf. The Horse of the Year Show had been staged there a few days earlier and there were huge divots on the surface. In the second game, it was a case of the survival of the fittest. Leeds could really put it about and we had lads who knew how to look after themselves. A Premiership referee recently studied the 'X'-rated replay video and said that, applying today's rules, there would only have been three players left on the pitch at the end of the game.

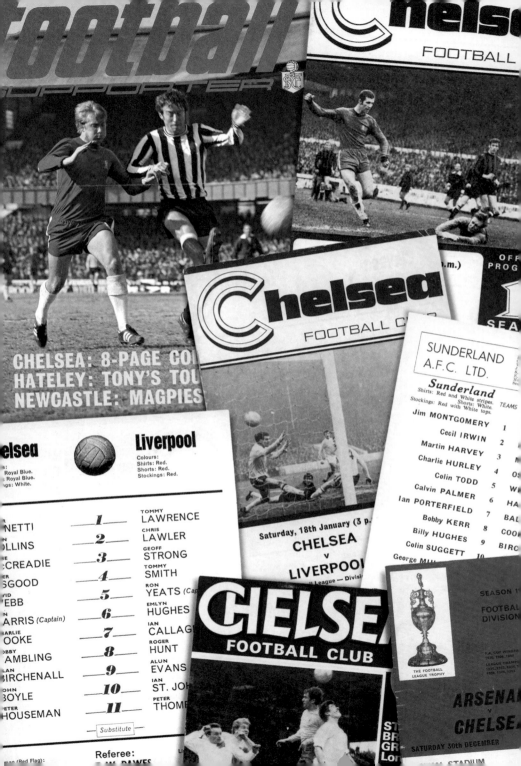

football
SUPPORTER

CHELSEA: 8-PAGE CO[LOUR]
HATELEY: TONY'S TOU[R]
NEWCASTLE: MAGPIES

Chelsea
FOOTBALL

Chelsea
FOOTBALL C[LUB]

[Ch]elsea • **Liverpool**

Colours:
[...] Royal Blue.
[...] Royal Blue.
[...]gs: White.

Colours:
Shirts: Red.
Shorts: Red.
Stockings: Red.

[...]NETTI	_1_	TOMMY LAWRENCE	
[...]LLINS	_2_	CHRIS LAWLER	
[...]CREADIE	_3_	GEOFF STRONG	
[...]SGOOD	_4_	TOMMY SMITH	
[...]VID [...]EBB	_5_	RON YEATS (Cap[t])	
[...]N [...]ARRIS (Captain)	_6_	EMLYN HUGHES	
[...]HARLIE [...]OOKE	_7_	IAN CALLAG[HAN]	
[...]BBY [...]AMBLING	_8_	ROGER HUNT	
[...]LAN [...]IRCHENALL	_9_	ALUN EVANS	
[...]HN [...]OYLE	_10_	IAN ST. JO[HN]	
[...]ETER [...]HOUSEMAN	_11_	PETER THOMP[SON]	
	Substitute		

Referee:
[...] W. DAWES

[...]en (Red Flag)

Saturday, 18th January (3 p.[m.)
CHELSEA
v
LIVERPOOL
[...]ll League — Divisi[on]

SUNDERLAND A.F.C. LTD.

Sunderland
Shirts: Red and White stripes.   TEAMS
Shorts: White.
Stockings: Red with White tops.

Jim MONTGOMERY	1	
Cecil IRWIN	2	N[...]
Martin HARVEY	3	O[...]
Charlie HURLEY	4	OS[...]
Colin TODD	5	W[...]
Calvin PALMER	6	HA[...]
Ian PORTERFIELD	7	BAL[...]
Bobby KERR	8	COO[...]
Billy HUGHES	9	BIRC[...]
Colin SUGGETT	10	
George MIL[...]		

(n.m.)
OFF[ICIAL]
PROG[RAMME]
SEA[SON]

CHELSEA
FOOTBALL CLUB

THE FOOTBALL
LEAGUE TROPHY

SEASON 1[...]
FOOTBALL
DIVISION

F.A. CUP WINNER
[...]
LEAGUE CHAMP[...]
[...]

ARSENAL
v
CHELSEA
SATURDAY 30th DECEMBER
[...]AM STADIUM

ST[...]
BR[...]
GR[...]
Lon[...]

Although the final was an extreme case, it was typical of what went on in those days. As the old saying goes, no quarter was asked for and none was given. As a striker, I knew that the first time the ball came to me in a game I was going to be crunched from behind. It was mandatory and you were expected to get up and carry on with the job. It was like a tester. Nowadays you have to be face to face to get away with any sort of tackle but the fans loved it.

I was talking to Ron Harris recently and asked him how he would fare in the modern era. "I'd miss three games Birch and be in for one, miss another three games and be in for one," he explained. Chopper was so hard he made Vinnie Jones look like Dale Winton but that approach was the norm. Every side had one and, in a perverse way, it almost bred skilful players. Crikey, you had to have bags of skill to avoid being crunched. And, for all those terrible tackles, how many players had their careers brought to a premature end? Certainly no more than suffer a similar fate in the modern game, I'll wager.

Come to think of it, I suffered my fair share of cup disappointment while I was at the Bridge. For the club, unquestionably the biggest blow was our performance in the Fairs Cup in my second season there. We all eagerly awaited the first round draw. Would it be Real Madrid or Juventus, Ajax or Bayern Munich? No, out of the hat came a trip over Hadrian's Wall to face Morton. At least I had the consolation of scoring in both games and the trip to Morton brought me into contact with Alex Ferguson for the first time.

He was an interested spectator and was subsequently to make a move for me and Lenny Glover later in my career at Leicester (at least, his judgement in players has improved with age!). In the second round we were drawn against Dutch side DWS Amsterdam but after two goalless draws we were eliminated on the toss of a coin.

As you're no doubt realising by now the Birch is struggling to recall too many individual games. However, there are the occasional matches which stick in the memory cells, mainly for the wrong reasons. A trip to Manchester United in my first full season is one which falls into that category. We had travelled up by train and

■ **FRONT PAGE NEWS:** It's not just in the modern game that there are plenty of football magazines around. Back in the sixties and seventies we had our fair share too. Football Supporter was clearly struggling for its August 1969 edition because they put Newcastle defender Frank Clark and me on the front cover....

....also reproduced are a selection of programmes including one from my Chelsea debut at Sunderland.

booked into the Grand Hotel on a Friday evening. Dinner was followed by a customary constitutional stroll for 20 minutes. I guess I should have realised something was wrong when we made our way to the revolving doors.

Trainer Norman Medhurst, nicknamed Tinks because of his jug-ears (he looked like he had been loaned out of a trophy cabinet), stretched his arms out wide and pleaded with Ossie not to go out onto the road. Ossie ignored him and together with me, Charlie Cooke, Tommy Baldwin, John Boyle, Marvin Hinton and Joe Fascione we set off. I innocently did some window-shopping while the rest of the crowd marched on ahead of us. Suddenly they disappeared into a building illuminated with a neon sign that read 'Mecca'. It certainly wasn't the religious establishment. No, it was the very trendy Locarno night club. Ossie waved me over and my jaw dropped. I knew I had a decision to make but Ossie shouted: "I've already got your ticket."

Here I am on a Friday night on the eve of one of our biggest games of the season and I'm going into a nightclub. It was the first time I'd ever done it and I was scared stiff. Ossie and the lads went straight to the bar and I ordered myself a pint of shandy. The rest of the group went off on a *Buffalo Bill Cody* leaving me on my own propping up the bar. A guy came up to me and shouted out: "Are we going to win tomorrow, Birch?" I didn't know where to look and mumbled a few words. "Well, we've got no chance have we? You getting sloshed and Ossie and the rest in all four corners of this club." The only thing that didn't quite add up was that the guy was speaking in a northern accent. I looked up and my eyes were immediately drawn to a little lapel badge which screamed out at me: Northern branch of the Chelsea Supporters' Club. He was the chairman and I was aghast at what he must have thought of me.

Joe Fascione came back to join me and we slid out and raced back to the hotel. Just as we came through the doors, Harry Medhurst pounced on us. "Get to bed! Where's the rest of them?" he shrieked. I protested I had no idea and dashed off to my room although I found it difficult to go to sleep immediately because I felt so guilty. A few hours later there was a banging on my door and it was Ossie and 'Sponge' Baldwin. "Let me in," shouted Ossie, "You'll have to go to Ena's room because me and Sponge are sleeping here." I was too tired to argue so I got out of bed and made a dash across the landing to room with John Hollins who had been tucked up in bed for the last 11 hours.

At breakfast there were a few sheepish looks across the cornflakes and, though I can't be sure, I think Dave Sexton had a fair idea the lads had been up to mischief. Onto the coach we got and I was feeling a little the worse for wear along with the rest of them. We were taking on a United side that included the likes of Best, Charlton and Law.

Unbelievably, early in the game, I let fly with a rasper from the edge of the penalty area to put us one goal up. Tommy Baldwin grabbed two and Bobby Tambling was also on the mark as we scored a quite incredible 4-0 victory to silence a 55,117 capacity crowd at Old Trafford. Easy game this football, isn't it? There has to be a moral to this story somewhere but I'm damned if I can work it out. Before you ask, it never happened again.

Anyway, that's enough of the football. The off-the-field stories are much more interesting... and I can remember them. There are more than a few to tell about my room-mate Peter Osgood. And, at this juncture, it's worth pointing out it was not just the showbiz set that was attracted to Chelsea. The Stamford Bridge club also had a few supporters from the other side of the law, if you know what I mean. The ones you don't mess with if you value your face and legs.

I lived in Ascot and Ossie lived in Windsor. Our local hostelry was the Queens Stag Hounds, a beautiful country pub run by a lovely landlady named Daisy. I spent many an enjoyable evening there, often in the company of a close friend, Tony Nutley. Tony was a Berkshire farmer who kept racing pigeons. He had no interest in football whatsoever and we often used to sit down and put the world to rights.

On one summer evening, two rather large gentlemen strode in. Wearing black Crombies, complete with silk handkerchiefs peeping from their top pockets, they exuded a certain presence and a menacing air. Their noses were squashed, one eye was higher than the other, they had teeth like dominoes and a few nasty-looking scars were etched across their foreheads. Their eyes settled on me and they came across. "Where's your mate?" they asked gruffly. "Who?" I replied. "Don't get funny. Where is he?" they insisted. At this juncture had I been wearing a nappy I would unquestionably have filled it. "You mean Ossie," I said timidly. "I've no idea." They signalled to me that I should pass on a message. I was certainly in no position to refuse. "Tell him he needs his legs for walking." With that, they were gone. Myself and Tony waited a few minutes to ensure the coast was clear. I had an inkling that Ossie was at a night meeting at Windsor races.

I drove down in my Daimler Jaguar and went to the main entrance. I asked to speak to Ossie and, sure enough, he was in the bar. He was a little surprised to see me because I wasn't a gambling man but wasted no time in offering me a drink. I explained I had to speak to him urgently. When I told him about my close encounter of the menacing kind, he turned ashen and instructed me to bring my car right up to the front door. As if in a spy film, he slipped into the back seat and disappeared from sight. Ossie lived two minute's away from the racecourse and as we turned into his road he told me to drive past and check the coast was clear. It was and we turned back up the road again. I slowed down and then saw Ossie move faster than at any point of his entire career. He disappeared up the drive into his house like a rat up a drainpipe. I tried ringing him later but the phone had been taken off the hook. The following morning I noticed he was not in for training. "Ossie's wife rang in and said he's not feeling well," Dave Sexton told me. To this day, I never did find out exactly what happened.

This was not my only brush with the underworld fraternity. I had arguably an even more scary experience after our European clash with DWS Amsterdam. It was a balmy autumn evening and we decided to stop off at the Lord Palmerston pub en route to one of our clubbing venues in Heathrow.

Because of the mild weather, we were in short-sleeves and I was propping up the bar with a pint minding my own business. "You were crap tonight," said a deep Cockney accent behind me. I turned around and vehemently agreed, for two reasons; firstly we had been rubbish and secondly this guy was as wide as he was tall. He was wearing a thick black Crombie overcoat, which I thought a shade unusual given that I was sweating in my short-sleeved shirt. I decided to change the topic of conversation and asked: "Aren't you a bit hot wearing that overcoat?" He gave me an icy stare and said: "Of course I am, but I've got to wear it." With that, he took a step back, pulled open the coat and beckoned me to look inside. I was mortified. I was now staring down the barrel of a sawn-off shotgun. He closed his coat and I beat a hasty retreat to see Ossie. Needless to say, we both rushed out of the pub.

We didn't think a great deal more about it until I picked up a paper the following day on the way back from training. Screaming headlines across the London Standard read: Gangland Shooting. A man, the article said, had been blasted in both legs in what had all the hallmarks of a gangland shooting. I can never be sure... but we certainly gave the Lord Palmerston a wide berth for a week or two.

Life was never dull for the Birch. Invariably more things have happened to me off the park. One of the most incredible has to be the tale of the confidence trickster who went around Ascot impersonating me. In those days, although many people had heard of me, there were few who recognised me face to face. There was no instant recognition because footballers were not the high-profile animals they have become. I may have been semi-recognised in Sheffield but, in the heart of Ascot, very few people knew the faces of professional footballers.

My problems started one day when I received a phone call from Ossie. "Ere, what you doing, Sherman? You owe £5 at Sunningdale Golf Club," he said. I had never been to Sunningdale in my life. I had never been a golfer. I insisted he had got the story wrong. A few weeks later he came round with his wife Rose to drop off some

A CASE OF MISTAKEN IDENTITY: Here's the photo I had to take around to a lady in Ascot to prove I was the real, one and only, Alan Birchenall. Unfortunately, an impostor went around impersonating me, and borrowed £400 to buy an engagement ring. The mother still didn't believe me and I had to contact the police to sort out the matter. Eventually the conman was caught and jailed. It could only happen to me.

eggs to the *tank commander*. "Why have you become engaged?" he asked, pulling me to one side. "No, I'm married. You've met the *tank commander* already," I replied. "No, you've also got engaged to another girl," repeated Ossie. "But why would I want to do that when I'm already married?" came my response. In a debate which assumed farcical proportions, Ossie went on to explain he had heard the story from his mum who lived in Windsor.

Apparently one of his mum's neighbours had boasted in the corner shop that her daughter had become engaged to the footballer Alan Birchenall. "Right," I said, "let's go around to her house and sort this out". Off we went and knocked on the neighbour's door. A woman answered and I asked whether she had a daughter who was marrying Alan Birchenall. "That's right," she said. "Well, I'm Alan Birchenall," I said. She delivered a fairly unequivocal reply:

MAKING THE NEWS: I was used to being in the headlines for scoring the occasional goal but not for being impersonated by a confidence trickster. Apparently, some geezer went around Thames Valley pretending to be me, stealing money and getting engaged to a local girl. Eventually the man was caught but not before I had some explaining to do to my real wife Heather.

"Piss off!" "Pardon?" was my token response. "Piss off!" she repeated aggressively. "And if you don't go now I'll call the police." I was more than a little taken aback by this response and walked back down the drive with Ossie.

THE IMPOSTER STORY MADE ALL THE PAPERS: Here's what the *Sunday Express* had to say on the matter on December 22.

To his thousands of fans and team colleagues, Chelsea's £100,000 star Alan Birchenall is a keen and dedicated footballer with only two interests in life, his career and his wife, Heather.

But to some people in the Thames Valley area where he lives he is a smooth-talking, beer-drinking confidence trickster who disappeared with a local girl leaving behind debts and angry former friends. Now police are investigating the case of the two footballers at the request of the real Alan Birchenall, for someone has been impersonating him. In a few weeks the mystery man has borrowed money claiming he was the footballer, signed autographs and even offered to give a talk to a school on team tactics. "If I ever catch up with this character he will wish he never started this business,' Mr Birchenall, 23-year-old former Sheffield United player told me at his home near Ascot, Berkshire. "I don't mind a bloke pretending to be me if he just wants to impress a new girlfriend at a dance or something. But this is different and has done my name a lot of harm". Mr Birchenall joined Chelsea in November last year. He married in June and moved into a pleasant modern detached house the next month. "Everything went well until about a fortnight ago. Then I got a phone call from my mate Peter Osgood who lives in Windsor. He said somebody had been impersonating me and people thought I had been going out with a girl and was going to marry her. I drove over to see Peter and we both went to see a friend of his where this chap had been staying. It was then that I heard what had

been going on and I was furious. This man was apparently an authority on Chelsea and knew my background well. I rang the police but I doubt if they will ever catch up with him." Peter Osgood, another Chelsea player and an under 23 international, told me: "Someone rang my mother and asked if Alan Birchenall was married. She said he was. Then this person said he could not be because he was going out with a girl and they were to be married." The woman the bogus footballer went out with is Eileen Evans, a former cinema cashier who lived with her parents in Bracknell. Her mother Ethel Evans said: "Eileen met this man in a pub in Bracknell where he was known as Alan Birchenall the footballer. He used to come around here nearly every day and his knowledge of football was exceptional. My husband, who is a keen fan, could not trip him. He was a smooth talker with lots of charm and nerve. He borrowed £25 off me. I took it out of the rent money I had saved. But he was always making excuses and when I asked about the money he said he had left his cheque book in his flat in Chelsea and was going to fetch it to repay me. He never did. My daughter was crazy about him and believed he was the Chelsea footballer. They were going to be married." Mr Harry Evans, Eileen's brother and a father of four, said: "He told me he had property in Bournemouth which he wanted me to decorate. He said he would give me £1,000 for the whole job. So, I packed my job in. Then he started making excuses and finally said the job would have to be postponed. Fortunately I got my job back but it cost me a week's wages, about £25. He had a nerve of iron." A police officer said: "We are investigating complaints about this man."

We agreed we'd go to Ossie's house, bring back the latest copy of the official Chelsea team photograph and demonstrate to the woman that I was the real Alan Birchenall. Half an hour later we returned. I unrolled the team photo and pointed to my *boat* but she still insisted it wasn't me. With that she slammed the door in our faces.

I was left with no alternative but to go to the police myself. I had to produce my driving licence and gas bill before the officers were satisfied and then we all marched round to the house for a third time. Eventually, the truth dawned on the woman. Her daughter was away for a few days with the impostor who had a flat in London. He had borrowed £400 off them to purchase an engagement ring, and had even signed the IOU 'Alan Birchenall'. Needless to say, the conman did a runner.

They eventually caught him some months later up in Birmingham after a string of scams across the Home Counties. He was six foot and blond but otherwise didn't look anything like me. What was particularly galling, however, was not the money. No, it was the sight of the daughter. Did anyone really think I would get engaged to a complete *clagthorpe* like that? Come to think of it, she was more of a *double doris clagthorpe*.

I fared little better in my first and only dealing with a soccer agent. In the late sixties only a handful of agents were operating, unlike the thousands currently flooding the new Millennium soccer market-place in the Premiership and Football League. As one of the very first six-figure transfers, I received a number of approaches and decided to work with a guy called Cyril Wayne.

One of my many failings is a general inability to remember names and faces, but in this particular instance the face of Cyril Wayne and his goatee beard is etched on my brain for the rest of my days and that memory will never diminish. I am unsure what happened to Cyril but if he is holed up on a desert island somewhere I sincerely hope this book gets washed up on the shore. And, even if all the other pages have been ravaged by the sea, I hope this one survives intact for him to peruse.

Cyril had some very plush offices in Gloucester Square, just around the corner from the American Embassy. For a while everything seemed to move along smoothly. I opened a few petrol stations, made some other personal appearances and even did some catalogue modelling. I suppose, as a young professional footballer, I was easily impressed but I should have smelled a rat on one of my first meetings with him.

Cyril took me to the Bag of Nails nightclub in Soho to meet some of his music acquaintances. There weren't too many people in the club but my attention was immediately drawn to a couple of famous faces from The Animals and The Beatles, some guys called Burdon and McCartney, I think. Muggins eagerly ordered the first round for about a dozen of us. The bill came to almost half my entire week's wages. Being a quick drinker, I was soon ready for another one. I looked around but nobody seemed interested in putting a hand in their pocket.

I decided on an old 'Northern' trick and ordered another round, waiting for someone to offer to pay. The silence was deafening and yes, you've guessed it, the other half of my week's wages was cleaned out as well. Having supped the two most expensive halves of lager of my life, I was now stony broke and incapable of ordering a third round. Cyril and I left as I berated my music idols for being the tightest skinflints on the planet.

MISS BAGSHOTT: Being a professional footballer did produce certain fringe benefits. One of these was the opportunity to judge beauty contests. Myself and the British boxing champion Billy Walker were invited to do the honours for the Bagshott carnival queen. Billy, myself and our two better halves plumped for this lucky young lady and are about to bestow her crown upon her. Actually, I voted for someone else but given Billy's ferocious left hook and right uppercut I certainly wasn't going to argue with him.

I had a slightly less expensive night when Cyril invited me to a *moriarty* back at his flat. This was the Swinging Sixties, remember, and I had already taken a liking for the occasional menthol cigarette. I'm not a heavy smoker - I doubt if I smoke 20 a week - but I do like a fag with a pint even to this day. Sitting beside me was an attractive young lady who proceeded to roll a joint. She passed it to the person on her left and then offered it to me. "No thanks. I'm fine with my menthol," came my naive reply. She must have thought I was a right plonker and gave me a funny look.

Only then did the penny drop but I was always so uncomfortable in that environment and must have stuck out like a sore thumb.

I popped into Cyril's offices once a month and, regular as clockwork, I'd enquire about the finances. He'd always tell me they were coming along nicely. "It's building up well. I've not touched a penny, not even my commission. We'll let it build up," he repeated. One day he asked for a few Chelsea photos for publicity purposes. I needed them back quickly and he told me to return the following day to collect them. A day later I turned up to be greeted by the sight of a padlocked door. and no sign of Cyril.

I spoke to other tenants in the offices who suggested he might have done a moonlight flit. All the furniture had been cleared out. Nothing was left. I have never seen Cyril since. I estimate that he fleeced me for between £15,000 and £20,000 - a considerable amount of money in those days. Based on five per cent interest, you owe me £1.6million, Cyril, and I really hope it was worth it. For the rest of my career, I never had another agent. Once bitten, twice shy, you might say.

One man I found to be much more reliable is a gentlemen many of you will have heard about. His name is Stan Flashman. Stan was the last word when it came to getting tickets and even in the sixties he had amassed a sizeable empire. My club, Leicester City, recently attracted a fair amount of adverse publicity over ticket arrangements for the 1999 Worthington Cup final against Spurs. Well, I'm telling you, players have been passing on tickets for decades. Anybody who says they didn't know about it in my day is lying. Some of the game's most respected ambassadors were involved. It was looked upon as a perk of the job.

For all the big games we would pool our tickets and then head off up to the Bowler Hat restaurant just off Fleet Street. There, we would meet up with one of Stan's representatives and be escorted to Stan's council house at the back of Charing Cross station. There were so many padlocks on the doors it took us five minutes to get inside. Eventually, you would be ushered into a dingy little room which was filled by the ample figure of Stan in this big chair. "Come on in, boys," he would say before peeling off a wad of notes to buy the tickets we had collected for him.

I'd done business with Stan on a couple of occasions and I was desperate to arrange something special for my dad. Dad was a huge Black and White Minstrels fan (for the uninitiated, a now politically incorrect dance troupe who appeared on Saturday night BBC television for years in the sixties and seventies) and was desperate to see them live.

Mum and Dad were coming down to see me play at Stamford Bridge so, the day before, I decided to ring up Stan to see if he could get me tickets. He was an

■ **SLEEVES ROLLED UP:** Please don't think I'm vain, but this is one of my favourite photos from my Chelsea days. It kind of encapsulates my approach to the game... plenty of effort and determination though not always a great deal of skill.

absolute diamond and told me a pair would be waiting at the Globe Theatre. Not only did Stan not charge me but he got my parents a pair of seats on the front row together with VIP passes for the after-show party. Mum and Dad were absolutely delighted and I'll always be grateful to Stan for making it such a special weekend for them.

In hindsight, my three seasons at Chelsea provided me with the highest standard of football and success I was to enjoy throughout my entire 17-season career. We never finished outside the top six, had a brief sojourn in Europe and won an FA Cup. Yet it's amazing how, when comparing it to Sheffield United and Leicester, you would not put my Chelsea chapter on an altogether different plane. These days, to finish in the top six for three successive seasons is a pretty major achievement. But in those days you didn't look at it like that. It was never really a topic of conversation as to whether you finished sixth or 17th. It was, believe it or not, largely immaterial.

In the modern era, every club with the exception of Manchester United, Arsenal and a few others go out to get those 42 points to guarantee Premiership survival. Most other things are considered a bonus. In the sixties and seventies we only lived from game to game. There were no targets, we simply went out on a Saturday afternoon and tried to play a good game of football. No monthly targets, monthly awards, or half-way progress reports. If you got two points on a Saturday, great; a draw was okay; and if you lost there was always next week. I never ever heard one of my managers say to me that the target was to get 42 points and when that was achieved we could start to enjoy ourselves.

The pressure we had was only on a game-to-game basis. It sounds stupid but if a team was relegated they probably didn't realise the enormity of it all until the final game. And, even then, to be relegated was not the end of the universe scenario which it now appears to be. The financial pressures of relegation and poor results certainly were not in evidence as they are today. Football was not a business in those days. It was a sport.

At Chelsea, however, I think it fair to say there was a clash of egos. There were so many hugely talented players it was almost impossible not to have some friction. It was, perhaps, those egos that were to ultimately lead to the demise of Dave Sexton. I will always retain a great deal of respect for Dave - remember I was his first signing at the Bridge. He was a supreme coach but I felt he did find it difficult trying to keep everyone happy - particularly Peter Osgood and Alan Hudson who didn't exactly see eye to eye.

Despite the egos, what talent we possessed! In the modern day the players might have been required to run around a little more but there was an abundance of skill. In today's marketplace you would have an array of footballers valued at £10 million or indeed, a lot more. Without wishing to sound patronising, it was a privilege for me to play alongside them. I never had ideas above my station and realised where I fitted in. In total I made 91 appearances and scored 26 goals in three seasons before moving on to Crystal Palace. On the field it was a privilege to be involved... off it I was introduced to the stars of Hollywood and the world of pop and show-business. Happy times.

Off to the Palace

Chapter 8

On the face of it, a transfer across London from Chelsea to Crystal Palace would hardly be considered the best of career moves. In the current football climate Chelsea are one of an elite band of Premiership clubs, while Crystal Palace are fighting for their financial lives. Yet, in much the same way as the fortunes of these two clubs have polarised, back in the sixties and early seventies there was very little to choose between them. The distribution of footballing wealth in that era was so much fairer and, as a consequence, quality players could be found at every club. As a result, the old First Division was extremely competitive with the comparative gap in class between top and bottom so much smaller than it is today. Sure, Chelsea has always been viewed as one of the more fashionable clubs but I did not consider my move to Selhurst Park to be a step down. No, I saw it as a glorious opportunity to continue playing my football at the highest level... and on a slightly more regular basis. At Chelsea I was a small fish in a big pond. At Crystal Palace I was a bigger fish in a smaller pond.

Please don't get the impression that Palace were the poor relations. I say 'a smaller pond' but that does the club a great disservice. Attendances at Selhurst Park averaged 30,000 which demonstrated the fantastic supporter base the club enjoyed. The ground was every bit as good as Stamford Bridge which, although large, was a little dilapidated in those days. Training facilities at Palace could not be bettered - we trained at the Crystal Palace national athletics track. First and foremost, though, must always be the players. As a newly-promoted club, Palace were hungry and ambitious to do well. They signed several new faces and I was impressed by their appetite to succeed - that and the fact the win bonuses were phenomenal. Although they did not possess the stars of Chelsea, there was undoubted quality throughout the team.

Young Stevie Kember was attracting rave reviews for his midfield performances while David Payne had won England Under-23 honours. I always put great emphasis on the quality of goalkeepers and throughout my career I was fortunate to play in front of the very best. John Jackson, I felt, was an excellent 'keeper. Up front, my strike partner was to be

■ **GREENSLEEVES:** Palace quickly got myself and Bobby Tambling down to work when they forced us to cover for the groundsmen in mowing the Selhurst Park turf. Both of us had travelled for talks with manager Bert Head not thinking for a moment that we would complete a deal. But after 20 minutes apiece in Bert's company we both signed on the dotted line and were paraded before the press a few hours later. Bobby and I joined from Chelsea in a £140,000 deal.

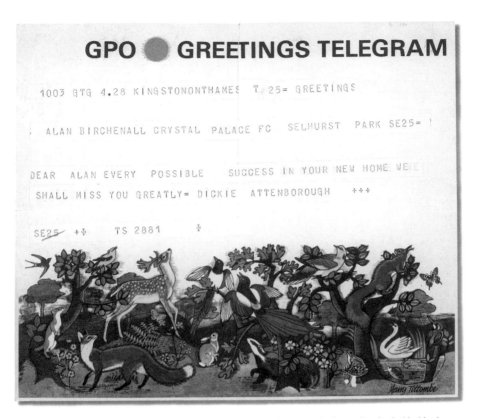

GPO ● GREETINGS TELEGRAM

1003 GTG 4.28 KINGSTONONTHAMES T 25= GREETINGS

ALAN BIRCHENALL CRYSTAL PALACE FC SELHURST PARK SE25= !

DEAR ALAN EVERY POSSIBLE SUCCESS IN YOUR NEW HOME WE

SHALL MISS YOU GREATLY= DICKIE ATTENBOROUGH +++

SE25 +% TS 2881 %

■ **BY ROYAL COMMAND:** No, this is not a telegram from the Queen but he's not that far behind in the celebrity stakes. Chelsea president and famous actor Richard Attenborough very kindly sent me this good luck telegram after my move from Stamford Bridge to Selhurst Park. It's a telegram I'll always cherish and has been kept in the Birchy loft for the past 30 years.

Gerry Queen, a tall centre forward who I considered I could work well alongside. I thought there was sufficient quality in the team to have a real crack at the First Division and, far from being disappointed at leaving Chelsea, I was intrigued and exhilarated about the prospect of playing my part in an exciting new chapter for Palace. Had I thought this was a team of no-hopers, neither I nor Bobby Tambling would have left Stamford Bridge.

Money, as they say, makes the world go around. And who would have thought that Palace could offer double the bonuses Chelsea were paying? At Stamford Bridge we were on £30 a point, at Palace the figure was £60. Yet that was indicative of the

PALACE POSE: Here's another of my model looks for the camera.

way the footballing money cake was divided up in those days. Palace were generating regular 30,000 crowds - not far short of Chelsea - and that meant quite a lot of dosh coming in once a fortnight. Big television money had not yet begun, and commercial revenues were still very much in their infancy. Nowadays gate receipts contribute only 30 per cent of a club's finances, but back in the sixties and seventies it was 99 per cent. With most sides attracting not incomparable size crowds there was not the disparity which currently exists between the big and the smaller clubs. There were no multi-million pound shirt sponsorship contracts, kit deals, merchandising stores or internet sites. It was a much more level playing field for everyone. Now we have a scenario where a handful of clubs generate a disproportionate amount of wealth and, as a result, are able to attract all the best players.

Those top-quality players may not even get a regular game but it is very hard for clubs outside that elite to prise them away because of the difficulty in matching their wage demands. Conversely, the top players at the smaller clubs are liable to become unsettled, either by their own thoughts or, if they needed prompting, from those of an agent. In my day there were only a handful of agents in operation and it had sadly been my misfortune to hire a spiv who did a runner.

Very early in my Chelsea career I had begun to realise and accept my own limitations. I like to think I never suffered from delusions of grandeur. I knew, deep down, that I was probably one rung short of climbing to the top of the international-standard soccer ladder. I was a good First Division pro capable of carving out a successful career for himself but sadly I did not quite have all the attributes necessary to reach the pinnacle of my profession. I likened myself to a 'jobbing' actor - an honest professional who could hopefully be relied upon to do a good steady job. Crystal Palace sold themselves to me in eloquent fashion: they spoke of filling the ground, of building a great team and really going for success. I was hooked. Everyone likes to be wanted and I desperately yearned to play my part in the Palace success story. I wanted to play regular First Division football. I was flattered they made such a big effort to persuade Bobby Tambling and myself to sign. Sadly, within 16 months of my arrival, I was to move on to Leicester City as things did not work out as I had hoped ... but more of that later in the chapter.

One of the perils of being a footballer is that you have to move house more often than most folk. By this time I had married the *tank commander* and we were forced to go through the obligatory rounds of house-hunting. Whilst at Chelsea we had lived in a lovely place, near Ascot, which we had bought for the princely sum of £7,500 (believe me, that was a lot of money). We had managed to sell it for a king's ransom of £10,500. Before the Palace move came up we had looked at a luxury

■ **HEAD TO HEAD:** Bobby Tambling and me get in some ball practice ahead of the start of the new 70-71 season. This photo was taken on the eve of Palace's first game back in the top flight after promotion - a trip to West Bromwich Albion. We earned a goalless draw at The Hawthorns, in which we both made our full debuts for the club, before rocketing up the table into the top three with a run of six wins in eight games.

bungalow which backed onto Ascot Racecourse. It was immaculate and set in two acres of land, but it was exorbitantly priced at £24,500. We vowed one day to aspire to such luxury. More pressing, though, was the need to find a suitable place in South London. The chairman of Crystal Palace, Arthur Wait, was a lovely fellow who, fortuitously for us, was also a builder. He showed us personally around all his houses before we settled on a Georgian mews terrace in the village of Banstead. As far as the location was concerned, it was perfect. To the right was a pub called The Mint and to our left was a hostelry known as The Woolpack. Backing on to the bottom of our garden was a bowling green and a public park.

As I've said before, the Birch never fancied golf. I was, however, fascinated by bowls. For a couple of weeks, I would potter out of my garden, take a seat on a park bench and watch the locals play. I was fascinated. One day, they invited me for a game. "Come on Birch, give it a try," invited one of the old boys who just happened to be a Palace fan. I eagerly accepted, played throughout the summer and really enjoyed myself, discovering it a brilliant form of relaxation. These days there are quite a few young men playing the sport, but in the early seventies I must have been the only guy under 60 south of Watford who had taken up such an 'elderly' pastime. Needless to say, I took a lot of stick from the rest of the lads who played their golf or snooker while I took my woods and flat cap onto the village green. Still, the Birch has always liked to stand out from the rest of the crowd. There was, however, one downside to this sea of domestic tranquillity in Banstead. At the chairman's suggestion, I paid him a fiver a week rent which, on the face of it, was a great deal. However, complications on my previous mortgage meant I got stung with a four-figure tax demand when I moved on from Palace so I was not exactly best pleased. It was something to do with the fact I was still inadvertently claiming tax relief on my mortgage payments. In those days, players had never heard of financial advisors.

One major difference at Crystal Palace was that it was a much more family-orientated club than Chelsea. There was an excellent team spirit on and off the pitch and the players would socialise at events with their wives. I struck up a friendship with Steve Kember, whom I nicknamed 'Gypo' because of his long straggly hair which gave him an unkempt Romany look. We got along famously and went out as couples or as lads together. On the sporting front away from the football pitch, cricket played a sizeable role. Steve Kember, David Payne and I all donned whites for Thornton Heath CC. Gypo, in particular, was an excellent cricketer and still turns his arm over today.

Of course, the lads could not share all their little secrets with their better halves. This was particularly true in the case of Bobby Tambling and his wife who were both Jehovah's Witnesses. Our main meeting point was The Glaziers social

FANCY FLICKS: The Birch puts the Claw through its paces in a pre-season warm-up.

213

■ **CRYSTAL PALACE 1970–71:** Meet the Palace class of 1970 about to embark on a brave new venture into the unknown of the First Division. As always, manager Bert Head was resplendent in his suit. We only ever used to see him once a week when he came in to pick the team on a Saturday afternoon.

club at Selhurst Park. We'd all scramble off the bus after an away game and dive in for a beer or two before being picked up by our partners. Not only did Bobby like a ciggie but he also liked a drop of alcohol. This was particularly bad news when your wife had converted you to a religious sect where alcohol and cigarettes were frowned upon. So, while he waited for his wife to collect him, he would religiously (sorry about that!) order a double vodka and orange. His wife would duly arrive, wait for him to finish what she thought was his healthy orange juice and escort him off the premises in blissful ignorance. To be fair to the lads, we never dropped him in it once (until now).

One tag Selhurst Park has unfortunately had to endure for quite a while is that it is without doubt one of the most inaccessible football grounds in the country. I can assure you it was exactly the same in my day. I can recall some horrific journeys back to my mum and dad in Nottingham. The M25 was not even a twinkle in a motorway builder's eye, so you had to embark on a four-hour trek through Streatham, Purley, Tooting, Hammersmith and Chiswick before you got anywhere near the MI. To football fans outside the capital, Palace is looked upon as just another London club. To Palace supporters, though, it has a separate individual identity. Croydon is a big city in its own right and Palace draw support from a highly localised area.

Getting to that little corner south of London was an achievement in itself. At the start of any season clubs scan the fixture lists and look out for the trip to Palace. Whenever it is scheduled there is always a groan. I think some clubs would genuinely rather play away at Torquay than go to Selhurst Park. Matters, of course, were further complicated when Wimbledon moved to the ground to play their home fixtures. I remember a couple of years ago my beloved Leicester City had to go there twice - drawing Palace away in the FA Cup, having already played Wimbledon in the Premiership.

Looking at the map, the trip seems innocuous enough but it is impossible to get a clean run into the ground. I should know, I tried just about every road permutation. Yet while visiting clubs only had to endure an annual trip, spare a thought for us at Palace - we had to make our way out of Croydon 23 times a season for away games. This probably explains why we had such a superlative home record and a pretty naff away one!

In our first season following promotion we collected three away victories - Huddersfield, Manchester United and Ipswich Town. Unfortunately the rot set in early the following season when we lost our first five away matches on the spin. I decided enough was enough and packed my bags to Leicester. The irony was Palace ended their losing away streak in the following game - you've guessed it, they earned a goalless draw at Filbert Street. Remember, too, there were no luxury coaches - we travelled in ancient bone-shakers with row upon row of uncomfortable hard-backed seats. There were no tables, televisions, videos, microwaves or toilets. To take four hours to get to the Midlands was not unusual, although we did travel by train to matches further North. Bear in mind, too, the road infrastructure was completely different to the present day. I'll swear that on a couple of occasions north of Stevenage we were ambushed by Dick Turpin!

Our inaccessibility, however, was compensated by the truly fantastic training facilities we enjoyed. At Sheffield I had been used to a windswept pitch at The Ball Inn training ground, while at Chelsea we trained out at Mitchum. Here, though, we had the full use of the national athletics stadium at Crystal Palace. Two days a week we would use the stadium itself and be trained by AAA coach Bob McNab. One of the top athletics coaches in the country, Bob really put us through our paces. Much technological advancement has been made in recent years but back in the early seventies Bob used to put a heavy harness on us and hold us back as we tried to run around the track. He was, quite literally, years ahead of his time. I enjoyed his sessions and Bob once told me he could have turned me into a useful athlete either at 400 metres or the long jump. "It's a shame you didn't 'cos I've not turned out to be much good as a footballer," I quipped.

Although I had a certain aptitude for track and field, my sporting prowess did not extend to the trampoline. Our coach George Petchey decided one day that it would be a good idea to change the routine and take us all into the gym for a session on one. I was nominated by George to try out the Olympic-size matting. I'd never been on a trampoline before in my life and happily bounced away for 30 seconds. My problems began, however, when I tried to stop. The canvas was so taut I was almost head-butting the ceiling and, in attempting to reduce my bounce, I lost my balance, was catapulted 30 feet across the gym and crashed in a crumpled heap into the wall-bars. All joking aside, I was quite badly shaken and George had to hastily cancel the session. To this day, I've never been back on a trampoline, but if I could see a replay now I'd probably kill myself laughing!

Ground wise, and this may surprise a few, Selhurst Park was probably the best of the three clubs to date I had played for. Facilities at just about every ground were woefully inadequate compared to the luxury of the many new stadia in the Premiership. Most fans like to stand and they didn't seem too worried about the hygiene in the toilets or the quality of the burger bars (both had similar standards. Sorry, the toilets were cleaner). Selhurst Park was a big ground and I remember a crowd in excess of 42,000 turning out to see us in an FA Cup third round tie against Chelsea.

My arrival at Selhurst Park marked a watershed in my career in terms of expectation levels. At both Sheffield United and Chelsea I had looked upon myself as the 'second' striker. At Bramall Lane, Mick Jones was the man who banged in most of the goals. It was a similar story at Stamford Bridge when I played a supporting role to Peter Osgood. At Palace, however, I was the man charged with scoring. I was the 'main man' and the support role was played by Gerry Queen. For someone who did not consider himself to be a natural goalscorer I knew the pressure was on me. That's why I was so pleased when I finished top scorer of the 1970-71 campaign with 13 goals. Now 13 might not sound prolific but to reach double figures in a newly-promoted team was no mean achievement. Strangely, too, it was to be the last time I scored double figures in a season and ultimately marked the end of my days when I could hit the back of the net with any real regularity.

I arrived at Palace at the same time as Bobby Tambling. I was valued at £100,000 and Bobby at £40,000 in the £140,000 double deal. Bobby was, and still remains, one of the goalscoring greats at the Bridge. He graduated through the youth team and

It's that time of the year again as we report to Selhurst Park for the pre-season photo-call with all the new signings. We're full of the joys of summer and, left to right are: Davy Provan, me, Peter Wall, Terry Wharton, Bobby Tambling and Gerry Humphreys.

■ **SHEER DELIGHT:** I take the congratulations of my team-mates after netting my first-ever goal for Crystal Palace following my £100,000 move from Chelsea. I scored the winner in a 1-0 victory over Newcastle which gave us our first success of the season after an opening-day draw at West Brom and a 1-0 home defeat by Manchester City.

spent over ten seasons at the club amassing over 250 goals. Strangely, you know, he operated wide on the left rather than as an out-and-out centre forward. As the younger player, I felt I had a little more to prove than Bobby. He had done so much at Chelsea that a little piece of him may well have stayed there. He was still a great player but ultimately his best seasons had already been played out.

As with any club, Palace had their fair share of diverse characters and showmen in the dressing room. Certainly, there was a keen sense of camaraderie both on and off the pitch which helped us to survive our first season back in the top flight. One of the players I most vividly recall, however, was not one who made too many first team appearances. Roger Hynd joined us from Birmingham City and if there was a bigger, harder man operating in the game at the time then I never saw him. Roger made Arnie Schwarzenegger look like Julian Clary. As the old saying goes, he could trap the ball further than I could kick it. His party trick was to try and catch you unawares when he walked into the dressing room in the morning. Most sane people content themselves with a polite 'good morning'. Not Hindy. He used to point his four fingers together and jab you underneath the rib cage. It was like being hit by four steel rivets and the pain was excruciating. 'Hindy' would then retire to the gymnasium before training where he would batter the weights into submission and work on developing his 28 inch neck. I think Sylvester Stallone must have modelled his Rocky character on 'Hindy'. His physique was awesome.

My big pal 'Gypo' Kember was a real pain in the *arris*. He had the knack of being inordinately successful at winding me up in a matter of seconds. One morning I was in the dressing room reading my fan mail and quietly minding my own business. Suddenly I smelt burning and moments later my letters began going up in flames. 'Gypo' had set fire to my mail with a box of matches. I raced after him down the tunnel and out onto the pitch. He was a spritely little bugger and I could never catch him. On this morning the sprinklers were out and 'Gypo' unfortunately failed to see the wire that pushed them across the playing surface. He tripped over it, and I pounced on him and gave him one of the biggest hidings of his life.

Shenanigans like this went on in the dressing-room all the time. Periodically, my best leather shoes would go missing only to re-appear floating calmly in the bath. On other occasions there would be a large hole cut out of the arse of my underpants.

GOAL: It's a race for the final touch between myself and Tony Taylor as West Bromwich Albion keeper Jim Cumbes desperately tries to make up the lost ground. I got the finishing touch for the goal as we eased home 3-0, in front of 28,330 fans at Selhurst Park, to record our sixth win in eight games and move into the First Division top three.

My shirts would often suffer too, the sleeves being hacked off at the elbows. Many a time I had to turn up at a lunch meeting in Croydon after training wearing my tracksuit while the rest of my clothes lay in a ruined and crumpled heap in the back of my car. 'Gypo' was always the instigator.

He did, however bite off more than he could chew when he messed with the club captain John Sewell. John, together with Eddie McCreadie, was the most immaculately dressed player I ever came across in my career (yes, much smarter than you, Elvis). I never saw him in anything less formal than a well-tailored three-piece suit, crisp collar and matching tie. Club captains, in those days, tended to keep a little distant from the rest of the players. They were invariably the senior player and were awarded the captaincy on the basis of longevity. John was a great bloke

HYPODERMIC GERRY: Scarves, gloves, coats, Gerry Queen looked every bit the eskimo - in Summer!

but you didn't mess with him. 'Gypo' only messed up his clothes once. John pulled him to one side and the straggly-haired one never dared stray again.

Centre-half Mel Blyth wins the Birchy vote for the tightest player in football. This is a massive statement to make given the number of people in football I have mixed with over a 20-year career in the game. I can say, quite categorically, that Mel is the biggest skinflint of all time. He perfected the art of appearing from nowhere just as someone else was about to order a round at the bar. It got so bad we used to call him 'get 'em in, Blyth' because he never did. I still believe he has the original five pound note - a white one - which he received in his first wage packet at Palace. Perversely, he happily revels in being labelled a tight-arse. I understand he's still the same around the pubs of Croydon today. I had heard that the University of Croydon runs a degree course in penny-pinching. A former honours graduate, Mel is now Dean of the Faculty.

If Mel was the stingiest penny-pincher I have ever come across, my strike partner Gerry Queen was the biggest hypochondriac. You could always spot him a mile off in summer. He was the only herbert dressed like an eskimo. Some modern-day players have this annoying habit of wearing gloves. Well, I swear Gerry used to wear a scarf as well as gloves when he was playing. I nicknamed him 'Hypodermic

Gerry'... and with good reason. There was one celebrated game in our first season when we won 2-0 at Ipswich. Peter Wall, the former Liverpool defender, chipped a ball down the line onto the chest of Gerry. Admittedly the ball was slightly over-hit but Gerry went down as if he'd been shot by a sniper. As his strike partner, I dutifully rushed over to check he was okay. He was wheezing away and complaining he couldn't breathe properly. We managed to persuade him to get up and carry on and thought little more about the incident. After the game we were all in high spirits and hardly noticed Gerry slumped gloomily in the corner feeling sorry for himself. On the coach back the heater was going full blast but there sat Gerry in overcoat, scarf and gloves. On the following Monday morning he failed to turn up for training. No-one knew where he was. Apparently, after getting off the team bus on Saturday night

Modern-day team buses are the ultimate in luxury. Microwave ovens, individual stereo points, toilets, beds, televisions and air conditioning. Well, this had absolutely none of those. The only similarities are seats and a set of wheels. We didn't even have a table to play cards to while away the long journeys to and from Selhurst Park. The only concession to luxury was that we received a packed lunch before we set off to games. The canteen staff wrapped us up a sandwich, apple, orange, drink and a Mars bar. Ever the joker, Steve 'Gypo' Kember is trying to swipe my crutches after I picked up an injury in an away game.

he had walked to the neighbouring Mayday Hospital and admitted himself into a ward overnight. He spent a total of four days detained for observation because he was so concerned he might have sustained a serious injury. Gerry was a great lad... but what a 'hypodermic' .

We had a fantastic cross-section of characters in the dressing room, as we did, I felt, at all the clubs for whom I played. Banter is a big part of football and we took the mickey every bit as much at Selhurst Park as anywhere else. Throughout my career I have always found goalkeepers to be some of the biggest eccentrics. John Jackson certainly fitted into that category. I'd have no hesitation in saying he was a complete loony, a sort of footballing John Cleese. His opposite was David Payne, a quiet, studious character. I've lost touch with many of them but I often wonder what they are doing now. I have this vision of Payney being a successful college lecturer and Jacko feeding the chimps at Whipsnade Zoo.

I'd like to tell you more about our manager Bert Head but, to be honest, I can't, I never saw him often enough. We would see him for an hour or two on a Saturday afternoon and, if you were lucky, you might bump into him at Selhurst Park during the week. George Petchey took day-to-day control of us but it couldn't have been easy for him. Even on Fridays he wouldn't have a clue as to who might be in the team. So, when we rehearsed free kicks and corners, George never used to know who to put where. Every Saturday lunchtime, before a home game, we would meet up at The Selsdon Park Hotel for our pre-match meal. Bert would arrive and announce the team and then George would hastily have to make changes to all his set-piece routines because the original players in his wall were not now playing! The Selsdon Park was a magnificent hotel. Set in a few hundred acres, it was looked on as one of the premier hotels in South London and, to this day, is still regularly used by Premiership and First Division clubs staying overnight for games at Selhurst Park. All the players would meet up at 12 noon and we would tuck into a hearty steak, a few rounds of toast and several pots of tea. Saturday lunchtime football preview programmes were in their infancy though the presenters of our era bore very little resemblance to Gabby Yorath. After Bert announced the team, we'd all jump into our cars and head off to the game.

Although my time at Palace was comparatively brief I did, as you might expect, do plenty of homework on the socialising and nightlife scenes. Nightclub headquarters was 'Doctor Jims' in Croydon where our players would regularly assemble and Mel Blyth would even more regularly avoid the bar. As a married man I never, of course, wished to stay out late. Unfortunately, being the shy and retiring type I was regularly led astray by 'Gypo' who insisted that, after the many evening club functions we had to attend, we popped into Doctor Jims on the way home. A

■ **KEEPING NORMAN AT ARM'S LENGTH:** Sadly, this is far closer to legendary Leeds hardman Norman Hunter than I would normally prefer to find myself. Realising the enormity of my mistake, I am desperately trying to fend him off with my right arm while also making a token jump to head the ball. My immediate concern was the plight of my legs when they landed back on the floor again. We fought out a 1-1 draw in front of 38,000 fans at Selhurst Park in November 1970.

quick drink became a flagon or two and there are many adventures I can vaguely recall through a misty drink-induced haze. Now I think about it, the Bali Hai in Streatham was also a popular haunt. This club was just around the corner from the ice rink and it's fair to say we were skating on thin ice when it came to the excuses we used to our wives and girlfriends for our early morning returns. Contrary to popular belief, I was not a heavy drinker. I am indebted to some advice given to me by the club doctor at Sheffield United. Doc O'Gorman used to ask me my tipple. "Stones bitter," I'd reply. "Very good," he'd comment. "You can train that out of yourself but you can't get rid of the spirits." Doc spoke with some authority because he operated on many people and had seen the damage spirits had done to their insides. I followed his advice for the rest of my career and, even, to this day. Lager, at this stage, was only just coming on to the market and although I graduated from bitter to lager I always steered clear of whisky, brandy, vodka and the like.

THE CLAW IN ACTION: Admire the technique. This is a lesson to all aspiring young footballers in how to get your body over the ball before letting fly with a long-distance exocet shot. I'd clearly got the body shape right for the camera angle but, unfortunately, my shot's final destination was nearer to East Croydon railway station than it was to the opposition goal.

I like to think that drink never significantly impaired my performance although my health did suffer on one occasion at Crystal Palace with some rather ill-advised rehabilitation work. Half-way through an away game - I think it was at Wolves but no-one seems too sure - I sustained a nasty knee injury, subsequently diagnosed as strained knee ligaments. I was stretchered off to our dressing room for treatment to continue at the hands of a physio. Despite the fact I was in considerable pain and had sustained the injury just ten minutes earlier, he told me to work the knee immediately. He proceeded to force me to do ten minutes of step-ups on a nearby bench. I was in agony but he insisted I continue. "You don't need any strappings, we just need to get the knee working straight away," he kept telling me. I knew I had to work the joint within 24 hours of an operation during my days at Chelsea and that course of action did pay off. But this was a completely different type of injury... and the physio was nowhere near as good to look at as the suspender-clad nurse in St Stephens Hospital. Suffice to say, I ended up spending double-time on the treatment table in the ensuing weeks before being fit enough to return. I have subsequently told this story to several members of the medical profession and all have expressed horror that my career could have been ended by such an inappropriate course of medical action.

As so often happens with clubs newly promoted to the top flight, we surprised ourselves by the magnificent start we made to the 1970-71 season. I scored our initial goal in the First Division with the winner against Newcastle in a 1-0 victory that set us on our way. In a remarkable sequence of results we won six out of eight matches in September and October, culminating in Bobby Tambling's winner in a 1-0 defeat of Manchester United at Old Trafford. Those other victories over Blackpool, Nottingham Forest, Huddersfield, Southampton and West Bromwich Albion moved us into the top three of the table. With bonuses running at £60 per point, we all agreed life had never been so sweet, and our wives and girlfriends had never bought so many new outfits. Sadly, these things never last. From mid-October through to the end of the season we were destined to win only five more League matches and end in 18th spot, just above the relegation zone. No matter, the first objective of any newly-promoted club is to survive and we had been assured of that at a relatively early stage of the season.

PRIVATES ON PARADE: Okay, okay. I know I said in the Sheffield United chapter that I never stood in a wall after being poleaxed by a Stan Lynn special for Birmingham. Well, in this game against Stoke in April 1971 I found myself cajoled into the wall alongside (left to right) Steve Kember, Jimmy Scott, myself and Bobby Tambling. I was determined not to take any chances as you can see from the position of my left hand. I was grasping them tighter than the squeeze which Vinnie Jones put on Paul Gascoigne a few years ago.

■ **BAD HAIR DAY:** I'm afraid that Steve Kember swiped my hair-drier before this official photo-call. As a result, I had to come out of the dressing room and get my head and shoulders portrait photo done looking a little the worse for wear.

There were some cracking interludes in cup competitions as well. In the FA Cup we were drawn against my former club Chelsea. An aggregate attendance of 97,000 watched our two third-round games - 42,000 at Selhurst Park and 55,000 at Stamford Bridge. Interesting that it's only recently, with the multi-million pound development of all-seater stadia, that clubs can once again begin to accommodate crowds of this magnitude. John McCormick and I scored in a 2-2 draw in the first game, before we went down 2-0 at The Bridge. The first game was memorable because of the footwear I wore. Heavy overnight frosts made for a rutted, bone-hard pitch. It was so hard the *namby-pambys* wouldn't play on it today but we just got on with the job. I wore a pair of black rubber-soled basketball boots with the laces tied around the ankle. In the League Cup we reached the fifth round before losing 4-2 to Manchester United. We'd beaten Rochdale, Lincoln and Arsenal en route to Old Trafford before finally bowing out of the competition.

Despite our disappointing end to the season - we got thumped 6-0 at Southampton on the final day - we still had plenty to look forward to with a rather special end-of-season competition. In previous chapters, you will recall, the Birch does not have the fondest memories of European football. However, it must be said that some of the hottest international highlights of my career belong to my days with Palace. After all, how many players can say they have beaten Inter Milan in the famous San Siro Stadium? That's exactly what happened to me and the rest of the Palace team when

we were entered into the Anglo-Italian Cup. My younger readers have probably never heard of the competition but in our day it was a reasonably prestigious event. Clubs from the English First Division and Italian Serie A would contest a tournament in the close season on a home and away basis.

In the summer of 1971 we were paired in Group Two with Italian giants Inter and Cagliari, and fellow English club West Bromwich Albion. Amazingly, we beat Inter in both games, home and away. It was the first time they had been beaten on home soil in European competition for over ten years but, from what I can remember, we gave them a right good kicking. Inter were bristling with Italian World Cup stars - no fewer than five of their side had played in the Italian national team hammered 4-1 by Brazil in the World Cup Final just a year earlier. They were

■ **LUIGI RIVA:** Just one of the World Cup stars we met during our Anglo-Italian Cup adventure with Palace.

THE CRYSTAL PALACE TEAM IN 1971-72: *Back row, left to right:* Terry Long (coach), Peter Wall, Mel Blyth, Phil Hoadley, John Jackson, yours truly, John Hardie, John McCormick, Gerry Queen, Alan Pinkney, Bert Head (Manager). *Front row:* John Loughlan, Terry Wharton, David Payne, Jimmy Scott, Steve Kember, Gerry Humphreys, Bobby Tambling, Tony Taylor.

Bertini, Mazzola, Boninsegna, Burgnich and Facchetti. We went over to the San Siro and won 1-0. The stadium was enormous and before the game we were all presented with a special limited edition Inter Milan black and blue watch. I sometimes still wear it to this day. In fact, I'm so proud of it I put it on my wrist even though the timepiece hasn't worked since 1984! In return, and showing the generous hospitality for which Palace were famous, we gave them a limited edition signed pennant - to be shared between all 14 of them!

Our success was not just confined to victory over the Milanese giants. We also beat Cagliari, who included the legendary Italian World Cup star Luigi Riva. Remember, this was not my first taste of competing against the Italians. As a teenager with Sheffield United we'd played Inter's arch rivals AC Milan in the Chilean capital of Santiago and beaten them 4-0. There was something about the Italians. They oozed class and always possessed an aura of superiority. They certainly looked the part, with their designer sun-glasses and Armani suits, eclipsing even the Birch's sartorial elegance. They were more like movie stars than footballers. Still, there can't be too many players who can say they have beaten both Milanese giants in club action.

So, my first season with Palace was one I viewed with a certain amount of satisfaction. However, when we should have been looking at building on the success of our first season back in

■ **NEW-STYLE KIT:** Bert Head had been so impressed by the performances of Dutch champions Ajax that he decided it was high time for some of their flair to rub off on us. However, instead of buying Cruyff and Neeskens, Bert decided to opt for the low-cost option of designing a new kit similar to that worn by Ajax. So, for the start of the 1971-72 season we found ourselves forsaking the customary claret shirts for a predominantly white kit with a claret and sky blue centre stripe. Here, we are wearing the new kit for the first time in our season-opener against Newcastle. It didn't quite have the desired effect. I left the club in October and Palace finished 20th in the table.

Division One, optimism was replaced by a mood of pessimism for our second campaign. Skipper Stevie Kember and I feared the worst and so it was to prove. We felt we needed to bring in some more big-name stars to strengthen the squad but there was a notable absence of new top-flight players. At the time, Palace had a close relationship with Scottish side Morton. Bert arranged with Morton boss Hal Stewart for a couple of Danish players to come down. The previous season Bobby Tambling and I had been the double signing, but now the club were thinking about a couple of Scandinavians no-one had ever heard of - Per Bartrum and Bar Thorup, I think, were their names. There was also a rumour of Gypo and myself moving on. Gypo was mentioned as a possible target for Chelsea, and I was linked with several clubs, including Leicester City. Significantly, Palace did not issue any 'hands-off' warnings through the media and we both began to feel the writing was on the wall.

ANGLO ITALIAN CUP ENCOUNTER: Although only half his body is in picture, I'm reliably informed this is the figure of Italian World Cup star Giacinto Facchetti tussling with the Birch in the home leg of our Group Two game with Inter Milan. We amazed the soccer world by completing a home and away double over the Italian aces.

It was also a shade unfortunate that the club also decided to introduce a new team strip following a summer tour to Holland in which we had played Feyenoord, ADO and PSV Eindhoven. Bert Head was a big fan of Dutch football and, in particular, Ajax. Ajax were one of Europe's top teams and included such greats as Johann Cruyff and Johann Neeskens. Bert obviously couldn't afford to bring in superstars (as I explained earlier, he preferred a more unconventional chain of supply via Morton) but did have the idea of replicating the famous Ajax strip into Palace's colours. The Ajax kit consisted of a white shirt with a broad red centre strip running down the middle. Palace brought in a white shirt with a centre band of claret and sky blue. We looked the business but unfortunately seldom played like it.

Our opening game of the season at home to Newcastle proved to be something of a false dawn. We eased to a 2-0 victory with goals from Tambling and Tony Taylor but were destined never to win again while Gypo and I were at the club. Our watershed was a 3-0 defeat by Spurs at White Hart Lane in September 1971

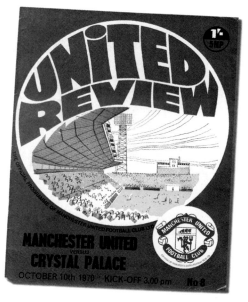

OLD TRAFFORD MEMORIES: Visiting Old Trafford in the seventies was just as intimidating as it is now. But we certainly enjoyed ourselves in our first season following promotion. Bobby Tambling scored the goal in a famous 1-0 victory.

after which we were both sold. 'Gypo' moved on to Chelsea for £180,000 while I went to Leicester in a £100,000 deal with Bobby Kellard (valued at £40,000) going in the opposite direction. In retrospect, the club clearly needed to raise some finance in order to underwrite the rebuilding of their playing squad. The first season in the top flight had not come cheaply with the amount of bonuses paid out and £280,000 was equivalent to a modern-day £10 million. Our departures genuinely did enable them to buy virtually a new team but unfortunately the players they were able to bring in found it hard to sustain First Division football.

Looking back on my career, it's a sobering statistic that most of my clubs ended up being relegated within a couple of years of my departure. Sheffield United went down the year after I left and even mighty Chelsea fell on hard times despite their cup triumphs. Palace too were relegated shortly after my demise and, incidentally, Leicester dropped out of the top flight too. This leads me to two conclusions. Firstly, I showed a surprising sense of good timing in getting out when I did, and secondly, I proved something of a lucky talisman for clubs while I was around the place. I certainly would not subscribe to the foolish notion that it had anything to do with the clubs being deprived of my services. I'm far too realistic about my own shortcomings for that.

Here's a couple of line-ups for the First Division games against Huddersfield and Arsenal. Look at the battle of the number nines in the Huddersfield game as I went head to head with Frank Worthington, later to become my colleague and firm friend at Leicester. Frank had the last laugh on this occasion as Town won 3-0 on our patch. Arsenal completed an historic league and cup double in this year so it was no real surprise when we crashed to a 2-0 home defeat, preceded by a 1-1 draw at Highbury earlier in the season.

Home Sweet Home

In every person's life there is, I believe, a defining era. A period in your existence which shapes the whole outlook of the rest of your life. Mine was unquestionably the five years I spent playing my football with Leicester City. Not only did it provide me with the most enjoyable time of my career but it also taught me many valuable lessons which have stood me in good stead for the rest of my life. Very simply, moving to Leicester was the best decision I ever made. I enjoyed my football at Filbert Street more than anywhere else and, off the field, I had a truly fantastic time with my family. So much so, that I pen these memoirs in my retirement home(!) still ensconced in Leicestershire some 25 years after finishing my playing days with the club.

At this early stage of the chapter, however, I must make a quite candid confession. Most Leicester fans will tell you that the seventies, under the managership of the late Jimmy Bloomfield, was the one truly golden era for the club. I'm afraid it was all a bit of a myth. Without doubt we were one of the great entertainers of the decade, we won a national newspaper award for being the most entertaining First Division side for three years in succession. But, to be honest, that was the only trophy we were ever going to win.

We were incapable of winning six consecutive games to reach an FA Cup final (although we did once get to a semi final) let alone able to show the required consistency over 20 games to force our way into the Division One top six and European qualification. But there are many matches which will live long in my memory and those of supporters, individual 90-minute performances which I believe will be very difficult for any Leicester City team to ever surpass.

I had many a long debate with the former Leicester manager Martin O'Neill about the true success we enjoyed as a team. Martin always teased me that the 'Bloomfield

Boys' never won a trophy, compared to his cup-winning exploits during an immensely successful five-year stint with the club. He was right. It's inevitable that we look into the past with our rose-tinted spectacles and perhaps forget the many games in which we struggled.

Only in two of the six seasons I spent with the club did we manage to finish in the top ten - I can remember a couple of tense relegation battles. But, boy, we certainly knew how not to win a trophy in style. Jimmy Bloomfield put together a collection of some of the greatest entertainers and flair players operating in the game at that time; Frank Worthington, Keith Weller, Steve Whitworth and Peter Shilton were all England internationals and we conjured up some truly magical performances.

One week we could be breathtaking, the next we'd go down by three goals to a side

CAPITAL CITY: Jon Sammels fills me in on the Leicester scene a day after I completed my move from Crystal Palace to Filbert Street. Jon had made the move out of London from Arsenal earlier in the season and was well placed to give me a few hints on life in the Midlands. Jon and I were two of the first London buys made by manager Jimmy Bloomfield. Previously, because of the large number of Scottish players signed by the club, City had been christened Leicester Thistle. Now, with all the new arrivals from the capital, the club was re-nicknamed Leicester Cockney.

struggling at the foot of the division. Leicester, in fact, almost became synonymous for our great displays against the bigger clubs only to let ourselves down against teams which we were fancied to beat. It would not have been unfair to say that out of a 42-game season, we would be brilliant in 20 matches and instantly forgettable in the other 20.

Ironic, too, isn't it that I should enjoy my football so much after hanging up my striking boots at the premature age of 28. I'd been kicked from pillar to post at

NAME: ALAN JOHN BIRCHENALL

Date of Birth: 28.8.45.

Date of Examination: 7.10.71.

PREVIOUS MEDICAL HISTORY

1)   Removal of Appendix when 3 years old.

2)   Tonsils and Adenoids removed in childhood.

3)   Broken toes when 12 years old.

4)   Broken wrist when 14 years old.

5)   Glandular Fever in 1963.

6)   Injured left knee joint October 1969. Off football
for 8 weeks - good recovery.

7)   Severe laceration - 3", above left knee joint -
seven stitches.

EXAMINATION

This player appears to be in good health - robust
physique and looks well.

Wt. - 12 st. 6 lbs.

Ht. - 6 ft.

Blood Pressure - 128/70 (Normal.

Urine - No Albumen. Np Sugar (Normal).

Vision - Rt. Eye 6/6 (Normal)
Left. Eye 6/18 (Slight weakness).
Not colour blind.

Teeth, Throat, Heart and lungs and Central
Nervous system - Normal.

His skin is clear and healthy - he has no Ruptures.

X-Rays of Hip, Knee and Ankle joints are normal.
The only condition I found was a slight weakness of his internal
Ligament of his left knee joint, due to a recent injury.

.H. t. hurley............

EMERGENCY WARD 10: Even back in the Jurassic period, we still had to undergo medical examinations, although they were far less stringent in the seventies. I had to get the all-clear from doctors Freer and Brit before completing my £100,000 move from Crystal Palace. As you can see, I suffered more than my share of misfortune as a youngster, when I had my tonsils, adenoids and appendix all removed before the age of eight.

Sheffield United, Chelsea and Crystal Palace, and Leicester marked my withdrawal from the front line into an anchorman midfield role. It worked like a dream as my vocal abilities to organise (ie my big mouth) were put to good use and I did my best to pull the strings of the side from my new-found rearguard position.

Happy, happy days at Leicester. And, for those of you who have managed to continue reading this far in the book without lapsing into a coma, there are more than the occasional few humorous tales to be recounted which even I find difficult to believe actually happened to all of the lads.

One of my better attributes, I believe, is that despite my rather outgoing personality I was always a fairly level-headed guy. I know I wore a few loud clothes and had a ridiculous bouffant hair-do but I never kidded myself about my true ability as a footballer. By the time Leicester came in for me, I was fully aware I was not destined to win a sideboard-full of League Championship trophies. Even to this day I afford myself a wry smile when players talk about how they need to be competing for top honours on a regular basis. It's great to aspire to such heights but for the overwhelming majority of all professional footballers the harsh truth is they will win bugger all. For every player who talks about cups, League titles and Champions League honours, there are another 20 just like me (well, not quite like me, thank goodness) -

PRAISE THE LORD: I sink to my knees and offer thanks to the man upstairs after netting the second goal in a 2-0 defeat of Manchester United in April 1972. On hand to offer me congratulations are Malcolm Manley and Jon Sammels. Jogging back to the centre circle is substitute Rodney Fern whom we nicknamed Gerson - because he had no similarity to the Brazilian genius whatsoever!

BOOTIFUL SPONSORSHIP: Modern players look upon boot deals and kit sponsorships as par for the course. But it was the seventies when boot contracts first started to be drawn up. Adidas and Puma were the main two football shoe manufacturers at the time so I signed up with... an unknown French firm called Hunga. Hunga paid me £250 for the privilege of wearing their boots. The left boot was worth £249.99 while the French manufacturers threw in the right boot for 1p. Couldn't exactly have been the greatest sponsorship ever... no-one has ever heard of them since.

journeyman footballers who make a living out of the game, glad just to be involved.

Only at Chelsea did I really think I had a genuine chance of picking up some silverware but sadly it didn't materialise. At Crystal Palace I knew there was very little chance of major success and it was a similar story at Leicester. But that didn't demotivate me. Far from it. I made it my goal and my ambition to go out and enjoy every single minute of my football. I was playing at the highest level, week in and week out and I was very privileged to be part of the scene. Every supporter who came to watch us, and all my old friends in Nottingham on Woodthorpe Park playing fields, would give their right arm just to have one fleeting taste of top professional football action. Here I was making my living from the game and living out those dreams on a weekly basis.

How could I not be happy? Sure, we would all love to win a Championship or two but I was quite literally taking part in a dream world.

I had known for some time that the writing was on the wall at Crystal Palace and jumped at the chance when Leicester came in for me shortly after the start of the 1971-72 season. Palace were struggling, the better players were being sold and I was hugely impressed when I met Jimmy Bloomfield. He had a terrific reputation as a coach and I admired his footballing background with Arsenal, West Ham and Orient. He sold the club to me very effectively and I still maintain that, important as the money is, equally so is the first impression a manager makes on a player. I suppose in the modern era we refer it to as charisma. Jimmy certainly had a presence and he quickly made me into a convert. Bobby Kellard moved in the opposite direction to Selhurst Park in a move valued at a total of £100,000. I signed for a weekly basic wage of £100 plus a bonus structure of £25 per point. I'm not saying it wasn't good money, but the salary was largely unimportant. I wasn't the top earner at the club by any means, but neither was I anywhere near being the best player. Footballers like to be where they are wanted, and clearly Leicester wanted me more than Palace.

I was subsequently often asked my views on moving out of the capital to come to the Midlands but my life was changing and I was happy to get away. I'd done the single man routine down the Kings Road with Chelsea, I had my wife Heather and young daughter and wanted a family life. Coming to Leicester suited me fine and with our respective parents 25 miles up the road in Nottingham it meant I was close enough to visit my mum but just far enough away to stay out of the way of the mother-in-law (only joking, she was a lovely lady). We were to settle very comfortably into a bungalow in the picturesque village of Cossington, just north of Leicester.

Due to a large influx of Scottish players in earlier seasons under the managership of Matt Gillies, Leicester had come to be affectionately looked upon as Leicester Thistle. My arrival along with several others from London clubs, however, was to change this nickname to Leicester Cockney.

Winger Lenny Glover had been one of the first Londoners to arrive, with Jon Sammels an influential buy from Arsenal by Jimmy at the start of the 1971 season. Jon was a double-winner with the Gunners and despite getting a bit of stick from the North Bank I always considered him to be a class act. Two months later Jimmy moved to sign me and a matter of days later Keith Weller also transferred out of the capital from Chelsea.

Unfortunately, it is to my discredit that I did not immediately begin to repay Jimmy's faith in my ability. The first game for which I was eligible was a rather daunting trip to Arsenal. I had been struggling with a groin injury (not a self-inflicted one, I hasten to add) but Jimmy was keen for me to play. Lenny was also being plagued by an injury and, on the morning of the game, Jimmy had us both in for fitness tests. He insisted that one of us had to play. As any footballer will tell you, they are always keen to make sure they make the best possible debut. "I'm not fit, I can't play," Lenny told Jimmy. My response to the manager was even more forthright. "Well, there's no way I can play because I'm the new signing," was my rather clumsy delivery. I won the day and Jimmy ruled me out but insisted Lenny played. Suffice to say, we got hammered 3-0 and Lenny limped off after 30 minutes with a pulled *jane*.

From this less than illustrious start was to a spring a Foxes career spanning 176 appearances and 14 goals yet those first few months at the club and in the city were far from easy ones. Perhaps it was because I had to work so hard to become accepted that I was able to appreciate the club and the area so much more in later years. At Sheffield I was instantly welcomed as one of their own, a recipient of true Yorkshire hospitality. At Chelsea and Palace I was very quickly able to get into the cosmopolitan swing of London life. Yet when I first came to Leicester I found the people more than a little guarded, perhaps even stand-offish. I likened the city of Leicester to a big club and I had to serve my apprenticeship before I was accepted. Once, of course, you were accepted into the fold, Leicestershire people look upon you as a friend for life. Even to this day, in my role at Filbert Street as club co-ordinator, I come across many players who found it very difficult to settle into the area in the first few months. Ironically, though, there are a vast number of ex-Leicester players who have chosen to settle in the region for the rest of their lives. From the fifties era Howard Riley, John Ogilvie and Davie Gibson have all made Leicester their home and, from my time, Lenny Glover and Jon Sammels are residents of the city. Jon is a driving instructor although goodness only knows what Lenny gets up to.

I was staying with Keith Weller at the Post House Hotel for several months after my arrival while we looked for our new homes. It was a real top-quality five-star hotel and let's just say that Keith and I didn't go hungry. We ate like kings, steak and lobster featuring regularly on the menu. Our only problem was that the food was so exquisite and rich we quickly became bored of it. Indeed, the highlight of our week was to dash home to our wives and get an honest basic home-cooked meal of egg and chips! Although we ensured we did not break the pre-game 48-hour curfew (I learned my lesson after that game at Manchester United), we did like to go out for a few drinks after our Saturday and Wednesday night games. This, of course, was all part of our social programme to integrate fully into the local community and for no other reason, you understand. With our families not yet moved up from London, we clearly didn't want to go back to the loneliness of an hotel room straight after a match. Our principal port of call was a nightclub in the city called Grannys. A few of the lads used to go there because the club staff looked after us and we could enjoy a quiet drink without being bothered too much. Or so I thought.

Nightclubs were still in their infancy. Grannys was a pokey little place where entry was gained by ascending a steep flight of stairs. The main benefit of a nightclub in the seventies was that it was one of only a handful of places where you could get a drink after 11pm. As you walked into the club, you turned left to the bar and right onto the dance-floor. In 500 visits to the club, I turned left on 499 occasions and on the other I headed for the toilets. One interesting little tit-bit of information is that

WE GOTTA LOTTA BOTTLE: You might say the local paper, the *Leicester Mercury,* was milking the publicity of the new arrivals of Keith Weller and myself. We arrived within days of each other and both made our debut in a goalless draw against Crystal Palace in October 1971. Keith moved up from Chelsea, and I joined from Crystal Palace. We both stayed the first few months in the Post House Hotel, Leicester, which was where this photo was taken. Needless to say, a few seconds after the photographer disappeared we got rid of the milk and ordered a couple of pints of lager.

the DJ was a guy called Mel Pace. Do you know, some 27 years later he's the PA announcer at Filbert Street. Still, I had better not be too derogatory about him because he saw me in action at the club, so to speak.

I was viewed by some of the locals in the club as a bit of a London flash 'arry. One group in particular, a shifty-looking lot, sporting a motley collection of scars and broken bones, took a dislike to yours truly and I was warned by the assistant manager to watch out for them because they had it in for me. One night I received a garbled message via Lenny Glover that they were going to 'sort me out'. Apparently a friend of a friend of one of the old players felt I was being too loud and trying to rule the roost at the football club. My only crime, as I saw it, was trying to organise some team spirit among the lads.

■ **1971-72 TEAM GROUP:** Here's my first appearance in an official Leicester City team photo: Back row (left to right) John Sjoberg, Alastair Brown, Steve Whitworth, Peter Shilton, Malcolm Munro, Graham Cross, Alan Woollett, Alan Birchenall, Malcolm Manley. (Front row) John Farrington, Rodney Fern, David Nish, David Tomlin, Jimmy Bloomfield (manager), Len Glover, Jon Sammels, Keith Weller.

Throughout my six years at Leicester there were always a few cliques in the dressing room, as there are at every football club to this day. Upon my arrival it was noticeable there was very much an 'us' and 'them' situation between the established Leicester players and the London boys. There was a mentality where some players came in, kept their noses clean, did the training, played the games and went home. I considered that far too mundane a way of living for a professional footballer, I wanted to squeeze every last drop of life and entertainment out of my career. I must have hit the older, established players like a hurricane. Within weeks I was planning social events, lads' nights out and organising a few practical jokes. I like to think that helped foster a great team spirit and I do believe 90 per cent of the players came around to my way of thinking.

Unfortunately my cavalier approach got me into a load of trouble with this section of local *pondlife*. As the weeks went by, the veiled threats became more menacing to the stage when I was informed by a third party not to turn up at Grannys on my own or I would get a good beating. Without wishing to sound too Rambo-ish (have I told you about the time I saved Sylvester Stallone from drowning in Hawaii? No, well I'll give you all the details in a later chapter), I will take anybody on face to face (Chopper Harris, excepted, of course) but I was a trifle concerned by the prospect of being set upon in the dark by a group of local thugs.

At this point, let me tell you about some of my business associates from London. Two types of people used to mainly frequent players' bars at football clubs - showbiz celebrities and villains. When I look in the bars today I don't think anything has really changed. At Chelsea I was befriended by 'associates' of one of the two most powerful gangland groups in London. I struck up a good friendship with one of these 'associates' who kept in touch with me after my move to Leicester. He asked how I was settling into life in the Midlands and I told him I was experiencing problems with one particular guy. "What's his name?" he asked. I told him that all I knew was his first name and that he worked for a tyre company.

Two weeks passed and I and a few of the lads found ourselves in Grannys again after a midweek game. Sure enough, across the bar was my mate and his cronies smirking at me. I ordered a round only to be told by the barman my drink had already been taken care of by 'the gentleman across the bar.' I looked up to see that familiar face leering at me. "Tonight's the night," I thought to myself, "he's got me a drink as some sort of prelude to giving me a good hiding." As he started to walk in my direction I instinctively grabbed a beer glass and was preparing to smash it on the bar in order to protect myself. I certainly wasn't going to go down without a fight. He came up to me and declared: "Birch, I think there's been a bit of a misunderstanding. We've not got off on the best possible terms and I'd just

■ **BEST IN THE BUSINESS:** Peter Shilton was in a league of his own and some of his performances were truly breathtaking. Myself and Newcastle defender Frank Clark stand and watch as Peter deals with another centre. Note the all white strip which Peter pioneered in the early seventies.

like to bury the hatchet and apologise to you for the hassle I've caused." I could hardly believe my ears. From getting a good pasting, I had now received a full apology.

Another week passed by and, a few days ahead of a game against Chelsea, my gangland enforcer called to request a couple of tickets. "No problem," I said. As an aside, he asked whether I was still having problems. "Funny you should say that ...." I started, before the penny suddenly dropped. My 'associate', acting on the scantest of information, had made a special journey up the M1 to track down the guy who was giving me the trouble, had a few quiet words in his shell-like and warned him about the error of his ways. "I don't think you'll be getting any more problems," he said, with typical understatement. The postscript to this story is that I now get on quite well with the guy, and if I bump into him in Leicester we exchange a few pleasantries.

Although I have great difficulty in remembering much of the on-the-field action, I have to confess there is one game which always sticks in my mind. It was only my second start for Leicester and after a goalless home draw on my debut against my old club Crystal Palace we travelled to West Ham. Leicester fans will know it has been the unluckiest ground for the club to visit over the past 30 years. Since winning the World Cup in 1966, we had to wait for Darren Eadie to give Leicester their first Upton Park triumph in the year 2000. It was the same in my era and on this particular afternoon the Hammers were in irresistible form. Geoff Hurst was creating chance after chance, Martin Peters was buzzing around and Bobby Moore was at his imperious best. We were hopelessly outclassed, scraping a 1-1 draw when we should have been beaten 8-1. We weren't because of the performance of one man, our 'keeper Peter Shilton. It was the finest goalkeeping performance I have ever witnessed in my life. Now bear in mind I'd been fortunate to play in sides with great custodians - Alan Hodgkinson at Sheffield United, Peter Bonetti at Chelsea and John Jackson at Palace. Shilts, however, was in a different league. On the team coach on the way home he must have thought I was a right pervert because I sat staring at him all the way around the North Circular. I could not believe this ordinary guy had produced a display of such Superman proportions. I'd heard he was a good young 'keeper but nothing had prepared me for that performance. I don't know whether that game lives in Peter's mind but it certainly does in mine.

Like all goalkeepers, Shilts was a bit of a loner. I actually got changed next to him in the dressing rooms and he would always report hours ahead of me in the morning. George Dewis, his youth team coach at Leicester, told me how Peter used to tie weights to his ankles and suspend himself from the wall-bars. Take a look at Peter and you'll notice he has freakishly long arms. He wasn't born like that but his dedication knew no bounds and all that stretching was designed to improve his reach by an inch or two. In training he was absolutely awesome but he was very much a man for doing his own thing. He trained separately to the rest of us. Bear in mind, this was in an era before goalkeeping coaches. I may be wrong, but I don't think Peter would have welcomed someone telling him what to do, or how to position his feet and cut down his angles. He was self-taught and would not have taken kindly to outside interference.

If Jimmy Bloomfield was responsible for one thing at Filbert Street, it was producing a cultural revolution within the club. Before Jimmy's arrival, the club was rather insular and the players had very little profile on the national stage. Jimmy brought a new type of player to the club - players from London, who were used to a different lifestyle and liked to burn the candle at both ends. As I have said earlier, there were two distinct groups when I arrived. The local boys like John Sjoberg, Graham Cross, Malcolm Manley, Alan Woollett and Steve Whitworth were all great

▢ Oh he of the trawlerman's jumper, **ALAN WOOLLETT** (above) and ladies man and Elvis fan **FRANK WORTHINGTON** (right).

lads but, shall we say, enjoyed the quiet life. They came in for training, played the games and got off home. I came from a breed who wanted to live the life of a professional footballer on and off the pitch and as Jimmy signed more and more players the balance of power shifted from 50-50 to more like 80-20. Dennis Rofe, Frank Worthington, Jeff Blockley and Chris Garland were four more Jimmy signings - all of whom had played the game on a slightly bigger stage, enjoyed higher profiles and possessed strong characters.

Arguably the difference in cultures was perhaps best summed up by Alan Woollett and Frank. To say they were poles apart would be something of a major understatement. In his Elvis gear, stetson hat, leather studded belt and cowboy boots, Frank was a fashion statement. Alan, by contrast, was more at home doing his shopping in Milletts, clad most often in a trawlerman's jumper and dungarees. He was a dead ringer for Compo from Last of the Summer Wine. Throughout the year there would be occasions when these two culture gaps would manifest themselves - end of season tours, especially.

Jimmy, pleased with the progress we had made, offered us an end of season trip to Barbados. Our only dilemma was whether we should take our wives or partners or, in Frank's case, wives and partners. Jimmy offered the decision to the players. There was some serious persuading to be done. I could see a lot of the Leicester lads were keen to take their wives or, to be more accurate, were afraid of the consequences if they didn't. As their arms twitched, I butted in. "Boss, lads only please because it will be better for team spirit. After all, we will be taking our wives on another holiday at the end of the season," I explained. It seemed to do the trick as the arms stayed down and the local boys spent the next 48 hours wondering how to break the news to their other halves.

Having already visited the Caribbean paradise while with Chelsea, I regaled the lads with stories of what they could expect, and on arrival proudly showed off the view to my room-mate Frank - sea view, golden sands and palm trees. Paradise personified. We went for a stroll along the beach and bumped into Alan Woollett and Graham Cross. As we were walking by, a microscopic cloud passed across the sun and lowered the temperature from 90 to 89 degrees fahrenheit. There was a solitary spit of rain. Woolly turned around and said to me: "Bet it's not raining in Wigston, Birch!" Those cliques never totally subsided, we never were one completely happy band of 16 professional footballers but there was a camaraderie among the lads and I like to think I played some small part in helping bring us all a little closer together.

Although Jimmy was far from being a revolutionary coach, he liked to be different. In the gym when we did warm-up routines he liked nothing better than to switch on a tape machine and start playing Glenn Miller tunes and the famous 'Little Brown Jug' song. At the time, only the Brazilians used music as part of their warm-up routines. Now, the Wimbledon ghetto blaster has become legendary and I don't think there is a single Premiership team which doesn't play music in the dressing room before a game as a way of relaxing the players. That was typical Jimmy, in many respects he was way ahead of his time.

One of his best signings had to be the acquisition of Frank Worthington. I had been there just over a season when he arrived. In typical Frank style, he scored on his debut at Old Trafford to earn us a 1-1 draw with Manchester United. He finished top scorer at the club for three successive seasons, banging in 48 goals in the process. Typically, he never let us forget about any one of the goals.

Frank's home debut was, in many ways, more memorable for his performance off the pitch than on it, a goalless draw with Coventry City. Our first watering hole after a match was invariably the players' bar. At Filbert Street, it was a dingy little room closeted away in the bowels of the main stand. During the week it was used as an administrative office but on match-days a table would be plonked in the middle of the room and two great City fans, Stan and Mary, would run a bar for us. I say 'bar', but truthfully it was a crate of beer and, if the girls were lucky, a bottle of white wine. On an average afternoon there would be a handful of players' wives, girlfriends and a few children.

Enter Frank after the game; the door creaked open and in he sauntered wearing a fedora, black t-shirt with 'Elvis' emblazoned across it in silver glitter, jacket covered in embroidered red roses, the tightest possible pair of jeans and knee-length black leather boots. Most of the wives and girlfriends were seated so as Frank walked in

they were treated to a pretty impressive pair of *testimonials* which were fairly bulging out of the crotch area of Frank's skin-tight pants. After the next game, for some inexplicable reason, there was an enormous surge in the players bar popularity with the female fraternity. It was standing room only. As Frank walked in, he turned to me and said: "A little bit busier this afternoon, lads," with a nudge and a wink.

Frank was a considerably more complex character than most people realise. I took a battering from him in his quaintly named autobiography One Hump or Two but myself and Lenny Glover were probably his only two real friends

▓ **SHARING A LAUGH AND A JOKE:**
Manager Jimmy Bloomfield reminds star striker Frank Worthington that he's forgotten to pay his car parking tickets. Frank assures the gaffer he'll deal with it as soon as he gets back home... and promptly forgets all about it.

at Filbert Street. Frank himself probably wouldn't disagree.

Frank got on well with Lenny because of their almost telepathic understanding on the pitch. Throughout all Frank's clubs (and there were plenty of them!) he says he never had a better understanding with any player than with Lenny. They always seemed to know exactly where each other was on the pitch. I think Frank liked me because of my extrovert nature and ability to entertain - it certainly had nothing to do with my footballing ability because he always used to crucify me.

Yet although Frank was an extrovert on the pitch, he was quite introverted during the week. Believe it or not, he used to keep himself to himself and was very softly spoken for much of the time. He did, however, have to raise his voice on more than one occasion with his first wife Birgitta. Their rows were legendary and what an oddball couple they made.

LENNY GLOVER: City's tricky winger enjoyed a almost telepathic understanding on the pitch with the Foxes charismatic centre-forward Frank Worthington.

When they first arrived the *tank commander* invited Birgitta over for dinner as a way of getting to know each other. *Tanko* put on a great spread although she was a little put out when Birgitta turned up on the door with the Worthington's pet alsatian. Undeterred, Heather took them through to the dining room and served up a delicious main course of fillet steak. Birgitta proceeded to chop up the steak into tiny pieces before putting the plate on the floor. A very grateful alsatian wolfed down the food while Birgitta took some muesli out of here handbag. "I don't eat meat," she said by way of explanation. Heather was stunned into silence as she watched a dog eat fillet steak off our best bone china.

Frank, in many ways, was very naive in the ways of the real world. He's a lovely chap, but he needs someone to look after his every need all of the time otherwise he finds it hard to cope. We very quickly found out about some of Frank's foibles after his arrival in Leicester. On his first day he roared up to the training ground in a Ford Mustang, complete with a leather strap tied around the bonnet. For those of you who can remember the Mustang, it sounded like a Sherman tank but was a very powerful motor car. After a short while, Frank was presented with a sponsored car. One day I was driving through Leicester when I heard on the radio that there had been a major traffic jam in Charles Street. I thought no more about it until Lenny Glover pulled me in the dressing room the following morning.

"Did you hear about Frank," he said. "He was driving through town yesterday when his car ran out of petrol. He thought it had broken down so he simply got out of the car, left it in the middle of the road and walked home!"

Frank's explanation was that as the car was not his property it was nothing to do with him.

He also had a blind spot when it came to parking, and thought that yellow lines did not apply to him. As a consequence Frank picked up parking tickets like confetti. Of course, he never thought you had to pay them either. So, once a month, regular as clockwork, there would be a visit by the boys in blue down to the training ground and the club were forced into settling Frank's unpaid parking fines. I don't think Frank did this out of big-headedness. He has simply always been in need of someone to take control of his life.

On the training ground, Frank was an education to watch as well. One of his greatest pleasures in life was to take out a bag of balls after the main session and rain in volleys and shots on Peter Shilton and, latterly, Mark Wallington. Frank insisted on quality crosses being delivered so that he could produce acrobatic bicycle kicks and other outrageous finishes. Of course, none of us were going to go out on a Monday afternoon in darkest January and feed Frank's ego by crossing ball after ball after ball. Instead, two members of the groundstaff would be despatched to supply Frank from either flank. Woe betide them if they did not deliver a good enough cross. When Frank scored, he would wheel away in triumph and raise his arms aloft as if he had just got the winner at Old Trafford. Whisper it quietly, but we all used to watch from inside the training ground because some of Frank's finishes were truly breathtaking. He also wellied quite a few out of the ground.

There was probably only one other person more obsessional on the training ground and that was Shilts. Many experts have spoken about his dedication and commitment being the reason behind his success. Untrue. You could not be as talented a 'keeper as Shilts unless you were born with a certain amount of natural ability. World-class is an over-used phrase but it probably doesn't do Shilts justice. Quite simply, he was the best in the world. Absolutely awesome. Some of the sessions had to be seen to be believed.

Often, on the Friday before a game, Frank, Lenny, myself, Jon Sammels and Keith Weller would line up and take shots at Peter from the edge of the box. Between us we'd pepper about fifty and it was all deadly serious. We'd blast them, curl them, bend them, do everything we could to beat Shilts from 18 yards. When Peter was really in the mood, he didn't let in a single goal. The odds of this happening are thousands to one. I often thought that if you filmed the session you'd have the perfect goalkeeping video.

Jimmy assembled a truly talented team. In my first season we finished twelfth but, with the arrival of Worthington and Rofe, it was in the 1973-74 campaign that things really began to take shape. This co-incided with the demise of my days as a striker. Although I had been signed to play up front, my partnership with Rodney Fern had, in truth, been less than prolific. Jimmy pulled me in training and suggested I might consider reverting to a central midfield role. Far from being outraged at having my striking abilities questioned, I was a keen advocate of the idea. To be honest, I'd had the shit kicked out of me as a forward. I slotted into a defensive midfield role just in front of the two centre halves and our formation really took shape from there.

It was in my final season as a recognised striker that I almost scored my only ever first-class

SWEATING UP: Jimmy Bloomfield was always keen to bring some light-hearted relief to training and here the squad went for a communal sauna to sweat off a few excess pounds. Jimmy is pictured centre with me in the background and (foreground) Alan Woollett in pole position.

■ **ON THE BALL:** I'll admit it, I do think I look rather good on this photo. I'd had a particularly good day with the blow-drier and got my bouffant just right. Not a bad facial expression although the lower lip is jutting out a little because of a cold sore. For the record, this was photo-call day for the start of the 1973-74 season.

hat-trick. It came in February 1973 when we beat the mighty Leeds 2-0 and I scored both goals in front of a capacity Filbert Street crowd. One in particular was an absolute scorcher. I collected the ball and unleashed a left-footed 30-yard thunderbolt that arrowed into the top corner. Over the years, the distance of that strike has become longer and longer, until a couple of years ago I was telling everyone I'd *larruped* it from the half-way line! Unfortunately, my fantasies were shattered when television's number one reporter Gary Newbon (he told me to put that in) was scouting through the Star Soccer archives and found footage of the goal. I was most crestfallen when I saw the strike was considerably closer to the 18-yard box than the half-way line.

ACTION REPLAY: For many years I recounted the story of my wonder goal against Leeds United. As the years passed by, so did the length of the shot to the point at which it reached the half-way line. Sadly, ITV sports controller Gary Newbon (he's the one in the middle) recently found the Star Soccer footage of the game to reveal the shot was, in actual fact, struck on the edge of the 18-yard-box. Cheers Gary, who here was sifting through some of his early fan-mail with club receptionists Sue Purple and Diane Benton.

Our tactics were very simple. We played a system I called the Birchy concertina. Our objective was basically to get everyone behind the ball, suck in teams and then counter-attack them with real pace and skill. We didn't bother chasing after the ball in the opposition half, we just let them come at us. It worked like a dream. Frank was up front banging in the goals, Weller produced the goods down the right and Lenny did the business down the left.

Unquestionably we had the two best wide men operating in England at that time. I played in midfield alongside Jon Sammels and everything worked wonderfully well. For the players we had at our disposal, it was the perfect system. I also happen to think it was a supremely balanced team, one of the most finely balanced I ever played in at any club.

■ **CITY ACES:** (Left to right) Jon Sammels, Steve Whitworth, Keith Weller and David Nish were all class acts in the Bloomfield Boys line-up.

Our achievements were recognised at international level with Frank, Wells and Steve Whitworth all winning call-ups for England. While that might not sound too spectacular by Liverpool and Manchester United standards, it was a tremendous feat for a club like Leicester City where we all had to work twice as hard to earn the same amount of recognition. Lenny was a fantastic player but he was also the only professional upon whom I never saw a bead of sweat. I was unsure whether this was attributable to his metabolism or his laziness. In the modern era, he might struggle with the tackling back element of the game but back in the seventies he was mustard. An intelligent player, he could go either way and had a telepathic understanding with Frank. Lenny, however, could also be viciously cutting. He was probably the most ruthless of anyone in the dressing room banter stakes.

Everything about Wells oozed class. He never seemed to sprint, but glided across the turf. He possessed an abundance of skill and once he had the ball we all piled forward because we knew he would go past players and get in a cross.

My midfield partner Jon Sammels was another class act. He arrived in Leicester after taking some stick at Highbury and he used to get a bit of barracking from the fans at Filbert Street too. But Jon was a players' player. He always wanted the ball and would never vanish out of a game. When some players are struggling they stay out of the way and don't want the ball. Jon would never, ever hide and earned a great deal of respect from everyone in the game.

David Nish was another, like Lenny, who never seemed to work up much of a sweat. He was a Rolls Royce of a player who, I naively felt, always played at one pace. This I found out to my cost to be untrue when I tried to race past him when he was at Derby and he simply cruised by me in the race for the ball. I knew I had to be right on the edge to be effective. Nishy always seemed to be playing within himself but it's often the sign of a talented player that they always have a little something in reserve.

As with all my other clubs, I wasted little time in giving a Birchy nickname to all the players. Some were straightforward like Elvis and Wells. Dennis Rofe became Syd because of his likeness to Carry On actor Sid James. Mark Wallington was The Duke and Steve Earle The Baron. Graham Cross was 'fatty', much to the intense dislike of his wife... so I used the name all the more. Shilts earned the nickname of 'The Mongol' after he was stung by a mosquito while on a pre-season tour of Sweden. The insect bit Peter on his chin on the morning of a game and by the time of kick off his chin had puffed up like a balloon.

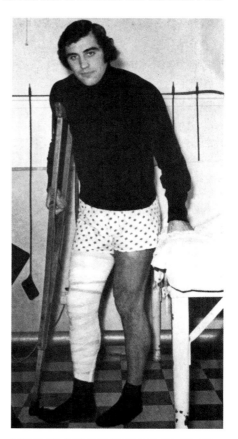

Rod Fern was nicknamed Gerson, after the famous Brazilian. Rod was a nice guy but never the most confident. You always kept having to give him a little boost. That's why I referred to him as Gerson. "You know, Rod, you remind me of Gerson the way you play sometimes," I told him. Frank and Lenny thought it was hilarious but it seemed to do the trick.

Arguably the most subtle and inventive was my christening of Lenny as 'Fido.' This stemmed from the time when Lenny rather unwisely told me of a Friday evening stroll he undertook with his red setter. On the night in question, he was walking along his estate in Evington when he chanced to look up into a window to see a rather attractive young lady clothing off in full view of the street. Every Friday evening after that for the next 36 years he patrolled the same streets in Evington waiting under the same lamp-post. The only problem is he hasn't got a dog any more!

WHERE DID YOU GET THOSE SHORTS, PETER?
Peter Shilton was undoubtedly the greatest goalkeeper in the world. I used to marvel at his acrobatics in training with Frank Worthington. But, as he recovered from a broken leg in the 1971-72 season you did have to question his judgement in boxer shorts.

It's often been said the seventies was a golden era for football. Certainly, the game was filled with characters and every team possessed its fair share. At Leicester we had more than most with Frank,

255

Wells, Lenny and myself often grabbing a headline or two, not always for the right reason. Don't ask why, but things just seemed to 'happen' to me. Believe it or not, I never set out with the intention of capturing any publicity for myself. It's not like a famous film star or singer - Madonna and Liz Hurley spring to mind - who appear to deliberately perform outrageous stunts with the sole intention of attracting publicity to enhance their career. I always seemed to be in the wrong place at the wrong time. Whatever I did on a football pitch was spontaneous because of my love for the game and I felt it should be played with a smile on your face.

At every available opportunity, I liked to use my sense of humour to diffuse tension. One of the ways in which I entertained the lads in what is undoubtedly the tensest time of the week for any professional footballer, the final hour before kick off, centred around a little routine I perfected with my left boot. I would tie together a few shoelaces on the boot and position it outside the dressing room door. Then, with Frank, Lenny, the manager and everyone looking on, I'd whistle to it and shout: "Come to daddy." I'd start to pull on the long lace hidden in my right hand and, sure enough, through the door came the boot. "Are you going to be a good boy today?" I'd quip as I reeled the boot across the dressing room floor. Frank used to be in hysterics and Jimmy would often stick his head around the door and afford himself a wry smile. Meanwhile, I'd look down in disdain on the right boot and spit on it in disgust. This became a ritual in our dressing room but it did serve a useful purpose as well, releasing players' tension at a crucial stage of the afternoon.

Even by my standards, the extraordinary case of the missing meat pies and the bobble hat takes some beating. Midway through the first half of a match against a side I can't remember, I do recall one of our players going down injured. It was quite a serious knock and the trainer was attending to him for what seemed an eternity. I propped myself against a wall on the East Stand and was chatting to a few fans. With nothing better to do, I borrowed a bobble hat and put it on my head. A few moments later a pie-man came walking around the perimeter track. For those of you who can remember this far back, you may recall the vendors, dressed in white smocks and carrying a large tray of pies. I spotted him and decided to give one of his pies - steak and kidney, I think - to a fan. "Thanks, Birch," smiled the fan and seconds later all the supporters around him were calling for me to hand them one as well. It was like the biblical story of the fishes and the loaves - I kept dipping into this poor kid's tray and giving his pies away for free. Within seconds I had cleared out his whole supply.

By this time, we were ready to re-start the game and, in response to the lad's plea, I told him to come and see me later and I would pay for the pies myself. The action started again only for, 60 seconds later, the irate referee to stop the game. He came up to me and shouted: "Get that bobble hat off your head, Birchenall. I knew I'd get some trouble from you as soon as I saw I'd got Leicester." Silly old me hadn't realised I had kept the hat on. So, in the space of two minutes, I'd donated a tray of pies and ponced around in a bobble hat!

Half time finally came and back in the dressing room Jimmy summoned up all his reserves of anger to give us a real rollocking. He was in full flow only for us to hear a knock on the door. Suddenly, it burst open and as I looked to my right I couldn't believe my eyes. There, coming through the door, was a pieman in a white smock. "'Ere, Birch!", he shouted at the top of his voice, "you owe me £2 five shillings and sixpence for all them pies. Are you going to pay me now or later?" I was staggered. Jimmy was completely dumbfounded and the rest of the lads were trying their hardest not to burst out laughing.

I recall a time when the rain was absolutely lashing down and we were waiting in the tunnel to go out for the start of the second half. I sheltered under the brolly of a couple of our lady supporters and, when we finally ran out, decided to borrow the umbrella. I took up my position on the pitch in front of our back four, the referee checked with both goalkeepers and whistled the start of the half. Half a second later there was another shrill blast on his whistle and he raced up to me. "Get rid of that umbrella now, Birchenall!" he bawled and proceeded to give me a mighty rollocking although, to be fair, he did stop short of putting my name in his notebook. The whole crowd erupted as he snatched the brolly and threw it back into the crowd.

Or what about the time when young centre forward Bob Lee was sent crashing to earth after an aerial challenge in a game against Arsenal? Bob lay unconscious in a crumpled heap on the floor and our physio, George Preston, raced swiftly across the pitch to give him some treatment. Bob looked quite bad and a few of us gathered around. After administering smelling salts, George said to us: "He's struggling. He doesn't know who he is or where he is". "Well,' I replied, "tell him he's George Best and he's playing for Manchester United!"

I would hasten to point out that I was not always the focal point of these incidents. Mark Wallington took centre stage during one pre-season. Mark was a top-class goalkeeper although he did have one or two problems with his weight. Endeavouring to shed a few pounds, he invested in a special weight-reduction rubber suit from a catalogue. Apparently , you put it on while you sat around the house and the manufacturers claimed it was possible to lose half a stone while watching Crossroads.

Mark decided to take this philosophy a stage further by wearing the rubber suit under his training kit and hopefully sweat off a few stone. This was a rather bold step when we were doing our pre-season around Bradgate Park - a famous country park in Leicestershire which has been the scene of arduous pre-season runs for City players during the past four decades. On the day in question, Jimmy told us there was to be one timed run around the perimeter of the park. There was only one message to us all: don't finish last. Off we hared and after about 40 minutes of hard slog we trickled back in and boarded the bus. Twenty minutes later the final stragglers limped home and the coach was ready to leave.

"Where's the Duke?" went up the shout. So we waited. And waited. And waited. Jimmy finally decided to send out some search parties and we went off in pairs to all four corners of the park to find Mark. One pair came across some walkers who looked extremely worried. "We've found a body!" they shrieked. "It's lying in a ditch and we don't know whether it's alive or dead. It's covered in a black plastic bag. Call the police!" Messages were flashed back and the lads raced over to the ditch. There, lying prostrate was Mark. He was unconscious and severely dehydrated. The physios helped him back to the bus and he spent the next two days recovering from the ordeal.

Football training grounds at that time tended to be havens for black market activities. With players receiving their money in cash, there was always scope to cut a deal or two. There seemed to be a constant procession of lorries and vans being driven into the Belvoir Drive training ground. Boots would be opened and invitations extended to sample the wares. You'd often see a roll of material being shifted out, a stereo system being exchanged. Hear no evil, see no evil, as they say. A player had only to drop the vaguest hint he was on the look-out for a piece of equipment and there'd be a choice of six available by the following morning. At one of the nightclubs we frequented, I christened a little alcove 'Criminals Corner' on account of the clientele it attracted. One of the lads mentioned he was eager to take up golf. The following morning an associate arrived armed with a new set of clubs and bag. "How much would you give for these?" he enquired of the player. "Well, really, I'd prefer another make," was the reply. "No problem," replied the associate who duly returned to the sports shop from where he had half-inched the clubs and gave a very plausible argument that he had received them as a present and didn't have a receipt. Of course, the shop staff were only too keen to exchange them and the following morning the player was presented with the bag and clubs of his preferred choice. Talk about brass neck!!

We've spoken at length about the banter and humour which exists among footballers at every club. A lot of the time it is very funny but there are times when it can be politely described as borderline. Many footballers thrive on banter. I had been lucky to be brought up in a good school at Chelsea where I learned how to handle myself. I would often knock myself as this would deflect any abuse being hurled in my

JUST A TRIM, PLEASE: One of my favourite haunts away from the football ground was a hairdressing salon on Narborough Road run by my close friend Franco Pizzolon. Franco looked after the barnets of most of the City players and here I am modelling his latest creation.

direction. Not all players, though, were as comfortable taking the stick. There were some strong characters and both Frank and Lenny were not averse to dishing out the abuse.

For one guy at Leicester, it all proved too much. Malcolm Munro was a promising young centre half who enjoyed a fantastic first full season in 1973-74. He started off the following campaign in similar vein until January. Malcolm, in fact, played a key role in keeping us in the FA Cup and ensuring we did not become one of the biggest FA Cup giantkilling victims of all time against Leatherhead. It was he who cleared off the line from the 'Leatherhead Lip' Chris Kelly with the non-leaguers already two goals up. Unfortunately, he also made a few mistakes and took a fair bit of abuse and stick.

Malcolm was left out of the side after the game and it was to prove his final one in a Leicester shirt. The following season he didn't turn up for pre-season training and no-one knew what had happened. It was the last we saw of him. The story was he couldn't handle the flak and went off to drive a truck across Australia. The last I heard he had returned to England and was working in the fire service in Nottingham. I suppose everyone assumes that all professional footballers love their life, but there is a small percentage of players who find the pressures and the banter in a dressing room too much. They can't handle it, don't enjoy themselves and, as in any other walk of life, simply want to get out.

From an early stage, as was the case with most clubs, I was elected social secretary and charged with the task of organising nights out. In the modern game, the demands and rigours are such that it is becoming increasingly difficult for players to attend social functions. Here at Leicester we have a department responsible for arranging player functions and everything is laid on for them. Back in the seventies, when clubs employed one man and his dog, players were left largely to their own devices.

Being a 'social animal' I was keen to establish a thriving social scene for the players and, having discovered very few of the lads went out in midweek, decided to take the bull by the horns. I placed an advertisement in the club programme asking for invitations from local pubs and clubs who were prepared to host darts and pool nights with the players.

In my naivety I expected only a few replies, but within a few days mail was arriving at Filbert Street by the sackload with invitations from all four corners of the county, and beyond. I had a word with the players and quite a few were up for the nights out, so I sifted through the letters and chose a few which looked promising. One, in particular, caught my eye. It was from the barman of a city centre pub who said his boss was a mad-keen Leicester fan and he would love to host a charity darts night with the players.

Excellent, I thought. I enlisted the help of Keith Weller, Dennis Rofe and Peter Shilton for a four-ball and the event was fixed up for a Wednesday evening, traditionally the best midweek night out in Leicester. Little did we know that the Dover Castle pub had a certain notoriety and reputation in the city.

I was the first to arrive on the night, to be greeted by an enthusiastic barman with peroxide blond hair wearing a particularly garish silver-spangled jacket. As I looked around there seemed an overwhelming number of blokes around the place. The friendly barman exchanged pleasantries with me and asked if I would care to meet Josie, a big Foxes fan. Well, I thought, this was an interesting proposition. She might be a real *desirable*. Expectantly, I made my way upstairs and into a darkened room only to be greeted by a high-pitched shriek: "Ooooooh, it's you Birchy. I can't believe it. To meet you in the flesh, it's one of the greatest moments of my life. Come here, pleeeease, darling," said Josie. Josie then proceeded to step out of the shadows and I was confronted by a fella with purple hair, dressed in a flouncy floral shirt and a pair of tight-fitting white trousers. To say I was shocked would be a major understatement. Josie was desperate to have a photograph taken with me so I sat down on a chair and he leapt on me with gay abandon. "Oooooh, this is fantastic. I can't believe it's really you, darling."

After the photo session we filed downstairs where the rest of the lads had now assembled in the darts room for our charity challenge match. There was not a single woman in the crowd. As we practised, we could feel our form being studied, and I don't mean our ability to hit double top. 'Wells' was always game for a laugh and he decided to take things one step further. Half-way through the game and with the scores fairly even, he turned to me with a smile on his face and whispered: "Watch this, Birch." He threw his first two darts at the treble 20 but then deliberately aimed his last into the wall. Naturally, the dart bounced off the wall and fell onto the floor. Wells went up to the board, pulled out the two arrows from treble 20 and then proceeded to very deliberately bend down and pick up the third dart. As he bent down, he wiggled his arse and very slowly got back up again. Well, there was a mighty 'Ooooooh' in the crowd and you could feel every set of eyes concentrating on Wells' buttocks. "We're never going to get out of here alive!" I said to him.

Shilts, meanwhile, having had a half of shandy, was now in desperate need of the toilet. "Birch," he whispered to me, "I need the loo. I'm desperate for a piddle." "Well," I replied, "what's stopping you?" "There's no way I'm going on my own. Can you come in with me, please," came the reply. Here I was, in a gay pub escorting the England goalkeeper to the toilets because he was frightened to go on his own. Off we trotted to the tiny toilet, only to be followed by eight other blokes. As we stood over the urinal, Shilts whispered out of the corner of his mouth. "I'm not getting it out in here."

■ **LADIES MAN:** Out in the county again on community service with the lady footballers of Ratcliffe Bombers. Only I, however, could end up on a Football Association disrepute charge. I offered to referee a ladies charity match involving the Bombers but my generosity backfired when some petty-minded individual complained to the Leicestershire FA that I was not a fully qualified referee. I received a letter of censure from the local FA warning me as to my future conduct. Oh, and by the way, I had no ulterior motives getting involved in ladies football. If I had been out on the pull I certainly wouldn't have worn that tank top.

■ **ANYONE FOR CRICKET:** Former Leicestershire and England skipper Ray Illingworth never forgot my impromptu performance in a turban disguised as Ben Ali Birchenheimer during a charity cricket match at Grace Road. A City team was taking on the county cricketers and, for a laugh, I blackened myself up with boot polish, put on a turban and went out to bat under my assumed name. As I got to the crease, I asked Illy to dolly me up one delivery. I dutifully smashed it for a six into an adjacent double decker bus. Even though this was a charity game, Illy's pride had been dented. He proceeded to call up fast bowler Ken Higgs. Ken, it appeared, retreated as far as Northampton, before steaming in to deliver his first ball. I never saw it and the ball shattered my stumps as if they were in a skittle alley. I have seldom been as frightened in my life... especially as I had left my 'box' back in the pavilion.

■ **GIVE US A JOB:**
It's December 1976 and I was invited along to perform the official opening of Coalville job centre. Little did I realise that a year later I would be paying a return visit. Only instead of making a speech and cutting a ribbon, I was stood in a mile long queue waiting to sign on. Funny, but after queueing up for half an hour I was so full of shame that I went home and vowed never ever to return again.

■ **COMMUNITY SERVICE:** On the day this photograph was taken by the Leicester Mercury, my five years' service with Leicester City was brought to an end when I was released to join San Jose Earthquakes. It was quite an emotional time for me after so many happy seasons at Filbert Street. But rather than moping around at home I ensured I honoured an appointment to present swimming certificates to youngsters at the Stafford Leys primary school in Leicester Forest East.

■ WHAT'S UP, NURSE:
The Birch and Keith Weller decide to carry out some medical research of our own with a nurse from Leicester's Groby Road hospital. The lads were on hand to present a cheque for £1,088 to purchase specialist equipment as part of our community programme.

■ BEATLES OUTFOXED: Here's Leicester City's own Fab Five who entertained supporters at the club's Take Your Pick lottery evenings in the function suite at Filbert Street. Jon Sammels is on guitar, Dennis Rofe is on drums, the singing duties are shared by Steve Earle and yours truly, while Keith Weller is a picture of concentration on his organ.

■ ON THE CATWALK:
My close friend Franco arranged for me to do some modelling appearances. I'm not quite sure how I allowed myself to be persuaded to wear this polka dot black velvet jacket, however.

■ **ON THE OCHE:** Eat your heart out, Leighton Rees, John Lowe and Eric Bristow. We honed our darts skills with a Leicester City players side which toured the local pubs and clubs playing a combination of darts, pool and skittles. Keith Weller, Dennis Rofe and Peter Shilton were among the mainstays of the team. We had some great nights out and the locals really enjoyed themselves. However, we did get more than we bargained for at one of our early nights when we went to the Dover Castle pub in Leicester. Unbeknown to us, it was a 'gay' pub and we all seemed to be very popular with the locals.

■ **FANCY A FLUTTER:** We're not quite sure who's paying who here but, from what I can remember, I was placing a charity bet with Corals. Not being much of a gambler myself, I decided to ask the expert opinion of Peter Shilton. On Shilts' advice, I laid £25 on Ching Dynasty to win the 2.15 at Newmarket. Of course, it didn't win. Mind you, it was still a pleasure to hand over my greenbacks to the lovely Corals representative Kay Nicholson. You know what they say about ladies in glasses, well I always made passes at them. Where are you now, Kay?

LEICESTER CITY FC 1973-74: We swapped the Filbert Street turf for the terracing on the Kop for our team photograph this year. Can you spot me in the second row (fifth one in from the right).

Now I'll concede I was more than a little intimidated by our male audience. "You're gonna have to," I told Shilts. Fortunately, a fella came out of a cubicle and Shilts darted inside like a rat up a drainpipe. In truth, we went on to have a great night and it was one of the very best evenings I was to enjoy in my five years as social secretary at the club . There was a good bit of banter and, the following morning in training, I went up to Graham Cross and Alan Woollett to ask them about the pub. They were amazed. "Didn't you know, that's the main gay pub in Leicestershire?" they said. I do now.

Nothing was subsequently to ever match proceedings of that evening but we did have some great times. We went to pubs and working men's clubs throughout the county in Oakham, Melton, Ashby, Market Harborough and Hinckley and everywhere we went we had a fantastic reception. Not only did we raise thousands of pounds for local charities but it was also a great way of keeping in touch with our fans and the local community. It also meant that the players, by enjoying each other's company, were able to bond together and share a good spirit. However, there was a secondary ulterior motive. We invariably arranged events for Wednesday nights and the unwritten rule was I had to ensure we were finished by 10.30pm. Nothing to do with a club curfew, you understand. No, it owed more to the fact we had to be at Grannys nightclub by 11pm for a few beers into the small hours. A lot of the publicans obviously wanted us to stay on for a late session at the pub but I had to quietly explain we were under club orders to be back home by 10.45pm. Little did they know the real truth.

This arrangement suited everyone. From a club perspective it was great public relations because we went out into the community, for the pubs their regulars loved shooting pool and playing darts with the lads, and for the players it meant we were guaranteed a good night out at Grannys. Only the wives and girlfriends lost out but we explained to them this was compulsory club business and we had no say in the matter.

Mind you, we always made it up to them after matches when we went out for social evenings. Custom and practice after midweek and Saturday games was to go out for a meal at the Costa Brava restaurant in Leicester. The owner is a guy called Ramon Fernandez who was well connected on the Spanish and European football scene. After midweek games especially, we would be there for the duration. I got to know Dave Bartram, lead singer of Showaddywaddy who were one of the country's top bands at the time - and still do the circuit these days. Dave would join us and we would be singing into the small hours. Ramon had an electronic organ in the restaurant and the organist would stay until about 2am. He'd leave the organ on remote control and we'd all take it in turns to play a tune. We always knew when it was time to leave... we'd hear the milkfloats rattling outside. Ramon was a fantastic host, I rarely recall us having to pay too many of our bills. His footballing connections meant we would often bump into the likes of Ron Atkinson, John Bond and Lawrie McMenemy. Having seen me in action in the restaurant, no wonder they never tried to sign me.

Unwinding with a few beers after a game is part and parcel of the English footballing culture. I know in this modern era that we hold up the continental players, with their diet of pasta and mineral water, as role-models but I genuinely believe that is not the English mentality. I've been involved in the game for nearly 40 years and 99 per cent of all English players love a beer after a match. It's their way of unwinding. Okay, they don't take it to the extremes we used to enjoy and take for granted, but I see nothing wrong with a few jars and a social. It's an accepted part of our game. Let the Europeans do what they want but we should still allow our players to relax in a manner in which they feel accustomed. They're not stupid, they know the physical demands put upon them in the game today, and as long as they do not abuse their bodies, let them get on with it. Anyway, enough of Birchy on his soapbox.

The seventies was a time when football commercialism was just beginning to manifest itself. Club sponsorships, sponsored cars, club lotteries and the like were all in their infancy. Needless to say, the lads wanted a cut of the action and requirements were placed on the players in return for these perks. Let's just set the record straight, there was no resemblance to today's commercial spin-offs and lucrative advertising deals. A Pontin's holiday, a four-pack of Everards and a sponsored Mini car were the extent of the offers. The lads, however, were grateful for anything.

Stuart Crooks was the commercial manager of the club and it's fair to say he had a hand in more pies than Ginsters as he juggled with a variety of television sets, tumble dryers and other lottery prizes. One of the main commercial operations at the club was the lottery with a weekly prize draw called 'Take Your Pick'. Compared to today's National Lottery, it was archaic but at the time it was one of the most successful football lotteries in the country. I and some of the players would make the draw along with one of the our celebrity supporters, Bill Maynard. A famous stand-up comedian in his own right, Bill was famed at the time for his role as Selwyn Froggatt in the national television series. He'd turn up each week, subject to work commitments, and get a bottle of champagne. I'd turn up and just get a thank you!

One of the first commercial perks on offer was a Pontin's holiday. Now, these days, most players would turn up their noses at this, but not back then. Each player got one Pontin's holiday a year. After a couple of years, however, this offer dried up until I bumped into Pontin's boss Captain Rowley at a function in London. The Captain was staggered to hear we no longer had the holidays - as he was continuing

■ **BEHIND THE WHEEL:** Here's the original advertisement which appeared in the Leicester Mercury about my sponsored car with local garage Trinity Motors. I'm pictured receiving the keys to my Fiat 131 from sales manager Ken Marshall and managing director Dennis Wattam. What was not so widely reported was that a few weeks later I wrote off the car after a collision with a lamp-post!

For family-man **ALAN BIRCHENALL** the **FIAT** 131 has some very interesting features.

A cordial send off as Alan Birchenall takes over the keys of his new FIAT 131 at Trinity Motors, Blackbird Road from Ken Marshall, Sales Manager, watched by Managing Director, Dennis Wattam.

For instance, it has a rigid passenger cage that's stronger than the ones you'll find on some cars twice the price. It has an underside completely sealed in a thick layer of PVC. Mechanically, it's deliberately been kept simple to keep servicing and maintenance bills down. For a car that's been built to cope with the problems that surround owning a car in times like these, we think you'll find it hard to beat. And we also think you'll find its price hard to resist.

A CAR LIKE THIS IS MONEY WELL SPENT

TM Trinity Motors (D.R.Wattam Ltd.)
47 Blackbird Road Leicester Phone 52137

to send them to the club. This caused quite a stir when I reported back to the lads and I was delegated to make the strongest possible protest. Apparently, it was blamed on an administrative oversight and the holidays were swiftly reinstated. Seems incredible today that an entire squad of First Division footballers were ready to go on strike over a one-week Pontin's family holiday!

If a holiday was deemed a major status symbol, a sponsored car was viewed with the same reverence as a 10-bedroom mansion. It was the ultimate accessory and unfortunately caused something of a division between the new boys and the local lads. Only myself, Frank Worthington, Keith Weller and the like were the recipients and this was the subject of some internal bickering.

It's ironic that in the modern era Premiership players are largely unconcerned about a sponsored car. With all the Aston Martins, BMWs, Jaguars and Porsches that inhabit training ground car parks, players wouldn't be seen dead in a Ford Mondeo... unless it could be used by their second cousin in the Outer Hebrides. Back in my day, I was made up when I received the keys to a Fiat 131 from a dealership in Blackbird Road, Leicester.

The car arrived in pristine condition but I'm afraid I wasn't able to keep it that way for very long. Flushed with the joys of my new five-seater, I made a rather bold offer to drive five of us to the Player of the Year awards in London.

This was one of the major events of the year and Keith Weller, Frank Worthington, Lenny Glover and Steve Earle all crammed into my car for the journey down to the Heathrow Hilton where we were to stay overnight. After showering and sprucing up, we hired a driver to take us into central London. A good time was had by all and, more than a little the worse for wear, we piled into the car for the 3am journey back to bed. I noticed the driver was about to miss a turn near the hotel and bawled at him to turn left. Unfortunately, the roads were wet from overnight rain and he was doing about 70mph. He skidded across the road and careered into a lamp-post, slicing it in two before bouncing across to the other side of the road. The top half of the lamp-post came crashing down on the roof of the car, and the stump of the post burst into flames. Not surprisingly, this woke the occupants of the car, with the exception of Frank. Shellshocked, we checked we were alive and then beat a hasty departure to the hotel.

We had to be up bright and early next morning to report for training at Leicester but, from the breakfast room, I noticed quite a crowd of people gathering in the car park. Finishing our egg, bacon and sausage, we made our way outside, laden with suit carriers and discovered the object of everyone's attention; my car. Or at least it was a heap of scrap that resembled my car. I doubt the vehicle would have been given the all-clear to run in a stock car race.

Every window was smashed, there were dents in all the body panels and a massive V shape was imprinted in the roof where the telegraph pole had landed. By this time, our driver had long since vanished, never to be seen again. Gingerly, I squeezed into the driver's seat while the rest clambered through doors and windows. The suit-carriers were tied down in the back of the boot. I looked across the car and couldn't see the passenger side because of the V-shaped roof. We had no alternative but to drive straight off because we daren't be late for training. I started the engine which sounded distinctly the worse for wear and we limped out of the car park, everyone staring in amazement. We tried really hard to act as if nothing was wrong but we must have looked complete idiots.

There was no M25 in those days so we headed off towards the M1 via Slough. I'd stopped at a set of traffic lights when, to my consternation, a police motorcyclist pulled alongside. He looked at me, I looked at him. He knew, from the perilous state of our vehicle, we had been involved in an accident . I feared the worst but I think he recognised us, gave us the benefit of the doubt and signalled us to move on. I pulled away from the traffic lights as quickly as possible given the car was only operational in third gear. It took us about four hours to get back from the Hilton but the worst was yet to come.

Now I had to explain to the car dealership that I had wrecked my sponsored car within a few weeks of taking delivery. Adopting the Birchy-larger-than-life approach, I walked into the showroom to meet the owner, a lovely old guy who always had a pipe in his mouth. "I've had a little accident with the car," I began. "Don't worry Birch, we'll get it into the workshop and have it as good as new for you again," he smiled. Off we went to see the car, but as we got nearer and it came into view, his jaw started to droop and the pipe fell out of his mouth in amazement. "Did anyone get out alive?" he asked. "Oh yes," I replied, "all five of us actually so you don't need to worry about that. "Mmmmmm. I don't know whether to be glad you survived or angry you've written off a brand new car." "You can't repair it, then?" I queried innocently. He gave me a withering look. To be fair, he took it extremely well, giving me a brand new Fiat 131 Mirafiori on condition I promised not to destroy any more lamp-posts. The fact that I also purchased a Fiat 127 for the *tank commander* may have also had something to do with easing his discomfort.

Another of the more lucrative perks of being a professional footballer was our involvement in beauty pageants. In the modern 'politically correct' era beauty contests have substantially reduced in popularity and are now almost frowned

YOU BEAUTY: Eat your heart out David Ginola. The Birch puts on his very best sultry pose for some modelling work. Contrary to the way this picture is cropped, I can assure you that the two desirables were definitely not *clothed off*. At least that's what I told the *tank commander*.

upon. In the seventies, however, Miss World was at its height and attracted one of the biggest television audiences of the year.

There were numerous local beauty contests including, of course, Miss Leicester City. Yours truly had the arduous task of sitting on a number of these judging panels. Out of a sense of loyalty to the Leicestershire public, I reluctantly agreed to give up my spare time and help the organisers with the judging.

I can safely say that no matter how much temptation was laid out in front of me, I never succumbed. I was a model of impartiality, you might say. Of course, I can't say the same about Frank and some of the other single lads.

There is one incident in my time at Leicester which I have been asked about more than any other. In many respects, it was a watershed (in more ways than one) and demonstrated the personality clashes which were often close to the surface during the Bloomfield era. With so many strong and forceful characters in the side, there were always going to be differences of opinion and the 'Weller in the bath' incident has now adopted legendary status.

It took place just five days before Christmas in the 1974-75 season though, in truth, the incident had been brewing for several weeks. We had suffered a nightmare run of five straight defeats and a draw leading up to a Friday night home game against Ipswich Town. A few harsh words had been spoken in the dressing room and 'Wells' staggered us by saying that the style of play we were adopting was not helping his chances of playing international football for England. I was more than a little surprised and the rest of the lads reminded him in no uncertain terms that we were in this together as a team.

Frank Worthington and Lenny Glover, in particular, were incensed by the comments and it was noticeable how Wells suddenly got to see a lot less of the ball. Let's just say that he didn't receive as many passes as he had previously enjoyed.

I could sense everyone was more than a little edgy in the dressing room before the Ipswich game. I went up to Frank and, in my usual jokey way, told him not to worry and that he would soon be scoring again. Frank turned round to me and yelled: "Don't worry about my game, concentrate on your own." "Oh well," I thought "we are going to be in for a fun night." And so it turned out.

We were pretty dire in the first 45 minutes and Wells was taking a bit of stick from fans in the East Stand. On the stroke of half time he was running down the right wing when a tackle came in and the referee blew his whistle. In sheer frustration, Weller carried on, volleying the ball into the crowd. It smacked straight into the face of a helpless nine-year-old and completely flattened him. The referee went over, St

John Ambulance helpers tended to the boy and there was general uproar. Of course, Wells had not aimed for the lad, he had simply kicked out in frustration. As the players went down the tunnel, Frank and a few others had a right go at Wells. We trooped into the dressing room and Jim proceeded to give us a rollocking, or as strong a rollocking as he could muster. Jimmy was such a lovely man he rarely lost his temper, but he had a dig at me and then looked around for Wells to enquire whether he could perhaps raise his game a little. There was no sign of Wells anywhere. I was sent to look for him and walked through into the shower and bath room. Wells was sitting naked in one of the individual baths. "Come on," I said, the gaffer wants you. "Sod off, I'm staying here," came the reply. I went back to the main dressing room with the unenviable task of telling Jimmy that Wells was in the bath and wasn't coming out. A startled Jimmy told our substitute Mike 'the Bolt' Stringfellow to warm up. The only problem was 'the Bolt' needed 30 minutes, five tubes of deep heat ointment and a sauna before he stood a chance of warming up his muscles. So, we despatched him into the drying room and told him to be ready in five minutes. The buzzer went telling us to leave the dressing room and as we filed out a few obscenities were hurled in the way of Wells who was still in the bath.

We lost the game 1-0 and Wells was left out for the next two matches. Jim had a word with Keith and tried to smooth things over. Upon his return it was rather embarrassing to see that several players in the team almost seemed to be concentrating on not giving him the ball. Those incidentally, were the only two games that Wells missed in what turned out to be a long and arduous season in which we only narrowly avoided relegation in 18th position.

A season or two earlier Wells had been involved in a much more public incident witnessed by a worldwide television audience of millions. I'm sure you remember the game against Norwich at Filbert Street when Wells played in a pair of white tights. Believe it or not, but none of the lads knew anything about it in advance. About twenty minutes before kick-off Wells came out of the physio's room and into the dressing room resplendent in a pair of white tights. All the lads cracked up laughing and thought it was a joke. Only when he walked out of the players tunnel did they realise he was being deadly serious. In subsequent years a rumour has circulated around Leicester that Keith's wife had found the tights in his car and, thinking rather quickly under a certain amount of pressure, Wells said he had bought them to wear for the game. This was a story Wells himself had related to some of the lads. For once in Leicester City's history, the reality was a lot more mundane. Wells had borrowed the tights off his missus with her full knowledge to protect against injury. At the time, there was a heavy cold snap and the pitch was frozen over. It was rock-hard so the tights were actually a brilliant idea and one subsequently copied by other players in more recent times.

■ **HOT AIR BALLOON:** Leicester City won worldwide acclaim for their hot-air balloon which allowed matches at Filbert Street to be played while the rest of the soccer programme was struck down by the big freeze. However, it was not quite as successful as you might think. Lots of holes appeared in the all-weather tarpaulin after we inadvertently ran over it in our running spikes during special training sessions put on by Jimmy Bloomfield.

It was during those famous mid-winter freezes that Leicester could often be relied upon to provide top-class football while the rest of the country shut down. Our all-weather pitch covering was the envy of everyone up and down the country. In truth, everything wasn't quite as straightforward. For starters, it required about 50 people to erect the tent so every time there was a cold snap we would put up a notice at the local labour exchange, issuing an appeal for supporters and workers to come to Filbert Street and spend a morning helping out.

Dismantling it was even more of a pain. Theoretically, there was a gulley around the perimeter track into which it was supposed to be lowered. However, it was all rather messy and in our haste to download the tarpaulin it would often be left unfurled around the running track.

Around this time, ever the innovative trainer, Jimmy had us all back one afternoon a week at Filbert Street to do sprint-training using proper spiked athletics shoes. Off we would race but as we slowed down we would scamper across the all-weather pitch covering. Very soon a large number of puncture holes appeared and, for some strange reason, it was never quite as effective after that. The club put it down to wear and tear but now you know the real reason.

By now you will have probably gathered that controversy and the Birch were the closest of bedfellows. I inadvertently found myself never far from the headlines for a variety of reasons, with the one notable exception of footballing talent. However, there is an incident which stands head and shoulders above the rest as the most dramatic and high-profile misdemeanour of my playing career. It led to questions being raised in the House of Commons, offers of a regular column in a German gay magazine, success in the European photograph of the year awards and death threats from an extremist right-wing political party.

I am, of course, referring to the celebrated kiss with my good friend (but not that close) Tony Currie during Leicester's end of season First Division game with Sheffield United in April 75. The scene was set on a balmy sunny Saturday afternoon at Bramall Lane. It was the last game of the campaign and the dry spell meant we were playing on a bone-hard pitch with very little grass.

The season had been long and hard and we were to finish 18th. Our cause was certainly not helped by the fact that, at the time of the incident, we were taking a right mauling and were losing 4-0. Given such a scoreline, most players would not be far off suicidal. So it gives you a clue as to the way I played that I still had time for a big grin on my face. I was charging through the middle of the park when I became aware of a United opponent tracking back to tackle me. We tripped over each other and did a neat somersault before coming to rest on the bone-hard pitch side by side. I glanced to my right and was amazed to see TC. Amazed because it must have been the only time in his 15-year career that Tony ever bothered to tackle anyone!

Tony was a great mate who had replaced me when I left Sheffield United for Chelsea for £100,000. Blades manager John Harris went down to Watford and brought back TC with him for £40,000. John must have thought he was quids in.

Now bear in mind this was the time when long blond hair was very fashionable and Tony and I were both blessed with a considerable amount. I looked across at him and said: "Give us a kiss." With that, we both puckered up and kissed each other full on. No tongues, I stress. The whole kiss lasted a fraction of a second. We dusted ourselves down, got back on our feet and got on with the game. Not another word was said and we forgot about the whole episode.

The following morning I was tucked up in bed usual, waiting for my Sunday treat when the *tank commander* would make a cup of *rosy* and bring me the newspapers to peruse. It was the one morning of the week when I could get a lie-in and I always looked forward to it immensely. Strangely, however, on this occasion the door

KISSING COUSINS: This is the photo that sent shockwaves through English society in May 1975 and scooped European sports photograph of the year. My kiss with Tony Currie during City's 4-0 defeat to Sheffield United at Bramall Lane is arguably the most controversial incident in which I have ever been involved. It only lasted a fraction of a second but our impromptu kiss led to death threats from a right wing political party, questions in the House of Commons and the offer of a column in a German gay magazine. Inset, three years ago TC and I decided to reproduce the fateful moment at Filbert Street in front of a 22,000 capacity crowd.

opened and a News of the World was hurled across the room at head height. *Tanko* disappeared, muttering: "You've done it this time." No tea, and a newspaper strewn across the bed. I was a shade concerned wondering what on earth I had done wrong now.

Anyway, couldn't be that important, I thought, as I sat down to study the match report of our game. One of the traditions was always to look at the bottom of the report where players were individually marked out of 10. Fearing the worst I looked for 'Birchenall' and saw a five against my name. Given the circumstances, I was quite pleased. Four was a stinker, three a disgrace. Five was below average, but acceptable. One surefire way of generating animosity between players and journalists were these marks. If you got a good mark, you loved them. If they gave you a bad one, you wanted to punch their lights out.

In common with all sports-orientated people, I always read my newspapers from the back page first. The last page I read was the front page ... and what a sight greeted my eyes when I finally worked my way to the front. There, screaming out of the page at me, was a large photograph of two footballers kissing lip to lip. I cringed as the enormity of the situation began to sink in. What had I done, I thought.

I knew instantly it was going to be a major issue. While the 21st century is a pretty tolerant society exposed as it is to a wide amount of sexual latitude, the seventies was a very different marketplace. A picture of two male sportsmen kissing full on the lips was deemed offensive, repulsive and sexually deviant. I knew the kiss had been a moment of fun that lasted a fraction of a second but, sadly, very few people shared my view.

The photograph featured on the national night-time television news and, as the debate rolled on for the next few days, questions were tabled by Members of Parliament in the House of Commons. Just what was happening to our national game? Had moral standards sunk so low? These were among the points debated. I was mortified.

Footballers being footballers I received a tremendous amount of sympathy when I reported for training on the Monday morning. Ha! You must be joking. The lads thought it was hilarious. Worthington, Glover and Weller were not going to miss this opportunity. It was bad enough losing 4-0 and receiving a dressing down from Jimmy Bloomfield but it was the final straw when I got to my car. The lads had borrowed their wives' lipsticks and daubed the windows with pink and red messages. My car looked like a walking advert for Max Factor.

Even Jimmy, never one to go overboard, called me over and said in a very controlled tone: "I think you've gone just a little too far this time, Alan."

■ **FULL STRETCH:** Not a bad *Buddy Holly* if I say so myself. A reasonable body shape from the Birch as I crack one in at Anfield watched by (left to right) Ian Callaghan, Steve Heighway, Steve Earle and Emlyn Hughes.

■ **ON THE BALL:** Alan Ball was the sort of person you loved or loathed. As a player I loathed him, now I love him. Without doubt, he was the best one-touch player I ever came up against. I could never get anywhere near him.

■ **DOUBLE WHAMMY:** Billy Bremner gives me a dig in the ribs with his outstretched right boot while at the same time delivering a right hand into my throat. Whenever you went into battle against Leeds, no quarter was asked and none was given. Look at Billy's flash tie-ups which characterised the Leeds side of the seventies.

■ **MY HAIR'S BETTER THAN YOURS:** A dispute breaks out between Spurs' Alfie Conn and myself. I can't remember the exact problem but it probably had something to do with the pair of us laying claim to the longest hair.

■ **GARISH KIT:** Without a doubt, this was the worst kit it was ever my misfortune to wear during my 20 years of playing professional football. It was an Admiral creation and aside from the garish logos and design it was so tight it was like playing in a girdle. This photograph was taken during a 1-0 victory over Stoke at the Victoria Ground in March 1977. I was to play only two more games before my Leicester career was finished.

■ **POETRY IN MOTION:** Or so I'd have myself believe. Look at the shape and the poise as *'the claw'* prepares to deliver another inch-perfect ball into the stand.

■ **BEADY-EYED:** October 1973 and the latest fashion accessory was to wear a string of beads around your neck. Never one to miss out on a fashion statement, myself and Frank Worthington bought a shedload.

One of the more dubious benefits of this whole episode was that there was a significant upturn in the amount of fan-mail I received. Sadly, not all of it was material I welcomed. One letter, in particular, came from the prospective MP of a prominent right-wing political organisation. I and TC were labelled a disgrace to the British nation and warned that if the party ever came to power we would be lined up against a wall and shot. Charming!

Another letter from Germany started more promisingly. "Dear Herr Birchenheimer (as well as the Americans, the Germans could never pronounce my name properly either), we are a German magazine and we have seen the recent photos of you playing football in England. We are very interested in you writing a regular weekly column for our magazine for which we would pay you a fee. Enclosed is a contract which we would like you to sign and return to us." I was just reaching for the currency convertor to work out how much German marks were worth in pounds sterling when I noticed the content of the magazine. It was not a football journal. It was a publication for gay men!

Six months later the story still had a few more twists and turns. I was contacted by the organisers of a prestigious European sports photographic competition. Apparently, the photograph of the two of us had been voted Best European Sports Photograph 1974-75. TC and I were invited to be present at the awards in Paris. It meant an overnight stay in the French capital... but as there was only one hotel room with a double bed for us to share we politely declined.

Younger, more sexually enlightened, readers of this book may wonder what all the fuss was about when they look at the photograph. But in the seventies homosexuality was a taboo subject and any faintly overt activity or imagery was just not mentioned or alluded to in public. It really did create an enormous furore. Perhaps the closest analogy I can draw was the huge outcry and exposure following the infamous photo of Vinnie Jones squeezing Paul Gascoigne's testicles more than 15 years later.

There is even a postscript to this story. A decade later, when Leicester were playing Sheffield United at Filbert Street, the editor of the programme thought it would be a jolly wheeze to reproduce the photograph with a suitably humorous caption.

Ten thousand programmes were duly printed and delivered but, on the Friday night, a change of heart involving the club chairman and secretary meant the photograph was no longer deemed suitable for a family magazine. Consequently, club officials stayed up the entire night performing the laborious task of cutting out the page containing the offending photograph from all 10,000 programmes.

WHAT A SICKENER: I'm striding out of the tunnel at Old Trafford for our 1974 FA Cup semi final with Liverpool. Unfortunately, a thigh strain meant that I missed out and young Joe Waters took my place. I'd been pumped full of cortisone two days before but all to no avail. Not only did I miss this tie, I sat out the replay at Villa Park when Liverpool won 3-1 four days later.

I began this book by telling you it most definitely would not be a tale of how many footballing trophies and medals I collected during my career. Nor do I have any complaints about that. I doubt there are many who have enjoyed playing professional football more than me, but it is fair to say I suffered from a slice of ill luck or two in the FA Cup - the oldest cup competition in the world. Injury ruled me out of playing any part in Chelsea's 1970 triumph and I was struck down by an injury jinx during Leicester's cup run of 1974.

I had been forced to sit out the quarter final defeat of Queen's Park Rangers in which my understudy Joe Waters scored both goals in a 2-0 success but hopes were high that I would be back in time for the semi against Liverpool.

I had been struggling for a few weeks with a thigh strain and a couple of days before the game a practice match was arranged to test out my fitness. This was in the era when if injuries did not heal quickly there was one overall solution; pump you full of cortisone. I understand there are now some legal cases with players suffering side-effects in later life from having received the drug. Still, in the seventies, what did us footballers care. I wanted to play and had the injection. I think I was probably given a shot that would have numbed a horse but I came through the practice game. the following morning, although I could hardly walk. I missed the first game at Old Trafford where we drew 0-0. I now had a second bite of the cherry in the replay at Villa Park four days later. Again, an injection but to no avail. We lost 3-1 and a miserable night was had by all. The full severity of the injury was only revealed a few days later when it transpired a thigh muscle had become detached from the bone and was hanging only by a few slender fibres. I came back for the last three games and we finished in an excellent ninth position but the semi final defeat was still a bitter pill to swallow as it was ultimately to prove the closest the Bloomfield Boys ever came to lifting a piece of silverware.

During my time at Leicester, I lost count of the innumerable social functions I organised and the personal appearances I made on behalf of the club. Many accusations are levelled at modern-day players that they do not do enough for the community. Here in Leicester, we are fortunate to have a very professional system operated by the club where players are booked out to attend a series of functions. Details are taken, maps are issued, instructions are given. It's all very slickly organised. Back in my day, requests used to come in and then it was left up to the players.

Believe it or not, I actually liked attending these functions. I went to schools to hand out certificates, old people's homes to pose for photographs, opened countless shops, community centres, job centres and you would never hear me complain once. Many a time the *tank commander* would whinge about the amount of time I spent on afternoons visiting far flung corners of Leicestershire. On some occasions, I'd turn up and the organisers didn't know who I was. They had written to the club, not received a reply and assumed no-one was coming. I would often dive into the office, gather up the requests and attend as many as I could. In a funny sort of way, it always gave me a buzz to see the excitement it brought to young people to meet a professional footballer.

I suppose I've always been a people person and never wanted to lose contact with my roots. I know what it's like to be a real fan and have always attempted to stay in touch with their feelings. One of the highlights of my week was watching my local Sunday morning football team, the Red Lion from Rothley. Although I was involved in football professionally, I found it a great way of relaxing. Indeed, on rare occasions I was pressed into action - much against Football Association rules. There were several occasions when, with 15 minutes to go, both sides agreed I could come on as a substitute. Here I was, a First Division footballer playing Sunday morning football less than 24 hours after lining up against Manchester United. Bear in mind that I had faced some of the hardest players in the game like Norman Hunter, Nobby Stiles, Ron Harris. Without fear of contradiction, I was never more afraid than on those Sunday games. The Sunday lads wanted their scalp and the tackles used to welly in from all angles. Thank goodness I was never injured or there would have been hell to pay.

If I have one regret in football - and I have tried very hard not to have any at all - it would have to be the way in which my association with Leicester City came to a bitterly disappointing end.

Following my arrival in September 1971 I had been a virtual ever-present for the following four seasons, and thought of myself as an important cog in a reasonably successful side during one of the most entertaining periods in the club's proud history.

Sadly, my departure and demise was ill-tempered, messy and downright embarrassing and one which I felt was not in keeping with what was otherwise the most enjoyable period of my career.

My problems started at the beginning of the 1975-76 season. We'd lost only one of our first six games - during which time we had played Liverpool and Arsenal - before I was sidelined with a knee injury. There was a considerable amount of conjecture and debate about the injury. I was actually suffering from fluid on the knee but the club felt there was very little wrong with me and it was a difficult condition to diagnose at that time.

I was on a collision course with Jimmy Bloomfield and we fell out in a major way as I have already explained in more detail elsewhere in this book. I was accused of 'swinging lead' and for those who know me they will tell you nothing could be further from the truth.

It was an accusation I took extremely personally and events spiralled to the extent that I took the matter to a League tribunal. A highly foolish course of action, I know, but at the time I felt I was completely in the right. The tribunal ruled against me and matters degenerated from there.

I was furious with Jimmy and put in a transfer request which was granted by the club. It was a hard time, not just for me but my family as well. Wife Heather was contacted by the national press and a headline article appeared in the Daily Mirror with the headline 'My Husband's No Cry-Baby!'

Much of this dispute was played out against a backdrop of me reaching the big

30. In the modern era, a not insubstantial amount of players carry on operating at the highest level until well into their mid-thirties. In the Jurassic era diets, stretches and fitness conditioning were unheard of. As a result, once you turned 30 you knew you were on the way out.

Wages in the seventies, while still good, bore no relation to the multi-million pound contracts being signed on a fairly regular basis today. The moment a reasonable player signs a four-year contract nowadays he effectively becomes a millionaire and, in most cases, need not worry about money for the rest of his life. He certainly doesn't have to spend time worrying about putting food on the table for his family. Even the biggest names of my era couldn't afford not to work when they finished the game. To me, the massive sums of money around must take a huge strain off players. No-one in our era had that security and peace of mind.

Put all these thoughts into the melting pot of a 30-year-old professional footballer and perhaps you can see how insecurity and uncertainty can creep in.

Looking back, I did think the world was against me. In these situations you tend to retreat into your shell and blame everyone but yourself. I even lashed out at the press which, given my previously excellent relations with them, was unheard of.

Our local reporter on the Leicester Mercury was Bill Anderson. Even to this day, he's still covering the club. He's the only Scotsman I know who doesn't drink and doesn't smoke. I played a game in an unaccustomed central defensive position as an experiment for Jimmy Bloomfield. It wasn't a resounding success and Bill wrote a piece in the Mercury saying it hadn't worked.

I was coming out of the ground with Frank Worthington one lunchtime when I saw Bill hanging around the car park. I'd read his report and was furious. "I'm not speaking to you again," I growled. And, for the next two months, I refused to have anything to do with him. The prospect of me being unable speak to anyone for such a length of time is bordering on the incomprehensible but that's exactly what I did (mind you, Bill must have thought he'd got a right result).

I thought Jimmy was against me. I thought Bill and the media was against me. I thought the world was against me. I've seen it happen a hundred times over with other players at Leicester City in subsequent years. And I'm sure it will continue to

ON THE WAY OUT: My Leicester career came to an end in 1977 and this injury (left) hardly helped my cause. To this day, I still have problems with my ankles and it was an ankle injury in this 1-1 draw with Coventry in October 1976 which hastened my demise. Frank Worthington, physio George Preston and Coventry's Mick Coop help me off but it was to be three months before I started another match. In fact, I started only five more games before my Filbert Street career was over after five seasons.

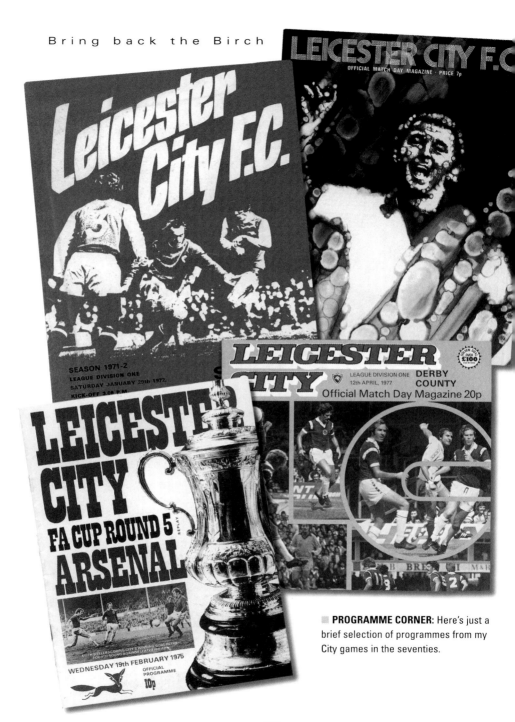

Leicester City F.C.

LEICESTER CITY F.C
OFFICIAL MATCH DAY MAGAZINE · PRICE 7p

SEASON 1971-2
LEAGUE DIVISION ONE
SATURDAY JANUARY 29th 1972.
KICK-OFF 3.00 P.M

LEICESTER
CITY
LEAGUE DIVISION ONE   DERBY
12th APRIL, 1977   COUNTY
Official Match Day Magazine 20p

LEICESTER
CITY
FA CUP ROUND 5
ARSENAL
KEITH WELLER SCORING CITY'S WINNING GOAL IN THE
FOURTH ROUND AGAINST LEATHERHEAD
WEDNESDAY 19th FEBRUARY 1975
OFFICIAL
PROGRAMME
10p

PROGRAMME CORNER: Here's just a
brief selection of programmes from my
City games in the seventies.

288

happen. In my role as club co-ordinator it really annoys me when I see players with their heads down and going through the motions. Yet I was doing exactly the same.

Players, like anyone in life, can become insecure. Most people in their working lives are just starting to come into their prime in their early thirties. They are gaining more confidence, stature and responsibility in their work environment and are beginning to grow into their jobs. Contrast this with the life of a professional footballer who's been living in a fantasy land since he was 16 years of age. He's been cosseted and molly-coddled and had everything done for him in life. He's earned good money and received much adulation.

Now, all of a sudden at the age of 30, he's on the downward slide. He's already peaked in his chosen career and there's only one way to go - down. No matter how hard he tries he knows his best days are behind him. The mind may be willing but the legs certainly aren't. It's a sobering thought and one which can weigh heavily and change a person's personality. It hits you like a brick and, faced with the uncertainty of how you are going to cope with the rest of your life, it's all too easy to panic and I think that is what happened to me and I did act out of character.

I found it very difficult to cope with the fact that one minute I was a regular first team player vital to the success of the football club, the next it felt as if I had been completely discarded and was ready for the knackers yard. I don't care who you are, that is a massive blow to your self esteem and self-confidence. Of course you feel like the world is against you.

The dilemma I faced was how to continue to live the kind of life myself and my family had enjoyed for several seasons. Football money was going to dry up and I - a secondary modern kid who grew up on a council estate in Nottingham - was now faced with rebuilding my life all over again. I made it my goal to try to continue to enjoy the same standard of living I enjoyed as a professional footballer. It was hard work but as we will find out in a later chapter I was fortunate enough to be able to do it.

Many of my peers in the game in the seventies have subsequently fallen on hard times. Many found they could not make that next - and most difficult - step. My heart goes out to them and I have never forgotten how tough were those months I was forced to endure while I was being frozen out at Leicester.

I still went to all the games but it was very hard to watch. Jimmy signed new players and it's impossible not to think that those players have stolen what you consider to be your rightful place.

I made only one substitute appearance during the rest of the 75-76 campaign - I came off the bench in a 1-0 defeat of Newcastle at Filbert Street. Jimmy called me into his office in March and said that Notts County had expressed an interest in taking me on loan. "You need some match fitness and we're going well enough here to cope without you," was how he phrased it.

After my stint at Meadow Lane I had the opportunity to go to America with the San Jose Earthquakes. I jumped at the chance to get away from Leicester for the summer and try to rebuild my career and enjoy a break from the English game.

In doing so, however, I inadvertently turned down the most successful manager of the modern footballing era.

Scottish club Aberdeen made enquiries for both myself and Lenny Glover, Jimmy told us. Aberdeen, of course, were managed at the time by Alex Ferguson. Neither of us fancied Aberdeen, especially when Lenny could go to Tampa Bay and I had an option of joining San Jose. I have always felt that Alex is such a shrewd judge of a player. Obviously at this early stage of his managerial career he was entitled to make a few mistakes.

In my final season in 1976-77 I was involved a little more, starting a total of 11 matches but by now the damage had been done. I was never the same player again. I did try to patch things up with Jimmy towards the end and we were fairly civilised about matters. He told me that another American franchise had come in for me - this time it was the Memphis Rogues. I accepted the offer of a second shot at American football although it was with a heavy heart that I said my final goodbyes to Leicester City as a professional player.

Ironically, Jimmy was not to last too much longer himself at Filbert Street. Despite all he had achieved with an entertaining brand of football, the supporters called for his head the following season. Jimmy was subsequently to be struck down by cancer and it has long been my opinion that because Jimmy bottled up so many of his emotions this may have contributed to his illness. There were some very strong characters in the dressing room but I take solace in the fact that I did make my peace with Jimmy.

The end to my Leicester career was a major disappointment but the manner of my departure never diminished my love affair with the club. I look upon Leicester as my home and Leicester City as my football club. Throughout all my business interests, I have never lost contact with the club and in my role as public relations officer and, more recently, club co-ordinator I like to think I have played a small part in maintaining close links between the club, supporters and the players of previous decades.

All stations to Trowbridge

Chapter 10

DURING my times with Sheffield United, Chelsea, Crystal Palace and Leicester, I was fortunate never to play a single match outside the old English First Division. Any illusions I might have had about being a pampered prima-donna rapidly disappeared in the twilight of my career. As I slid down the slippery slope, the marbled halls of Highbury were swapped for the wooden railway sleepers of Hartlepool. Capacity crowds at Anfield were exchanged for the spartan surrounds of Bootham Crescent. Lush pitches like Old Trafford were replaced by threadbare playing surfaces in Bournemouth. And, you know, I wouldn't have changed it for the world. I made my father's dream come true at Notts County, I sampled the best meat pies of my life in Blackburn, I was reunited with my former Nottingham Schoolboys team-mate David Pleat at Luton and at Hereford... well, they served a decent pint of scrumpy.

I'll never forget the first two thoughts which came into my head when Jimmy Bloomfield called me into his office one afternoon to explain that Notts County had expressed an interest in taking me on loan. Firstly, I immediately thought of my father's love affair with the Magpies. Secondly, it was only 30 minutes up the A46. What more could I ask for? Strangely, it did not bother me that I would be dropping out of the First Division for the first time in my professional career. Life had turned sour at Filbert Street and a month at Meadow Lane was a great way of regaining some match fitness and achieving a boyhood dream.

I raced up to Mum and Dad's house in Top Valley to tell them the news, casually explaining to my dad that I was going out on loan. Even in the late seventies, loan deals were quite unusual. "Great idea, son," he told me. "Where are you going?"

When I told them it was Notts County his jaw dropped. There was a long pause. It had always been his wish to see his son run out in the black and white stripes of Notts County at Meadow Lane. I genuinely believe that if you had given him the choice of winning £1 million on the pools or seeing his son play for County, at that precise moment he would have plumped for the latter. This was to be the culmination of all those years watching the Magpies, rolling back the clock 20 years to when we walked the six miles from Sherwood to Meadow Lane to see them in action on Saturday afternoons.

Reality, however, began to settle in at 3pm on Saturday March 13 at the Manor Ground when I made my Magpies debut in Division Two action against Oxford United. Enthused by the emotions of playing for my boyhood club, allied to my top flight experience, I had a stinker and we got beaten 2-1. My Meadow Lane debut was to come a week later when we were playing Blackpool. There was still a lot to play for because the club were pushing for promotion and a crowd of over 10,000 came down. There was no Birchenall senior, however, in the Directors' Box. I'd wanted to make it an extra-special day out for my dad and arranged for Directors Box and VIP tea-room passes for him in the Main Stand. When I rang him on the Thursday to give him the good news, there was another pause. "No thanks, lad," he said. "What do you mean?" I replied. "Well, if it's all the same to you I'll stand where I've always stood for the past 30 years but thanks anyway."

And that's what he did. When I ran out I spied him on the Spion Kop in his customary position, 20 steps up in line with the right-hand goalpost looking down towards the Meadow Lane end. My mind flitted back to when I was dropped in the junior pen while my dad took up the same spot from where he had seen Lawton, Sewell, Leuty and company. In truth, it was quite an emotional moment for me. Sadly, this did not translate itself into a result. We slipped to a successive 2-1 beating and again I was out of sorts. At Blackburn the following week we slumped to a third straight defeat and, things went from bad to worse in our big promotion showdown with Sunderland.

Nearly 15,000 fans crammed into Meadow Lane for a real six-pointer against a Sunderland side that contained several players who had lifted the FA Cup just a few seasons earlier. With the game evenly poised at 0-0, we won a second-half penalty. Brian Stubbs walked up to me and handed me the ball. I'd never scored a penalty in my life. The last one I had taken was eight years ago in the last minute of a game for Chelsea against Arsenal. I'd scored two goals and the lads gave me the spot kick to complete my hat-trick. Well, I nearly hit the corner flag!

Undeterred, I was carried away by the emotion of the occasion. Here was an opportunity to score my first goal for Notts County in front of my dad at Meadow

Lane. I thought the gods were shining on me. I precisely placed the ball on the spot and took five steps backward. As I ran towards the ball I can remember not having a clue what to do with *the claw*. Should I blast it, curl it or chip it? In front of me was Sunderland 'keeper Jim Montgomery and I sidefooted the ball to Jim's right. Jim didn't even bother diving for it. He knew there was no need. Instead, he threw his cap on it. It was a horrible penalty. I squirmed with embarrassment and the match ended goalless. My dad was so embarrassed he never ever brought the subject up in conversation. One person, however, who has not allowed me to forget it is my co-author on this book, Paul Mace. Macey grew up as a Notts fan and was among the crowd right behind the goal. He was only 12 at the time but when our paths crossed at Filbert Street for the first time in a professional capacity 10 years ago it was his opening gambit to me!

To complete a less than illustrious five-game loan spell with the Magpies, we drew 1-1 at Luton and fell out of the promotion picture. I headed back to Leicester and then on to a summer with the San Jose Earthquakes in the North American Soccer League. I'll be honest, the Birch did suffer a little crisis of confidence as a result of my stint at Meadow Lane. In that short spell I found myself questioning my own abilities. I wondered how I'd managed to survive for so long in the top flight. I had played against the biggest names in the country for 10 years - George Best, Bobby Charlton, Bobby Moore, Billy Bremner, to name a few - and I'd never had an inferiority complex playing against any of them. But all of a sudden I wondered if I had been cheating a living out of the game. I couldn't understand why I wasn't playing better. I had terrible problems adjusting and it wasn't just me. After my career was over, I began to understand a little more about the changes but at the time I couldn't see the wood for the trees. Lots of other established First Division players found it difficult to adjust to the lower divisions. For me, the single biggest difference was the mental toughness required in the top flight. Physically, the lower divisions could be every bit as intimidating as Division One, but there was a mental edge which set apart players from the top flight and those below. Going to America did help me cope with the adjustment but I was still nevertheless highly surprised when Notts County came back in for me on a permanent basis.

I went to Nottingham for a meeting with County Chairman Jack Dunnett to discuss terms. After my experiences at Chelsea, I had long since dispensed with the services of agents and was happy to represent myself. Going up against Mr Dunnett, a Labour MP for Nottingham East and a trained barrister, was a rather serious mistake. I felt I had three principal areas of appeal to the Magpies: I came cheap, lived nearby (thereby saving on relocation costs) and the club could use the emotional blackmail of my father's support to bring me to the Lane. At the meeting I stated my case for an increased salary. Mr Dunnett listened intently and then told me I would be getting

■ Here I am flying high as a Magpie in our official team photo for the 1977-78 Division Two season: Back row (left to right) are Colin Murphy (assistant manager), Ian Scanlon, David McVay, John Sims, Les Bradd, Eric McManus, Sammy Chapman, Brian Stubbs, Tristan Benjamin, Ray O'Brien, Jack Wheeler (trainer); (front row) Mick Vinter, Birch, Pedro Richards, Steve Carter, Jimmy Sirrel (manager), Arthur Mann, David Smith, Paul Hooks, Lloyd Richards.

exactly the same wage as I had been on at Leicester. Obviously, he had spoken to his Foxes counterpart and knew every detail of my former contract. Vainly, I tried to negotiate a signing-on fee. Eager to lay claim that I had at least bartered some cash out of him, I did manage to agree an appearance bonus. It was something ridiculous such as earning an extra hundred quid if I made 100 appearances. Given that I only signed a one year contract this was always going to be a shade difficult! Mr Dunnett also conceded that there would be a signing-on fee if I signed a new deal at the end of the season. Little did naive Birch realise there was never a snowflake in hell's chance of that happening!

My dad was overcome with emotion when he heard I had signed the one year deal. "That's great, son, only I sincerely hope you play better than you did while on loan because I've got to go to work in the morning after every game you play." Returning to Meadow Lane signalled to me that my playing career had turned full circle. Seventeen years earlier as a spotty 14-year-old oik I used to go down to the ground two evenings a week to train with the youngsters. The dressing rooms were exactly as I pictured them all those years ago - nothing had changed, and they'd not even received a lick of paint. It was just the same, right down to the large green bricks of carbolic soap in the corners of the bath. County's dressing rooms should have carried a government health warning. Still, I suppose it was character-building, as they say.

Although there is considerably more money in the modern era of football, not too many clubs I had played for previously could have been described as being on the poverty line. We were treated well and afforded the best facilities and creature comforts. Notts, by contrast, struggled to make ends meet. Their small supporter base meant they were always fighting an uphill battle and under Jimmy Sirrel in many respects they were over-achieving by establishing themselves in the Second Division. Remember, the Magpies were only one rung below the top flight.

The financial constraints exerted on the club were best illustrated on the morning of my first training session. I'd donned training kit and noticed a pile of tie-ups being placed on the physio's treatment couch. Whoosh, out shot a load of hands and the tie-ups swiftly vanished. Unruffled, I asked County physio Jack Wheeler for some more. In a scene reminiscent of the classic Oliver Twist sketch when the young urchin asks for more food, Jack gave me a quizzical look. "There ain't no more Birch, that's all we've got." Not wishing to make a scene, I trained with my socks around my ankles! Returning to the dressing room, I noticed one of the groundstaff gathering up the tie-ups and putting them into a bath, washing them and then laying them out to dry. At every other club, tie ups were used and thrown away. Not at County. They were recycled to the point where they literally fell to bits. My training kit felt as if it had first been used by Tommy Lawton and my jockstrap had certainly seen better days. Welcome to the frugal world of Notts County.

My own demeanour and standards of dress sense were in sharp contrast to the surrounds of the dressing room area and I do like to take just a little bit of credit for introducing some new standards of hygiene to the rest of the lads. Even to this day, Birch attaches a great deal of importance to his appearance and it's not unheard of for me to have three showers a day. In the late seventies I was the king of the hairdryer and designer toiletries. Among the professional footballing fraternity I am as famous for my Moulinex turbo 100 as I am for my left foot!

This was the era of long hair and after every training session and match I had to ensured I coiffeured the *barnet* properly. I had very fine hair (as in thinness, not quality) so the hairdryer was a most important accessory Whenever I walked into any dressing room I always looked for a three-pin socket so I could plug it in. At Notts there was only one plug and it was my misfortune that it was under the seat of the peg of Sammy Chapman.

For those of you unfamiliar with Sammy, he spent most of his career at Nottingham Forest before moving over the Trent for a season or two. A legendary hard-man, he made Vinnie Jones look like Little Lord Fauntleroy. I used to sidle up to his seat as close as I dare and plug in the drier for a quick *BJ*. The first time Sammy clocked me he gave me a withering look and dismissed me as a 'woofter'. Initially I took a fair amount of stick from the rest of the players. Many, like Brian Stubbs, David Needham and Ian Scanlon, had never even seen a comb let alone a top-of-the-range twin-speed Moulinex, but the banter was like water off a duck's back to me. I had been brought up in tough schools like Chelsea. If I could cope with Ron Harris having a dig, I could certainly cope with these fellows. And, sure enough, several of the players began asking if they could borrow the drier. Indeed, this was a scenario acted out at most of my clubs. Whenever I left, I would always bequeath my hairdryer to the dressing room. I can safely say that I left my mark on every club I played for ... and not just on the pitch. By the time I'd finished there must have been a dozen hairdryers left at clubs across all four points of the country!

My toiletry collection also proved extremely popular with my team-mates. At Leicester, most of the players used to bring in a bag of smellies and shampoo. At Notts County I was the only one, and I very quickly found out why. Pre-Birchenall, the Notts lads had relied on green carbolic soap. Not only did they wash themselves with it, they even shampooed their hair with the stuff. No wonder they needed a hair-drier to restore some shape to their *barnets* after years of carbolic abuse. The Birch arrived, complete with scented shampoo, underarm deodorant and the latest designer after-shave - I had no intention of going within a sniff of carbolic. And very quickly the lads decided to borrow my toiletries. My entire supply was used up inside a week. Foolishly I replenished my stock before realising this would prove a costly exercise. I hadn't bargained on being the official toiletry supplier to the entire Notts County squad. To be fair, Stubbsy never used my after-shave. He considered it 'puff-ish'. Indeed, if he ever smelt after-shave on any player during a game I'm sure he used to give them an extra whack for being a 'nancy'.

Although County was not considered a fashionable club, Jimmy had bought extremely wisely and had assembled a talented team that knocked on the door of promotion from Division Two for several seasons: Needham and Stubbs were a fantastic central defensive partnership, Ray O'Brien had a left foot almost to rival *the*

MOULINEX MAGPIE: The famed hairdryer was clearly given some major stick before I posed for this 1977-78 bubble-gum card collection!

claw, Eric McManus was an excellent 'keeper, Les Bradd a superb goalscorer and a real gentle giant and, out on the wing, Steve Carter could hit a great ball.

In midfield was a lovely fella called Arthur Mann who sadly passed away a couple of years ago. I'm sure Arthur wouldn't mind me relating the following anecdote because he was a solid, down-to-earth guy and always enjoyed a laugh at his own expense. In the dressing room was a large bath and after one of my first training sessions, myself and Arthur were having a good old soak. I was shampooing the *barnet* and ducked my head under the water to clear the suds. As I came back to the surface I spotted a rat in the middle of the bath. I let out a yelp and clambered out faster than a ferret up a drainpipe.

Still in a state of shock, I turned around and was staggered to see Arthur washing the rat. "Oh my godfathers. What on earth is happening?" I thought to myself. Arthur looked at me quizzically. "Best way to keep 'em clean," he said in a matter-of-fact voice. It was then I noticed something rather different about Arthur's appearance.

The penny dropped - Arthur's thick head of hair had disappeared and there were now just a couple of tufts poking out over each ear. It wasn't a rat at all. Arthur was washing his *syrup* in the bath. I didn't know whether to laugh or cry. I raced into the dressing room and shouted out to the lads: "What about Arthur's wig?" "Yes", they replied, "it's not a very good one, is it?" Well, it certainly had me fooled!

My biggest source of amazement was reserved for the way he managed to play matches without it coming off. I don't know what he used to stick it down with but it worked well. He very rarely headed the ball for obvious reasons but you could never say wearing a wig adversely affected his performance. In many respects, Arthur was probably 20 years ahead of his time. Now players with a full thatch of hair shave it off a la David Beckham. The bald look is all the rage. Just think, Arthur could have been a cult figure had he been around in the new Millennium!

On the pitch, my Notts career carried on from where it had left off during my loan period. After the initial five games without a win, I had to wait another seven before finally tasting victory in a black and white shirt and my dad could breathe a little more easily. The success came in a 3-1 victory over local rivals Mansfield Town at Field Mill.

Although our League form was a disappointment throughout the campaign - we ended up finishing 15th - we did almost break my barren run in cup competitions. Equalling my previous best achievement of reaching the last four of the FA Cup, we sailed through to the semi-finals of the Anglo Scottish Cup - a competition, as the name suggests, featuring English and Scottish sides in a knock-out competition. We had beaten Motherwell over two legs to set up a semi with St Mirren. I played in the first leg in which a Mick Vinter goal gave us a 1-0 victory at Meadow Lane but I missed the return trip north of the border with injury and it was just as well. We lost 2-0 and went out 2-1 on aggregate. Bang went another Birchy dream of playing in a cup final.

My farewell game in a Magpies shirt was a 1-1 draw at home to Millwall on 9th April, 1977 before I jetted back over the Atlantic for my second taste of Stateside soccer with Memphis. Upon my return I suffered a severe dose of reality when I signed on the dole at the local labour exchange, or at least I nearly did before I was rescued from my misery by Blackburn manager Jim Iley.

I signed the same day as Celtic striker Joe Craig. It was a Friday, and we made our debuts in a 2-1 home defeat by Charlton on the Saturday but, on the Monday, Jim was sacked. Welcome to Blackburn Rovers!

I'll always be eternally gratefully to Jim for rescuing me from my dole queue nightmare. His call came completely out of the blue and, the way I felt at that time,

I would have signed for absolutely anyone. I travelled up to meet Jim and again the football cartel appeared to be in operation because he told me I would be signing for exactly the same money as I had been on at Notts County. However, I would also get travelling expenses and an hotel allowance.

I had fond memories of Ewood Park. Indeed, the ground had provided me with one of the pinnacles of my career when I made my England debut in an Under 23 international under Sir Alf Ramsey. The memories came flooding back when I made the arduous drive from the Midlands up the M1 and M62 into Blackburn for the first time. When you came off the motorway and dropped into Blackburn through places such as Accrington it was a real culture shock. It was a very harsh landscape with the mills and the terraced houses, but the people were very friendly and made you feel tremendously welcome. Ewood Park was a real traditional type of ground - you could almost smell its history.

BLACKBURN ROVERS 1978-79: You'll notice I have lost my place on the front row of team photographs and have been relegated to the end of the back row. Take a look too at the state of the Ewood Park pitch. There's hardly a blade of grass on it. The full team caption is: (back row) Birch, Paul Maguire, Tim Parkin, John Butcher, Neil Ramsbottom, John Radford, Derek Fazackerley, Martin Fowler; (second row) Martin Hickson, Peter Morris, John Bailey, Joe Craig, Jack Marshall (physio), John Aston, Paul Round, John Waddington, Brian Morley. (third row) Simon Garner, Noel Brotherston, Tony Parkes, John Pickering (manager), Glenn Keeley, Stuart Metcalfe, Kevin Hird. (front row) Brian Moran, Mark Shipley, Nigel Smith.

One of the game's oldest clubs, they had fallen on hard times and were now battling to keep their heads above water in Division Two. As I had signed on the same day as Joe Craig, he and I were to become firm friends during our short stay there. My agreement with Blackburn was that I would train in Leicester three days a week and travel up to Blackburn for a couple of nights. Joe and I were accommodated in an hotel for the first couple of months before Blackburn decided we weren't worth such five-star treatment and transferred us to a local boarding house. It turned out to be a great move. The landlord effectively left us in charge of the establishment. We'd serve drinks behind the bar to other residents and we enjoyed the freedom of the kitchen to cook our own food whenever we wanted. Many a night we would come in after a few drinks and rustle up a few bacon butties. I was always tremendously impressed by the hospitality of Lancashire folk. They led comparatively hard lives and money was not always plentiful but they loved their football and always made me feel so welcome.

On the pitch, if results had been hard to come by at Meadow Lane, they were damn near impossible at Ewood Park. In my 20-game career for Rovers, we managed only three victories. John Pickering, who took over from Jim, was a shrewd tactician. It was his first managerial job but we could hardly get a result to save our lives. Joe had been top scorer for Celtic the previous season but even he was unable to stem the tide of draws and defeats as we tumbled down the table.

My own personal highlight of my short stay with Rovers had to be our FA Cup trip to Liverpool. Somehow we had scraped past Millwall 2-1 in the third round to earn ourselves a plum visit to Anfield. Liverpool were at the height of their powers and no-one gave us a chance, but we put up a fantastic performance and made the Merseysiders really sweat for their narrow 1-0 victory. Kenny Dalglish scored a late winner but I really enjoyed myself that night. After so many years in the old First Division with my previous clubs, it felt like I was going home and, if I say so myself, I had a pretty decent game. Given my other run of performances, you might say it was distinctly overdue!

We did at least manage some sort of consistency by the time I left the club for Luton. We were in the middle of a run of five consecutive League defeats. I knew I wasn't doing myself any favours and the travelling from Leicester was wearing me down. I was mentally preparing to drop down another division if I was to continue my League career because, even at the age of 33, all I wanted to do was play regular football. So, it all came as something of a surprise when Jim Pickering called me one afternoon to say that a Second Division club had come in for me. He told me it was Luton and immediately I realised their manager was my former Nottingham Schools team-mate David Pleat.

MAD AS A HATTER: I'd trudged around Filbert Street for six years in a Leicester City shirt... but this was my debut in a Luton jersey, quite literally. By an incredible quirk of fate, my first game after signing for David Pleat at Luton was a trip to Leicester. We got hammered 3-0 and seconds after this photo I was about to be deluged by a hundred snowballs from City supporters eager to get their own back on me for all my performances down the years.

David gave me a call later that afternoon and we arranged to meet at Trowell services on the M1. We had a long chat as David explained the plans he had for the Kenilworth Road club and I was quickly sold on them. This had as much to do with the fact Luton was a straightforward one-hour drive down the M1 compared to the much more arduous two-and-a-half-hour trek across the Pennines to Ewood Park. Again, the arrangement was that I could train in Leicester for a couple of days a week so all that was left to discuss were terms. Unbelievably, David offered me exactly the same wage I had been on at Blackburn, Notts County and Leicester. I naively thought this was the maximum wage for players in the lower divisions, so naturally, I agreed.

The following morning I reported for training and bumped into David Coates, who I had known from our days together at Filbert Street. "Birchy, your first job is to give everyone a lift in the dressing room. We've got some good lads but they're all a bit down. Give everyone a gee-up," he told me. I thought little more about it. Wherever I went I was always the same loudmouth in the dressing room and I wasn't going to change at this late stage of my career. The club had suffered some heavy defeats and were hovering on the edges of the relegation zone. Incredibly, my first game was a trip to my beloved Leicester.

This surely had to be an omen, I thought. The gods were shining on me and the stage was set to make a triumphant return to one of my old stamping grounds and instantly ingratiate myself with my new club's supporters. Silly me. It was a horrible night: sleet and snow were lashing down and to cap it all we were slaughtered 3-0, although I did enjoy some friendly banter with the Leicester fans. While we were warming up I chucked a couple of snowballs at fans behind the home team dug-out. As I left the pitch at half time, I was pelted by around 100 snowballs!

THE BLOND BOMBSHELL: Here it is folks, the worst photograph of a professional footballer ever taken in the history of the game. I have spent the past 21 years desperately trying to get hold of the negative but always without success. A combination of the Spanish sun and some dodgy curlers produced this rather unique look. What made it all the worse was that this photograph was used as my official head and shoulders shot for all the newspaper photos and sticker cards for the whole of the season. Even to this day, I have not really lived this photo down. If you look really closely, you'll also see that I was having a pretty dire attempt at growing a blond moustache.

After such an inauspicious start I feared the worst. But I managed to weave some of my magic in the dressing room and, thanks to a few victories and several draws, we managed to stay up by the skin of our teeth.

I worked really hard in the close season and was looking forward to playing my part in a promotion push during the 1979-80 season. Pleaty was a shrewd judge of a player's worth and we had some excellent men on our books. Although he was pushing on a bit, Bob Hatton was still a quality striker. Young Ricky Hill and Brian Stein were just making their way in the game and winger David Moss was one of the most under-rated players of his generation. He struck a really sweet ball. Paul Price went on to carve out an excellent career for himself at Spurs, and Kirk Stephens was a hard-as-nails defender. I felt more confident about success than I had for a long while. Sadly, things went wrong from the moment I set foot at the pre-season photo-call.

In the late seventies the demi-perm, as worn by Kevin Keegan, was all the rage. Kevin had dark hair, however, I had blond and, take a tip from me, don't ever have a perm if you've got blond hair. A few days before the start of the season I paid a visit to my hairdresser and asked for a demi-perm. At the time, I thought it tremendously fashionable. This effect lasted for all of half an hour before I saw the end result in the mirror. I looked an absolute disgrace. My appearance was not helped by the fact I was also vainly trying to grow a moustache (another major mistake). For those of you old enough to remember him, I looked like Mr Pastry - a massive mop of blond fuzzy hair flopping all over my head.

Two days later Luton were holding their official photo call so I had no alternative but to turn up modelling my new hair-style. Strangely, I did not look quite so bad alongside my team-mates because two other fools - Paul Price and Kirk Stephens - also had similar blond perms. The three of us looked like fuzzy-wuzzies on the team photo. At this stage I also have to say that the Luton kit did not do me any favours, either. My fair hair and complexion clashed badly with Luton's white and orange shirts. Their colour scheme didn't suit me at all, I much preferred the blue of Chelsea and Leicester.

As the photographs began to circulate so the number of calls I received began to increase. It reached a stage where at least twice a day the phone would ring and the person on the other end of the line would not say a word. I would hear a succession of cackles of laughter coming down the line before they could finally manage to bring themselves to speak coherently about my *barnet*. Just about everyone I ever played with in football rang me in that four-week period. My life was a nightmare, but one that wouldn't go away. All the newspapers and just about every football magazine I opened had that unflattering head and shoulders photo. I've spent the last 21 years desperately trying to get hold of the negative and I've come very close on many occasions but always just missed out. A succession of Leicester City programme editors (Macey included) have sneaked it into their publications and ribbing has been undertaken by a new generation of players and supporters. I promise that after this book is finished I will lay my hands on the offending negative and burn it.

■ **COURT JESTER:** Here I am in April 1979 neatly controlling a ball in Luton Town colours. I thought they wanted me for my footballing skills but it emerged that my old mate David Pleat just needed the Birch to give the dressing-room a bit of a lift!

I had been very impressed with David Pleat as a manager. Of course, we went back a long way but I didn't have any problems playing under him. He had a fantastic knowledge about the game and I had a very healthy respect for him. His coaching methods were excellent and he had gathered a strong team around him with John Moore, Ken Gutteridge and David Coates. David was arguably the most methodical of all the managers I played under. He knew absolutely everything, not just about his own players, but about everyone else's. In fact, he probably knew more about your own business than you did yourself. David was very intense and had dossiers on players around the world. He had an almost encyclopaedic knowledge of the game and those involved in it.

Nothing, however, quite braced me for the manner of my departure from Kenilworth Road. David called me in to say that another club had expressed an interest and Luton were prepared to release me. I was most put out. I protested that I wanted to stay and fight for my place. It was a case of the old adage that the mind was willing even if the body was hesitating a little. But I genuinely didn't want to go.

"No, Birch, you don't understand," David Coates told me. "Your job is done here." "No it's not," I retorted, "I want to help you get promotion. We're only a month into the season." Replied Coatesy: "Your job is done. You were brought in to give the dressing room a lift. Everyone was down when you came but now the players are buzzing again. You've done your job. There's nothing more for you to do here." It slowly dawned on me that Pleaty had not brought me into the club for my footballing abilities but for my motivational skills in the dressing room. At the time I was mortified that people thought I couldn't play the game. Looking back, I agree it was probably a clever move by David. Luton narrowly avoided relegation and went on to have some tremendously successful years - arguably the best in their history. Court jester Birch, meanwhile, was allowed to move further on down to Hereford United.

Hereford were struggling in Division Four and I had little intention of going there but I agreed to meet up with their manager Mike Bailey and his assistant, a very young Bobby Gould. It was probably a very shrewd move on the part of Mike to arrange to meet me in the Post House Hotel in Luton, just off the M1. Had they asked me to travel to Hereford, I would have quickly realised it was like travelling to the end of the world and would have been most unlikely to agree to a move. Mike and Bobby explained the situation and how they needed an older head to steady the ship. Again, they agreed I could stay in Leicester and travel over for a couple of days a week. And, again, it was still the same wage. However, I felt that was reasonable under the circumstances, given that Hereford were a lowly Division Four side.

My first journey over there is one I will not easily forget - it took me over four hours. The first two, from Leicester to Birmingham and Worcester, were predominantly motorway but after Worcester it was more a case of Farmer Giles country. The roads twisted and turned incessantly and there were arguably more tractors per square mile in that region than in any other throughout the land. As those who know me well will tell you, I lose all patience in a car. I get irritable and angry and my blood would boil during those last 30 miles into Hereford.

Fourth Division football was a real culture shock to the Birch. I made my debut in a goalless draw at home to Torquay and 10 days later I completed the 450th League appearance of my career in a 2-0 victory over Crewe. My jinx with managers, however, was to strike again when Mike Bailey quit Edgar Street to go back to Charlton Athletic. This effectively sounded the death knell on my League career. I had been at Hereford a mere five games when Mike left and new manager Frank Lord appeared to take an instant dislike to me. Although I was only in Hereford a couple of days a week, I was looked upon as the lead voice in the dressing room. I was again the lads' social secretary and players' night outs generally co-incided with when I was in town. Unfortunately, one of my nocturnal excursions got a little out of hand.

We were having a few quiet drinks in the town centre on a Wednesday night and in our party was a young lad called Andy Feeley who had been an England youth international and was now being tipped as a hot prospect. He had captained Hereford at the age of 16 and was a skilful midfielder. His only problem was he could be a little over-exuberant after downing a few drinks. Sure enough, he started to get into an argument with a chap at the bar. This guy was quiet and unassuming and didn't want to get involved but Andy insisted on winding him up. At this point, we should remember that Hereford is home base for the SAS regiment, a point obviously lost on Andy. Four deftly delivered punches later Andy was unconscious at the feet of this modest, unassuming SAS man. Anyway, we continued to have an enjoyable evening but paid well for it the following morning.

Frank had heard about our night out and was determined to stamp his authority on the squad. He ran us ragged in one of the hardest sessions I had ever undertaken in my career. I would have struggled to finish it when I was a teenager, let alone at 34 years of age. I was physically sick and, from that point on, knew I was on borrowed time. I think Frank viewed me as a threat. He thought I might undermine his authority and after a handful of games I found myself frozen out of the team. It was one thing not to make the side at Chelsea, but to be out of the picture at Hereford was another. Frank was unhappy with me and I with him.

It eventually transpired that my last taste of senior action came as a second half substitute for Hereford in a 2-1 FA Cup second round defeat at home to Aldershot

…AND NOW THE END IS NEAR:
As Frank Sinatra so famously says in one of his great records, the writing was on the wall by the time I arrived at Hereford. The game at Hartlepool on Saturday November 10, 1979 marked my third last game in the Football League. The Victoria Ground proved to be my final away League match.

I saw recently that the ground was voted one of the most hospitable in the country. Not for me it wasn't. We got thumped 3-0, I never got a kick and the winds off the North Sea nearly blew my knackers off.

on December 15, 1979. Actually, my last game should have been at Lincoln a few weeks later. Frank named me in the team but the game was postponed because the Sincil Bank pitch was unfit. A word too on my final senior away game at Hartlepool. Down the years I have played at every major ground - Highbury, Anfield, Old Trafford, Stamford Bridge and St James Park. As you might expect, most of those had some pretty impressive dressing rooms; Highbury was probably my favourite. But, without a shadow of a doubt, the worst dressing rooms I had the misfortune to get changed in were at Hartlepool's Victoria Ground. There was a big hole in the side of the wall which faced out directly onto the main road outside. Consequently, the

Birch could be seen struggling into his jock strap while a multitude of fans peered through the gap. What a sight! To compound the afternoon's woes, we lost 3-0 and the wind off the North Sea was one of the most bitingly cold I ever experienced.

My contract was due to run until the end of the season but it was clear something had to give. I had talks with Frank after Christmas. The club put a package to me and I accepted. My contract was cancelled in January 1980 and so ended a 16-year career in the Football League. In truth, it was a sad end, but every professional player will tell you it is a poignant moment when they hang up their boots.

After my Hereford experience the last thing I would have contemplated was a spell in non-League football. However, a couple of weeks after finishing at Edgar Street, I received a phone call from Tony Senter, General Manager of Trowbridge Town. I had to look on a map to see where Trowbridge was located! My first reaction to Tony was: "You must be joking!!" But he was very persuasive. He told me about the club, where it was going, what he wanted to achieve and how he viewed me as a key component in that success story. He also told me I would be paid £100 a week. "C'mon down and see what you think," he said. Eventually I was browbeaten into submission and said I would play a couple of games.

After I'd put down the phone I couldn't believe I had actually assented to all this. I had said yes to a guy I had never even seen, and agreed to play for a team I had never heard of. Only the Birch could do this. Trowbridge, I later discovered, were one of the country's oldest non-League clubs having been founded in 1880. They were playing their football in the Southern League Midland Division and averaging gates of less than 100 at their Frome Road ground in Wiltshire. The population of Trowbridge amounted to only 20,000 people and it was a minor miracle the club was able to hold its head above water in the Southern League, let alone the dizzy heights of the Alliance which we were to reach in 18 months time.

If a little earlier I was complaining about the drive to Hereford, let me tell you the journey to Trowbridge was every bit as bad. Basically, it entailed following part of the old Fosse Way, built by the Romans from Wiltshire to Leicester and beyond. I doubt it could have been much slower to go by chariot 2,000 years ago. Needless to say, I didn't really bother about training. I turned up on matchdays and Tony and the board seemed to happy with the way things were going. In our second season we managed to rise above the nether regions and put together a promotion campaign. During this time, Tony approached me after a night game against Corby. "Birch, we'd like you to become player-manager," he said. I laughed him out of court. How could I be manager living 120 miles away in Leicester? "No," Tony persisted, "we can sort something out for you." After hurried consultations with the board they offered me a package, saying it did not matter if I couldn't manage more than one night a week for training. Flattered they were so keen to keep my services, I agreed. I travelled down two nights a week for training and turned up for matches. Do you know, I never saw a reserve game in my three-and-a-half years with the club!

Although we enjoyed a successful season, we never really entertained thoughts about promotion to the Alliance. We ended up finishing third and I thought little more about it during the summer as I prepared for another season in the Southern League. A bizarre set of circumstances followed, however. Alvechurch won the championship but did not bother to apply for promotion. Runners-up Bedford Town applied, but their ground did not come up to scratch. By default, Trowbridge were next in line. Tony told me the grading committee members would be coming for a ground inspection on a Friday afternoon. Not for one minute did I think there was the remotest chance we would get in. Our ground was barely Southern League standard... but I reckoned without the guile of Tony Senter. He had joined the club from Walsall in 1977 and was one of the shrewdest and cleverest football

TROWBRIDGE 1982: Trust you like the kit. As part of my managerial duties, I blagged a free all blue strip from Patrick as we were unable to afford a new one for ourselves. I've got my accustomed position back again on the front row of the team pic. On the far right of the front row is former Arsenal star George Armstrong. 'Geordie' was a great guy and, as I was finishing off this book, I was deeply saddened to hear of his death. The full caption is: (back row), Parrott, Collicut, Davies, Harding, Smeulders, Feeley, Tainton, Senter (front row) Speck, Tanner, Wright, Birch, Harris, Maynard, Armstrong.

administrators I ever came across during my life in football. As general manager he was responsible for the day-to-day running of the club and operated one of the most successful lottery schemes in the West Country. It was this lottery that effectively bank-rolled the club, because we certainly struggled to get adequate money through the gate.

One of the principal barriers to our progress into the Alliance was an absence of proper turnstiles. We simply didn't have any! Undeterred, Tony acquired a couple from his 'contacts' and literally plonked them on some spare land adjacent to the entrance. They weren't cemented in, they just sat there like telephone kiosks. Along came the grading committee and Tony gave them a whistle-stop tour of the ground before taking them into the boardroom where he plied them with considerable 'hospitality'. I'm not sure how much everyone had to drink but a couple of hours later a jubilant Tony rang me. "Birch, we're in the Alliance," he declared triumphantly. "You what?" I spluttered, "But I haven't got a team!" "Well, you'd better go out and get one," he retorted!

And so it came to pass that little Trowbridge Town were promoted into the Alliance Premier for the first time in their history. We would be rubbing shoulders with non-League giants such as Altrincham, Scarborough, Kettering and Barry Fry's Barnet. When we got the fixture list, I nearly passed out, but after only four matches we were in the top six after spectacular victories over champions Altrincham and Boston and a point from a game with Worcester City. We managed to assemble a fairly decent side containing several players with League experience, relying heavily on my former club Hereford by taking on defender Steve Strong and striker Paul Hunter. Goalkeeper John Smeulders came from Bournemouth, Paul Collicutt and Keith Tanner arrived from Swindon and Gary Harris joined us from Cardiff. Probably the biggest coup, however, was signing my old mucker Andy Feeley. Fully recovered from his work-out with the SAS, Andy had been in dispute with Hereford and we managed to secure his services on loan. As a former England youth international and veteran of League football at the age of 16, Andy was far too good for the Alliance but he was a mate and he agreed to turn out for us. Thanks to the guile of Tony Senter we even managed to sign him permanently. Although on loan with us, Hereford were prepared to sell him for £40,000 but there was no way in a million years tiny Trowbridge could ever have afforded him. However, Hereford made an administrative cock-up which was swiftly spotted by the wily Tony and, as a result, we were able to sign Andy on a free. Hereford were not best pleased!

I took a fairly maverick approach to management and picked up one or two tips from my days in America with San Jose and Memphis. My half-time team talks adopted legendary status. On many an occasion I would troop off at half time and go into the public address box. I'd grab the microphone and broadcast my views on the first half to the fans. "Stick with us," I'd tell the bemused crowd. "I know we were crap in the first half but we'll get better. Just keep on getting behind the lads."

In the dressing room, I'd tell the lads to sit on the floor and raise their legs up onto the benches. That way the blood would drain out and circulate better so that when they got up again they wouldn't feel heavy-legged. I know it probably breaks every medical code in the book but it seemed to work for us. My powers of motivation were fairly straightforward and direct. "I'm the oldest player in this team. None of you should be less fit than me. If you stop running before me then you're dropped," I used to say. Pretty basic stuff, but it had the desired effect. Against all the odds, we managed to

stop up in our first season in 17th spot. Our performances seemed to capture the imagination of the Trowbridge public (no easy thing to achieve). For the bigger games we managed to attract four-figure gates - our home game with Boston drew a crowd of 1,047!

I have to say I really did take well to management. It suited my personality and, if there's one thing I am good at, then it is being able to get into people's psyche. To this day, many still continue to dismiss me as a court jester. I may not be the most educated man in the world but I like to think I'm streetwise. Put me in a room and I can converse as easily with a managing director as I can a bus conductor. To me, one of the biggest assets in a football boss is the ability to manage people. There are only a set number of ways, tactically, that you can play the game. The trick is to get the best out of players and that means being able to understand them and command their respect.

■ **GOLDEN OLDIES:** Meet my midfield engine room for the start of the 1982-83 Alliance season. On the left is my old Leicester team-mate Jon Sammels, centre is the former Bristol City player Trevor Tainton and (right) is the ex-Arsenal star George Armstrong. Coupled with myself in midfield, our average age was 36 and our average weight was 14 stone 6 pounds.

The following season we attempted to improve further. I opted for experience and brought in former Leicester team-mates Jon Sammels and George Armstrong, and ex-Bristol City man Trevor Tainton. Our average age was 36 and our average weight was around 14 stone six pounds. I doubt there has ever been an older midfield put out in the Alliance. You can't beat a bit of experience, that's what I say! And we certainly got off to a flier. After 15 games we were rooted to the bottom without a win and had acquired only five points. How we ever managed to survive after such a terrible start I'll never know but we did. It must have been our experience!

Never one to miss a psychological trick, I ensured a striker I signed from Kidderminister Harriers had a profound effect on matches. Bernie Wright was a fearsome-looking forward. With his bushy beard and curly black hair he was a dead ringer for Grizzly Adams. Before a match I made sure I left our dressing room door slightly ajar while the opposition ran out. As it was quite cramped they had to exit in single file so I told Bernie to stick his head around our door and growl at the opposition as they ran out. It used to put the fear of God into quite a few of them, I can tell you!

I also never used to miss a trick when it came to handling the press. Trowbridge, it's fair to say, never had much of a media presence before my arrival. We were on a distant planet to Bristol City and Bristol Rovers and were a long way behind our nearest neighbours Bath City too. But local journalists quickly cottoned on to the fact that I made good 'copy'. If they rang me, I always produced a story from somewhere. I used to be quite proud of the tales I manufactured to get Trowbridge into the papers and it soon got to a point where I was the first manager they would ring. I took the view that our supporters wanted to read about Trowbridge and everything that went into the papers was free publicity for the club.

All good things, however, must come to an end. The travelling was beginning to wear me down and opportunities were presenting themselves to me back in Leicester. I am often asked whether I would have fancied a crack at League management. There were reports the two Bristol clubs had expressed an interest in my services but it was not something I ever actively pushed. At the time I had no inclination to relocate my family and looked upon Leicester as my home. Kettering, too, were reportedly interested in me but after two seasons as player manager with Trowbridge I took the view it was time to hang up my boots. I had an excellent opportunity to go into the importing business and this co-incided with an offer from my beloved Leicester City to return in a public relations role. This position, suggested by chairman Terry Shipman, was an exciting and innovative one. It was a dual role I decided to take and I've not had any regrets, although there is still a part of me that wonders what might have been had I gone down the managerial route...

Happy Families

THROUGHOUT my life an image has been painted of The Birch. To the vast majority of people, I am a larger-than-life showman who has led a showbiz-style life in the game of football. My celebrated kiss with Tony Currie, my long blond locks, my singing prowess, my fashion sense and my rather loud exterior have all combined to give a certain picture of yours truly. As those closest to me will tell you, the real story is a little different. I like to think I'm not quite that superficial or two-dimensional. Come to think of it, I'm a lot more boring away from the spotlight than you might think. Believe it or not, stability and a very closely knit family have played vitally important roles in my life. I've known my wife since I was 15 years old, and away from football I liked nothing better than playing with my kids as they grew up. As a youngster myself, I benefited from a fantastically supportive family who travelled everywhere to watch me play. I attach a great deal of importance to my parents' support in shaping me into the way I am. I think I am a loyal person and there have been many constants throughout my life, none more so than my marriage, my children and my parents. They, undoubtedly, are the most important things. I'm sorry if this shatters a few illusions of your persona of the Birch as a party animal but that's the way I am and I make no apologies.

I was only 15 years old when I first clapped eyes on Heather. I'd just started work with Carlton Engineering Works and my regular Sunday night haunt was the Colemans Club at the back of the Black Boy Inn, just off Slab Square in the centre of Nottingham. Throughout the day I'd play football on Woodthorpe Park and, by evening, I'd have worked up quite a thirst. All the football lads would make the journey into Nottingham on the bus resplendent in our best 'pulling' gear; mine was

■ **MODEL LOOKS:** Heather did a bit of modelling as a youngster... and very pretty she was too. This is a particularly fetching portrait pic taken by the Daily Mirror. However, having heard what these fashion photographers get up to, I have to admit, I didn't exactly give Heather my full backing on the modelling route.

a shiny grey mohair suit, a shirt with detachable collar which ripped into my neck, a thin pinstripe tie and winklepickers. We'd go into a special bar in the Black Boy designated 'men only'. Funny, but at the time we thought it was really macho to drink in there. We might as well have had 'gay' tattooed on our foreheads!

Although I loved the taste of mixed fruit, I was out with the rest of the football lads so, to save face, I used to drink a quite ridiculous alcoholic concoction called Black Velvet. Nowadays, it more commonly comprises Guinness and cider. My preference was cider and Mackeson - three pints of that and you were ready to throw up, guaranteed! I lost count of the number of times I *belle-vued* over Slab Square.

After three pints I staggered through to the Colemans disco which resembled a church hall. The lads would walk around the dance floor while the girls sat on chairs around the edge. Spotting a good-looking girl, however, was never easy. This was the era when hooped skirts were all the rage. Layer upon layer of petticoat would be draped over the hoops. When the girls sat down the hoops would rise up and the girl's entire body would be obscured, with the exception of the top half of their face, just visible behind the billowing ranks of lace-trimmed under-garments.

One set of eyes and forehead, in particular, appealed to me but such was my lack of self esteem I didn't have enough confidence to make the first tentative approach. Heather and her friend Cindy were regulars like ourselves and I thought my luck was about to change when I discovered one of my footballing friends, John Webster, hung around with Heather in Bulwell. John played in the same Nottingham Boys side and went on to play professionally for Rotherham. I was picking his brains about Heather one night when my heart sank. You know how it is - every disco or dance hall has at least one flash 'arry, a suave, good-looking smoothie after whom all the girls longingly lust. The heart-throb of Colemans was Haydn Parmenter - he had the looks and, I believe, his father used to run an electrical shop in the city centre so he had a few bob as well. Not only that but he was also a couple of years older and owned a car. Consequently I was mortified when he approached Heather and she spent the rest of the evening cavorting on the dance floor with him. I was suffering from a terrible inferiority complex, what with my crew cut, buck teeth and *muldoons* all over my neck.

The following week I was talking to John again about Heather and asking whether he could put in a good word for me. He told me to go and speak to Heather myself. "You stand a good chance. She wants you to go over and ask her out." I was gobsmacked and spent the next hour trying to build up enough confidence to break the ice. I was with Webbo, Micky Somers and Eddie McGlory. Eddie also fancied Heather and, being a strong, confident Irish lad, he told us he was going to make a move. He and I had a big row but it did at least prompt me into rushing up to Heather.

I was so nervous I hardly knew what to say. "John's told me all about you," said Heather. "You play in the same Nottingham Boys football team. We all hang out together in the Penguin Cafe in Bulwell." She told me she worked in the electrical department of the Co-op on Parliament Street and asked what I did. Pleased as punch, I blurted out that I was employed by an engineering company. She caught me out when she asked my age, telling me she was '16 going on 17'. I replied I was a mere 15. Little did I realise that Heather was actually nine months younger than me.

We had a great dance and, growing in confidence, I asked if I could escort her home to Bulwell. For those of you who know Nottingham, Council House Square was where all the buses headed off to various points of the city and on Sundays the last ones left at 10.30pm. It was quite a sight to see these corporation buses making a dash for the corner - a sort of double-decker grand prix, if you like. Heather's friend hopped on a bus to Bestwood while we caught the Bulwell flier. I was in heaven, sitting on the back seat with my dream girl. Little did it matter that in eight hours I had to be clocking on for work in Carlton. We arrived back in Bulwell and I walked Heather to the gate of her house. "You'd better not come in because my dad is still up," Heather told me. I was so nervous I gave her the briefest of pecks on the cheek before setting off home.

From Bulwell to Sherwood is about five miles and, as I had missed the last bus, there was no option but to make my way home on foot. Fortified by three pints of Black Velvet, I started out. Don't ask me why, but I set myself the nonsensical challenge of running all the way home without once setting my feet down on the cracks in the paving stones. For nearly five miles I pounded along avoiding all the cracks.

I'd get home just before midnight and lay out my overalls in readiness for an early start the following morning. Mum would leave out sandwiches for me to collect on the way to work. This ritual continued for five Sundays before Heather finally asked me into her parents house.

The first time I stepped over the threshold I was absolutely petrified. Heather sat me down and her mum Golda offered me a cup of tea. Heather's dad was called George and when I learned he was a miner I feared the worst. He was a big strong man but soft as grease underneath. He dozed in the armchair while I sipped my tea and all I wanted to do was finish my rosy and get away before he woke up. I wasn't so lucky. Awakening from his slumbers, one eye opened and out of the corner of his mouth he said: "So you're Lal, our daughter has been telling us all about you." They were great people and I went on to develop a wonderful relationship with them both. Sadly, neither is still with us.

Our relationship blossomed although, like any other young courting couples, we had our occasional disagreements. Heather's parents moved house across Bulwell to a place in Lime Street. As I began to get my feet under the table with the family, my visits became more regular. On many a night we would sit downstairs in the lounge and wait for the rest of the family to go to bed. Heather would then make her way up upstairs, while I was left to fend for myself on the sofa downstairs with only an eiderdown for comfort. Suffice to say, when I thought the coast was clear, I gingerly made my way up to her room. This, remember, was the Sixties and such antics were frowned upon in a big way. In the new Millennium it's no big deal to most people, but back then you had to be very careful.

Unfortunately, I was seldom careful enough. No matter how delicately I inched up those stairs, I would always fall foul of at least one creaking floorboard. Little did I know that Golda and George were wide awake and listening to me. Of course, come morning time I was back under the eiderdown on the settee in the lounge. What happened in the meantime is mine and Heather's business!

Lime Street hosted some great parties with several of my colleagues from Sheffield United coming down for nights out in Nottingham. Heather was not one to come and watch every game. She was seldom interested in football but we enjoyed some great times in that house.

You're probably wondering what hospitality the Birchenall household laid on for Heather. Well, in truth, she was never a regular visitor. This had nothing to do with the lack of a warm reception. In fact, it was quite the opposite. My mum comes from the school brought up to think every visitor has been starved of food for a fortnight. Her prowess as a cook was legendary, not just in terms of quality but also in quantity. Plates would be piled three feet high and course after course served, followed by mountains of biscuits. Heather was only a small girl with a petite, sylph-like figure. As soon as Mum clapped eyes on her she was off to the kitchen to slave away over the stove. All this food was too much for Heather. She couldn't eat it such quantities and if there was one thing my mother disliked it was to see food left on a plate. She was mortally offended if a couple of peas were uneaten! So, Heather used to be more than a little intimidated by the sight of Birch tucking into his favourite meal of toad in the hole, mashed potato, peas, carrots and lashings of gravy, followed by a large helping of apple pie with dollops of custard, and a few biscuits thrown in for good measure. The Birch lapped it all up but Heather, anxious not to offend mum, used to be a little selective with her visits and certainly ensured they didn't co-incide with meal times.

Our relationship grew and one of the ultimate adventures proved to be our first-ever holiday together in the exotic climes of the Isle of Wight. We joined forces with my best pal Micky Somers and his girlfriend June, a real feisty little character who made Heather look like Mary Poppins. Micky and June, incidentally, went on to get married and now live in the Mapperley Plains district of Nottingham. I digress. We booked into a hotel, or to be more accurate, a boarding house. We two lads checked into one room and the two girls into another. Or at least that's what we did for appearances' sake. Once we got up to our rooms, we each chucked out a suitcase and paired off into our couples. It seems prudish in the modern era, but back in the Jurassic period it wasn't the done thing to advertise the fact you shared a room with anyone of the opposite sex unless they happened to be your wife.

Micky was a somewhat jealous type and hated anyone else to pay attention to the girls. One day a couple of French lads took an interest in Heather and June and poor old Micky got most upset. He followed them everywhere and was ready to start a fight. Although Micky was only a short-arse he was always ready for a ruck. The biggest drama, however, was reserved for the end of the holiday when I almost set the boarding house on fire. I'd discovered cigarettes by the age of 17 and was enjoying a ciggie in my room when I thought I heard someone about to come in. I hastily dropped my fag into the waste paper bin where it soon set fire to the curtains. There was smoke everywhere and the flames started licking up the material. We managed to keep it under control... but only just, otherwise Birch may have found himself a convicted arsonist!

Not that Heather was a total angel during our relationship. She was a pupil at Manning Girls School, and while Birch was bunking off to play football, Heather embarked on a few of her own extra-curricular excursions. She was not averse to using a lunchtime or two to make an impromptu visit to the discos at The Locarno in Nottingham city centre. Many of you I know will comment on how incongruous a disco at lunchtime sounds but they were all the rage in the early Sixties. Not surprisingly, afternoon attendance records at school among the teenage fraternity were not all they might have been. Heather would pack a change of clothing in her bag and take off her school uniform during lunch break, donning something a little more racy. Then, along with her friends, she'd dive on a bus and have an hour or two at The Locarno.

Heather was always a very bright girl. While my football career was blossoming she was graduating up the career ladder too. She left the Co-op to work at a printing company and, within a matter of months, had been put in day-to-day charge of the operation. In the absence of the boss, and at just 17, Heather was virtually running the company . She has always been well-organised and quietly efficient, properties she has used to good effect in later life running hostelries in Swithland and Quorn.

Aside from Mum's mealtimes, Heather and I became a permanent fixture by each other's side and I can honestly say that taking the first rungs on the road to becoming a professional footballer did not jeopardise our relationship in any way. Heather was not fazed nor did she view me as a different person now I had become a footballer.

As she has told me down the years - and she's perfectly correct - she certainly didn't marry me because I was a footballer as she knew me when I worked for an engineering company. I'd better be careful about what I say here, but, to my mind, professional sportsmen have to be very careful about whom they marry. I know of many instances where relationships have blossomed after a sportsman has become famous. It can put an immense strain on a marriage when a career is finished. Please don't take this the wrong way, but there are some women out there who fall in love with the lifestyle and trappings of a footballer as much as they do with the person. One of the great strengths of my relationship with Heather was that we knew each other before my sporting success came along. I knew full well she didn't want me just for my footballing ability and the wealth that brought.

I do have to admit I made something of a tactical error leading up to our marriage. We'd been engaged for a little while and my agreement with Heather was that we'd get hitched if I got a big move from Sheffield United. I thought I was on reasonably safe ground here as, just a few weeks earlier, manager John Harris had turned down my transfer request. "You're not goings bloomin' anywhere, son," he told me in no uncertain terms. A few months later Chelsea came in for me and I was on my way to Stamford Bridge for £100,000. My first call was to my parents to tell them the news, the second to Heather. She was delighted... and quickly added: "Don't forget the promise you made me!" "Of course not," I replied. "Damn!" I thought at the time (only joking). Nine months later we tied the knot at St Mary's Church in Bulwell. Ironically, John Harris had always been very keen for his younger players to get married. He felt marriage was a stabilising influence. If they were single, they were far more likely to be out on the town, succumbing to the sins of drink and clubbing. Once they were married, these natural instincts were far more likely to be curbed by 'er indoors'. Even to this day, it's a philosophy preached by many of our most senior and successful managers. Funny how some things never change.

I've spoken in an earlier chapter about those few months I spent in Barnes, bored out of my mind to the extent that I deliberately went out drinking on several nights just to get out of the house. During this time, Heather and I were house-hunting and we quickly plumped for Ascot, an area where Peter Osgood lived. We settled on a beautiful chalet-type house in a leafy lane called Mill Ride which backed onto Ascot racecourse

■ **CUTTING THE CAKE:** Myself and the *tank commander* pose for the obligatory picture (right), cutting the cake at our reception above the Co-op in Mapperley.

■ **HERE COMES THE BRIDE:** Husband and wife Heather and Alan Birchenall pose for their first photograph as a married couple on the steps of the church (left). Ever the showman, you'll notice the Birch broke with tradition by opting for a four-button jacket (most people had three). Take a look at the silver tie as well. I'd forgotten to get my *peckham* and had to dive into a shop in Arnold on route to the church and purchase a tie for eight shillings and a tanner.

■ **FAMILY GROUP:** From left to right (below): cousin Jean Williams, best man Len Badger, Mum and Dad, Birch, *Tank Commander*, Golda and George Philp (Heather's parents), June Somers, Ian Philp and Jean Philp.

A STAR WEDS

Bulwell bride for Chelsea footballer

CHELSEA'S £100,000 football star Alan Birchenall was married at St. Mary's Church, Bulwell, on Saturday to local girl Heather Elizabeth Philp.

Alan, who joined the First Division side from Sheffield United, lived locally for many years and his parents, Mr. and Mrs. L. Birchenall live at 45 Montfort Crescent, Sherwood.

The bride's parents, Mr. and Mrs. G. Philp, live at 54 Lime Street, Bulwell.

The bride has not seen her husband play since he joined Chelsea nine months ago.

The service was conducted by the Rev. N. Hill and the bride who was given in marriage by her father, wore a full-length dress in heavy white satin. Her bouquet was of pink roses, white stephanotis and lily of the valley.

The matrons of honour were Mrs. Jean Philp and Mrs. June Summers and the bridesmaid was Miss Jean Williams.

They all wore full-length dresses in pink brocade and carried bouquets of mixed white flowers.

Page-boy was a one-year-old

Alan Birchenall and his bride, Heather Elizabeth Philp after their wedding at Bulwell.

■ Here's how the wedding was reported in the Nottingham Guardian Journal.

It cost us the then princely sum of £7,750, although now it would probably set you back more than half a million quid. Heather was in charge of interior design and in the late sixties Habitat was the in-company for furnishings. Vivid orange settees, racy purple chairs and bright yellow tables winged their way into our house. If my contribution to our new home was minimal, then my input into the wedding was almost non-existent. Most fellas can't be bothered with wedding arrangements and I was no exception. I was quite happy for Heather and her family to organise the big day.

I did however offer my services in just one respect... and was most concerned that my offer was not accepted by my dad. After all, how many couples can say they could have had the legendary Joe Cocker as the cabaret for their wedding reception. I'd kept in touch with Joe since our nights out together in Sheffield when his Grease band were just starting out. They had a number one hit with 'A little help from your friends' and were starting to earn national recognition. Joe offered to come along to play at my wedding so I had a word with Dad. He didn't exactly give me the encouragement I'd been looking for. "Sorry son I've already booked the act. There's a lad at work whose dad is in a jazz band and I've booked 'em." I politely enquired whether he could unbook them but he was adamant there was no changing the schedule. I was then faced with having to make an embarrassing phone call to Joe to tell him that although his offer was very kind I could not avail myself of his services.

The wedding itself went like a dream on that fateful day of Saturday July 6th 1968 and off we all trooped afterwards for the evening reception in the Co-op Rooms in Mapperley Plains in Nottingham. There was a large footballing turn-out with players from Sheffield United and Chelsea making the journey. The jazz band arrived too, worse luck. One by one they got out their instruments and proceeded to set up. At a push, I could have coped with an Acker Bilk-type performance but these guys were into modern jazz and it was painful to listen to them for their first 30 minutes. Word got out that I had turned down Joe Cocker and I was slaughtered by the lads. After the first slot, I attempted to redeem the situation and hastily brought the disco music on early. After that the party went with a real swing. It swung so much that, following a series of complaints from local neighbours, the police were called on three occasions to request we keep the noise down.

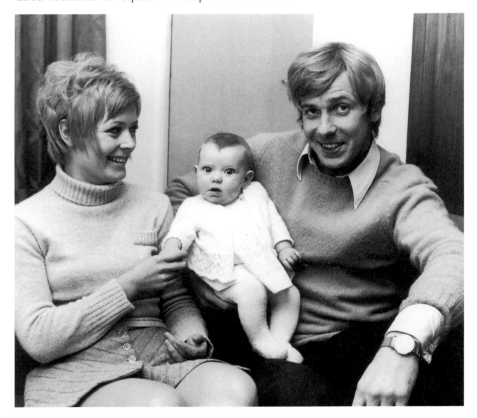

FAMILY THREESOME: Here's one of the first pictures of our daughter Laura. Mum, Dad and baby are captured on film at our home in Ascot.

Here we all are at home in Banstead during my time with Crystal Palace. These pics were taken during a photo session for a Palace programme. Look at the fashion statements being made by myself and *tanko*. I've got the slim-jim shirt with detachable collar wide enough to achieve take-off into a prevailing wind. *Tanko* has a tunic top and *blairs*. Laura is sporting her best little velvet number. I always used to like inviting people around to my home but these days it can be very different with players who safeguard their family privacy. At Leicester City, the most popular feature in our programme is the 'At Home With' article where players allow a cameraman into their home for some family pics. You only have to look at other club programmes to see that we're almost unique in this respect. I was always very accommodating and used to enjoy the banter the photos would promote among the lads.

As the wedding had taken place in early July and we were due to report back for pre-season training a few days earlier, we skipped the honeymoon and drove down to Ascot the following morning for our first day of married life, albeit feeling more than a little the worse for wear. People often ask me how I took to married life but, in truth, I welcomed it. I'd done the single man routine for six months in London and I was fed up with that. I enjoyed the prospect of going home to the *tank commander* after training, pottering around the house, going out for a drink or a nice meal and generally just unwinding.

■ **COLOURING BY NUMBERS:** Daughter Laura and son Dean earn top marks for artistic impression. If truth be told, the painting book actually belongs to the Birch. I'd just been getting art lessons from the *tank commander* when our kids walked in and nicked all my felt tip pens.

Married life quickly led to family life with the birth of our first child, Laura. My daughter's timing was immaculate - she decided to make her debut appearance on the day of a Chelsea midweek game against London derby rivals West Ham United. Heather woke up in the morning and I had to make the dash in the car to our local hospital in Ascot. When we got there, the nursing staff told me nothing was likely to happen for several hours so I was sent home. I went back to bed for a few hours ahead of the game only to receive a 'phone call to say I had become the proud father of a bouncing baby daughter. I rushed to the hospital to get my first glimpse of Laura. The local press came along to get a photo and, a few hours later, I went back home, got my kit ready and picked up Peter Osgood en route to Stamford Bridge. I played that evening and, as I recounted earlier, was tremendously touched by on-field congratulations on our new arrival from the legendary Bobby Moore.

For those of you thinking the Birch was not overly involved in the birth, it was a little different in those days. It was almost frowned upon to be at the birth of

■ **LITTLE ANGEL:** Don't you believe it. Laura had some terrible tantrums... like the time it needed a doctor, two nurses and myself to hold her down when she needed stitches in a cut head.

your child, and the father was very much kept at arm's length. I must also own up to a certain degree of squeamishness but please don't think I didn't do my bit at home. I've washed nappies with the best of them, I can tell you. And not these new disposable Pampers, either. Mums and Dads of today have it too easy. You should have tried washing those cotton nappies, they didn't half *pen and ink*.

Four years later, Birchenall family life was complete when son Dean arrived on the scene. By this time, we had moved to Leicester and Dean came into this world in the maternity ward at Kirby Muxloe hospital. Again, the Birch was not overly involved at the birth, but this time I was actually in the same building rather than fast asleep at home. Nursing staff left me in a waiting room, only showing me through to meet my son after Heather's exertions. In footballing parlance I was 'over the moon'. Two kids, one boy and one girl. The family was complete. Laura and Dean, however, ensured they kept Mum and Dad on their toes at all times.

Like all toddlers they could be right little sods. Laura's tantrums were legendary, typified by her antics after cutting her head in an accident at home. The incident happened on the night of a midweek game while I was with Crystal Palace. Laura came careering along the floor and cracked her head open on the corner of a door. There was blood everywhere and we made an emergency dash to the Mayday Hospital in Croydon. Laura was in a right state and no fewer than one doctor, two nurses and Dad were all unable to pin her down for stitches to be inserted into the wound. Eventually, the nurses got a blanket and enveloped Laura in a form of straight-jacket. Still she kicked and screamed and although the stitches eventually went in they were so rushed that Laura sports the scar to this day.

Dean had a particular aversion to sand which was a pretty monumental problem when we went on a beach holiday to Cala Millor in Spain. He couldn't bear the sand going in between his toes so Birch had to hire a bicycle, prop Dean in the carry-bag on the front handle bars and cycle along the promenade for two hours at a time. All the shopkeepers used to come out and laugh at the mad Englishman who cycled up and down in the midday sun with temperatures nudging 100 degrees fahrenheit.

One of the biggest advantages of being a professional footballer was the amount of time I was able to spend with my children. Most people tend to focus on the financial rewards that come with the profession but, for me, one of the single biggest benefits was that I was able to see Laura and Dean both grow up. After training in the morning, I had the rest of the day to myself and, in their early days of infants school, I was invariably the one who picked them up and dropped them off. It was a great feeling and those are the sort of things you can only do once. I'm well aware that many less fortunate Dads spend hours working to bring in the weekly wage and are only able to see their kids at night. I was very lucky and enjoyed my time with them immensely. The kids themselves used to get away quite a bit too. My in-laws had a caravan at Chapel St Leonards (one resort up the coast from Skegness) and Heather and the children would spend many a happy week away.

Dad, meanwhile, charted new territories when he decided that, despite his advancing years and a free bus pass, he would take driving lessons. What possessed him I'll never really know, but after a year of lessons he finally managed to get rid of the L-plates. To celebrate, I bought him a Mini Traveller. Obviously the novelty of being a car driver quickly wore off and the car spent virtually it's entire life abandoned, half on the pavement and half on the road outside my parents' house. Mum only travelled with him once. "Never again!" she said. I took her advice and don't think I ever once got in the car with my dad behind the wheel. When I bought the vehicle there were 41,000 miles on the clock, and when my dad sold it a few years later, the mileometer read 40,284 miles. Mind you, it was a miracle he ever managed to navigate those 284 miles without hitting another vehicle, pedestrian or lamp post!

At this stage my entire life had been one long success story. Domestically and professionally, things could hardly be bettered. I was playing First Division football and I had a fantastic family but I was soon to be hit by the hardest blow of my life so far - the death of my sister Christine. While I had been developing my football career, Christine had married husband Howard, had three great kids - Claire, Karen and Mark - and was living in Bulwell. We used to meet when we all popped around to visit Mum and Dad on Sunday afternoons. Although we had not been close when we grew up, there was now a real bond between us.

Christine had been ill for quite a while; she was suffering from bowel problems which had been diagnosed as cystitis. Mum, however, was a little sceptical. Chris had been suffering for years and the medication prescribed seemed to do very little to ease her suffering. Mum told me she was concerned about the advice Chris had been getting from her local doctor. I decided to have a word with the club doctor at Leicester City Football Club and mentioned my concern to Doc Lenten but he said it was a fundamental rule that you never treated someone else's patient. After much persuasion, however, he finally agreed to see Chris. I picked her up from Nottingham and drove over to Leicester. I'll never forget the day, it's forever etched on my memory. My 'sis looked really gaunt and was in his room for around 20 minutes. After she came out Doc Lenten gave me a letter in a sealed envelope and told me to give it to my sister's doctor. "I can't tell you any more, but take this to him straight away," he said in a grave voice.

Within a matter of days Christine was admitted to hospital in Nottingham. Doc Lenten had diagnosed my sister as suffering from bowel cancer and, in his letter to her GP had advised he strongly reconsider his course of treatment. Unfortunately, by this time it was all too late. Though I did not realise the full extent of the illness until after her death, the cancer had already begun to spread through her body. I remember the last time I went to visit Christine in hospital. I walked straight past her until I heard this voice shout "Lal". She had become so thin and gaunt I was not able to instantly recognise her. This was a few days before I was due to travel out with Leicester on a pre-season trip to the Canary Isles. I didn't really want to go but Heather and Mum persuaded me.

I was rooming with Lenny Glover and one afternoon Doc Lenten came in and said there was a telephone call I needed to take. It was Heather. She told me there was no easy way to break the news but that my sister was dead. All I wanted to do was get back home as quickly as possible but the club were unable to get a flight out for me for two days. It was the longest weekend of my life while I waited to get that plane home. Sensing my distress Lenny kindly came along with me. The club sent a car to pick us up at Heathrow airport and I raced up to Nottingham to be with my family. It was a very tearful occasion and I set about making all the funeral arrangements.

I don't think I really hate anyone but I must admit to having very strong feelings against that doctor. I think of him as a buffoon - responsible for misdiagnosing my sister for over two years. I can't help but wonder that my sister might still be with us today if her illness had been diagnosed earlier. I always said I would go and see the doctor concerned but I never really trusted myself to be in the same room as him. I don't know what I might have done to him. I felt so helpless and frustrated that my sister's life had been taken away from us and her children. It was a very new experience for me. Other than the death of my Auntie Anne, this was the first time I had to cope with the loss of someone close to me. You sort of brace yourself for someone to die when they are old but at such at early age it seems so much harder to bear.

However bad it was for us, think about the effect on my mum and dad and Christine's three children. They were subsequently brought up by Christine's husband Howard with a lot of help from my mum. It's heartwarming to this day that Claire, Karen and Mark still pay regular visits around to Mum's house in Top Valley. Karen is the dead spit of my mum and mum is now a great-grandma to Karen's son Liam. Mum refers to Liam as 'the little tornado' and, to quote one of her sayings, she's on her 'chin-straps' whenever he's around. I'm also pleased to report that Liam is being brought up the right way on a diet of Birch's favourite food, toad in the hole. It's also great for mum that they keep up such a good contact because it is through her grand-children she is able to maintain a link with her daughter.

Throughout our married and family life, it would be fair to say there was seldom a dull moment in the Birchenall household. Heather was a truly fantastic mum to our children and, at the same time, we certainly enjoyed life to the full. In all my years of playing football, I can count on one hand the number of times we failed to go out on a Saturday night after a game. Heather and I were both great socialisers and we had a fantastic circle of friends and relations. Every Saturday we'd go out for either a meal or a drink with friends and footballing team-mates and we had truly marvellous times. Heather was one of that rare breed of people who was completely nonplussed by the advent of television. She is not concerned about it in the slightest. I have to admit that the Birch, for all my socialising, does like to put on his carpet slippers and unwind in front of 'the box'. One of my cherished relaxations is to sit back and watch Coronation Street. I hardly ever miss an episode. Eastenders I find rather heavy going, but I love 'The Street' because of its sense of humour. Jack Duckworth is probably my favourite character.

Not so the *tank commander*. It was full steam ahead at all times and, over the years, her organisational skills assumed legendary status when it came to putting together house parties. In particular, the Birchenalls' Boxing Day bash became one of the highlights of the entire social calender. It started off in the first year with a handful of family and friends but, at its peak, attracted a crowd of in excess of 150 people - no mean achievement when you consider we only lived in a four-bedroom house. Guests would even re-arrange their Christmas breaks around their availability for this event.

General Montgomery would have been proud of the planning Heather put in. Preparations began weeks in advance. Every cooking utensil, pot and pan would be utilised to prepare a gastronomic feast, breweries would be contacted to deliver booze by the tanker load. The guest list became more and more impressive as the years went by. On one memorable occasion Gary Lineker and Willie Thorne came along. Snooker ace Willie, as many of you will know, is not over-endowed on the barnet stakes. This, however, did not stop him trying to grow a pony tail over the Christmas break. I say pony-tail, but it looked more like a pig-tail. The football lads could hardly contain themselves and one player, who shall remain anonymous, set fire to the pony-tail with a lighter. Willie was not best amused. The only downside to these memorable occasions was the six days it took to get the house back into some semblance of working order.

The death of my sister had a fundamental bearing on my life but when we lost Dad years later it was to have an even more profound effect. I had always looked upon my father as such a fit guy that it came as a terrible shock when he passed away. Right from my childhood days, when I used to yomp with him from Sherwood to Meadow Lane, I always thought he would be around. I could not envisage a time when he would not be there.

Sure, Dad liked to smoke his Park Drive but he seldom drank and kept himself in good condition. His only problem - as I discovered after his death - was that he would lapse into unconsciousness now and again while he sat in his chair. None of us paid too much attention to it at first as after a few minutes he would always come round again. Eventually my mum became very worried as the condition persisted and urged Dad to go to the doctors to check out whether there was a problem. Dad was one of that breed of person who hated going to see a doctor. "There's nothing wrong with me. I'll be alright," he always used to say. Then, one afternoon, he was travelling home from work at Bartons where he was employed in the wages department. He was on a bus going back to Top Valley when he passed out. Only this time he did not regain consciousness. His heart had stopped one time too many and he died while he was on that bus. There was a certain amount of poignancy

■ **SPLASHING AROUND:** If I was forced into naming my favourite family pic, this would get my vote. It was taken in the back garden of our house in Coalville during my time with Leicester City. As you can see, the house backed on to open fields and was very peaceful. I'm splashing water over Laura as *tanko* and son Dean look on.

given that he had spent most of his life working for a bus company. Not unlike my sister's passing away, it transpired the wonders of medical science could have saved my dad. Heart bypass operations have now become relatively common and friends of mine have had a whole new lease of life after undergoing the operation. It could have been the same for my father but sadly he never did go to see the doctor.

Dad's departure came as a massive shock to us all, especially to mum. We're a close-knit family, however, and we have all pulled together. Dad's death has unquestionably left a big hole in my life and I can't help but wonder that he might be here now, still going to watch his beloved Notts County, if only he had sought medical advice.

Given that we were such a football-orientated family, I suppose it was almost inevitable Dean would take a keen interest in football. From the age of about three, he'd always be kicking a ball around and, as he became older, his interest and the competitive element increased. I can, hand on my heart, say I never blindly pushed him down a football route. Dean is entitled to live his own life and make his own decisions but it's fair to say he did receive a fair amount of support from his dad.

He played for the local boys' teams around Birstall and became quite a talented player. At the age of 14 he was invited for a trial with Nottingham Forest but this co-incided with the family holiday and he wasn't able to make it to the City Ground. Ironic, isn't it, that his father failed to take up an offer from Forest 25 years earlier?

Dean, for me, had the skill to be a professional footballer but he was probably just one rung short when it came to dedication. These days there are so many distractions around and Dean just didn't quite have that edge needed to force your way into the profession. Still, he continues to play his Sunday football regularly and enjoys a game of five-a-side. Together with his mum, he's very happy running a pub in Quorn and I'm proud of the way things have turned out for him. Dean is settling down with his girlfriend Nicki and together they make a great couple.

Although both our offspring gave us their fair share of problems, it's probably fair to say that Laura handed us slightly more heart-ache. I can assure you I love Laura every bit as much as I do Dean but, in hindsight, I can perhaps see how she felt slightly left out whilst growing up. Dean and I spent so much time talking and playing football that I can see now why Laura might have thought she was not getting her fair share of attention. If we weren't out playing football, we'd be talking football, or we would be preparing Dean's kit for football. During Laura's teenage years, there were a few strains placed on the Birchenall domestic life but now I'm glad to say everything is excellent again.

Laura has settled down with a great guy called Dave who, incidentally, is a big Leicester City fan. Laura has helped get her own back on her dad by ensuring that he now has to be called Grandad. This, I can tell you, came as a big shock to the Birch's system, especially as Laura took great delight in coming into the pub to announce the event to the world. Little Caitlin is a real darling although I've seldom seen her when she isn't crying (she must take after her mum).

Looking back on our marriage I take a great deal of pride in what Heather and I achieved together. We brought up two lovely children and celebrated our silver wedding which, given the large number of people who currently seem to stay together for a considerably shorter period of time, I think is a quite major achievement. After I finished football it was always my ambition to maintain a similar standard of living and that is something I was fortunate enough to achieve. Without ever being mega-rich, we were able to enjoy a good standard of living throughout our married and family lives. However, over such a long period of time I suppose it is inevitable people change. I know I changed, and I know that Heather did too. As our children grew up, so our working lifestyles began to change too. Heather became more independent and self-sufficient and had a high-ranking job in the city council offices at Leicester. My working patterns changed too with my

involvement in the shoe business and my many nights out on community business for the football club.

Don't forget there can be few other professions in which a man can spend as much time with his wife as there is when you're a footballer. For 13 years we lived in each other's pockets and maybe we almost saw too much of each other in the early years. In truth, our decision to take on the running of a public house was not one

RELAXING IN THE GARDEN: The Birchenall family unwind after a leisurely game of cricket in the garden of our home in Cossington.

of the greatest moves of my life. I had more than enough on my plate with the shoe business and the football club to contemplate becoming a publican. However, we took over The Griffin in the Leicestershire village of Swithland and it all became too much for me. There weren't enough hours in the day to fulfil all three roles and something had to give.

We reached a stage where we felt it was best we separated and went in our own directions. I was going to use the phrase 'give each other space' but I think that is such a cop out. It's a cliche but we are still friends. Heather and Dean now run a pub in Quorn, just down the road from where I live. After 40 years of knowing each other there is no bitterness between us. We have a grown-up family who are still around us and they all know that Dad is on hand nearby to lend a helping hand if needed.

In some respects I suppose it is sad that after 40 years we are now apart. But, having been in a profession which can place a high toll on married life, I certainly don't think we can complain that we have not had a good innings. We have had

STANDING TO ATTENTION: A good friend of mine was top photographer Eric Swayne. We met while I was at Chelsea and he was one of the very top guys in his profession. He was commissioned to shoot the Pirelli calendar and rubbed shoulders with Lord Lichfield and David Bailey. Eric came up to Leicester and shot a series of family portrait pictures. This picture (left) was one of my favourites in the back garden of our Coalville house. Mind you, I'm not too sure about the sweater.

many, many fantastic times together and I don't regret a moment of our marriage. I take a fair amount of pride in the fact that the girl I met when I was 15 should be destined to spend the majority of her entire life with me.

Without a doubt, the one question Heather was constantly asked throughout her marriage was how did she manage to put up with me? "If only they knew the real you," she would always tell me. To most people I am a complete extrovert. Yes, I am loud and the life and soul of the party. When I am around football people I come alive. But Heather has seen a side of me over the years that few other people have witnessed or appreciated. At home, I can be quite sombre and quiet. I like nothing better than to curl up and watch my favourite soap Coronation Street in complete silence. I suppose too I am a lot thinner-skinned than many people give me credit for. I have a public persona that is quite a long way removed from the inner me. Heather knows that side and knows me better than just about anyone else on the planet.

Since we parted I think we have both been able to get on with our separate lives. We can take a lot of pride and satisfaction from what we have achieved together. We have a near-lifetime of memories to treasure and I hope that neither of us becomes too embittered in our later life. I certainly don't think we have any reason to.

Life for the Birch, these days, is a three-bedroomed house on a new estate in Mountsorrel, a village north of Leicester towards Loughborough. I live on my own and, though it's very different, I cope okay. Throughout my life I've been fairly independent so the washing, cooking and cleaning doesn't worry me too much. My one area of domestic weakness, however, is my cooking abilities - Delia Smith, I definitely ain't. However, I have my own 'meals on wheels' service from Leicester City training ground where chef Gary plates up a meal for me and I microwave it at home later that night. I still regularly partake of my mum's excellent cooking. I like to pay a visit once a week to her home in Nottingham. She still makes the best egg butty in the world. Mum was incredibly supportive of me when I grew up and I feel it's important I keep in regular touch with my visits.

At home, I like to unwind watching the television or reading a good sports biography. My work with Leicester City keeps me busy and I am out and about the county on a fairly regular basis. Please, don't think I'm crying for the sympathy vote here. It's a big culture shock after 40 years of living with the same person but you have to get on with life. As for settling down again with someone else, I think that highly unlikely. As Heather might remark: "Who'd put up with you?" You know, she's probably right.

Life After Football

C h a p t e r   1 2

I made a promise to myself that when I finished football I would do everything possible to maintain the same standard of lifestyle to which my family had become accustomed. Although there was not the money in the game back then that there is now, it was still a reasonably tall order. Heather, myself and the kids never had to worry unduly about whether we could afford to go out for a meal or pop along to the cinema. It was that lifestyle I wanted to continue. I had seen many of my contemporaries finish the game and quickly fall on hard times.

The people who had hung on your shirt-tails while you were playing invariably didn't last long once your career was over. There was something rather sad, too, about seeing ex-great players hanging around clubs waiting to get a boardroom pass. Or travelling hundreds of miles and claiming a few quid in expenses for scouting missions to Hartlepool or Brighton. Call me stupid, but I had too much pride for that. I didn't want to outstay my welcome in the game. So, at the age of 37, I was facing a major crossroads not only in my career but in my whole life. I decided to embark along the route signposted 'Business'. For me, a one-time teenage bus mechanic, this was quite a momentous step.

I was coming to the end of my player-manager career with Trowbridge when I had a chance meeting with a local East Midlands business entrepreneur Keith Childs. My great friend AJ Bull and his wife Vaneesha organised a string of great dinner parties and it was at one of these that Heather and I met Keith and his wife Valerie. We got chatting and he gave me his business card and asked me to give him a call. I duly arranged to meet him in his offices in Coalville the following week.

■ **BEST FOOT FORWARD:** The training gear has been replaced by a smart suit and a dapper *peckham* as the Birch begins a new business career in the shoe business. Here I am modelling a few of my lines for the Leicester Mercury after signing up...

By this time I had already accepted the new position of part-time Public Relations Officer at Leicester City although that was more for pin money than a career. I'd found out from AJ that Keith had a finger in many pies. He ran a nightclub called Camelots in Nottingham and also owned a wine company, a clothing company and a shoe company.

My first business meeting with Keith was like something from a Monty Python sketch. Outside the offices was a gleaming Rolls Royce, and the first thing I noticed when I walked in was the luxuriously thick cream shagpile carpet. Sat behind one of the biggest desks I had ever seen in one of the largest chairs I had ever viewed was KC. I decamped myself into a sprawling leather sofa and found myself slumped about six inches off the floor and craning my neck upwards to see KC behind his desk (one of the oldest corporate tricks in the box is for the boss to ensure he's always sat looking down at his staff). To say I was intimidated would be an understatement. As a professional footballer, everything in your life is done for you. When you travel abroad you don't even have to carry your own passport. Now I was involved in the first business interview of my life.

KC did not seem bothered in the slightest about my lack of business acumen. He said he wanted to give me a chance in his company because of my personality and ability to get on with people. We agreed to give each other a six month trial and I opted for his clothing company. Sadly, my first business venture did not go exactly as planned. It started out exceptionally well when I came up with the idea of producing high quality lambswool sweaters customised in football club colours. It might not sound too original in this modern era of high-tech merchandising but in the eighties it was fairly innovative. I rang around my football contacts and signed up about 30 clubs including the likes of Arsenal, Glasgow Rangers and, of course, Leicester City. The orders came pouring in and KC sent out one of his associates with letters of credit to get the sweaters manufactured in the Far East. Delivery time was about eight weeks and, as the days ticked by, we saw some samples and everything looked great. The days turned into weeks but the samples didn't materialise into deliveries. Clubs became increasingly irate and we lost all contact with KC's associate. He had done a runner with the letters of credit, and those sweaters never did appear. I was left with the horrible task of ringing everyone up to say we could not complete the order. I was devastated. My first business venture had turned into a nightmare.

While I was still licking my business wounds, I bumped into the manager of the Nottingham nightclub who was waiting outside his office to see KC. He was most concerned that KC would not give him the time off to take a holiday his girlfriend had won in a competition. He was right. I offered to help and went in to see KC only to discover he was not in the best of moods. "There's only two people I'd trust to run the club for a week. One of them is me - and I can't afford the time - and the other one is you," he barked. I was rather surprised by his confidence in my business abilities. "Well, you've spent enough time in nightclubs over the past few years to understand what's needed," he reasoned. I reluctantly decided to give it a go only for KC to hit me with the whammy that he was going away on a six week cruise.

All of a sudden I found myself running a nightclub for a week while the boss was away on holiday. My first night was a Friday and, don't forget, I was still trying to preserve Trowbridge's status in the Alliance and had a 250-mile round trip to

Wiltshire the following day. Camelots was a smart club with a restaurant and, understandably, I was very nervous. At 10pm there was no-one in the club and, even though from my own experiences I knew no-one came in until at least 11pm, I was still petrified that Nottingham clubbers had decided to boycott the venue on my first night in charge. Come 2am we had had a great night, the club was packed and I had not experienced any problems.

After closing, though, the difficulties began. For the first time in my new business life I was wholly responsible for checking the till receipts matched the cash in the tills. This was a job KC had impressed upon me I had to do myself. Under no circumstances could I delegate the responsibility. It was also one of KC's rules that no member of staff left the club until the monies tallied up. Clunk, I put the key into the till and the receipt printed out. I heaved a huge sigh of relief when the monies tallied. Likewise for tills two and three. But on the fourth till there was a massive discrepancy of the best part of £500. I couldn't believe it. By this time the staff were desperate to leave. Three huge bouncers were shouting that their taxi was waiting outside but I stuck to my guns and told them they were going nowhere. It's fair to say I was feeling the pressure. After my fiasco with the lambswool sweaters, I couldn't ring KC on his cruise liner to tell I had lost £500 on my first night. One of the girls came up to double check and said that we were short. Still I held firm and refused to let anyone go home. Then, out of the blue, another waitress came up, checked the till receipt and gave me some excuse about notes being miscounted and that the money was all there. What she actually did I'll never know but the figures now tallied and off everybody dashed. With over £2,000 stashed in a money bag I gingerly locked up and made my way to my car. When I got back home in Leicester, I stashed the money under my bed and went to sleep before heading off to Trowbridge the following morning.

I might not have a business degree but I like to think I'm fairly streetwise. I believe the staff were testing me out that night and for the rest of the week I had no problems. I faxed over the week's figures to KC on his cruise liner and got a call back almost immediately. I feared the worst but he shouted down the phone: "They're the best week's takings I've had at the club for years. Well done! I want you to run the club full time." I politely told him there was no way I was going to run it on a permanent basis.

Having had my fingers burned in his clothing business and decided that a week was more than enough of running his nightclub, I now had two choices - the wine business or the shoe business. I looked at the wine company for a while before deciding it was not for me. I was a forsyth man myself and I knew how cut-throat the business was. One of the biggest accounts was with the Army in London and that entailed going down to the capital on most Friday evenings and getting sloshed in the Officers' Mess to ensure the company kept the order. Punting out a few crates of Blue Nun was not exactly my idea of business heaven. So, more by luck than judgement, I was left with the shoe business. It proved to be the best decision I ever made.

KC was not known as the slipper king of Britain for nothing. In the ensuing eight years I was to travel the world again at KC's side doing deals for literally millions of pairs of shoes. During that time I learned very little about shoes but I did learn what made the wheels go around in the shoe business. It was a murky world and throughout

LIFE IS A CABARET: Even after I retired from football, I still found myself in the limelight with a bevy of beautiful girls. Down the years at Leicester, we've had quite a few dancing troupes and cheerleading girls. For my money, this lot was the best. From left to right, the Foxy Ladies are Caroline Marie McHugh, Lesley Eales, Sonia Dalby and Miss Leicester City 1983 Michellann Pidcock.

my career in the business I can honestly say it left me disillusioned on more than one occasion. Ironic, isn't it, that football and professional sport are often accused of being riddled with bungs, corruption and brown paper envelopes. Without pointing the finger, I came across far more brown envelopes in the shoe game than I ever did in football. Maybe it was because I was a little naive. Perhaps the shoe game is no different to any other business. But let's just say I had my eyes opened.

As a professional footballer I travelled the world in four-star style. With KC I went one better and travelled five-star. Sourcing new shoes for the European markets took us from as far afield as Japan to Brazil and Hong Kong to the Seychelles. My first trip with KC to Hong Kong was one I will never forget. We were going out to conclude a few deals and I was the muggins left to join the queue to catch our Cathay Pacific flight to the Far East from Heathrow Airport. I had been standing in the queue for about half an hour when KC re-appeared, gave me a funny look and proceeded straight to the business class check-in . "Ah... Mr Childs, so pleased to see you again," said the stewardess. We were going first class. KC always knew how to travel in style. On the plane, a hostess came around with a tray of Champagne. None of your cheap rubbish, this was Dom Perignon. KC took a glass but, never one to forget my roots, I asked for a beer. KC grimaced and bawled at me: "I've not paid all this money for you to turn down Champagne and have a beer." I politely declined and stuck to my guns.

When we arrived in Hong Kong after a nightmare flight into the airport KC hailed a taxi and went straight to the top hotel on the island, the Excelsior. I was then to witness for the first time his fantastic gift of the gab when it came to hotel reservations. He asked to see the manager and proceeded to enquire whether there were any suites available. We were informed there were four categories of suite. "Perhaps I could see one," he politely enquired. We were shown around a mightily impressive suite only for KC to ask if we could view a slightly more expensive suite. Two more rungs up the suite ladder we were finally shown the Penthouse Suite. It was bigger than my house and had a view to die for overlooking Kowloon.

Having checked the accommodation was available for a week, KC proceeded to browbeat the manager into submission about taking the very best suite at a junior suite rate. If he didn't accept, he would be forced to take out two ordinary rooms. After much persuasion, the manager agreed and for the next 10 days we stayed in the best suite in the most exclusive hotel in Hong Kong. We used the suite to entertain our business clients and, as you might expect, it created a fantastic impression. KC, you see, oozed style.

The irony of our location, however, was never lost on me. I'd go out onto the balcony with a glass of Champagne (sorry, bottle of beer) and look down 30 floors to see young locals hop from sandpan to sandpan trying to eke out a living. The contrast could not be more vivid and were even more obvious when we ventured out to look at shoe factories who might be responsible for making our orders. There is much debate about child labour in the modern world. Well, 20 years ago I don't think I ever saw anyone on a production line over the age of 16 in all the factories we ever visited. The conditions were pitiful. There were no toilet facilities and young children slaved away, 14 hours a day, in stinking conditions. It was, to be truthful, quite humbling.

I'd sampled Hong Kong on several occasions, both as a footballer and now as a businessman, but a fresh port of call in my new profession was Taiwan. South of Hong Kong, Taipei was another island with a vibrantly cosmopolitan culture. There was a marvellous sub-culture in place at night. Many of the single Western men would make their way to the many nightclubs which tended to be frequented by Taiwanese ladies of the night. Boring old fuddy duddies like myself would pop along to a local bar and enjoy a quiet drink or two. After the clubs closed all the dodgiest hookers who had been unable to attract clients would come into the bars and have a drink to drown their sorrows. They would be confronted by the even sadder sight of Birch and KC enjoying a game of darts!

KC loved to live life to the full and I have to admit that his liking for food crossed wider boundaries than my own. During our visits to Seoul, we would always stay at the luxurious Lotte hotel. In the restaurant he would order a plate of 'kimchi'. It looked like raw cabbage but tasted far, far worse. On the first and only time I tried it, I bit into a chunk and had to rush at full speed to the bathroom and belle-vued down the toilet.

Travelling with KC was never ever dull but, even by our standards, the trip to Hawaii took some beating. We'd been to Japan and had just concluded a very successful business trip. On booking our return journey via San Francisco, we were told there were no direct flights and the only option was a one-night stop-over in Hawaii. What a hard life! I was gutted however when I realised my American visa had expired. My only hope was to dash across Tokyo and get one from the American Embassy. I had just one hour in which to do this. Anyone who has been to the Japanese capital will tell you that their traffic problems are even worse than those of London. We leapt into a cab and headed speedily for the Embassy. Needless to say, we got stuck in traffic but, as the minutes ticked by, I noticed out of the window the American flag about a mile away in the distance. What a stroke of luck!

Rolling back the years, I recalled the days when my Sheffield United manager John Harris told me how to run up The Moor shopping district in Sheffield, dodging pedestrians by dropping a shoulder and doing a little shimmy. Off I hared, weaving my way around hundreds of Tokyo shoppers and residents. As I sprinted up the Embassy steps, the clock struck noon and a smartly dressed US Marine shut the doors. I had missed out by a matter of seconds. Noticing my discomfort, the Marine started talking to me. "Australian, sir?," he enquired. "No, English," I replied a little wearily. He embarked on a five minute conversation about his cousin in Birmingham before belatedly asking me what I wanted. I explained my dilemma and he very kindly let me join the back of the queue of about 150 Japanese all

■ **WHO'S WHO:** This was a real who's who event of Leicestershire sporting stars. Again hosted by my late great friend, Franco Pizzolon, we attracted local aces from the world of boxing, cricket, football and showbiz. Holding the microphone is Showaddywaddy lead singer Dave Bartram, ably assisted by former Leicestershire and England skipper David Gower. L to R (back row) are Jeff Blockley, former boxing champ Tony Sibson, David Gower, Dave Bartram, the compere, Birch, Franco and Paul Ramsey; (front row) dunno, dunno, dunno, Ian Butcher, very fit bunny girl, very unfit Andy Feeley, Mark Bright and Bobby Smith.

waiting for visas. My heart sank because I knew I would not get the document processed in time to catch the afternoon flight. Suddenly, there was an announcement over the tannoy. "Would Mr Birchenall please come to gate 13." I walked straight to the front, a clerk asked me for 35 dollars and promptly stamped my passport. My newly-discovered Marine friend had done me proud!

Seconds later KC pulled up in the taxi outside and we were on our way to Hawaii for the trip of a lifetime. After all, it's not every holiday that you can say you saved the life of the son of one of the greatest movie stars in the world, is it? Intrigued, then please read on.

Upon touching down in Hawaii, I was determined not to be outdone by KC, having already visited the island on several occasions during my footballing career. KC did his usual trick of asking the cabbie for the best hotel. "Diamondhead, sir," said the cabbie and went on to inform us that this was where President Reagan stayed en route to summit talks with Russian Premier Mikhail Gorbachev. I said I preferred the Waikiki Beach because of its proximity to the coast. For once I won the argument, so you can imagine how crestfallen I was when we arrived at the hotel only to be told there were no rooms available. Off we went to the Diamondhead. By this time I had sampled some of the best hotels in the world, but this unquestionably was in a different league.

When we checked in at the open air reception there was a stream behind us with dolphins swimming through it. Needless to say, KC tried his 'suite trick' again with the manager and succeeded in booking us into the very same Presidential Suite as used by Mr Reagan just a few months earlier. On the first night, we went down for dinner and found ourselves seated in the focal point of the dining room. Musical accompaniment was provided by a 20-piece band and, everywhere you looked, there was an American millionaire dripping with gold. I began to feel slightly self-conscious and noticed that most of the other guests were staring at us. Everyone else was a male and female couple. "They think we're a couple of woofters," I said to KC, who found the whole episode highly amusing!

That evening we went into town and sampled one of the greatest nightclubs it has ever been my pleasure to venture into. Bobby McGees was a class act. When you walked into the club you were announced to the rest of the guests. The DJ made a special point of telling everyone that Alan and Keith were over from England and everyone was under orders to make us feel really happy.

Our one-night stay expanded into a 10-day holiday but nothing could have prepared me for what was to happen the following morning. We decided to try out the legendary Waikiki Beach so we hopped into a cab and prepared to soak up some rays. KC quickly became engrossed with a couple of middle-aged American millionairesses. There was no chance they would ever get sunburnt, they were wearing too much gold!

Left to my own devices, I decided to go for a swim. I spied a bathing platform about 400 metres out in the sea and headed off towards it. While idly lounging there in the brilliant sunshine I noticed a couple of young boys, both about nine years old, who were floating out to the staging on their lilos. After a while I became aware of a man on the shoreline shouting to the lads. I pointed this out to the boys but they didn't pay too much attention to me. Their lilos began drifting further out to sea and, seeing they were a little worried, I swam out to them and began pushing the lilo back to safety and the shore. By this time the man was becoming more irate and was gesticulating furiously. I carried on pushing the lads and, as I got closer to the beach, I recognised the dark-haired man in the water. "Is that your dad?" I asked one of the lads. "Yes, that's my pa," he said. I was looking at the world-famous actor Sylvester Stallone. He

CAUGHT OUT: For once the boot was on the other foot when my late friend Franco Pizzolon organised a surprise presentation to mark my charity work at one of his fashion nights. Left to right are (standing) commercial manager Peter Hill, Andy Feeley, Steve Moran, John Ogilvie, Davie Gibson, Bryan Hamilton, Franco Pizzolon, Ian Wilson, Guy Morris, Ali Mauchlen and Richie Norman. Front, Ian Andrews, Birch and Russell Osman.

gathered up his kid, said a hasty thanks and rushed out of the water. I couldn't believe what had happened. At that time, Stallone was one of the biggest movie stars in the world.

I later discovered he was taking a vacation on Hawaii while studying the script for Rocky 3. The following day, I swam out to the bathing platform from where I could see his holiday flat by the side of the beach. I watched him for half an hour and during that time he skipped and performed one-armed press-ups non-stop in preparation for the next Rocky film. Mid-way through his routine, a beautiful woman swam up to the platform and hauled herself aboard. Despite what you might think, the Birch is very shy and I was too tongue-tied to start up a conversation other than to say hello. "Excuse me, but aren't you the guy who saved my son's life yesterday?" she enquired. "Well, I wouldn't say that. I just helped get the boys back to the shore," I said, rather embarrassed. "Oh well, we're very grateful. I don't know what Sylvester would have done without you," she went on. Plucking up my courage I politely enquired why Mr Stallone had not been able to swim out himself. After all, it wasn't dangerous. "Don't tell anyone, but he's not a very good swimmer. In fact, he's rather afraid of water," came the reply. With that, she plunged back into the water and a wry smile crossed my lips.

Sylvester Stallone was arguably one of the most macho men in the world. He was an undisputed world boxing champion who had wiped out Vietnam single-handedly... yet he was afraid to go further than knee high in the sea. The story is not quite finished yet. That evening we were again seated in the centre of the restaurant, the residents all convinced by now we really were a couple of millionaire woofters. The head waiter came up and delivered a magnum of vintage Champagne to our table. "With the compliments of the gentleman over there," he said. I looked across and there was Sylvester with his entourage. I nodded our thanks and he nodded back. What a holiday!

An equally eventful, if slightly less star-studded, time was had by the Birch when we stopped off at the Seychelles en route from another Far East business trip. We enjoyed a relaxing few days in Mahe before KC dropped a surprise on me. He had arranged for us to spend three days on Bird Island, reputedly one of the most exclusive and romantic island paradises anywhere on the planet.

On the day we were due to fly out, KC went down with food poisoning (must have been the kimchi!) but he insisted I fly out on my own. I hopped into a tiny plane with five honeymooning couples. As you might imagine, the island was very popular with newly-weds. When we arrived there, after a 20 minute flight skimming over the Indian Ocean waves, we were met by two servants who showed us to our rooms. It was like something out of a 'Bounty' advert. Waves lapping gently over white sandy beaches, tropical palm trees swaying in the breeze, lush vegetation and de-luxe beach houses set back in the jungle. There was no electricity on the island. No televisions, no radios, no link with the outside world. An atomic bomb could have dropped on India and we would have been none the wiser. This was probably about as close to paradise as I had ever been. You could walk around the entire island in about 20 minutes and it was on one of these little jaunts that my embarrassing adventures began.

I was ambling quietly along the sand when I noticed two logs in the distance. Only as I got closer could I see they appeared to be moving. I had virtually trampled on the 'logs' by the time I realised it was a honeymooning couple deep in the throes of passion. Not wishing to look like a complete pervert, I brazened it out and started whistling as I passed by. "Morning," I said as I went by. They were so engrossed I don't even think they noticed I was there!

Further around the shoreline, I decided to lie down on the warm sand myself and soon found myself drifting off to sleep. I woke an hour later to be greeted by the sight of a giant turtle staring at me from about three feet away. I'm not sure who moved the quicker, me or the turtle, as I hared back into the jungle and the turtle turned flipper and scuttled back into the sea.

Dinner was served between 7pm and 9pm. For obvious reasons, I had not seen many other people during the day. They had other things to be getting up to, didn't they. But everyone turned out for a sumptuous dinner cooked on open fires. By 9.15 pm everyone had disappeared again back into their houses to continue their recreational activities. I was left on my own and was mortified when I was told the bar was shutting at 9.30pm. The barman relented and agreed to play pool with me for an hour. I was made up. Everyone else on Bird Island was busy love-making and the Birch was ecstatic because he'd found someone to play a game of pool with him!

An hour later my pool partner informed me that it was lights out. I thought he was joking. He wasn't. And when he said lights out, it really was lights out. He let me scamper most of the way back to my accommodation before the island was plunged into total darkness. I was left to stumble around for a few minutes before I finally discovered my beach house. What ensued is straight out of a Carry On film. I walked up the steps and hunted for the key only to hear the frantic amorous sounds of a couple romantically engaged. Wrong hut. Never mind. I scampered back down the steps and up into the next house. I was fiddling around with the key when I heard an American woman scream: "Geoff, there's a man at the door watching us." I panicked and, in my rush to escape, I fell off the verandah and into the jungle, landing on a particularly spiky tree. With rows of thorns embedded in my leg I raced away, desperate to avoid being caught and branded a 'peeping tom'. Thankfully, the third house was mine. I rushed inside, clothed off, flung myself on the bed and heaved a huge sigh of relief. My leg was beginning to throb but the drama was not over yet. I heard a lot of flapping and a parrot descended on one of the beams right outside my window. Trust my luck to cop for the noisiest bird on the island. The parrot squawked away to his heart's content. I tried to doze off but the noise became louder and louder. More than a little peeved, I felt around on the floor for one of my sandals, took aim and caught the parrot flush on the beak. The force knocked him off the perch and sent him flapping to the floor. I now had one seriously pissed-off parrot. If he was loud before, he was now uncontrollable. 'Squawk! Squawk! Squawk!' He raised such a commotion he woke up half the newly-weds. Everyone wanted to know what was going on. Instead of being branded a pervert, the entire population of Bird Island now thought I was a parrot-molester. That darned parrot wouldn't shut up all night. It drove me crazy. I was the subject of many inquisitive glances over the next few days and despite being one of the most idyllic spots I have ever visited I was mightily relieved to catch the plane back to the Seychelles and clap eyes on KC again.

I had six magnificent years working with KC but I am the first to admit there was a painful parting of the ways. I don't regret too many of the decisions I have made in my entire life but I rued the day I left KC's companies. Business associates approached me to join their companies. I would not have entertained the proposition but they told me KC was going through a difficult financial time and the future of his businesses was insecure. Actually, they weren't wrong. I made a decision to hand in my resignation in the best interests of my family. I had a mortgage and I wanted to continue providing them with a good lifestyle. For two years afterwards KC and I did not speak.

Now we're good friends again, keep in constant touch, and I'm godfather to his sons who are both big City fans. It would have been quite easy for me to omit to mention of my fall-out with KC in the book but I didn't want to do that. I made a grave mistake and I don't mind admitting it. It's the only time I've ever left a friend in the lurch and I am determined it shall never ever happen again. Although I left KC, I stayed in the same line of work. I still travelled extensively - but not quite so stylishly - and, to this day, I retain an interest in the shoe business. Now I confine myself to looking after accounts with 30 football clubs for branded slippers. If I'm honest, I have never been that enamoured with the shoe business. My first love was always football and Leicester City. But the shoe game taught me an awful lot about people and business.

In truth my heart has always been with Leicester City from the first couple of years after I joined the club back in 1971. When I was approached to become Public Relations Officer by then chairman Terry Shipman I was tremendously flattered and did not need too much persuading. The Shipman family themselves have always been great supporters of the club. They truly have blue blood running through their veins. Terry's dad Len was President of the Football League and Terry's daughter Maxine carries on the City blood-line. At the time, the appointment was one of the very first of its kind in the country. In the modern era every club has a former player involved in some capacity on matchdays. Back in the early eighties it was almost unheard of and I can genuinely say I would not have missed my time at the club for all the tea in China.

One of the principal roles of my job down the years has been working with the footballers on community initiatives. As a player in the seventies I had trawled around all four corners of the county on personal appearances. Now, a large proportion of my new job meant I went out to those same hostelries and working mens' clubs with a new generation of City players. I have always maintained that most squads of 18 professional footballers, will fall into three distinct groups. The first six are the lads who will do anything for you at the drop of a hat. The second group, while not wildly enthusiastic, appreciate their responsibilities as professional sportsmen. And the last six wouldn't ever bother to turn up at a party in their own house!

SOFT-SHOE SHUFFLE: My love of football and my shoe interests finally bore fruit when I produced a new official Leicester City slipper range. Modelling the slippers are, left to right, Muzzy Izzet, Graham Fenton, Julian Watts, Ian Marshall, Neil Lennon and Garry Parker.

One player I would put in that first group was a young lad called Gary Lineker. Gary was a just a young lad breaking into the first team when he used to make his first appearances out on the county circuit with the Birch. He was always up for a game of pool in a local hostelry and was an excellent ambassador for the football club. Pontus Kaamark is probably the most recent example of the model professional. Fluent in five languages, I don't think there was a community scheme or voluntary organisation in which Pontus did not become involved during his four-year stay at Leicester. He was an absolute diamond.

Gary McAllister, now enjoying an Indian summer in his career with Liverpool, is another with whom I forged a close working relationship. I have the utmost respect for Gary and he has been a fantastic model professional down the years. He arrived at Filbert Street from Motherwell at the same time as Ali Mauchlen and quickly earned an excellent reputation for himself. We always used to have a special banter between us. I would say to him: "Hur der fur." He would reply 'Say de four'. None of us would have a clue what we were talking about but even to this day when we bump into each other we immediately lapse into our silly language!

Inevitably down the years, the Birch has been on the receiving end of some good-natured banter from the lads. It's part and parcel of the game and I love every minute of it. I've lost count of the number of times I've had my best clothes ruined by being thrown into a bath or dragged head-first backwards along a muddy pitch. I must admit that I have been suffering at the hands of Robbie Savage in recent times, however. Our Welsh international has been responsible for decimating my underwear drawer. While undergoing a heavy session in the gym at the training ground, Robbie has twice broken into my office and cut large holes in my Calvin Klein underpants. Now I know Lil and the lads might be able to order their CKs by the sackload but to a former footballer down on his uppers I'm afraid I can't afford to keep shelling out another £15 on designer boxer shorts. Enough is enough and I have now promised revenge on the long-haired Welsh one. Many people have crossed me down the years and none have ever got away with it scot-free. I'll tell you this Robbie lad, I might wait a while before I exact revenge but you know it's coming, don't you?

The lads, occasionally, can go too far with their dressing-room antics. I'm reminded of the tale of the phantom Filbert Street flasher some years ago. Apparently, one of the players thought it was a great ruse in the days of the old main stand to pop out of the tunnel and go into the main reception area, open up his overcoat and give everyone an eyeful, so to speak. Unfortunately, this put our receptionists and secretarial staff off their lunches and words were mentioned at the highest level that this practice had to be curtailed pronto.

■ **GUESS WHO**: These days he's a well-known BBC football presenter and one of Leicestershire's most famous sporting sons. But can you recognise the figure on the right before he hit the big time? The ears are covered up by his long hair so there's no clue there. Of course, it's former Leicester and England ace Gary Lineker. Gary came along with other City players to a night I organised at the Blue Lion pub in Thrussington in 1984. Gary, Bobby Smith, Ian Wilson and Mark Wallington played a few games of darts and pool to raise money for local charities. In those days, we'd be out once a week holding social functions with the players at pubs and clubs throughout the county.

In my 18 years as Public Relations Officer with the club, I have worked with a total of seven managers - Gordon Milne, Bryan Hamilton, David Pleat, Brian Little, Mark McGhee, Martin O'Neill and Peter Taylor. A word briefly first, however, about Gordon's predecessor Jock Wallace. While still at Trowbridge, I approached Leicester about training with them on a part-time basis. Jock normally only allowed his own players to train but made an exception in my case. On some days I wished I hadn't bothered. During the warm-up I was chatting to Mark Wallington when Jock bawled me out and gave me one of the biggest rollockings of my life for talking out of school. I was also subjected to some of the hardest running sessions I ever undertook when we went up and down the hills in Bradgate Park.

By contrast, Gordon Milne was a quiet and methodical man. I often thought he never really got the praise he deserved for the work he did at Leicester. He had kept Coventry in the top flight for many years and did the same at Filbert Street after gaining promotion from Division Two. The club were never relegated from Division One during his time and he spent very little money. He was almost too unspectacular for supporters. A real gentlemen, he's still a regular visitor to the boardroom and after great success coaching abroad in Turkey is now director of football at Newcastle United.

Gordon's successor was Bryan Hamilton and it's fair to say that Bryan found life a little difficult. The club was relegated and didn't return to the top flight for a good few years. Bryan made some inspired signings, notably bringing Steve Walsh from his former club Wigan Athletic, but his tenure at the club was not to be a long one. At this point I would point out that any new manager would invariably take a close look at the Birch when they first arrived. As a former professional player with the club, it's only natural they might be a little concerned about 'my angle'. But any thoughts they might have had about me undermining their authority could not have been further from the truth. As far as I am concerned, the manager is the 'main man' at the club and I can truthfully say I have given every Leicester City manager my complete, total and utter support.

Of course, it was interesting when David Pleat arrived. One-time team-mates in the same Nottingham Schoolboys side, manager and player at Luton Town and now a third instalment in our professional relationship. When David arrived I think everyone in Leicester thought we were destined for an immediate return to the higher echelons. David had an impeccable managerial and coaching pedigree and having left Spurs it seemed a perfect move for the club and for him. Sadly, it did not turn out that way. After a couple of weeks, I recall David bumping into me in the tea room off the tunnel area in the old Main Stand. "You didn't tell me it was this bad," said David. "You never asked me!" I replied.

At Spurs Pleaty had Hoddle, Waddle and Ardiles - three players all tremendously comfortable on the ball. Unfortunately, although David wanted to play a similar passing style at Leicester, he had vastly different and rather less accomplished personnel. Results, shall we say, were not quite as encouraging as the fans had

■ **SAVAGED:** Over the years I've had to contend with quite a few dressings down at the hands of the players. After our Worthington Cup semi-final victory over Sunderland in 1998 I was leading the community singing at the end of the game when along came that Welsh prankster Robbie Savage and caked my favourite black Armani suit in Filbert Street mud.

hoped. Even David and I had a slight disagreement over my appearances in front of a microphone for BBC Radio Leicester. David felt it was not really possible to combine the duties of working for the club with offering unbiased views on radio commentaries when I was being asked to comment truthfully on playing performances. He was absolutely right.

It was with the appointment of Brian Little that I felt the club began to emerge from a darker period of its modern history. I remembered Brian from his days as a winger with Aston Villa. Long flowing hair, shirt outside his shorts - exactly the opposite persona to the one which arrived at Filbert Street. Clean-shaven, immaculately dressed, a strict disciplinarian and very articulate. With a minimal amount of money spent, a Wembley play-off final was achieved in the first season. That trip to the Twin Towers demonstrated the fantastic latent support for the club which was just waiting to get involved on a more regular basis. We took 40,000 fans for our 1-0 defeat to Blackburn in what was to be the start of a run of three successive play-off finals.

At the third attempt we beat Derby County and were back in the promised land of the Premiership. Just a few months into the campaign, however, Ron Atkinson was shown the door by Doug Ellis at Aston Villa. Villa was Brian's club. It was where his heart lay. From the moment I heard of Big Ron's departure I always thought Brian would end up there.

Along with Allan Evans and John Gregory, they made the trip along the M69 and M6 to Villa Park. It was at this moment that, for the very first time, I can reveal how the Birch became part of a caretaker management team at the club, albeit only for a matter of hours.

After Brian's departure, I had been speaking with chairman Martin George. My only concern was the well-being of the club. From my own playing days there I knew how important it was for the players not to be too distracted or sidetracked from their main purpose of winning matches. I knew the lads and the lads knew me. I spoke with Martin and he asked me if I would help in the management and coaching duties for the team on a short-term basis while the club sought a successor to Brian. I was only too pleased to be able to help and my first duty was to be present at a training session on the Friday and travel with the team for an overnight trip to Norwich.

I had an important business meeting early on the Friday morning but said I would get to the training ground as quickly as possible. When I arrived at I found the kitman, got some kit on and walked over to take a look at the lads in training. On my way over I was met by two fellow members of the management team, Tony McAndrew and Kevin Macdonald, who had previously been working with the club's youth squad. They did not seem best pleased to see me. "Have you spoken with the chairman this morning?" they said. "Things have changed, so you'd better have a word with him." Rather puzzled, I went back into the offices and rang the chairman. Apparently, Tony and Kevin had not been happy about my involvement. Although the chairman wanted me to travel to Norwich, I didn't want to make up the numbers and stand in the dug-out at Carrow Road like a spare part. So, instead, I stayed at home and listened to the match on BBC Radio Leicester. We lost 1-0. A few weeks later Tony and Kevin both joined up with Brian again at Aston Villa. That was it, the sole extent of my managerial involvement at Filbert Street.

Mark McGhee was the man appointed to succeed Brian and he faced the almost impossible task of keeping the club in the Premiership. Unfortunately, he didn't hang around long enough to take the club back out of the First Division. Mark moved on to Wolves just four months into the First Division season. Mark has subsequently admitted himself that he did not handle his departure from Leicester well. It came too soon after his arrival and the fans were always wary of anyone looking to use their club as a 'stepping stone' to bigger things.

■ **WATER WONDERLAND:** Sheer delight after winning the Worthington Cup with a 2-1 victory over Tranmere Rovers at Wembley in March 2000. The lads decided I needed an early bath after the game so I was flung in while still wearing my best Wembley suit. Left to right are, Emile Heskey, Robbie Savage, me, Tony Cottee, Ian Marshall and Garry Parker.

Mark's early departure paved the way for the arrival of Martin O'Neill, arguably the most successful manager in the club's history. He enjoyed five years of almost total success at the club, lifting the League Cup twice and establishing the Foxes in the top 10 of the Premiership for four successful seasons. I say almost total success, the first three months at the club were something of a war zone.

I remembered Martin from his days at Nottingham Forest as a very articulate Championship and European Cup winner. He was never shy of saying his piece and was almost like a shop steward figure among the lads under the inimitable Brian Clough. Martin was certainly his own man at Leicester but he would be the first to admit he found it tough going in the early months.

Try as he might, he couldn't get a victory and the fans were not slow to vent their feelings. There were after-match demonstrations following the Port Vale and Sheffield United home games and let's just say the natives were restless. I personally felt that Martin copped for several seasons of fans' frustrations. But, as he used to say, when it was his name they were chanting to 'fxxx off' I do suppose you take that rather personally. A few weeks into his reign at the club, I took Martin, his wife Geraldine and the family out to my hostelry in Swithland. They needed to get away from the pressures and I remember saying to him that it would all come good. Little did I imagine how good.

I must thank Martin at this point for giving me some of the best moments I have ever enjoyed during my 29-year association with the club. For the play-off final against Crystal Palace, Martin allowed me to sit on the team coach as it went down Wembley Way. There I was standing on the corner of the Harrow Road outside Wembley waiting to be picked up by the team bus. That five-minute ride was magical and I wouldn't have missed seeing that sea of Leicester City blue as we banked into the famous Wembley gates for anything in the world. Magical!

Arguably the biggest thrill of all was winning the Coca-Cola Cup in a replay at Hillsborough. I was sitting in the press box when I saw Steve Claridge net the extra-time winning goal. By the final whistle I had made my way to pitchside and was in my element as I danced away in triumph on the pitch. The ride home on the team bus was a dream come true for me. All those years as a player at Filbert Street, I had dreamed of travelling home with a piece of silverware on board. I had rehearsed all the songs I would sing. Sadly, we never won anything.

But on this particular night I enjoyed every minute of the drive back. I sat next to Macey, Kasey Keller and Spencer Prior and, sure enough, I led the lads in a spot of community singing on the way home. Even though it was about 3am, City fans were hanging out of windows all the way up the Narborough Road and drivers were honking their horns. It was a fantastic sight to behold. Even tee-total Emile Heskey was persuaded to sample a drop of bubbly on the way home! Unfortunately he was more than a little the worse for wear when he got off the bus and was quickly bundled into a car and driven home by his dad. The rest of us went on partying well into the early hours. I had not kicked a ball in anger but I'd definitely say it was my proudest-ever moment connected with the club.

Given everything that went off during Martin's reign, it would be fair to say he performed nothing short of a miracle on the resources available. As well as being a magician when it came to results, Martin was also an extremely articulate and intelligent man. He never missed a trick while he was there, but what may not be so widely known is his intense dislike of losing. Martin has to be a winner at everything he does. Even in a staff football match, he had to be on the winning side or else everyone risked his wrath. Two games, in particular, spring to mind.

The first was a staff versus journalists game organised during the club's UEFA Cup trip to Atletico Madrid. Our travelling band of English journalists had arranged to play their Spanish counterparts the day before the match. Training

CHEERS MARTIN: When I opened a new bar at my hostelry, The Griffin, in the Leicestershire village of Swithland who better to invite along than the then Leicester City manager Martin O'Neill. Martin pulled the first pint from the pumps and ensured the opening night went with a real swing.

■ **OVER THE BAR:** If I'm honest, my decision to go into the pub business was not one of the best of my life. With the footwear and my involvement at the football club, I found there weren't enough hours in the day to juggle the three jobs. I started out full of the joys of spring as this picture shows shortly after we took over the tenancy at The Griffin in Swithland.

finished but only a couple of Spanish media-men turned up. As the Leicester players trooped onto the bus to return to their hotel, Martin decided his coaching staff would take on the media in a seven-a-side match. Shirts and bibs were handed out and a little loosener ensued before we decided to play the match for real.

All professional sportsmen are competitive by their very nature but Martin takes this to a different level. The coaching side included Martin, John Robertson, Steve Walford, myself, Seamus McDonagh, physio Alan Smith, Jim Melrose and Paul Franklin. Up against us was Macey, Bill Anderson of the Leicester Mercury, Mark Regan of Leicester Sound, Ivan Gaskell of BBC East Midlands, Ralph Ellis of the Daily Star, club secretary Ian Silvester and the club doctor... aged 67. Oh, and they also seconded goalkeeper Pegguy Arphexad.

After 35 minutes the hacks were leading 5-1 and Martin was becoming increasingly concerned. As temperatures nudged the high nineties, Leicester City's coaching staff were going hell for leather to recover a four goal deficit just 36 hours before taking on one of the top club sides in Europe. The agreement had been that the game ended when the team coach came back to pick us up.

With the score at 5-3 Martin spotted the coach in the distance and frantically signalled for the driver to carry on around the ring road! I think the coach driver completed another three circuits of Madrid before he was finally allowed to come back in and Martin's team scraped home 6-5. I have to put my hand up and admit I was a disgrace. Undeniably my worst moment came when I was the last man against the club doctor who, defying his 67 years, nutmegged me, and I promptly fell over on my arse!

If tensions were raised in Madrid, they were at boiling point during the annual Christmas staff match at the training ground. Each year a coaching team would take on a side from the office staff which Macey was generally charged with organising. It was invariably a rout, although hopes had been raised one year when Macey pulled a flanker and signed up the world ball-juggling champion, Hristo, from Bulgaria. You may remember him entertaining the crowd at Filbert Street before a couple of games. He could juggle a ball for the best part of two days without a rest. Great ball-juggler he may be, but when it came to actually playing the game he couldn't trap a bag of cement! Three years ago it looked as if the fixture would have to be cancelled when then chief executive Barrie Pierpoint, displaying a rather Scrooge-like mentality, would not give the office staff time off to play the game in their lunch hour.

Down at the training ground, we scraped together a couple of sides to play each other. Needless to say, the gaffer's team was more than a shade stronger. In Martin's ranks were Jim Melrose, Steve Walford, Paul Franklin, John Robertson, Alan Smith and Melrose's brother. Macey put together a side which included the youth coaching staff, myself, the chef and the kitman. You would have thought we were planning World War Three. Macey might not be the most talented footballer in the world but he comes a close second to Martin in the competitive stakes. Tackles were flying and we all played as if our lives depended on the result. Martin's team lost and there was much rejoicing among our boys as we trooped off. Amid our delight, however, we had not realised how badly the gaffer had taken the defeat.

Martin was beside himself. He called his side into the dressing room and proceeded to berate them for their lack of effort, skill and conviction. He was absolutely livid and was so determined to exact revenge he insisted there be a re-match a week later. There was even talk of Premier League referee Pete Jones being brought in to ensure fair play! Several of Martin's team were mortified that instead of tucking into the Christmas pud they might be embarking on a fitness drive over the festive period. Thankfully for all of us the re-match was called off but I know that, even though Martin is now at Celtic some 18 months later, the defeat still rankles with him.

In much the same way as I feared the worst about Brian's departure to Aston Villa, I have to admit I thought the writing was on the wall when Celtic came in for Martin. All good things come to an end and in this day and age five years is a long time by managerial standards to stay at one club. Given his family background, Celtic was always going to be a very strong lure and so it proved.

HIGH NOON IN MADRID: Deep in thought, we are all contemplating the big match on a Madrid training ground. No, not the UEFA Cup game between Atletico and City. We're talking the LCFC coaching staff taking on a media side. It was every bit as serious as the main event and lasted for more than two hours as temperatures nudged 100 degrees fahrenheit in the midday sun. Left to right are physio Alan Smith, Martin O'Neill, David Nish, Birch and Paul Mace.

Many believed the Leicester City bubble would burst but the biggest compliment I can pay the new manager Peter Taylor is that he has not only avoided a bursting bubble but continued the club's development. In many respects Peter and Martin are not dissimilar. They are both players' managers. They have banter with the lads and enjoy the 'craic' but, equally, the players know there is a line they must not cross or risk the consequences. Where the pair differ, I feel, however, is that Peter is very much a coach who likes to be out on the training ground every minute of every session. Martin is what many might refer to as a more traditional manager - the type I now believe are becoming increasingly rare.

Peter made a truly fantastic start to his managerial career at Leicester and just five months into the job he was given the ultimate accolade when he was appointed manager of England for a game against Italy in Turin. Down the years Leicester City has been fortunate to have appointed some of the game's truly great managers and Peter looks set to continue that tradition.

One of the most rewarding aspects about my job as Public Relations Officer at Filbert Street has been my ability, albeit in a very small way, to make a difference. In particular, I've been fortunate enough to have helped raise a not inconsiderable amount of money for local charities. My great friend and loyal helper in most of my fund-raising activities down the years has been a guy called Derek 'Del Boy' Norton. Derek was doing his sums not long ago and reckons we have generated in excess of £300,000 for charitable causes in recent years.

Perhaps the single highest profile fund-raiser has been my end-of-season run. What started out as a jolly wheeze 18 years ago has snowballed into an annual marathon that takes an ever-increasing toll on the Birch's legs each year. They say '...from little acorns grow' and I recall opening my mail 18 years ago at the football club and being really touched by a little girl's letter and appeal for help. I was determined to do something and hit upon the idea of an end-of-season run around the pitch at Filbert Street. I figured that as the match lasted 90 minutes, I should be able to run for 90 minutes before kick-off. The groundstaff coned off a track and that day was born the Birchy Charity Run. My first year was very ad-hoc and raised only a few hundred pounds. Supporters' Club chairman Cliff Ginetta and his wife Linda handed buckets around the crowd and supporters lobbed in a few coins.

Yet, as the years went by, the fund-raising became much more professional. I was inundated with requests from charities to run for their particular organisation and as word got around so the event attracted more sponsorship, publicity and runners. Last year John Motson even gave the event a mention on BBC Grandstand. It got to the stage where I felt like Forrest Gump when he ran across America and picked up hundreds of other runners along the way. In the end I had to cut it back a little because the managers were getting a trifle concerned about the detrimental effect to the pitch.

Each year City players would join me for a few laps as part of their warm-up and that tradition extended to our opponents too. I'd write a letter to the visiting manager in midweek and, without fail, they would send out the players to join in. On many occasions, as it was the final home game of the season, there was often a lot resting on the outcome of the game - relegations, promotions, the destinations of the Premiership. But what the run did do was generate a marvellous community spirit among both sets of supporters. Kevin Keegan joined me for a few laps when he was at Newcastle and Peter Schmeichel and the Manchester United lads ran alongside as well. I'll never forget a conversation I had with Swindon's Jan Aage Fjortoft. He knew all about me and my career with Leicester. Given that he had grown up in Norway, I was most impressed and asked how he knew so much about me. "Birchy, when I was growing up I used to watch you on Norwegian television playing for Leicester," he said. My, that boy must have led an unhappy childhood!

As well as famous sportsmen, stars from the world of showbiz have joined in as well; Coronation Street cafe owner Roy Cropper, alias David Neilsen, has accompanied me and Macey for the last three years. David is a keen Leicester supporter and has been forced to endure a certain amount of stick from the fans while doing the run. One of the more witty remarks from The Kop was: "What's it like to shag a bloke?" in obvious reference to his on-screen relationship with trans-sexual Hayley.

Hand on my heart, I can genuinely say I have never not finished a charity run nor have I ever stopped for as much as a yard. There is something inside which drives me on although I have to admit I have come close on more than one occasion. One of the big hurdles to overcome has been the weather. For every run, the sun is shining and, at pitchside, the temperatures are nudging into the eighties. The smell of the 'burger bar in the North Stand makes you want to *belle-vue* on every lap around that corner.

Probably my worst experience was five years ago when I failed to drink enough water. No sooner had I finished than I began feeling sick and dizzy. I careered down the tunnel and the St John Ambulance first-aiders laid me out and gave me an oxygen mask. I was suffering from severe dehydration and heat exhaustion and was flat out in the medical room. I have never felt as ill in my life as I did for the following 90 minutes. In fact I was close to being taken by ambulance to the Leicester Royal Infirmary but did just enough to stay at the ground. After the game, the chief executive Barrie Pierpoint poked his head around the door and asked why I wasn't doing the sponsors' presentations. The medical people didn't want me to move but I was stung into action and managed to haul myself upstairs to compere presentations to the match sponsors.

One of the beneficiaries over the years has been the Leicester Royal Infirmary. Proceeds from one of my runs went towards purchasing a specialist breathing unit for newly-born babies and the fruits of my labours were brought home just last year when Matt Elliott's baby son, Alfie, was one of the youngsters to benefit from the specialist equipment. Over the years I have supported a number of local organisations - LOROS, the Rainbows Hospice, the NSPCC and many others.

The Running Man

■ I can just about manage to clench my fist in triumph after completing another charity run in 1991.

OVER THE PAST TWO DECADES the final home fixture of the season at Filbert Street has been synonymous with one event... Birch's annual charity run. Every year I say it's going to be my last... and each time I have wound up the old *stumps* for another 90-minute trek around the Filbert Street pitch. I estimate I've raised over £200,000 for various charities and down the years I must thank everyone for their fantastic support. The fans have been brilliant and the management and players of the various opposing clubs have been fantastic too. Alex Ferguson and Manchester United, Kevin Keegan and Newcastle, they've all been magnificent.

■ Here I am being carried off on a stretcher after completing 60 laps. Well, I certainly couldn't have jogged down the players tunnel. On the far left is Leicester City director Bill Shooter who deserves special praise. Although in his seventies Bill is one of the fittest septuagenarians I know. He's taken part in every run for more than 12 years and during that time he's not aged one little bit.

■ I don't think Gary McAllister (yes it's really him) will thank me for using this photo from one of my early charity runs. My mistake here in 1988 was to invite top middle distance runners from the Leicester Coritanians Athletics Club along. They certainly put me and Gary to shame.

■ The Filbert Street faithful (left) are magnificent and without their support I doubt I could have kept going down the years.

■ Here's the proceeds from my 1993 run (above). A cheque for £13,190.24p is handed over to the Leicester Royal Infirmary to help purchase a vital piece of surgical equipment for the children's ward.

■ Peter Schmeichel was a great sport along with the rest of the Manchester United lads when they joined in for a few laps during my 1997 run. Also pictured is Brian Kidd.

■ For the first and only time in his life, the Birch is speechless as he is interviewed by BBC Radio Leicester sports heart-throb John Sinclair (above) after completing my Millennium run.

■ I'm performing my best Bugs Bunny impression as Martin O'Neill joins in for a couple of laps during the Millennium Run before our final home game against Bradford City (right).

Each year I insist it will be my last. Each year, I am persuaded to carry on for just one more time. I swore that my Millennium charity run in 2000 would definitely be an appropriate time to hang up my running shoes. Club director Bill Shooter believes we should carry on the run indefinitely, with or without me. But, you never know, I might be persuaded to give it just one more try in 2001.

I reckon the average distance I cover during the 90 minutes is 13 miles - just less than half the distance of a full marathon. Well, I was persuaded to do one of those as well. But, unlike my charity run, this really was a one-off. I was contacted by the NSPCC who told me they had a spare slot for a sponsored runner in the 1989 London Marathon. This was only a couple of months before the event and, rather foolishly, at the age of 44 I agreed to take part.

My preparations were less than professional. I travelled down on Saturday night to stay with my good friend Trevor 'Dead Dog' Davies. Trevor used to run a wine bar in Leicester and is very much a 'party animal'. A good-looking Irish guy, he's a self-made single man who has had more success with women than anyone I have ever come across. I'm digressing here, but he tells me his best picking-up point is Sainsbury's on a Friday night at 7pm! I was expecting a nice steaming cup of cocoa and to be cosily tucked up in bed in Trevor's Kensington penthouse by 10pm. 'Dead Dog' had different ideas. At 11pm we were on our sixth pint of lager in one of my favourite pubs, Churchills.

At 9am the following morning I meandered across London to Greenwich, ready for the off. There were so many runners it took me 20 minutes to get past the starting line. By the time I rounded the Cutty Sark (only a handful of miles) I was already breathing heavily. Gradually, though, I started to get my second wind and felt fairly comfortable until I reached the 17 mile mark. There was a great camaraderie among the runners and the spectators and it really encouraged you. It was then I hit the legendary 'wall' . The remaining nine miles and 385 yards were absolute purgatory. Again, my inner self refused to let me give up but by the time I crossed the finishing line I was a complete wreck. As soon as you finished, you were jumped on by helpers and given an aluminum foil sheet to keep warm, an apple, an orange, a Mars bar and, most importantly of all, your medal. It was about this point I realised I had made a severe tactical error. Everyone else had partners, children and friends waiting to pick them up. I had no-one.

I walked into a nearby park and collapsed onto a bench, munching my apple and orange and looking for all the world like a local vagrant. Still huddled in the foil wrap, I was approached three times by first-aiders who checked if I was okay. At this point, I was virtually incapable of movement, and as the crowd thinned out, I knew I had to make a move. I hobbled for a mile or so in vain pursuit of a taxi. Just when you

■ **MARATHON MAN:** In 1989 I rather recklessly promised to run the London Marathon for charity. I managed to complete the 26 mile 385 yard course in a time of four hours and 20 minutes. Sponsorship monies from Leicester City supporters went towards building an NSPCC hostel in Beaumont Leys in Leicester. I'm pictured in the old Main Stand at Filbert Street with my marathon medal. In case you're wondering, it was my first and only marathon.

needed a London black cab, you could not find one for love nor money. Eventually, I hailed a cabbie and clambered into the back. I looked a sorry, forlorn mess with my foil jacket and plastic carrier-bag of clothes. "You're Alan Birchenall, aren't you?" he said with a cheery smile and explained that he was a Chelsea fan. "Been running the marathon, have we?" he added. I managed a wry smile. My biggest problem now was that I had no money and was preparing to break the news to him gently.

We arrived back at Dead Dog's in Kensington and I was just about to explain my financial dilemma when he said: "There's no charge, mate. You were one of my heroes and it's great to say I've given you a lift. Besides, I'm going in for a triple heart by-pass operation tomorrow so one less fare is not really going to make much of a difference, is it?" I waved him goodbye and reflected on life's little ironies.

My day was not quite over yet, however, I still had the small matter of the drive back up to Leicester. After a long soak in the bath, I got changed and headed back up the M1. I remember feeling a warm glow of pride as, still wearing my medal proudly around my neck, I basked in the glory of having completed a marathon. Suddenly, I was stricken by intense, excruciating cramp in my right leg. My foot shot onto the accelerator pedal and I rocketed forward from 70 to 110mph in the outside lane. Weaving in and out of the traffic, wracked by the pains shooting down my leg, I veered onto the hard shoulder and screeched to a halt. I clambered out of the car and lay flat out on the motorway banking, trying to get rid of the cramp. As other cars flashed by, the drivers must have taken me for a real loony, stretched out on the verge like that.

Aside from my running, we were also able to raise a considerable amount of money for charitable causes during the sporting dinners held at the club for the best part of 20 years. At each event, a raffle was held, with proceeds going to a local charity and over the years the club's corporate supporters have contributed well over £100,000. As well as hosting the events, it also fell to me to book the guest speakers. I've been fortunate to commission just about everyone at Filbert Street over the years - George Best, Terry Venables, Kevin Keegan, Bobby Charlton, Jack Charlton, Alan Ball, Sir Stanley Matthews and Ian Botham, to name but a few. Many came at a reduced fee as a favour to myself but one celebrity actually donated his fee to the charity of the evening. The legendary Malcolm MacDonald, former Newcastle United and England centre-forward, was the speaker at one of our events and when it came time to pay him, he simply said: "No Birch, give it to the charity." A true gent, Malcolm.

Everyone has their own 'George Best story' and George didn't disappoint when he came along with his good friend Rodney Marsh. It was a packed house when he arrived. He had a couple of drinks and then a couple more. Rodney was desperate for him to go on stage before the meal was served and it quickly became apparent why. Questions and answers were eventually fired at George and let's just say he wasn't quite on top of his form. I feared the worst but after the show several people came up to me and said they had enjoyed a truly great evening. It is perhaps a sad indictment of the state of our society that some people in the audience had turned up in the hope they would see George the worse the wear for drink. They hadn't gone home disappointed.

Sir Stanley Matthews, however, was a completely different kettle of fish. He came along to a night when we had the former England manager Terry Venables. Sir Stanley was a true gent in every sense of the word. I had grown up when he was the king of football and, although not usually fazed by famous sportsmen, I was a little in awe of him. I politely asked if he remembered me playing in the same team as him for a testimonial at Stockport when my career with Sheffield United was just starting. To my amazement, he said he did. I felt a warm glow of pride run through my body. "Aye son, I remember because you were rubbish." And then a broad smile lit up his face! Sir Stanley might have been nearly 80 but he was certainly still too quick for me.

As is customary at these events, large crowds gathered at the end of the night to collect autographs. There was a longer line than usual for Sir Stanley. I was worried he might feel a little under pressure but he said he would be delighted to sign them all. Only he didn't just given them a quick flourish of his pen. He engaged every person in conversation, asked them whether they wanted a dedication, when it was their birthday, how many children they had, who they supported as a boy. It was quite enchanting to watch and Sir Stanley stayed seated until the small hours until everyone in the room had received their autograph.

Over the years the Birch has received valuable assistance in carrying out his public relations duties for the club. During my time with the football club and my various shoe companies, I've engaged the services of many secretaries. I daresay I'm not the easiest of people to work for but I'd have no hesitation in saying that my current secretary is the best of the lot. Rachel Cluley is a real diamond and, for the past five years, she's worked for the Birch, Macey and even fitted in the Chairman's work as well. Rachel has been invaluable in processing all my correspondence from supporters, charities and local groups. There's only one problem though; she's the only woman who frightens me almost as much as the *tank commander*!

One of the highest-profile parts of my job has been my banter on the microphone before games and at half-time. What started out as a few brief seconds has now mushroomed into five-minute 'Birchy Banter' slots. As those of you who know me will testify, none of this is ever scripted. I do it all off the cuff and I have to concede this has caused one or two problems with the media and officialdom in recent times.

My most celebrated dispute with the Football Association came as a result of half-time comments made during a Premiership game with Coventry City which, to my misfortune, was also beamed live across the country by Sky. Welsh referee Keith Cooper took charge of the game and, controversially, had sent off two players by half-time. Both sets of supporters were booing and jeering and I felt it only appropriate to make mention of the incident so I spoke about the direction I felt the game was going in regarding the approach of referees. Little did I know my comments on the public address system were being heard, word for word, by the referee while he supped his half-time cuppa in the refs room. Needless to say, we didn't see eye to eye.

The national press also had a field day with headlines such as 'Bring Back the Birch'. Sure enough, a few days later a letter dropped through the Filbert Street letterbox informing that the FA were considering charging me for bringing the game into disrepute. What a load of nonsense. I was hardly in a mood to back down but, against my better judgement, I allowed a letter of apology to be submitted to the FA. As a result of this letter, no further action was taken against me.

Most recently, my pre-game comments about Manchester United received a prominent airing in the national media. I sometimes wonder if our entire nation hasn't lost its sense of humour. Before the game, our manager Peter Taylor and goalkeeper Tim Flowers were to receive their Carling Manager of the Month and Player of the Month awards. In between the presentations, I indulged in a little lighthearted banter with the United players as they ran out on to the pitch. I likened goalkeeper Fabien Barthez to our physio Mick Yeoman (they've both got the same amount of hair), I reminded a few of them that it wasn't only United who were capable of winning trophies and I thanked the United fans for making the long journey up from Plymouth. Mark Bosnich was a little less than pleased when he aimed a ball at the trophies on the table beside the pitch. Even more so when he missed by a mile!

As far as I was concerned, this was all good-natured banter. Well, we lost 3-0 and I was being held personally responsible by some sections of the media for winding up the United players before the game. Perhaps I missed my vocation. If I was that successful I should have become a motivational coach! United are the best team in the country, fact. They have supremely talented players. But these players have to run a gauntlet of hate and abuse at every away game. I sincerely doubt my comments would have made the slightest difference to them.

Down the years I have lost count of the number of times people have come up to me and asked why on earth I didn't set up my own sports agency. Given my outgoing personality and contacts in the game, they cannot understand why I did not have a dabble in the profession. The limit of my commercial dealings with sportsmen extended to booking them for functions at my beloved Leicester City.

However, a couple of years ago I finally decided to take the plunge. Well, it was more a case of tentatively dipping my teeniest tootsie in the water. I set up my own little sports agency to organise a few local functions involving Leicester City players past and present. Together with my co-author, we devised a very basic format with myself acting as compere and hosting a question and answer session with an audience.

At that time Martin O'Neill was the highest-profile sporting celebrity in the East Midlands. As Leicester City manager he was afforded God-like status so we invited him to be our first guest. We called the night 'An Audience with Martin O'Neill' and booked a function room at Jongleurs in Leicester's city centre.

Jongleurs is a national chain of comedy clubs and they were responsible for selling the tickets. Within 24 hours, all 320 had been sold. We knew Martin was popular but nothing had prepared us for this surge in demand among supporters. Crikey, there were even touts selling black market tickets on the night of the function! Martin was superb. All 320 supporters filled in their question sheets but, given Martin's gift of the blarney, we only managed to get through about 11 of them in two hours!

■ **ON THE MIKE:** When the civil war which erupted during Filbert Street in 1999 was at its height, I decided to go out on the pitch to do my half-time draw wearing a tin helmet and flak jacket. Eat your heart out, Captain Mainwaring! On another occasion, I went out with a scarf muffling my mouth because I was concerned I was being gagged.

Building on this success we went on to organise a series of player nights. Our first event featured Kasey Keller, Pontus Kaamark and Matt Elliott. All were picked because we knew they were excellent talkers. Kasey, in keeping with most American professional sportsmen, was extremely articulate, Pontus with his Swedish good-looks was a real wow with the female audience, and Matt was one of our most talented and popular players.

Another great night was had by all but unfortunately we became victims of our own success when we organised a third night entitled 'An Englishman, a Welshman, an Irishman and a Turk'. In case you're wondering, our hapless quartet were Steve Walsh, Robbie Savage, Neil Lennon and Muzzy Izzet. The entire first team squad decided to make a night of it and those not on the stage came to take their seats in the crowd. Unfortunately, during the day the squad had gone to Leicester Races and, shall we say, took the opportunity to unwind and de-stress themselves from the rigours of the Premiership.

Several arrived at Jongleurs considerably the worse for wear including, you've guessed it, Steve, Robbie, Neil and Muzzy. Sav is a little on the loud side when he's

stone cold sober so you can imagine what he was like with a couple of bottles of lager inside him. Muzzy arrived five minutes before he was due to go on stage and was barely conscious. Steve, for all his years at the club and leadership skills on the pitch, is extremely shy in front of a microphone, while Neil had supped a fair bit but was slightly more capable than the rest when it came to holding his liquor.

Word of the success of our sporting gigs had reached Sky television and it was on this, of all nights, that they chose to send along a reporter and cameraman to film proceedings. Well, the first half was an absolute disaster. The players in the audience continually heckled the lads on stage, Muzzy fell asleep after the fifth question and Sav was uncontrollable. I managed to get through until the interval and then whisked the lads upstairs. Something had to be done and I read the riot act. Fair play to the lads, the second half was a big improvement and Lennie, in particular, showed remarkable powers of recovery.

■ **A LAUGH AND A JOKE:** Matt Elliott, Kasey Keller and Pontus Kaamark are in fine spirits during a question and answer night in Leicester. We held a series of audiences with Leicester City players, all of which proved extremely popular.

The drama, however, was not quite over. Sky were producing a short three-minute clip for their Friday night Sports Centre show and the last thing we could afford was for the cameras to show the players half-cut. Without going into too much detail, there were a series of phone calls to Sky headquarters to ensure the lads' integrity wasn't compromised.

■ **GOALKEEPING UNION:** Leicester has always been synonymous with the production of the very best 'keepers. Here's a fine trio of England international custodians: (left to right) Tim Flowers, Gordon Banks and Peter Shilton. Mind you, all of them together in the same goalmouth would have been powerless to stop a Birchy piledriver from 20 yards when *The Claw* was in its heyday!

After our successes in Leicestershire, we decided to branch out further afield. 'An Audience with Harry Redknapp' was our next function in East London. The Hammers boss and I have been good friends for many years and Harry was certainly up for the night. We held it at Jongleurs Comedy Club in Bow and I must admit to being extremely nervous. Everyone knew me in Leicestershire but I was a little unsure about how West Ham fans would take to me, even though I had been born just a few streets away from Upton Park all those years ago. My anxieties were heightened when I learned that a similar question and answer session involving West Ham players had ended in a brawl a few months previously. Thankfully I need not have worried and the night appeared to be a huge success.

Our next night was with Jim Smith at Derby. Jim is a great guy and again I was a little worried about how Rams' supporters might take to an ex Leicester player compering an evening at Pride Park. That was the least of my worries. The questions came thick and fast and Jim answered them all as honestly as he could. This was one of the great successes of the nights - fans could hear what managers and players really felt rather than listening to short sound bytes on television and radio interviews.

Unfortunately, there was a slight altercation as a result of Jim mis-hearing one of the questions and he upset a female member of the audience. She thought Jim had cast aspersions on women in football when, in fact, Jim was talking about a specific female reporter. This found its way into the papers and onto local radio the following day as an attack by Jim on all women connected with football.

Perhaps the most emotional and passionate night of all was our second date with Martin which we held at the football club. It had been organised for several weeks and all 400 tickets sold out within a matter of hours. This was around the time of the World Cup in France when Martin shot to prominence with his pundit's views on BBC television. It was also the time when stories linking him with a move to Everton were at their height. To Leicester fans, the end of the world was nigh.

Despite all the speculation, Martin was keen to honour the engagement and the atmosphere was electric. When we collected the questions from the audience, every single one of them asked: "Are you staying or leaving, Martin?" When Martin walked onto the stage the entire Belvoir Suite room got to their feet and gave him a standing ovation. Even by Martin's standards he was in breathtaking form and dropped the broadest possible hint that he would stay with the club. The audience went wild.

I finally went international with the concept when we took out the former Leicester, Arsenal and England striker Alan Smith for a gig in the Swedish capital of Stockholm. I never cease to be amazed by the knowledge and appetite Scandinavians have for our English game. The night was a great success and former Swedish international Martin Dahlin also paid a surprise visit. After the show, we went to the Cafe Opera nightclub in the centre of Stockholm. I doubt I have ever seen a higher concentration of beautiful blonde women anywhere in my life. Indeed, this turned out to be the highspot of the two-day trip because the organisers ran out of kroners and, to this day, we've still not been paid!

Increased commitments with the club mean that our audiences with footballing celebrities have been temporarily shelved. But if there are a few managers out there who fancy a good night, and earning a few quid into the bargain, please drop the Birch a line. I guarantee they turn into nights you will never forget.

By this time I had already travelled the world twice over. Once as a player and, more recently, as a shoe salesman with Keith Childs. Incredibly, a third trip beckoned in the last couple of years. Veterans' soccer tournaments have grown significantly in popularity recently. In common with many other sports - notably golf - there has been a big clamour to see the old-timers out in action again, and in football the age limit is normally over-35s. I have to admit there are very few over-50s who have been operational. You've guessed it - the Birch is one of them. In the past few years I've flown out for tournaments in Singapore, Mauritius and Trinidad and Tobago. Hard life, isn't it?

■ AN AUDIENCE WITH JIM SMITH: I'll admit I was more than a shade nervous when I compered an evening with the Derby manager in the backyard of Leicester's main rivals. Thankfully, I got a great reception at Pride Park but the night grabbed the headlines for all the wrong reasons the following day. Jim found himself on the wrong end of local media stories accusing him of having said there was no place in football for women. As if Jim would ever say that...

■ AN AUDIENCE WITH MARTIN O'NEILL: The former City boss brought the house down with his performance at one of our question and answer nights. It was a sell-out event and most of Leicester wanted to know whether he was going to stay at Filbert Street or move on to Everton. With speculation at fever pitch, Martin said he planned to stay at Leicester. Although the evening lasted nearly three hours, I only needed to ask him six questions. Crikey, even The Birch couldn't get a word in edgeways.

■ **UNITED MAN:** All those years after Alex Ferguson first took a look at me during his early managerial days with Aberdeen, he finally got his man. Yes, the Birch poses for a signing photograph with the obligatory shirt. Mind you, after my recent touchline antics with United fans, I'm not too sure how well I'd go down at Old Trafford. This photo was taken when Sir Alex came along to speak at a special benefit dinner for the former Leicester City boss Jock Wallace.

I'll be the first to concede that I've been picked more for my social and organisational skills than any lingering remnants of footballing ability. Still, I do like to pull on the old boots now and again. One of my first veterans' experiences was courtesy of by big pal and arguably Leicester's number one travelling fan Mark 'the big man' Cain. Mark makes many a trip from Singapore to Leicester to see his beloved Foxes in action. But it was us who made the journey in the opposite direction to take part in a veterans event at the Singapore Cricket Club in 1995.

Mark attracted a great line up of former players - Frank Worthington, Martin Peters, Martin Chivers, Mick Mills, Peter Bonetti, Gerry Armstrong and Alan Kennedy all flew out ,along with the famous Van de Kerkhof twins Rene and Willie from Holland. As I've said before, assemble a group of footballers, plonk them down anywhere in the world with a few bottles and they'll be happy. When the venue is the Raffles Hotel in Singapore, they're damned ecstatic, I can tell you. Forget the football, one of the highlights was Frank discovering there was an Elvis theme bar in the town. Naturally, we all had to visit it and Frank spent two hours giving us his Elvis repertoire!

Having spent 12 hours on a 'plane flying across the Indian Ocean for a Soccer Sevens tournament in Mauritius, we all hoped for a sun-kissed island paradise. I'm sure it is paradise when the sun shines but for the 10 days we were out there it pelted down with rain for nine of them. No matter, footballers are adept at keeping themselves amused or, in this case, tanked up. Local brewery Tiger were one of the main sponsors and had laid on a lorry-load of free beer for the 50 players travelling over from England. As it was raining so heavily, the lads found themselves having to have a drink to pass the time and we had drunk the entire shipment dry after the fourth day!

That evening we had a sponsors' function and I hit upon the idea of making an impassioned plea to the brewery big-wigs to supply some more beer. I got all the lads up on stage and to the tune of 'For he's a jolly good fellow' we made a cheery request for a few more bottles. I was most disappointed when the brewery big cheese just laughed at us. The following day, however, I glanced down the approach road to the hotel and saw a Tiger truck weaving its way towards us - our brewery friends had not let us down at all. They had sent up another container load of beer. The lads, needless to say, were made up.

Our third veterans' excursion was to the Caribbean holiday isle of Trinidad & Tobago. The 'plane ride over was hardly the most comfortable I have enjoyed thanks to David Speedie. David is a great lad but when he's had a couple of bottles of pop he can be a right pest. Upon arrival in the Caribbean I was paired to room with comedian Stan Boardman. He was absolutely fantastic company and we got on really well... but I did scare him to death one night. Our two single beds had been closed together so it was a little more intimate than we would have liked. In the small hours of one morning, I couldn't find my watch so I leaned over to try and see Stan's alarm clock. I peeped over him without success, so leaned further over to see the clock. I was in the process of straddling him when Stan woke up and got the shock of his life to find me, stark naked, lying on top of him. "I was only trying to see what the time was," I protested rather sheepishly. I think he was slightly worried about the Birch for the next couple of nights and hardly slept a wink.

■ **OSSIE AND BIRCH:** Reunited at Filbert Street 25 years after we played together at Stamford Bridge. Unfortunately, Peter Osgood incurred the wrath of the Filbert Street faithful. He slaughtered the City players at half-time and was booed down the tunnel. Diplomacy never was one of Ossie's stronger points.

As the elder statesmen of the tour, Martin Chivers and myself tended to concentrate on the social, rather than the football, element of the tour. I did however make a fleeting appearance for my team - with devastating effect - against the competition favourites, an ex-Liverpool side. A deft flick set up a Dennis Wise goal for which I claimed the assist of the tournament. As well as Dennis, I also got to know Vinnie Jones quite well during the tour. I must admit I hadn't thought I would see eye to eye with Vinnie but after we broke the ice I was really impressed with him. I got a shout to join him and his wife for dinner one night at a fantastic restaurant. I was getting ready to pouch for my *munjaro* when I was told: "Don't bother, Vinnie's taken care of it all."

And, I'm afraid, that just about takes care of this book. In the past 12 months, I have accepted an expanded role at Filbert Street to act as the club's co-ordinator. After the civil war that blighted the club during 1999, one of my responsibilities has been to unite the footballing and commercial departments. I do not feel this book is an appropriate vehicle in which to wash the club's dirty laundry in public. Dependent, however, on how many of you buy it - in addition to my mother - I may be persuaded to write another publication solely on my times with Leicester City. We'll see.

For this offering it's ironic that much of the subject matter stems from the masses of scrapbooks and memorabilia I kept throughout my life. From my very first days as a youngster at Notts County, I have endeavoured to keep every photo, news article, medal, photograph, certificate and programme relating to my footballing achievements. Deep down, I did it to show a complete record of their father's career to my children. Son Dean is now 25 years of age and he's never so much as looked inside a single carrier bag of my life story (I wonder if he'll bother reading this book). Still, I'm delighted to say that my scrapbooks have finally come of age in the research. Most of the photographs and newspaper cuttings reproduced in this publication have come from my own collection.

As I now look back on 55 years of life, I can count the number of regrets I still have on one hand. Fate has dealt me a fine set of cards. From humble beginnings in the East End of London, I have lived out many of the dreams I had as a young boy. I became a professional footballer. I travelled the world. I got married and had children. I've eaten in some of the best restaurants in the world and stayed in the finest hotels. Yet I like to think I have never forgotten my roots. To me, one of life's pleasures is to eat my favourite toad in the hole, have a couple of *sherbets* down the local and watch a good game of football. I'm well aware some see me as a court jester. Personally, I like to think I've got a little more to offer than that.

In bringing the curtain down on this little offering, I can't help but be reminded of the words of many folk when describing near-death spiritual experiences - a

YOU BEAUTY: If you pushed me to name the best sporting moment of my life since I first joined up with Leicester City 29 years ago, then I would say the night in Sheffield when we won the 1997 Coca Cola Cup by beating Middlesbrough in extra time was probably my crowning glory. At the final whistle, I raced onto the pitch and led the City faithful in their singing. What a night. I'm pictured with (right) goalscorer Steve Claridge and (left) Steve Walsh with the beloved Football League trophy.

feeling of going down a long tunnel but glimpsing light at the end of it. Well, forgive the sporting analogy, but I reckon it must be a football tunnel leading out onto a pitch with the floodlights on for a night match. It's a tunnel I've trodden many a time and I can genuinely tell you that every time I came out of that tunnel I had a fantastic time before walking back down it again some two hours later. Sadly, my professional playing days are over but, thanks to my duties as Club Co-ordinator at Filbert Street, it's a tunnel I still regularly pop in and out of. You know, when I stop going up and down that tunnel, I really will know my time is up.

But this is not a time to be morose or pessimistic. I want this book to be a celebration of my life. I'm no embittered old footballer with a chip on his shoulder. Hopefully, these words have given you an opportunity to share some of the amusing moments that have happened to me down the years. I can truthfully say I have given the football of life a damn good kicking. And *the claw*, even though it might be creaking a little, is not quite finished yet. As the proverb hanging up on the office wall in my little home says: "Old footballers never die, they just don't score as often!"

■ **FINAL WORD:** An aerial tussle with Liverpool's John Toshack during our 1-1 draw with the Reds at Filbert Street in September 1973. What was not widely known was that John signed for Leicester from the Reds. He was introduced to the players by Jimmy Bloomfield on the eve of a trip to Everton. He came on the coach with us and the pair of us shared a room overnight. We travelled to Goodison Park only for John to disappear, never to be seen by us again. To this day, I've not spoken to him about a most unusual turn of events. Maybe it was the prospect of rooming with me on away trips. Happy days!

ALAN BIRCHENALL - *Career Summary*

Club	Season	League Apps	League Gls	FA Cup Apps	FA Cup Gls	Lge Cup Apps	Lge Cup Gls
SHEFFIELD UNITED	1964-65	31	12	3	-	1	1
Joined June 1963	1965-66	27(1)	8	2	2	1	-
	1966-67	31	10	3	-	3	-
	1967-68	17	1	-	-	1	1
	Total	**106(1)**	**31**	**8**	**2**	**6**	**2**
CHELSEA	1967-68	21	5	5	2	-	-
Joined Nov 1967 £100,000	1968-69	39	12	5	1	3	1
	1969-70	14(1)	3	-	-	4	2
	Total	**74(1)**	**20**	**10**	**3**	**7**	**3**
CRYSTAL PALACE	1970-71	36	10	2	1	5	2
Joined June 1970 £100,000	1971-72	5	1	-	-	-	-
	Total	**41**	**11**	**2**	**1**	**5**	**2**
LEICESTER CITY	1971-72	29	4	3	-	-	-
Joined Sept 1971	1972-73	36	5	2	-	-	-
£45,450 plus Bobby Kellard	1973-74	33	2	4	-	2	-
	1974-75	40	1	5	1	2	1
	1975-76	7(1)	-	-	-	1	-
	1976-77	11(6)	-	-	-	1	-
	Total	**156(7)**	**12**	**14**	**1**	**6**	**1**
NOTTS COUNTY (loan)	1975-76	5	-	-	-	-	-
Joined Mar 1976	**Total**	**5**	**-**	**-**	**-**	**-**	**-**

Club	Season	Regular Season Apps	Regular Season Gls	Play-offs Apps	Play-offs Gls		
SAN JOSE EARTHQUAKES							
Joined Apr 1977 (loan)	1977	16(1)	3	1	-		
	Total	**16(1)**	**3**	**1**	**-**		

Club	Season	League Apps	League Gls	FA Cup Apps	FA Cup Gls	Lge Cup Apps	Lge Cup Gls
NOTTS COUNTY	1977-78	28	-	3	-	-	-
Joined Sept 1977	**Total**	**28**	**-**	**3**	**-**	**-**	**-**

Club	Season	Regular Season Apps	Regular Season Gls				
MEMPHIS ROGUES							
Joined Apr 1978	1978	21(3)	2				
	Total	**21(3)**	**2**				

Club	Season	League Apps	League Gls	FA Cup Apps	FA Cup Gls	Lge Cup Apps	Lge Cup Gls
BLACKBURN ROVERS	1978-79	17(1)	-	2	-	-	-
Joined Sept 1978	**Total**	**17(1)**	**-**	**2**	**-**	**-**	**-**
LUTON TOWN	1978-79	8	-	-	-	-	-
Joined Mar 1979	1979-80	1(1)	-	-	-	-	-
	Total	**9(1)**	**-**	**-**	**-**	**-**	**-**
HEREFORD UNITED	1979-80	11	-	-(1)	-	-	-
Joined Oct 1979	**Total**	**11**	**-**	**-(1)**	**-**	**-**	**-**
ENGLISH CAREER TOTALS		**447(11)**	**74**	**39(1)**	**7**	**24**	**8**

US CAREER TOTALS	REGULAR SEASON Apps	REGULAR SEASON Gls	PLAY-OFFS Apps	PLAY-OFFS Gls
	37(4)	**5**	**1**	**-**

International Caps: ENGLAND UNDER-23
With **SHEFFIELD UNITED**: 20/04/1966 v **Turkey** (at Blackburn) 2-0, 01/11/1967 v **Wales** (at Swansea) 2-1
With **CHELSEA**: 25/05/1968 v **Italy** (in Trieste) 1-1, 03/06/1968 v **West Germany** (in Kassel) 1-0 *(scored)*.

Glossary

Alan Whickers - ladies knickers.

Aristotle - Not our Greek philosopher friend but a 'Birchyism' to refer to a bottom. In easy stages, we go from Aristotle to bottle, to bottle and glass, arse and finally bottom.

Barnet - Hair or Hairstyle.

BJ - A blow-dry with the Birch's Moulinex 200 Turbo De luxe hairdryer. Not to be confused with connotations of a more sexual nature.

Belle Vue - nothing to do with the Manchester speedway track, more to do with being sick. A derivative of cockney rhyme for spew.

Bins - a pair of spectacles. Even the Birch wears 'em these days.

Blairs - Flares - as in on your trousers.

Boat - Cockney rhyme for face. Boat race, geddit?

Borussias - short for the German club Borussia Monchengladbach and refers to a lady's chest. Hence the phrase, 'she's got a great pair of Borussias'. Arguably the best borussias I ever saw at close quarters were those of Raquel Welch.

Buffalo-ing - embarking on a scouting mission (football or nightclub). Short for Buffalo Bill Cody.

Clagthorpe - A female not considered to be the greatest looker in the world.

Claw, The - A term of endearment for my left foot. As the old saying goes, it could open up a can of beans from 30 yards.

Desireable - A female with a certain amount of class and style.

Double Doris Clagthorpe - even worse looking than a clagthorpe.

Elvis - Frank Worthington

Fido - Lenny Glover, 'cos of his pervy dog-walking antics around Evington.

Forsyth - a pint of lager, cockney rhyme derived from television programme Forsyth Saga.

Jurassic period - an era when Birch walked planet Earth as a teenager.

Larrup - A word that covers a multitude of meanings. Larruping most commonly refers to a bout of sexual actitivity or can also be used to describe kicking a football. Hence, she was a good 'larrup' or I 'larruped' one in from 30 yards.

Muldoons - The spots which I was afflicted with during my early life. Spotty muldoons, geddit?

Minging - absolutely terrible.

Moriarty - Not to be confused with the great adversary of Sherlock Holmes. This was rhyming slang for party, of which the tank commander organised none better.

Munjaro - Food

Peckham - Cockney rhyme for tie, as in Peckham Rye.

Pen and Ink - A major stink.

Pondlife - a general descriptive term for a wide category of sub-standard people it has been my misfortune to come across.

Scotches - Legs, derivative from Cockney rhyme Scotch Eggs.

Sherbet - a pint of alcoholic beverage.

Syrup - Wig. As worn by Arthur Mann at Notts County.

Tank Commander - the wife. Heather earned the nickname for her fearsome organisational skills ... and her ability to put the fear of God into me.

Tanko - abbreviation of above.